# MUTED

## The Dimity Horse Mysteries
## Book 1

## LEANNE OWENS

ISBN-13: 978-1-7950-1466-3

# DEDICATION

For our children – Robert, Kate, and Michael

# CONTENTS

# ACKNOWLEDGMENTS

Thank you to the people who encouraged me.
Thank you to all the horses I've ever known, loved, and learned from, as well as all the horse people – I've been lucky enough to know some of the best in so many disciplines.
Thank you to the students of Rosewood High who like listening to my stories when their work is done.

# PROLOGUE

*If your soul came from a perfect place, a place we might call heaven, and resided here on Earth for a brief flash of life, it would not want a long life of perfection here; otherwise, it would never get to experience the full scope of being human. The best and bravest of souls would choose the lives that bring about change for the better, and these lives would know grief and suffering, as those depths allow you to climb to great heights and point the way for others to follow.*

**Social media post by Lane Dimity, over twenty million shares**

## Ellamanga Station - Outback Queensland
### The Saddest Day

Lane stopped speaking on his eighth birthday.

He woke that morning with a smile bursting out of him. He was eight. There would be cake and presents, and his parents would be happy on this day. He would see his father smile. He would hear his mother laugh. For a brief time, the drought and the bank and the money and the grassless paddocks and the dying animals and the anger and the sadness would be forgotten because it was his birthday.

Lane ran barefoot to the kitchen, still in his pajamas. The bare wooden floors were icy cold under his feet. Outback Queensland in June could be frosty at night, even though the days were hot and dusty. He made a quick detour to the bathroom, his excitement almost bursting, and then continued down the long corridors.

A grin split his face as he reached the big, open kitchen and his eyes spied four presents in bright paper on the table. He did not notice that the paper was wrinkled and creased from repeated use; he simply saw gifts. For ten seconds, he stood spellbound by the sight of presents. What could they be? Please not books and clothes again, but if they

1

were, he knew he'd make his parents believe they were just what he wanted. But maybe there were toys… or a gun… or a bow and arrows. No, not a bow and arrows; there was nothing that shape. Maybe books and clothes – but that would be good, yes, it would, and he would see his mother smile as he showed her how much he liked them.

His mother. She was sitting on a chair at the far end of the kitchen, staring out the window at the brown plains that stretched away forever. She wasn't smiling. She was crying. She hadn't noticed him, and she was staring out the window and crying. Lane felt a chill of terror grip his chest. This wasn't supposed to happen on his birthday. She should look up and smile and laugh, open her arms to hug him and wish him a happy birthday. His breath started to choke in his throat, his lips quivered, and he felt tears burning his eyes. If his mother was crying on his birthday, it must be bad. Very bad. Very, very bad.

'Mummy?' he asked, his voice shaking.

Marion Dimity turned slowly to look at her son. Her beautiful son with the face of an angel and a smile that lifted hearts to the heavens. Her gifted, talented, loving, amazing son. An agonized cry was strangled from her throat as she looked at him and thought of the hurt he would suffer that day. She had failed him. She had failed Joe, her husband. She had failed Ellamanga, their property.

'Mummy?' he asked again, walking slowly towards her, his large brown eyes melting into pools of tears, his tousled sun-bleached hair framing a face that was now filled with fear.

Unable to speak, Marion simply opened her arms and let her son walk into them, and she enclosed him in a hug that she wished could protect him from the world, the drought, and all the sadness that was yet to come. It had gone on so long. So long. Wet season after wet season had come and gone without enough rain to break the drought, and now, in the tenth year, there was no grass left. The dams were dry, there was no money remaining to buy hay, the bank was about to take Ellamanga, and there was nothing left but slow starvation ahead for the remaining stock. What would they do without Ellamanga? Joe had been born here, like his father before him; he *was* Ellamanga, and he was dying with his land because she didn't know how to help.

They had sold most of the cattle years ago, and Joe had been driving a truck to make the money to buy feed for the last of the horses and make the bank repayments, but the truck company had collapsed, and now there was nothing. No one to help. No rain coming. A long wait until the next wet season. And the horses were starving. They had given away all that they could, but no one else had feed, and people on the coast were too far away to drive out for skinny horses, even free ones.

A distant gunshot broke the silence. Then another.

'Not the horses, Mummy? Not the horses?' He gripped his mother's arms with tiny hands that squeezed her flesh so tight that little bruises would be left to mark the moment he realized what was happening.

The shots stabbed into his soul. His breath was punched out of him by a third shot. His mother held him tight, but he struggled free, like a small wild creature desperate to escape a trap. Then, without another thought for his presents, he bolted from the house. A high-pitched wail wrung from somewhere deep within, as his feet carried him as fast as he could run, down the dusty roadway, past the sheds, down through the dry creek crossing, and up under the parched eucalypts that bowed sadly on the cold morning.

He did not notice how cold the air was that morning. He did not notice how his throat burned as he struggled to feed oxygen into his body. He did not even realize that words were wrung from him as he ran and ran and ran.

'Daddy! No! Not the horses! Not the horses! Not Punkin! Punkin! Jess! Dusty!'

He did notice the shots. Another one. And another. And another.

It was five hundred meters from the homestead to the cattle yards, and he reached them on pure adrenalin and fear, his young body pushed beyond the normal limits of endurance. His chest was on fire with pain, and his breath rattled inwards and exploded out in clouds of steam in the cold air, but he kept running. He could see horses in the yards. Some were standing, heads high in terror as they crowded into a corner. Most of the horses were on the ground. Lying on the ground. Still. Unmoving. Another shot. Another horse fell to the ground, its legs just dissolving under it so that it dropped like a puppet with cut strings.

'No, Daddy! No!' he sobbed, climbing through the first of the rails, slipping and falling to the dust, the clouds of finely ground powder puffing up to coat his face and turn his tears to mud. He struggled to stand, but his exhausted little legs would not support him, so he crawled towards his father, begging him to stop.

Joe Dimity was reloading his .357 magnum revolver with six cartridges. He stopped for a moment to look at his son crawling towards him in the pulverized dirt of the old cattle yards, his little face twisted in agony, mud lines streaking his face from the tears. He had hoped to have this done before Lane woke up. He was going to have it done so that when Lane woke, he would be in the kitchen with Marion, and they would open the presents, and then they would go for a drive.

And keep driving. Today they would drive away from Ellamanga for a picnic and just keep going.

Ellamanga. His home. His life. His blood. For long seconds he gazed at his son as he felt his soul dying alongside his animals.

'Go home, Lane,' he spoke softly, his voice deep and gentle. It was a voice that calmed horses and coaxed wild horses into loyal workers on Ellamanga. It was a voice they trusted. And now he was killing the last of them. His horses. His soul.

'Please stop, Daddy,' Lane begged as he crawled through the next set of rails to enter the yard where some of the horses stood in terror, their heads high and nostrils snorting at the smell of blood, while others lay silent in death, their eyes open as though questioning the skies. More tears pushed trails through the dust on his face, and he tried to stand, but his muscles were failing him, so he continued on his hands and knees.

'I'm sorry, Lane,' he shook his head, speaking in the voice that had soothed Lane to sleep so many nights as he read a book or told a story. 'Go home. Turn away. This has to be done.'

Reaching the body of Salamanca, a ten-year-old chestnut mare who had been bred at Ellamanga, like her dam, and her dam before her, and her dam before that, Lane pressed his face into the warm hair of her back and thought of his father riding her, laughing, once, long ago. Now, she was so still, the bones pushing gauntly at her skin from within. Using her body, Lane pulled himself to his feet, his trembling legs struggling to support him.

He walked between his father and the horses. His horses. He had grown up with these horses. They had carried him from the time his father put him as a baby in front of him in the stock saddle and took him for rides around the station. They were his friends. His best friends. They spoke to him of rides, and peace, and moments when their spirits melded together in gallops across the plains. They were the soft muzzles who reached out to touch him when he walked among them. They were the companions who knew he would keep them safe. They were the soaring souls of freedom who carried him safely when they raced life itself. They were beauty and strength, kindness and curiosity; they were knowledge and innocence. They were his friends.

'Don't shoot anymore, Dad. Please.' He raised his hands out by his sides as though to shield the remaining horses from the bullets. 'We can feed them. We can save them.'

'No, we can't, Lane,' Joe hung his head, unable to meet the pleading, tearful eyes of his son, seeing his own shattered soul in their depths. 'They are starving. We can't get feed for them. We have no money left. They are hungry, and they are suffering. I've tried. God, I've tried. But I've lost. I can't leave them to die slowly; it's just too cruel. Too damned cruel. Go back to the house, and we'll go for a drive later, OK? We'll go somewhere where there's grass. We'll drive and leave this behind. Go.'

'No, Dad, no,' Lane shook his head emphatically and stepped closer to his pinto pony, Punkin, who buried his muzzle in the boy's back for protection, pressing gently against him as though he could hide his soft brown eyes from the death around him, 'Punkin's my best friend. You can't shoot him. He's my best friend. Don't shoot him.'

'No more words,' Joe commanded, an edge of anger sharpening his voice. 'I don't want to hear another word out of you, you hear? Not another word. This is killing me, too, but words won't help. Get back to the house, Lane.'

Lane half turned, wrapped his arms around Punkin's neck, and hugged him desperately, 'Not Punkin. Or Jess. Or Dusty.' He looked at the remaining horses, their ribs sticking out starkly, their hollow eyes showing how scared they were of the blood and death around them, but they would not hurt him. He was their friend. He would convince his father to save them. He would find the words that would keep them safe. He would find the words that could turn back time so that the other horses were still alive. The words had to be there. 'We can take them somewhere, Dad. We can take them to where there is grass.'

Joe did not reply. There was no grass. The horses were too weak to travel far. He had sold the farm truck a year ago to buy more feed. There was no way out of this suffering except death. He knew his son was too young to understand, but he still felt angry at him for not understanding. He stepped forward and grabbed Lane, dragging his arms away from the neck of the pony.

'Get back to the house, Lane.'

'I can't leave them, Daddy; I have to save them. I have to. We can do something; I know we can. You can't shoot them.'

Joe raised his right hand and slapped Lane across the mouth, hard enough to snap the child's head back and split his lip, sending him reeling away to land on his back under his pony's legs. Punkin froze, careful to keep his hooves pressed to the ground so that he did not step on his boy.

Lane stared up at his father in shock. Never had a hand been raised to him before. Never had Joe used violence. This was not his father, this was an angry man who was killing his best friends, and Lane's eyes glittered with the fear of this stranger.

As a drop of blood trickled from the corner of Lane's mouth, Joe backed away.

'You don't understand, Lane.'

'I do, Daddy, I do. We don't have to kill them. We can save them. We'll take them somewhere safe. Someone will give us feed for them.'

Joe raised his hands to his ears, not caring where the barrel of the revolver pointed, and he covered his ears to try and block the voice of his son. 'Just shut up, Lane. Just shut up. Shut up. Shut up. Shut up.'

He reached out his free hand to grab Lane by the arm and drag him away from the horses. Lane screamed and kicked, but his father was a big man, and the child was powerless against him. Shoving him roughly into the dirt, Joe turned back towards the horses, and as Lane sat frozen with shock in the cold on the shortest day of the year, his birthday, he watched his father shoot the last of the Ellamanga horses. His chest tightened so that he couldn't breathe, and he couldn't find the words to stop his father. And they fell. One after another. His horses fell.

As Punkin collapsed to the ground, blood pouring from his nostrils and the hole between his eyes, Lane started to scream. A high-pitched, unearthly scream of grief. He rocked back and forth, staring at his pony. Screaming. And screaming. Screaming.

'Shut the hell up, Lane!' Joe yelled at him, 'Just shut the hell up. I told you to go back to the house.'

Lane rocked back and forth, noises of grief emptying from his soul, his eyes fixed on the glazing eyes of his pony.

Joe's shoulders sagged. He had failed them all. He was a failure. He had hit his own son. He was nothing. He was no more than a grain of sand on the ground. He was without meaning, without soul. He had failed his animals. He had failed his family. He wasn't a man anymore, and he knew they would be better off without him. He knew their lives would be better without him there. They could start a new life without him dragging them down and failing them.

Raising the gun one last time, Joe stared at the barrel for a few black seconds, unaware of Lane launching himself off the ground and throwing himself at the gun. He pulled the trigger.

It was an hour before Marion found them. She had sat, despondent, in the kitchen after Lane had bolted from the house, staring out at the grassless dirt of the station and quietly telling herself to get up and go after him, repeating it over and over until the words no longer had meaning, they were just sounds in the blackness. When the gunfire stopped, she waited. They would come home soon, and then they would go for that drive. The three of them would drive away from this dead place.

Her heart slowly turned to cold porridge in her chest. Finally, she forced herself to stir from the comfort of nothingness and went to the door. She waited. She stared down the road. They would be back soon.

For another ten minutes, her mind went back and forth between the decision of driving the car down to the yards or walking, drive or walk, drive, or walk. What to choose… to drive or walk. Drive or walk. She looked at the car and saw it had a flat tire, so she walked. For twenty meters, she walked, her running shoes padding softly on the road as she walked slowly, then she broke into a jog, then a run. A mad run. A frantic race against time. Why did I wait? Why did I wait? Why did I wait? Her mind repeated over and over as she bolted.

The yards were silent with death when she arrived. She called the names of her husband and son, but there was only silence. She yelled their names as she clambered through the rails to the main yard to where the bodies of skinny horses lay, her terror rising. *This isn't real,* her mind kept saying, *it isn't real, it isn't real.*

When she saw her husband and son lying bloodied and still in the dirt of the yards, she started screaming their names, but there was no response from either of them, no word, no movement, no life. Her own breath was squeezed from her lungs as a mountain of grief landed on her chest, and she staggered towards their bodies before her legs gave way, leaving her on her knees within an arm's length of Lane.

Anguished cries wailed from her throat, and she battled to breathe as pain crushed her chest. With shaking hands, she reached out and touched her son's upturned face. It was so cold. His eyes stared unseeing at the sky, and there was so much blood on him and under him and around him. So much blood. Sobbing his name, she shook him, but his body was soft and unresponsive, like a large rag doll. She clutched his body to her chest, his arms dangling limply, and murmured his name over and over.

She stared at the hole in the front of her husband's face with the blood congealing around it, and did not want to even touch him. He had done this. He had killed them all. There was nothing left of life.

When neighbors, Jill and Trevor Moreton, arrived at Ellamanga some hours later with a birthday present for their godson, Lane, they found Marion unconscious on the floor in the kitchen, her hands, arms, and clothes covered in blood, an empty bottle of pills beside her. They could not wake her. The phone had been disconnected a few weeks earlier, so Jill ran back to the car and used her mobile to call for help while Trevor searched the house for Joe and Lane.

Her first call was to a nearby station, about ten kilometers away, because one of the owners, Jasmine, was a nurse and could reach Ellamanga faster than any emergency service. Then she dialed the emergency number to call in the police and a medical team. She was put through to the Royal Flying Doctor Service and was advised that there was a plane with a doctor in the air less than half an hour away, and it would divert to Ellamanga.

'Is there an airstrip there?' the operator asked.

'They use the road north of the house,' Jill said. 'It'll be clear from the air when they see it. There's the house and sheds with Ellamanga written on the roof of the house, and due north of that, about a kilometer from the house, there's a straight stretch of road that doubles as an airstrip.'

'And is there one person who's overdosed, or three?'

'One person we know of,' Jill's voice caught on the words, and she took a deep breath before continuing. 'There's an eight-year-old boy and his father missing. It's the boy's birthday, so they should be here, and we found Marion, the mother, on the floor in the house, and it looks as though she's lost a lot of blood and has taken tablets.'

While she was trying to explain what they had found, Trevor carried Marion out to the car and carefully laid her on the back seat, turning her on her side, and handed the empty pill bottle to Jill so that she could describe what she had taken.

'They're going to land on the road north of the house,' Jill told him, holding the phone away from her mouth while she spoke to her husband. 'I'll take Marion there and wait for them. Jasmine will be here soon. You can look for Joe and Lane.'

Looking at the blood that now stained Trevor's clothes, she shook her head, 'Damn, how much blood has she lost?'

Trevor's face was pale, and he replied quietly, 'It's not her blood, Jill. She's not bleeding.'

'Oh, God,' Jill's arms dropped to her side, the phone in her hand forgotten, the color draining from her face as she leaned heavily against the car. 'Lane.'

'I called him, but he didn't answer,' Trevor told her as he headed back to the house. 'I'll check the house, but she's covered in dust as though she's been out in the paddock somewhere.'

'It's not her blood,' Jill told the operator, 'and we have a little boy and his father missing, and Marion is covered in someone else's blood. Oh, dear God, this is…' Her voice failed her.

Instead of taking Marion to the airstrip, Jill joined her husband, looking for Lane and Joe. Together, they hurried through the homestead, calling for them and looking in all rooms, in cupboards, and under beds, in case Lane was hiding.

Jasmine and two jackaroos arrived in her Toyota ute, spewing a cloud of dust across the scene as she slammed on the brakes to pull up next to the Moreton's car. With her wild red hair held back in a ponytail and jammed under an Akubra, she strode straight to where Marion lay, her intelligent green eyes assessing everything she was seeing. Jill ran out of the house to give a run-down of what they had found and what they hadn't found.

'Go help the Moretons look for Lane and Joe,' she instructed the jackaroos, lanky young men in Wranglers and blue shirts, with neat brown hair and eyes that looked beyond the horizon from long days of working on the vast plains.

With a glance at the empty tablet bottle, she ran her hands over Marion, seeing that the blood wasn't hers and feeling the same sense of fear that had struck her neighbors when they realized that Lane and Joe could have been the source of that blood.

'She's not coming back from this,' Jasmine looked at Jill, her face pinched with worry, 'she hardly has a pulse now, and that,' she nodded at the pill bottle, 'is a new script for Joe's beta-blockers, so she could have taken the lot.'

'Can we make her vomit it up?' asked Jill.

Jasmine shook her head sadly, 'No. She's in a coma, and her heart is close to stopping already. A single tablet lowers Joe's blood pressure. A whole bottle…'

'Over here!' Trevor yelled, pointing to footprints on the dry track that led to the cattle yards.

Everyone ran to him and stared down at the ground. The breeze through the night had wiped the dirt clean of yesterday's tracks, so this morning's footprints were clear to read. There were the large boot prints of Joe heading down to the yard. Over them were laid the small, bare footprints of Lane, mainly the toes and balls of his feet as though he was running…running with the desperation of a little boy trying to catch his father. On top of those prints were the tracks belonging to the patterned soles of Marion's shoes, heading out from the house in a direct line. The marks of her journey home staggered from side to side, and there were occasional hand and knee prints showing she had fallen.

'Wait here with Marion,' Trevor instructed the women and the jackaroos as he took off at a run following the footprints, his heart thudding like a drum that was about to rip open from the pressure of the beats. 'I'll find them.'

Instead of waiting, Jill cast a telling glance at Jasmine, who nodded in reply; she would remain behind. Jill followed Trevor towards the yards. The jackaroos began to follow, but Jasmine called them back - they were young, and she had a notion of what horror might be at the yards, and they didn't need to see that.

Jill raced after her husband and saw him hesitate on the stony crossing of the creek as he wondered if they had gone left, right, or straight ahead. It didn't take long to see that the tracks continued out the far side, and he was off again. She caught him up, and they ran side by side, their eyes on the trail of footprints that told a tragic story of three people heading out and one broken one returning.

'No, no, no...' Jill moaned when they were about a hundred meters from the yards, and they could see crows and hawks landing on the rails overlooking the carcasses of the horses. The scavengers would not land if there were people alive in the yards.

They ran harder.

They waved their hands and yelled at the birds as they approached, and the birds took to the air with cries of complaint. They raced through the gates that Marion had left open when she left. Joe was on his back next to Lane's pony, the blood of man and horse mixed in coagulated lumps on the earth around them. Lane lay over his pony, his pajamas stained and dirty, his arms around Punkin's neck, his face against his mane, his eyes closed as though he was sleeping.

A mighty sob tore from Jill's chest as she saw Lane. She stopped, her hands over her mouth. She and Trevor could not have children of their own, and this little boy had been a blessing in their lives, their godson, a dear child they had loved as though he had been their gift from heaven. He was an angel, the child of their dreams, the one they wanted to watch grow up, and here he was, covered in blood, lying on the body of his pony in the dry dust of the drought.

Looking at the dust, Trevor could see that Lane's crawl marks dragged through the dust from his father to the pony. His eyes pinched in thought as he saw that the child's tracks covered some of Marion's footprints. The child had moved after Marion had been here. Had she died because she thought her son was dead when he had still been alive?

Trevor did not bother to touch Joe. The blue, grey, and purple tones to his skin and wound made it evident that he was dead, but he stepped up to Lane and gently, reverently, laid his hand on the small, bloodstained cheek, observing, sadly, how dark the birthmark on his neck stood out against the pale skin. Angel's wings, Jill called them, but Lane liked to call it his flying bird.

'His skin is like ice,' he whispered. Then, looking from father to son and back again, he noticed something different between them. He carefully turned Lane, the child's body limp and cold. Too cold. And his skin. It was white. He was cold and white, like someone in deep shock.

'Jill!' his voice shook, 'Jill – he's alive.'

# CHAPTER ONE

*Time Magazine asked Lane Dimity how much harder life was for him because of his selective mutism, and he wrote: "The spoken word cannot truly capture the feel of sunshine on your body or the wind in your hair. To speak aloud of love does not make it any more real. To tell someone about the sensation of riding a horse you trust across the plains in a storm does not make the moment more special. We spend so much time speaking and trying to capture the indefinable in sounds and syllables, which merely seek to confine the infinite, that sometimes we forget to just be and do and love. I like to hear the stories of others as they are important, but my own story is played out in actions, and I don't find life harder in my silence, only more introspective and peaceful."*

**This was their biggest selling issue of the year. The on-line version of the Lane Dimity interview had twice as many hits as the next most popular article of the year.**

### The Pilatos Building - New York

Thirty stories up makes the pavement people look so small, Karen mused as she rested her forehead on the cold glass of the window. Tiny little people, rushing about their tiny little lives, climbing in and out of toy taxis, and hastening in and out of the buildings on Water Street. The clear view was suddenly blurred as the rain tumbled past the window. When it reached the street, there was a silent explosion of umbrellas, transforming the footpaths into rivers of black circles bumping past each other, broken occasionally by the brightness of a rebellious, colorful umbrella. From above, it was a meaningless flow of life, something to look down upon with the emptiness of a lesser god watching leaves blow across a dead lawn.

'With less than six months to go,' a voice rabbited on, forming a background to her thoughts, 'we need to be aware that the risk factor to Stablex is now in the red zone.'

She hadn't been listening to Phillip Reach's dramatic monologue. In her opinion, he was a sneaky little man, and she didn't trust him. He was always trying to take the glory for good decisions made by others and blaming them for his bad ones. She despised the way he looked at her - she could almost feel his drool on her flesh. When she spoke to him, she tended to focus on his tie because everything else about him was distasteful. His eyes were watery blue, weak, and cold. His lips were too narrow and wet-looking from his constant lizard-like licking. His hair was expensively dyed and implanted, and he sported a youthful windblown style that could have been attractive on another man. Karen would prefer to run her fingers through fly-blown entrails than touch that manicured mop. His face, in general, was a shifting kaleidoscope of cunning, lust, greed, envy, pride, and wrath, and every expression turned her stomach a little. So, she gazed at his tie when she had to look at him; at least, it was always impeccably knotted.

'Then we ramp up our defenses,' a voice of frozen steel pulled her attention back from the view outside to the office. She looked at the table where four men discussed the latest pharmaceutical product released by Pilatos Industries as the hard voice continued. 'I will not have those animal rights fools interfering in this, so you do whatever is needed to keep our image clean.' 'John,' said Phillip, the point of his tongue sneaking out to dampen his thin lips, 'we are doing everything possible. We've had two animal welfare groups and several equine veterinary specialists out to inspect the horses, as well as our own team of specialists, of course. As far as any of them are concerned, we're doing everything right. ADOR, Animals Deserving Our Respect, is one of the toughest animal groups around at the moment, and they have signed off on everything we've done there. Of course, we have given them some substantial donations to show our appreciation, and, consequently, they've approved everything. We've got that in writing. It's freely available to anyone who looks at our websites. I'm not saying that the extremists can harm our image because we have all our bases covered, just that they will try.'

John Lawford slammed a fist down on the aged oak of the conference table and glared at the three men sitting opposite him, 'How the hell can they even try? If you've done your job properly, no one can touch our image. The reality is, there are no welfare issues with these horses!'

'They don't care about reality,' pointed out Jeremy Murray, the Chief Financial Officer of Pilatos Industries. Patting down the styled flick of his blonde hair over his alarmingly dark, fake-tanned forehead, he let his baby blue eyes sweep all in the room, including Karen. 'They don't care that the Stablex horses are better looked after than ninety-nine percent of the horses in the world; they only care about disrupting the profits of a pharmaceutical company. There's no rhyme nor reason to them – they attack because they can and because pharmaceuticals are the latest whipping boy in this let's-blame-someone world.'

Karen didn't like him, either. Phillip was a sneaky sod, and Jeremy was far too full of himself. He would have been a bully at school, she told herself, someone who picked on the kids who didn't have as much money, or who weren't as good at sport, or who weren't as good looking. He was a natural-born bully, and Phillip would have been his sniveling off-sider, kicking someone once Jeremy had flattened them to the ground. How did men with such despicable characters climb so high up the corporate ladder? Sociopathic tendencies, her inner voice answered her unspoken question.

'It's simply a chess game,' Karen wandered back from the window, smoothed her grey Alexander McQueen skirt down. She sat on the chair to the right of John Lawford, facing the other three men. Her dark blue eyes flecked with winter grey calculated the worth of each of the men and found two of the three wanting, so she turned her gaze to Joe Kaiphas, the head of the company's security.

'There are a certain number of moves to be made,' she continued in her cool and efficient tone, the smooth fall of her mahogany hair bobbing around her aristocratic features as she spoke, 'and it's our job always to be several steps ahead of our opponents, knocking their pieces off the board, protecting our pieces, making certain sacrifices when necessary, and winning the game.'

Joe regarded her with a stony face, the only expression she ever saw him use. There was no flicker of desire in his eyes as they rested on the woman who had been described by many as hauntingly beautiful and by some as the ice princess of the corporate kingdom. His dark brown eyes gave nothing away, and she never knew what he was about to say. The other two, they were predictable in their utterances as well as their desires, but Joe ran like a deep, shadowed river, and she had no idea what thoughts lurked in the depths until he brought them out as words.

There was something primally dangerous about him, from the way he moved with the languid grace of a leopard to the slow turning of his head as his eyes gathered every iota of information from every situation in which he was placed. He seemed all-knowing, and Karen knew she should be scared of the man, but there was something strangely protective about him, and she had an innate trust of him. She knew little about his private life apart from the fact that he had a young daughter, Karina, whom she had never met. There was no overlap at all between his personal life and his work for Pilatos.

'There are a few pieces that need to be removed from the board in this game,' he spoke to Karen, his voice flat. 'You'll need to decide if those pieces are to be taken out of all future games or if they are just to be put to one side for this game.'

'I don't think we need anything drastic,' Karen tilted her head back and forth as she weighed up the options. 'We need to start by checkmating some of their predictable moves. They will say our horses are suffering, so we have to prove to all that they are better cared for than ninety-nine percent of the horses in the world. They are going to state that there is cruelty, so we need to prove beyond doubt that there is no cruelty, that we work with the best welfare groups in the world to ensure that the lives of these stallions are good. I want the public to know that our horses are the best looked after horses in the entire history of horses, so let's get the images of our happy horses out there to combat the negative press before it even starts.'

'Who poses the biggest problem?' John asked her. He had complete faith in her analytical ability and knew that she would have assessed who was likely to try and discredit their company.

Karen met his gaze, so like her own with the grey-flecked dark blue eyes that regarded the world with cool detachment. She did not smile at him as theirs was not a relationship built on smiles and emotion; it was built on blood ties and ambition.

Before Karen could reply, Joe gave details in his featureless voice. 'The horseman, Lane Dimity, is in Arizona at present, and he has targeted similar equine establishments to ours, so he heads our list.'

'The mute Australian?' scoffed Phillip, leaning back in his chair and rolling his eyes, 'That boy's just a touchy-feely, new-age show pony. He's not going to be a problem. What about some of the bigger organizations? Those animal-loving, tree-hugging charities - they're going to be the ones to screw us over.'

Joe turned his expressionless gaze to Phillip, waiting until his voice faded away before speaking. 'The Australian has over seventy million social media followers. He never asks for money, but when he asks for change, it happens. All he has to do is tell his followers not to buy our products, and he destroys us. It's as simple as that. That's the sort of power he has.'

'Does he abuse his power?' John leaned forward in his seat, steepling his fingers in front of his face as he considered the potential enemy. 'What are his weaknesses? Has he been snooping around

Pilatos? How do we reach him? Can we invite him to a meeting and pay him off?'

'He doesn't operate like anyone else I've seen,' Joe shrugged off the barrage of questions. 'I'm at the point of believing he really is there for the welfare of the animals. He makes his money from the sales of his books, which are international bestsellers. He doesn't seem to accrue any wealth from his work with animals or from his army of followers. He just is.'

'I call bull,' Jeremy sneered, 'you don't have that much power without making money from it. And how do we even know he's interested in our company? And, if he is, why not buy him off? Get someone in close to him and find out what his price is.'

'He has a small group of trusted friends,' Joe tapped the phone in front of him, and a photo of four laughing people took up half the wall at one end of the office, 'and then a big ring of long-term friends. New people don't get close to him – he is protected by loyal guard dogs who keep him safe. His followers are fanatical about him.'

He scrolled an arrow across the photo, starting from the left with the tall, lean, tanned man with sun-bleached honey hair in an out-of-control tousle that would have been the envy of movie stars. He had a smile that brought sunshine into the room on this dreary New York day. 'That's Lane. He's thirty-two. Not married. Sexual preference unknown. Travels the world staying with friends – he rarely uses a hotel, just stays with people and borrows vehicles. He does own a cattle property in outback Queensland, but it's managed by the neighbors, and he mainly runs it as a wildlife refuge, not a money-making enterprise. He seems to have friends in every country, usually people with horses, from Native Americans to circus folk in England to Hungarian horse studs.'

Karen examined his face, so open and happy, and she struggled for another word…innocent, yes, something in that face and crinkled brown eyes looked innocent compared to the world-weary men around her. He was only three years younger than she was, so she didn't know how he could maintain such a childlike innocence in his eyes when the world was what she knew it to be. Innocence belonged in childhood, not in people who wielded great power.

Danger came in many guises, so she was not beguiled by this open-faced Australian who charmed so many millions with his messages of positivity and hope. He was a threat to Pilatos Industries; she was Pilatos Industries; therefore, he was a threat to her. In the last few days, she had made it her business to learn something about this enigmatic man, and she failed to understand what motivated him. Money?

Fame? Power? Greed? The need to be the center of attention? She did not trust what she could not understand.

Staring at his smiling image, she considered what Joe had said about working with people who made a living from horses, and asked, 'Then, he's not so extremist that he wants to stop people using horses altogether?'

Joe nodded, 'He rides them himself, and he's fine with them being used as long as, in his words, their spirits are not in chains.'

A derisive snort came from Phillip, 'Spirits in chains,' his narrow lips curled back in a mocking snarl. 'What sort of new-age crap is that man smoking? So, a freaking circus horse in England has spiritual freedom, but our horses don't? How do we even know he's interested in our horses? Maybe he's no threat at all, and we need to move on to the bigger organizations that have an agenda, not some smiling golden boy from the outback.'

'I'll come to that,' Joe said quietly, his cold gaze freezing Phillip's words. The arrow on the photo moved to the next person whose arm was draped over Lane's shoulder, a dark-haired, dark-eyed, dark-skinned man with a smile even bigger than Lane's and a look of mischief in his expression. He wasn't as tall as Lane but was still taller than average and was more muscular.

'Matt McLeay. Twenty-five years old. A horseman like Lane. He's performed in circuses and horse spectaculars around the world. He's Aboriginal, single, a sought-after horse trainer, doesn't seem to care much about money, and these days he mainly travels with Lane and gives voice to him when needed.'

'Are they gay? A couple?' Phillip asked.

'Is that important?' asked Karen, wondering what their sexuality had to do with them being a threat to Pilatos.

'It could be leverage,' he replied.

'It's not 1950 anymore, Phillip,' Karen said dryly.

He glared at her, licking his lips as though he wanted to say something, but kept his words to himself.

The arrow moved to the woman standing next to Matt, her arm reaching behind him to grab Lane on the shoulder. Her black hair hung in silky tendrils past her shoulders, and her face was worthy of gracing magazine covers. She was strikingly beautiful. 'Andrea McLeay, Matt's twin sister. Photographer. Well-known and respected for her wildlife photography and is considered one of the leading equine photographers in the world. These past two years, when she's not on assignment, she's spent most of her time with her twin, Lane, and Tom, the fourth in this group.'

Joe indicated the stern and chiseled warrior face of the tallest of the men. His arms were folded across his chest, and he stared through the camera and into the souls of anyone looking at the image. His sleek dark hair was pulled back in a ponytail, and his Native American features were unmistakable.

'Tom Claw,' Joe continued, 'Navajo, or *Diné*. Arizona born. Age thirty. He's a climatologist who worked briefly with NASA and is currently a successful author of environmental books. For the past three years, he has spent a lot of his time with Lane when he's not on book tours. He's also an accomplished horseman who was shortlisted for our Olympic team in show jumping some years back.'

'You mean to tell me,' Jeremy shook his head as he turned from the photo of the four friends to face Joe, 'that this mute cowboy and his little band of indigenous, horse-mad groupies pose a threat to Pilatos Industries? I'm not buying it. They're not organized. They're not powerful. They're nothing compared to us. They're no threat.'

'I agree,' chimed in Phillip, always happy to stick his boot into an enemy once Jeremy had punched them down. 'We're wasting our time even looking at them. We might be in the red zone as far as potential attacks on Pilatos and Stablex are concerned, but a social media guru who can't talk and his little gang of three are not stepping into that red zone. They'll bad-mouth us on social media, like every other anti-vaxing, flat-earther, and move on to their next ludicrous hate campaign against some other pharmaceutical company.'

The room fell silent when he stopped talking. John Lawford's attention moved from the photo and slowly scanned the three men at the table before settling on Karen, who was still regarding the image of the four friends, her expression slightly troubled.

'Karen?' he asked, trusting her insight.

'They're a problem,' she said quietly, and Joe nodded slightly as the other two men threw scornful looks at her. 'I think they're a really big problem. Seventy million followers. How many of those are men in the Stablex target market? How many have fathers or grandfathers in that demographic? He is a cult figure, so all he has to do is bad mouth us on social media, like Phillip said, and his followers bring us down. I think once Stablex hits the market, there'll be no stopping it, so they will want to stop us before it's on the shelves.'

'He might think he's a twenty-first-century Jesus-of-the-horses,' sniffed Phillip, 'but he's just a man running a con like any other publicity-hungry figure. Buy him off or get rid of him - people have accidents.'

'Cult leaders who have accidents become martyrs,' Karen pointed out, casting Phillip's tie a condescending look. 'If there's any chance he's already started working on a campaign against us, those three,' she indicated the photo on the wall, 'will turn the world against us. They're not stupid – it wouldn't take a case of paranoia to link an accident to the pharmaceutical company he was about to damage.'

'Then what do we do?' Jeremy asked. He still didn't believe that a silent man who liked horses could pose any threat to a multi-billion-dollar company like Pilatos, but he was smart enough to play along with Karen and John Lawford.

'Invite him in on our terms,' John said decisively, 'employ him as an advisor on horse health or spiritual chains or equine happiness. I know we don't have a welfare issue with the Stablex horses, so let's get him on-side and throw money at him. I want him neutralized.'

Joe shook his head, 'That's how I know he does pose a threat,' he flicked a glance at Phillip in recognition of the earlier question, 'I rang him a few days ago and spoke to Matt McLeay. Lane was there, of course, and I put forward our interest in having him as a consultant to assist with the best practices in caring for our horses.'

He paused and began tapping at the screen on his phone.

'And?' urged Jeremy.

'And I'll play the conversation,' Joe said, 'it will be easier than explaining.'

The room fell silent as Joe fast-forwarded through the start of the phone conversation where he spoke to someone who connected him to someone else who put him through to Matt, then started the recording from that point.

'Matt McLeay here,' drawled an Australian voice with an outback twang to it.

'Hi, Matt. Joe Kaiphas here. I'm associated with Pilatos Industries.'

'I know who you are, Mr. Kaiphas.'

Significant looks were cast around the office. Not many people outside of this room knew who Joe was or knew about his role in Pilatos.

'Call me, Joe, please,' Joe's voice was affable and friendly, unlike the flat voice he'd been using in the office. 'Since you know who I am, I'm assuming you also know about Pilatos and our equine facility.'

'You'd be assuming correctly.'

'Good. I was hoping to organize a meeting with you and Mr. Dimity to discuss the equine facility. We've had several leading welfare organizations approve of the facility, including ADOR. It's our belief it would be advantageous to all if we could have you inspect it and advise of any changes you feel could improve the welfare of the horses. There would, of course, be a generous consulting fee to compensate for your time and input.'

'One moment, please.'

There was an eight-second silence that dragged slowly. Karen guessed that Lane must have been present, and some communication was going on between him and Matt.

'Thank you for your offer,' Matt's voice was careful, with less drawl than before, 'but Lane has already seen the facility, and his only advice would be to shut it down.'

Everyone looked surprised at that. The equine facility was closed and extremely well-guarded. No one could see it without going through security checks, and Lane Dimity had definitely not been on any visiting lists. It was alarming to hear that he had somehow visited the farm where the Pilatos horses were located.

'That's not an option,' Joe's voice had become firmer, hinting at the stoniness that usually occupied his expression, 'so let's work together on this for the benefit of the horses. Let us know what needs to be changed, and we'll work with you.'

'The facility will shut,' Matt's voice was cold and quite at odds with the smiling face that was still on the office wall. 'Lane will not be associated in any way with Stablex except to assist in its demise. Good day, Mr. Kaiphas.'

The phone call ended before Joe could say anything else.

His dark eyes regarded the others at the table. Both Jeremy and Phillip had shocked expressions on their faces, and he knew why: although many knew that Pilatos was working on a new wonder drug, only a handful of people outside of this room knew that the trade name for this particular product was Stablex. The fact that Matt and Lane knew the name indicated that they had inside information, which could amount to industrial espionage.

John Lawford stood, his considerable height towering threateningly over everyone else in the room, his eyes stormy with anger as he stared at the smiling faces in the photo on the office wall. How dare they threaten his kingdom. He looked down at Karen like a hunting dog signaling to the pack that the hunt was about to start. She looked back at him, unblinking.

'Get close to him,' he commanded. 'Talk to him. Find out what he's planning. Stop him. Do whatever it takes to neutralize that bleeding-heart Australian and his gang. I will not have them damage this product or our company.'

'No one gets close to him,' Joe warned.

'Karen will, won't you?'

Karen glanced at the photo on the wall, thought of what she had learned of Lane and his beliefs so far, and felt a protective surge of fury. This company was her company, and he threatened it. She would reach him, and she would protect Pilatos.

'Yes, Dad.'

Several hours later, Karen left the Pilatos building and stood in the drab, drizzly street, her grey outfit blending with the grey world around her. She had intended to walk briskly to a meeting a block away, but there was something about the dreary day that robbed her of motion. She stood and looked at her world of cement and bitumen and glass - a grey sky above and shades of grey below. People dodged around her like salmon dodging a rock in their stream, and she stood, motionless, feeling grey.

Across the street in the glassed foyer of the opposing building, flashes of color caught her eye. Her gaze was drawn to the reds and yellows and oranges of sunsets, the blues of sea and skies, and the greens of grasslands and forests. She stared at the posters as though they were windows to worlds far removed from this dull metropolitan landscape. They seemed to call to her, and she found herself dodging between cars to cross the street. Some part of her needed to be closer to the color that contrasted so brightly to the scene around her.

They were posters advertising an exhibition of photographs by the world-renowned equine photographer, Andrea McLeay. Each one was a magnificent landscape, and within each of the vast scenes were horses, so small as to be unnoticed from a distance. As she approached, it seemed as though every object in each image pointed to the horses, and their tiny shapes became the focal points of each poster. It was quite remarkable.

Karen thought of that smiling face that Joe had cast onto the wall of the office. Andrea McLeay was indeed an exceptional artist with her camera. It was then that the pieces dropped into place in her mind. This was how she would get close to Lane, not by approaching him directly but by contacting Andrea, one of his trusted confidantes.

A thousand thoughts fire-worked in her brain, and within a minute, she had her phone out, calling her assistant for a number for Andrea McLeay, the equine photographer. She hung up and continued gazing at these islands of color until she received the number. She rang it, expecting an answering service or assistant, but was pleasantly surprised to have Andrea answer the phone in her cheery Australian voice.

'Hiya. Andy here – how can I help?'

'Hello, Andrea McLeay?'

'That's me. What can I do you for?'

Karen winced at the bright, bold voice, every bit as colorful as the posters in front of her. 'I was hoping to interest you in a couple of projects, Miss McLeay. A few horse magazines want to do feature articles on my mother's horses, so I wanted a good portfolio of photos from her farm in Kentucky.'

'What magazines are we talking about?' Andrea asked.

Karen named a couple of leading equine magazines that she had subscribed to when she was younger and had the time to ride horses and read magazines.

'They would normally have their own photographers, ah, sorry, who am I speaking to?'

'Karen from Bisente Farms. That's my mother's farm. She breeds showjumpers, and we have a few Bisente bred horses likely to compete at the next Olympics. She doesn't ride them herself – perhaps you've heard of Julian O'Sullivan? He's her main rider.'

'Karen Lawford,' the color drained from the voice, and it was as cold and grey as the water flowing past in the gutter.

'That's correct.'

'Sorry, not interested,' Andrea said flatly, 'the magazines will have their own photographers, and I'm sure you already know that any equine photographer would jump at the chance to photograph Julian. I'm really not interested in working for the Lawfords.'

Quickly reorganizing her tactics, Karen asked, 'Because of the Stablex horses?'

Since her twin brother had already used the secret trade name, she felt sure Andrea would be aware of it.

'Yes.'

'I was hoping you would come on board to photograph them as well. There's a six-figure fee on offer for half a day's photography, and since I believe you are the best in the business, I wanted to offer you the work.'

Andrea snorted, 'You've got to be kidding. Have you even looked at my work? Is there any photo you can see of mine that even faintly hints that I'd be interested in photographing what you are doing to those horses?'

Firm in her belief that the Stablex horses lived good lives with expert care and no suffering, Karen countered with, 'Your photos show you care about horses. I care about horses. I want someone to take photos that show that care.'

'Sorry, Luv,' Andrea said briskly without any hint of apology in her voice, 'you've got the wrong person here. See ya later.'

The phone went dead.

Placing her phone back in her handbag, Karen turned her back on the images of horses in wild landscapes and looked bleakly at the passing cars. Her hunches were rarely incorrect, and when she had seen these posters for Andrea's exhibition, she was sure this was the track that would lead her to Lane Dimity. It was unexpected to have her hunch go so wrong. It was unfamiliar and unsettling to be treated with the disrespect that Andrea had shown once she realized her identity. Usually, her name engendered deference and admiration, not a 'sorry, Luv' and a hang-up. This was...she frowned. This was unacceptable. She would meet this Andrea McLeay, and she would get her to photograph horses – she didn't care if it was her mother's Bisente horses or the Pilatos horses or the carousel horses in the park, but it would happen.

Drawing back her shoulders, she set off down the street, the misting rain in no way concerning her as she strode with purpose through the crowd of shuffling pedestrians who parted around her.

# CHAPTER TWO

*'So, tell me, I've heard you have an unusual thing about showers,' the host of the popular U.S. breakfast show asked.*

*Lane looked at Matt and began signing. Matt interpreted for the host and audience, 'I wouldn't call it a thing so much as an awareness. As the water pours over me, I realize that it connects me to the entire world through almost all of its history. In that shower are atoms that have been in glaciers and every ocean and river, every lake and stream, that have gone through the leaves of forests a million years ago and gone through the bodies of dinosaurs sixty million years ago. There are atoms that have been breathed in and out of almost every living creature on this planet, which have been locked up in ice caps and hurled around in millions of years of storms. I'm not just showering in water that came out of a pipe; I am immersed in atoms that connect me to everything through all of time with this planet.'*

*'Wow, just wow…' the host stopped, lost for words at the enormity of this awareness.*

**The YouTube version of this episode was their most-watched interview of the year.**

## Arizona

With his arms thrown back, Lane raised his face to the sun and felt the power that had left the star eight minutes ago surge through the skin on his face, arms, and bare torso. For several minutes, he sat on his unmoving horse as though they were a monument in honor of the sun's reign. The shadows cast by the high sun highlighted the pattern of muscles on his taut abdomen and sculpted the definition of his fit and muscular body. A sharp, black shade line marked the point where his blue jeans met the bare back and sides of the golden horse.

He gave thanks to the sun as he sat on his horse in the brilliant desert light. He was thankful for every breath he took, connecting him to all life that had ever been on Earth. He was glad to be a part of this universe, made from the same atoms that coalesced into everything else. He was humbled by the fact that, at an atomic level, he was connected to it all and made immortal through his atoms.

A call from below the steep hill brought him out of his reflections, and he sat on the bridleless horse, alerting the animal to action. Taking the almost invisible neck rope in one hand, he closed his legs lightly, and the horse launched over the edge of the precipice to land on the soft scree. Sitting down on its haunches, it slid and scrabbled down the hill, its ears pricked with the joy of being alive with a rider who melded as one with his mount. With one hand on the neck rope to guide the horse, Lane let him break into a canter once the footing was surer. He laughed with the exhilaration of being alive on the back of a good horse in the fleeting moment when the world seemed perfect.

The shrill *bring-bring* of a phone shattered the moment, and he looked over at Andrea, who lowered her camera and answered her phone. He hoped she had her shots as it was the third time he'd ridden his horse down the slope, and he didn't want to do it again. His horse had already given a flawless performance and deserved a rest.

Cantering back to where his friends stood, he grinned at Matt and Tom as he asked for some flying changes, and his horse did five two-time changes with the precision of a Grand Prix horse while he guided with the neck rope.

'Let's get back to taking photos,' Andrea smiled at her three male models as she slid her phone back in her pocket and picked up her camera.

'Who was that?' Matt asked, nodding at her pocket where she'd put the phone.

'No one important. Now, sexy faces, sexy thoughts. Sexy cowboys sell jeans, so I want you to be sexy.'

'Should you say that about your brother?' Tom pulled a face and raised his brows at her. 'It just doesn't seem right.'

'Right now, you are merely objects to me,' she said grandly, waving one hand airily around. 'You exist to sell those jeans, to make all who see you in those jeans want those jeans. You are the jeans, and the world wants you.'

'You are so full of crap, Andy' her twin, Matt, shook his head at her. 'Get on with the photos so we can get out of these jeans.'

Andy's gaze slid to Tom, and she gave him a wicked smile, 'And yet you stay silent when my brother tells me he wants to get out of his jeans. What's with that?'

'I'll tell you what's with it,' Tom glared at her, the twinkle in his eyes belying his fierce look, 'he hits a lot harder than you do if I tease him.'

'Fair enough,' she shrugged before stepping back to eye the scene with her artist's eye. 'I'm done with the Lane-god-of-the-sun shots, and I want some of the half-naked cowboys, now.'

Tom and Matt were shirtless in their blue jeans, their chiseled abs glistening in the Arizona sun, their faces shaded under the brims of their western hats. Tilting her head, Andy took in the whole scene - the colors of the sky and desert, the two palomino horses standing next to the men without as much as a rope around their necks to prevent them from moving away, the tanned torsos, the blue jeans, the dusty boots, the tufts of grass at their feet. They were the paints on her pallet, and she simply had to move them around to create a work of art that would satisfy her client and stimulate the sale of these jeans.

'Lane, can you get both the horses to look that direction and prick their ears?' she pointed to her left and threw him a smile as he moved his mount to change the line of sight of the other two horses and raised his hand, clicking his fingers. Both horses instantly came to attention, their eyes riveted on him.

'Yep, that's it. That's how I want them looking. Ah, let's see…good… now, hats off so I can see your faces. Hold them in your left hands. Now, Matt, you sort of half face your horse and lean your right hand on his wither and look into his eye as though you're speaking to him. OK. That's good; you hold that. Tom, can you bring that saddle in and put it down in front of and between the horses. No, both saddles, and the bridles and ropes. That looks better. Now, squat down and put your left hand with the hat on the horn of the closest saddle and look up at Matt's horse.'

As she spoke, she began to click, capturing images that might meet the marketing requirements.

'Matt, look down at Tom. Smile. No, don't laugh, you dingbats, just smile at each other in a Brokeback kinda way. Good. Tom, stand up between the horses and face me, and both of you look at Lane like the horses are doing, like you are all watching something unusual and interesting coming over the horizon…'

The horses came to attention, their eyes wide, and Matt and Tom started to laugh. Andy swung around quickly to catch Lane hunched over like an ape next to his horse, his hands trailing in the dust as he did a remarkably life-like imitation of a gorilla.

He immediately straightened and shot her a chagrined look when he met her unamused gaze, then signed, *I was unusual and interesting.*

'You were a doofus,' she told him, rolling her eyes. 'You were lucky the horses didn't bolt.'

*They thought I was interesting.*

'I think you're unusual, but that's me being polite,' her face split into a grin as she couldn't hide her amusement for long. 'Let's get back to this shoot. Sexy cowboys and palominos sell jeans. The money the advertising agency pays me covers my bills and buys you all food and drink.'

*OK, I'll be serious.*

'No need to be serious, just don't be a gorilla and send our horses off into the desert,' she told him, turning back to the half-naked cowboys and their horses, continuing her instructions as she clicked away.

Twenty minutes later, they were done. As Andy packed her camera equipment away, Matt and Tom carried the saddles and bridles back to the horse trailer parked nearby. The three horses followed Lane as he walked them back to the trailer. Andy raised her head from her camera case to watch Lane touch each horse above the eyes in a caress that spoke to the horses, and they relaxed trustingly into his touch. He closed his eyes and breathed in the essence of horse, connecting himself to these three, then stepped to one side of the trailer ramp and pointed for the first horse to step up. Although she'd seen it many times before, it always brought a bubble of emotion to her chest as she watched the horses load themselves. They followed Lane's silent instructions as though he was speaking as clearly to them as she spoke to others when she used her voice.

The first horse stood at an angle in the trailer, and Lane clicked the divider shut. Then he nodded to the second horse, and it stepped up and maneuvered into position so he could shut the next divider. He closed the third divider onto the last horse and raised the trailer ramp to enclose them, checked all the catches, and went to help Andy load the camera equipment.

*That was Karen L. on the phone*, he signed once everything was loaded.

'Yes, it was,' she sighed. She had spoken softly on the phone but should have realized that even though her brother and Tom hadn't heard her, Lane's hearing was more acute than theirs.

'What was?' asked Matt, joining them at the back of the pickup, his chest now covered with a tan cotton shirt, the photo-shoot Stetson replaced with his own work-worn Akubra, and the tight new city jeans traded for a comfortable riding pair.

'Karen Lawford from Pilatos was on the phone,' she told him, loud enough so that Tom could hear from the back door of the truck where he was putting his shirt on.

'You're kidding!' Matt opened his mouth in a cartoon gape.

Tom stepped into view, adjusting the belt on his faded jeans, his expression interested, 'What did she want?'

'She had some story about wanting me to photograph her mother's horses, and-slash-or the Stablex ones.'

*She used the name Stablex?*

'Yes, she did.'

Tom narrowed his eyes, thinking of the recent contact made by Joe Kaiphas. 'So, their security top-dog contacts Matt wanting to reach Lane. Now the heir-to-the-throne contacts you and is open with the name of the product that they've gone to such lengths to keep secret …they're worried.'

'So am I,' Andy looked into the depths of Tom's eyes, knowing that they shared the same thoughts: the people at the top of Pilatos Industries knew about them and knew they were planning something in relation to Stablex, and the feelers were coming out. 'They're powerful, they're greedy, and they have billions tied up in Stablex – they are going to want to stop us.'

Matt cocked his head to one side like a dog considering a problem, 'Shouldn't they be more worried about the big organizations that exist for the welfare of animals? We're just three Aussies and an American climatologist. We're not that much of a big deal.'

'Yes, we are,' Andy punched his arm none too lightly, 'we have Lane, and he's the big deal. He tells people to avoid Stablex, and there are tens of millions wiped off their profits immediately. He tells people to avoid Pilatos products, and there are hundreds of millions taken away from them. That's a big deal.'

Lane shook his head, his brown eyes thoughtful as he looked at the horizon and beyond. He knew there had to be more than a social media campaign telling people to avoid a product that hadn't even been released yet. He wanted everything to do with those Pilatos horses ripped down and thrown to the winds, not only to stop Pilatos from what they were doing but as a clear message to all companies with similar plans that it would no longer be accepted. It would be stopped. A 'don't buy this' campaign was not enough as there were always people who wanted to buy a product regardless of the damage and heartache it caused in production.

*Call her back,* his hands and expression spoke slowly at first, then picked up speed as the thoughts gelled in his mind, *tell her you'll photograph both her mother's horses and the Pilatos horses. Say you'll need your full photographic team. They're playing chess with us, trying to stay two moves ahead, so we need to be four, five, and six moves ahead of them. They have to think they are checkmating us without knowing what we have planned.*

'And that is?' Matt asked.

*I don't know yet,* Lane threw him a lop-sided grin and shrugged, *I'm not that far ahead, but it'll be good, it'll be big, and it will hurt them.*

'Please tell me you're not talking bombs,' Andy wrinkled her nose at him, 'you sound like a terrorist.'

'He's more your Jack Russell Terrorist than a bombs-and-guns terrorist,' Matt slapped his friend on the back, and they smirked at each other. 'Just point him at a shed, say *rat,* and he'll dig the place up with his bare hands, or paws, I guess, since we're talking Jack Russells.'

'Yeah, but this is not a rat in a shed,' Andy grumbled at her brother, 'this is one of the big pharmaceutical companies, and they can make little dogs like us vanish.'

*It'll be fine,* Lane charmed her with his irresistible smile, then laughed when she pulled a face at him instead of succumbing to the charm of his smile. Andy was one of the few who could resist him.

'It probably won't be fine at all,' she said, moving towards the front of the vehicle so she could drive, 'but I'm on board with it. I'll ring her back tonight after she's had time to try and plan another move that won't be needed after I ring.'

'Cun-ning,' her twin broke the word into two syllables to emphasize it.

'I like the way you think,' Tom winked at her, his face, so somber in photographs, falling into the easy smile that he reserved for his friends. 'What chance does that corporate giant have against us with you on our team?'

'Chance, indeed,' she huffed as she opened the driver's door and instructed them to get in.

They drove back to Tom's family's house, where the horses were released into a paddock behind the buildings with a dozen other palominos and buckskins. Lane spread a few bales of hay out to feed them, and Tom checked their water.

While Andy loaded her photos onto her computer and began editing them for the client, the men helped Tom's older brother fix some of the horse yard fencing. Tom's parents began preparing food for the barbecue to which surrounding Navajo families had been invited. It was a peaceful and productive afternoon in Arizona.

# CHAPTER THREE

*Think with your mind. Act with your heart. Be true to your soul.*
**Meme of Lane Dimity sitting on a horse in front of a spectacular sunset.**
**Shared over thirty million times.**

## The Pilatos Building - New York

After lunch with some of the research and development team, and several meetings throughout the afternoon, Karen instructed her favorite assistant, Sandy, to gather any more information she could find on Lane and his three friends and add it to their files. At four, she did a half-hour workout in the executive gym. After showering, she put on an expensive pantsuit in the usual grey and cream, adding her grandmother's single-strand of pearls to finish the look.

At five, she met with her father and some of the Chinese investors who were taking Pilatos products through to the Asian markets. Her gift for languages was a valuable asset when conducting business with those whose first language was not English. Karen did not speak Mandarin at the meeting. The investors had no idea that she was fluent in their language. The meeting was undertaken in English with one of the investors translating for the two who preferred to speak in their language while Karen remained quiet, taking notes and only talking when her father asked her a question.

After the Chinese left, she spent an intense half-hour with her father filling him in on anything that had been uttered in Mandarin, which had been said with the assumption that the Americans did not understand. Her ability with languages was something known only to her father and perhaps her mother, and it did not turn up in any background search that an investigator might do as she was self-taught and simply had a natural ability to decode languages. It was a useful tool in the presence of associates and competitors who spoke other languages, and it wasn't too difficult to keep the skill hidden.

Then, there were contracts to inspect. Since her Harvard degree was in Law and she specialized in contract law, it had become one of her tasks to check the more critical contracts from their legal department before the company signed off on them. John Lawford did not trust anyone, but he did trust his daughter more than most, and if she indicated to sign, it would be done.

It was almost eight when she left her office and took the private stairs up to her apartment in the residential section of the Pilatos building. There were ten apartments on the top three levels, with hers being the second-largest behind her father's full-floor penthouse two stories above. Her apartment was on the floor immediately above her office and had a private lift and a direct stairway to her office. She usually chose the stairs for the exercise. The facial recognition scan opened the door for her, and she stepped into the privacy of her apartment. Gently, she closed the door behind her and leaned against it for a moment, her eyes shut, her mind running through the memories of all that had happened that day.

'That you, honey?'

Karen had forgotten that Marcus was home tonight from his European conference. She had been looking forward to another quiet night alone.

'Yes, it is,' she forced her voice to sound cheerier than she felt as she straightened up to walk into the living room where he waited, still in his travel suit, with a glass of wine in each hand and a welcoming smile.

'I've missed you,' he stepped in to give her a kiss, the glasses of wine held out to each side.

Karen briefly pressed her lips to his and stepped back to remove one of the glasses of wine from him, raising it in a silent toast to his return. As far as partners went, he ticked all the boxes: Harvard medical where she was Harvard law, wealthy and respected family, older brother a Senator, handsome, urbane, controlled, a considerate lover in the bedroom, an accomplished cook in the kitchen, a sought-after guest at dinner parties, a generous donor at charity events, taller than her, in peak physical condition, blonde and blue-eyed with the slight tan of someone who plays tennis and golf and enjoys a spot of sailing. Could he be more perfect? He fitted into her life as though they were made for each other, and yet…and yet…she pushed those thoughts away and asked him about the conference.

Two glasses of wine were spent with Marcus regaling her with amusing stories from the events in Paris and Berlin, funny things other doctors had shared, insights into the topics covered, excitement over a few new procedures he was keen to try out. He then asked her about Pilatos, and she spent two sips telling him about the five days he was absent.

'Don't forget,' he moved to sit on the arm of her oversized chair, placing a gentle hand on her arm as he gazed down at her, 'we're dining at Cochrane's tonight. It's only a small affair, no more than forty guests, but it is formal, so we'd better change into something more suitable.'

'Do we have to?' she raised her winter ocean eyes to his baby blues, wishing he'd cancel the outing and make some excuse to the Cochranes. There'd be plenty of other people there; it's not as though they had to be present.

'Yes, we do. We accepted this nearly a month ago. Come along – you can leave your work for one evening. I'm sure you spent every night while I was away poring over your work instead of relaxing.'

'Getting my work done is what relaxes me,' she sniffed, placing her glass down on a side table and rising to go to her bathroom. One thing she really enjoyed about this apartment was private bathrooms – she was happy to share a bedroom with a man, but she did like the privacy of her own bathroom.

'Formal, remember,' he reminded her as she shut herself into her sanctuary of the combined bathroom and dressing room to one side of their bedroom.

Looking at herself in the full wall mirror, she parodied Marcus by mouthing, 'Formal, remember,' at herself, then shook her head at her puerile behavior. He was a wonderful man and undeserving of her mockery.

Showering quickly, since it was only a few hours since her last shower in the gym downstairs, she dried off and briefly admired her athletic body in the mirror, turning left and right and deciding it was looking healthier since her daily gym workouts. She selected a silver-grey cocktail-length dress in shimmering folds of silk, black high-heeled shoes, and a string of black pearls. She swept her hair up onto the top of her head and used some black pearl clips to hold it in place, then picked up a black clutch and walked out to the bedroom.

Marcus was still showering, so she went to the living room and opened her laptop to peruse the files on the Dimity gang. She was lost in the action and color of their alien world, where smiles were thrown joyfully at the camera and horses galloped across open plains, when she heard a cough and looked up to see Marcus standing in front of her. In contrast to the jeans and casual shirts favored by Lane, Matt, and Tom, Marcus was wearing an exquisitely cut suit that was probably worth more than all their wardrobes put together. He smiled at her, another glass of wine in his hand.

'Number three, Marcus?' her brows twitched upwards as she regarded the half-empty glass.

'Four, actually,' he smiled at her, and she noticed how similar it was to his brother's Senator's smile, all teeth and very little warmth. 'It feels like one of those nights when the secret to an enjoyable evening will be alcoholic lubrication.'

'I wish we hadn't agreed to go to the Cochrane's tonight,' she removed the glass from his hand and took it to the kitchen, talking as she walked. 'I have a lot of work I want to catch up on, and you need to rest after your travel.'

'You always have a lot of work,' he eyed her morosely as she tipped his wine down the sink and rinsed the glass, 'but you're right, it would have been preferable to be at home tonight. No matter, we'll simply make the best of it. Do you want me to drive, or will you drive, or shall we organize one of your drivers?'

Karen looked from the glass to Marcus and back to the glass, ignoring the slight undertone of malice as he spoke of 'her' drivers. 'I really don't think you should drive. I think Pearce is on duty tonight; I'll give the basement a call.'

She phoned the car park where the company cars were kept and where at least one driver was always on duty, ready to take Pilatos executives or associates wherever they needed. Pearce, her father's personal driver for more than twenty years, was working, and he said he'd have a vehicle ready to go in a few minutes. They caught the private lift down to the basement and engaged in small talk as Pearce helped them into the black BMW.

'How are Alicia's studies going?' Karen asked Pearce as they accelerated away from the Pilatos building.

His eldest daughter was studying at the New York Academy of Art, with the fees funded by the artworks she was selling to Karen, which then went on display in Pilatos buildings across the country. It wasn't totally altruistic - Karen believed her talent was such that, in years to come, the pieces would increase in value and prove to be an excellent investment.

'There's an exhibition on at present, Karen,' he spoke without looking around at her, his eyes performing a constant circuit of scanning left and right and ahead, side mirrors, rear-view mirror, and repeat, 'and she's received some excellent feedback. She has five pieces in, and three have sold already.'

'Wonderful!' Karen was genuinely pleased, and she ignored the hint of an eye-roll from Marcus, who disliked employees calling her by her first name. 'Please let her know that I'll buy the other works if they don't sell.'

'Alicia said she wanted to give them to  you, to thank you for all your support and kindness.'

'Nonsense, it's not kind to invest in art; it's financially sensible.'

'It is kind,' he gave a rare glance at her in the rear-view mirror. He'd known her since she was a serious-eyed child trying to win the affection of her remote father, and he saw beneath the cool, detached exterior that she had developed as an armor against the world in which she operated. 'Don't sell yourself short, Karen. You've supported a lot of young artists, none so much as Alicia, and it is greatly appreciated.'

'George and Felicity will be at Cochrane's tonight,' Marcus spoke over the top of Pearce's last few words, keen to bring Karen's attention back to him. He understood that Pearce had known Karen since she was a child, but he was still just the driver.

Returning her gaze to Marcus, she hid her inward sigh. She didn't particularly like his brother George, the Senator - he was such a politician, so chatty and yet so cagey, so open and yet so secretive, so friendly and yet so distant. She didn't know what he was; he lived for his public image, and she didn't know what lay beneath, or if anything lay beneath the surface, except that her instinct was to draw back from whatever was there. Felicity was the perfect politician's wife, so polite and politically correct, neatly groomed, and dedicated to making everyone feel comfortable around her husband. Karen wondered if there was still a school where they taught beautiful young women that their life's purpose was to be a stage prop for their husbands.

Her gaze slid past Marcus to the night outside the window, and she murmured, 'I thought George wouldn't be leaving Washington while they were debating the reforms on approaches to environmental issues.'

'It's a flying visit. Here this afternoon to meet with Mother, then the Cochrane's tonight since there will be a few power players there, and then back early in the morning.'

'Do you know what his approach is to the environment and wildlife? I have asked him, but he replied with a lot of words and not a lot of information.'

Marcus laughed, 'Sounds like George. He was born a politician. When we were kids, Mum would ask him what he wanted for dinner, and he'd mention ten dishes in the space of two minutes without leaving any idea of which one he wanted, but you felt that he'd support you in your decision, and that your decision was the one he wanted all along.'

'Is that what it takes to be a politician?' she mused, thinking that all the talk without purpose would have been tiresome. 'Being able to talk in circles without saying anything?'

'At least half the time,' Marcus grinned at her, and his genuine warm smile helped lift the touch of melancholy that seemed to have settled on her this grey day.

As Pearce pulled up outside the building where the Cochranes lived, Karen's phone rang. She looked at the number, ready to ignore the call. It was from Andrea McLeay. In any spare minute that afternoon and evening, Karen had been trying to think of ways to meet with Matt or Tom since she'd struck out with Andrea. It felt important to meet Lane Dimity and assess him in person so that she could work out what level of risk he posed to Pilatos. He's just one person, part of her mind said, while another part felt scared of what that one person might be capable of if he decided to go through with an attack on Pilatos. Perhaps not knowing how to approach these unusual people was partly behind her strange mood that afternoon.

Hesitantly, not knowing where this call was going, and disliking not knowing, Karen accepted the call and said hello.

'Hi, Karen, look, it's Andy McLeay here.'

'Good evening, Andrea. How can I help you?'

'I've had a cancellation next week, so I have two days available if you're still interested in photographing your mother's horses and the Pilatos horses.'

'I certainly am interested, so please lock us in for both days.'

'Excellent. I'll have a camera crew of three or four if that's alright.'

Matt, Tom, Lane, and perhaps someone else, Karen's lip twitched; that would be perfect.

'That would be fine. I'll text you my private email details, and please let me know what days and times suit. I'll work around you.'

'No need to put yourself out, Karen. Just have someone point us at the horses, and we'll get the job done.'

'It's not putting me out. I'm always happy to visit my mother on Bisente Farm, as well as check in on the Pilatos horses.'

'I'm looking forward to meeting you, then.'

'Before you go, Andrea, tell me, what changed your mind? You seemed quite adamant earlier that you wanted nothing to do with me or our horses.'

If Karen had expected her to be taken aback by the question or at all discomforted by it, she was sadly mistaken.

Andrea laughed with good humor and replied, 'Well, Lane, of course. He changes everything.'

'Ah, I see. I hope to meet him.'

'You will.'

The call ended on a friendlier basis than their first conversation. Karen slowly put the phone back in her bag. Her mind ran in many directions, trying to work out what moves were being made in this game. She wanted to meet Lane and have the opportunity to judge his views and change his mind, perhaps buy him off, or decide to hand the project over to Joe Kaiphas, who seemed particularly adept at removing threats to Pilatos. Her thoughts stalled on Joe and his work - she didn't want to know how he achieved it sometimes.

As long as she had a good security team in place, there wasn't any chance the Australians could sabotage anything at the farm or Pilatos. Each of them would have security watching them at all times, and everything would be on security cameras. She couldn't see what they hoped to achieve by coming to her like this as they must know they wouldn't be in a position to damage anything, and she knew there could be no exposé on the conditions of the horses at Pilatos as they were exceptionally well cared for and had passed all welfare inspections. Perhaps Lane just wanted to meet with her and attempt to change her mind as she wanted to change his.

'Are you coming, dear?' Marcus repeated for the third time, his voice a touch testy after being ignored twice.

'Uh? Oh, sorry, Marcus. Lost in thought.'

'I could see that. Perhaps the night air will refresh you a little.'

She accepted his arm as she gracefully folded her long legs out of the car and rose to her feet. Turning to speak to Pearce, she noted the pinched look on his face and correctly guessed that he didn't like the way Marcus spoke to her. 'We'll only be about two hours, Pearce...'

'More like three,' Marcus interrupted her.

'So, if you want to go home to Pilatos, that's fine. If you are due to knock off, would you mind letting the next driver know that we'll be calling when we're ready to go – in about two hours?'

Pearce gave her an approving look and nodded, 'I'll be nearby, Karen. Just give a call when you're ready.' He held up two fingers to indicate two hours and winked at her.

She chuckled and gently shut the door behind her and walked with Marcus into the gathering of power people. Usually, it would excite her to be the Pilatos representative at an assembly like this, winning approval and buttering-up the people who could make things easier for the company, but tonight it seemed…it seemed unimportant. Her mind wandered to those colorful images of the men and women riding horses in the wilderness, and something about that seemed so much more vital than pouring saccharine on the power brokers.

When the two hours of wine, food, talk, and endless admiring of others were up, Karen made her excuses to her hosts and told Marcus she was going home. She added that he was welcome to stay. He had spent most of the evening with his brother and sister-in-law, so it wasn't as though he would miss her company.

'I might stay,' he smiled at her in a way that may have looked warm to those watching, but Karen could see a distinct coolness in his eyes.

'Just give Pearce a call when you're ready to come home,' she nodded to him and began to head towards the door.

'I'll walk you down,' he put a hand to her elbow, bowing briefly to the people he was standing with as he left.

In the lift, Karen dialed Pearce and informed him she was ready to be picked up, and he told her that he'd be there in under two minutes.

'Are you sure you won't come home, Marcus?' she asked politely.

'Actually, I don't think I will,' he replied civilly. 'I thought I might stay in my own apartment tonight.'

'That's fine,' she nodded, 'I won't wait up then. Shall I see you tomorrow?'

'If you want to. Perhaps we should have a break from each other. You don't seem to have missed me while I was away, and tonight I may as well have been here with a stranger.'

'Yes, I agree,' she shrugged, a little alarmed at her complete lack of emotion. This was a fight, wasn't it? A polite one, but still a fight. Her partner didn't want to come home with her. He wanted a break from her. That certainly was not a healthy sign in a relationship. Instead of feeling upset, all she could think of was that she could enjoy stretching out across the bed again tonight.

'I can pick up my things tomorrow if you like,' he regarded her with sad eyes that were a touch bleary from travel and alcohol.

'Perhaps that would be for the best,' she responded, 'I think you deserve a partner more like Felicity, and I'm just not inclined that way.'

'No, you're not,' he sighed, 'you're better than Felicity. You're independent, strong, and amazing. I love all that about you, but you don't need me to make your life whole.'

Karen sniffed in slight amusement and laid a hand on his arm, 'No woman needs a man in her life to be whole. We are whole people by ourselves, not half people.'

'But you don't even need me. I want to feel needed.'

'How odd,' she shook her head, thinking about his words. 'Why do you want to be needed? Is that a fault with you or with me?'

'Perhaps with both of us, Karen.'

'Yes, perhaps.'

Karen stopped in the foyer and told him to go back to the party, 'I'll wait out front for Pearce...or not, that's him now.'

'So, should we talk about this tomorrow?' he asked her, hoping to see some sign that she was desperate to make things work between them, but Karen never seemed desperate for anything except to keep Pilatos Industries growing.

'I don't think there is any need,' she replied. 'I can pack up your things and have someone take them round to your place.'

'We could have had a life together, Karen; we still could.'

'I have a life, Marcus. You were a part of that life, and now, it seems, you're not, but life will go on.'

'Your obsession with the company will go on,' he said, a tinge of bitterness in his voice, for he knew that she would never walk away from Pilatos. That was her obsession and her real love, while she seemed unmoved by the notion of walking away from him.

'Yes, it probably will,' she offered him a small smile and reached up to plant a light kiss on his cheek. 'I'd appreciate it if we could remain friends. I enjoy your company.'

'Friends,' he inclined his head and looked down at the pattern on the carpet as he realized that where there was no passion, there was likely to be no hatred so that friendship could exist. 'Yes, we'll be friends.'

They parted, and he watched her go to the car where Pearce held the back door open for her, but she shook her head at him and opened the front door for herself.

'Everything OK?' Pearce asked as he settled behind the steering wheel and pulled into the traffic.

'I think Marcus and I have broken up. I'm not one hundred percent sure, but he's not coming home, and I'm packing his things up tomorrow to send over to his place.'

'I'd call that a breakup,' Pearce nodded, his eyes doing the continual roaming check of everything around them in case there was any danger. 'You don't appear to be very upset, but are you sure you're OK? I can get Alicia to come and stay the night with you if you'd like company.'

'That's sweet of you, Pearce, but, really, I'm fine,' she leaned her head back and closed her eyes, wondering why she felt nothing: no sadness, anger, or confusion, or even a sense of having said goodbye. It wasn't *a nothing* made up of emptiness, and it wasn't a numbness from shock; it was as if the lady who worked in the deli where she occasionally bought some olives and cheese had told her that she was no longer going to work there. It had no impact on her life at all.

Perhaps there's something intrinsically wrong with me, she thought when she entered her apartment and looked at the photos of her and Marcus together on a yacht, on an island, playing tennis, and in other settings looking companionable and well-matched. She walked to her bedroom, seeing the evidence of Marcus in her life in the photos and his possessions, but she still had no reaction except one of inconvenience. She wanted to do some more research on Lane Dimity and his friends but felt she should take care of the Marcus things first.

Changing into grey jeans and a white t-shirt, she found a couple of folded-down boxes in a cupboard, snapped them back into shape, and began walking around, packing up anything that belonged to Marcus. There weren't many things, just some clothes and some books, a couple of decorator items, bathroom products, and some of the photos. It was as though he had just been passing through. After she sealed the boxes, she went around and gathered up all the images that had him in them and put them in a cupboard, and, like that, he was gone. There was no sign of Marcus in her apartment, and the few years they'd been together hadn't even left a footprint on her heart.

Maybe I'm as sociopathic as Phillip and Jeremy, Karen thought as she sat down at her desk and flicked through the files on her laptop to find the ones that Sandy had been adding this afternoon, this complete lack of emotion would certainly support that. Does it even matter? Would I be happy to spend the rest of my life alone like this?

She looked around at the perfect neatness of her living space, the quiet, and the peace, and decided it might be the life for her. Tapping on a file of photos Sandy had put together on Lane and his friends, Karen began skipping through them, once more drawn into the color and intensity of the images, which were mostly photos taken by Andrea. There was one that she came back to several times, showing a shirtless Lane astride an Appaloosa, his arms outstretched and his face turned skywards as he galloped in front of an endless sky. He looked so free.

It would be an excellent image for Stablex, she thought, seeing how it could be used in a marketing campaign. Even if Andrea refused to take photos like that for Pilatos, she decided she would find someone who would. Picking up her stylus, she wrote across the screen over the picture in her flowing script, *Stablex: secret men's business.* Yes, that would work as a slogan over a series of images of young, virile men who set pulses racing.

Tapping a video clip of the four friends being interviewed on an Australian television breakfast show, Karen stared closely at Lane as his hands answered questions, and Matt and Andrea explained the answers to the journalist. Karen did not know sign language, but she was beginning to pick out words and expressions after only a few minutes, so she decided it was time to learn another language.

Her mind was particularly attuned to decoding languages, and she was confident that, given a week of study in her spare hours, she could have a basic understanding of what Lane was signing by the time they met. Looking at the empty spot on her desk where a photo of Marcus had sat until this evening, she told herself that she had a few extra hours now that their relationship was over.

# CHAPTER FOUR

*You can get excellent results by using brute force with your horse, you can even win Olympic Gold, but true beauty comes from the harmony of horse and rider working together towards a common goal. One of the amazing attributes of horses is that they want to work in partnership with us. Of course, you are in charge of the partnership, but you respect and listen to your partner; you don't force them to subjugate themselves to your whip and spur and rein - you use those things to guide their will, not force it. You cannot ride with heart if you ride with heartless force.*

**'Ride With Heart' by Lane Dimity, p.25**
**A best-seller worldwide, translated into twenty-five languages.**

### Bisente Farm - Kentucky

Karen had Pearce fly her in one of the Pilatos helicopters to Bisente Farm where her mother lived, a half-hour by road outside Lexington. There was a helipad on the roof of the New York Pilatos building, so it was a convenient mode of transport for out-of-state visits. Her father rarely visited Bisente, even though he remained married to Karen's mother Isabella, but he often went to Pilatos Farm on the other side of Lexington to check on progress there.

'Darling,' Isabella greeted her daughter with open arms as Karen stepped away from the helicopter on the landing pad between the main house and the show jumping arena. 'I am ecstatic that you managed to organize Andrea McLeay for these photos. Julian is so pleased; I swear he's changed his outfit six times this morning to find the best look for the magazines. And you look so beautiful.'

In her dove grey pantsuit, cream shirt, and black accessories, her rich mahogany hair swept up and clasped in place with black pearl combs, Karen thought she looked the perfect executive, but if her mother thought she was beautiful, she wouldn't argue.

Karen hugged her mother a little stiffly. Physical affection had never come easy to her. When she was younger, her mother seemed so busy that she had little time for hugging and closeness, and her father thought it was a sign of weakness. Only in the past ten years, since Isabella had retired to life on Bisente with her team of horses and all her other animals, had she become a hugger, and Karen was still not used to it.

Isabella was not as tall as Karen and had the trim athletic build of a horse rider, a look accentuated by her white shirt, jodhpurs, and knee-high black riding boots. Her dark hair was tied back in a ponytail, and the radiant skin on her aristocratic Spanish face was worthy of a woman twenty years younger.

'I wasn't sure it would happen, but I'm glad it did,' Karen allowed her mother to tuck her arm into hers and lead her back to the house, a sprawling white hacienda overlooking the gardens, show jump arena, dressage arenas, lush paddocks, and cross-country course, with views to the mountains beyond.

'I thought she might change her mind because of your father's horses over at Pilatos Farm,' Isabella shook her head, 'I know for a fact that her friend, the outback boy Lane Dimity, is not the sort to accept what is going on there.'

'I think he's thirty-two, Mother, not exactly a boy. Also, nothing is *going on* there,' Karen protested. 'You make it sound as though the horses are being beaten to a pulp before being slowly roasted. All the welfare checks so far have come out in our favor – the horses are happy.'

'You used to love horses, dear.'

'I still do, Mother, so stop thinking there's anything wrong with how the Pilatos horses are being treated. In fact, I've managed to score a shoot with Andrea over there tomorrow, and I'm hoping she'll see for herself that the horses are perfectly happy.'

'Will Lane be with her?'

'I'm hoping so,' Karen followed her mother into the vast expanse of the main living area, turning to admire the view back down over the show jumping arena and cross-country course set up around the lake below the house. 'I have a feeling he's going to try and cause problems for Pilatos.'

'I *know* he's going to cause problems,' her mother smiled and offered a glass of green juice to her daughter. 'You'll love that – my latest recipe with banana and kale, apples, ginger, and plenty of other things.'

Karen sniffed the drink and sipped it tentatively. Thank goodness it wasn't as bad as it looked. Her mother was always following some fad or other when it came to healthy eating, and raw foods with lots of juices seemed to be her latest. Since Isabella looked more like Karen's sister than her mother, it was probably working quite well.

'How do you know he's going to cause problems? Is it because he's a complete trouble maker when it comes to animal rights, or is there something specific?'

'Specific,' Isabella took a mouthful of her own drink and motioned Karen to sit on one of the white leather armchairs that faced the view.

Pearce entered the house with two small cases, his own and Karen's, and Isabella went to him, placing her glass on a table before sweeping her arms up to give him a hug. Pearce, still holding the bags, did the best he could to return the friendliness without hitting Isabella with luggage or dropping them on her feet. Karen met his eyes and grinned wickedly, knowing he was as uncomfortable with Isabella's physical displays of affection as she was.

'So wonderful to see you, Pearce,' Isabella enthused, 'I have your usual room made up for you. I wish Alicia could have made the trip, perhaps next time. Look, I have one of her paintings right there.'

She waved an elegant finger at one of the walls featuring a large canvas of abstract autumnal colored horses frolicking on bluegrass.

Pearce nodded at his daughter's painting. 'I'll let her know, Isabella. And lovely to see you, too. You are looking wonderful, as always.'

'Ever the charmer,' Isabella smiled up at him from under lowered lashes. 'Leave the bags there and join us, please.'

'I'd love to, Isabella,' he kept a firm hold on the bags, 'but I need to drop these in the rooms and fly straight over to Pilatos Farm. Joe rang a few minutes ago and said there was a bit of a demonstration starting up over there, people with placards and that sort of stuff. He wants me to check it out for him and let him know if he needs to bring more security down.'

Concern clouded Karen's eyes as he spoke. This was a new development and a worrying one. They didn't want attention there as the media, always desperate for views, hits, likes, follows, shares, and comments, would sensationalize what was going on to make a scandal where none existed. Many of the media heads were friends with her father, and they could minimize a lot of troublesome stories, but there were always those he couldn't control and those who didn't let the truth get in the way of a ratings-winning story.

'That would be the specific problem,' Isabella nodded to her daughter as Pearce left to take the bags into their bedrooms.

'What do you mean?'

'You won't find any public proof of Lane Dimity asking people to go there and demonstrate,' Isabella informed them, 'but Julian told me this morning that quite a few horse people he knows have received calls from Lane's friends in the last twenty-four hours, asking them to show their support for the Pilatos horses by picketing the gates at the farm.'

With lips narrowed in anger, Karen considered the new tactic that had come into play on the day she was likely to meet this outback man who didn't talk. Had the demonstration been the plan all along, and it was coincidental that it started today? Or had he chosen to press her buttons with this demonstration to see her response when they met? If so, he would be disappointed as he would see nothing except calm, cool leadership. She would not give in to any emotions in front of this self-styled, social media attention-seeking, equine guru. Repeating the description to herself, she found she liked it and filed it away to be brought out to his face or perhaps in an interview – it was the right mix of disdain, condescension, and accuracy.

'I don't know what they hope to achieve,' Karen exhaled and controlled her anger. 'Those horses are perfectly happy and extremely well cared for. We've proven that repeatedly. They're just seeking attention for themselves.'

'That may be,' Pearce nodded as he returned empty-handed, 'but it's working. Joe said that there are already a few media people there, and the number will grow. We need to find a way to shut this down.'

'Let me know what is going on when you report into Joe,' Karen told him as he left. 'I'll see if I can organize some of the heads of the welfare organizations who've inspected the stables to turn up and speak to whoever has been conned into demonstrating. Surely, once they know that the horses are fine, they'll leave.'

Shrugging, Pearce replied, 'It's been my experience that crowd mentality in a demonstration doesn't listen to truth and logic – they are running on emotions and are hungry for conflict, not conciliation. But you can try.'

Glancing at her watch, Karen nodded, 'I will try. I have two hours before Andrea gets here, so I'll see what can be achieved in that time. I want those protesters looking like fools, not looking like they are revealing some big secret to the public.'

Pearce left to start the helicopter back up and fly the twenty minutes to Pilatos Farm, while Karen caught up with the Bisente news with her mother. A new German Warmblood stallion was due to arrive to improve the jumping lines in the horses, one of the current stallions had been sold to Australia, and a team of five show jumpers had been sold to China for a total of ten million dollars. Julian and one of the other Bisente riders were shortlisted for the U.S. Olympic Show Jumping Team, and three other Bisente horses were likely to compete for two other countries. In all, Isabella's interest in show jumping was an international success.

'All wonderful news, Mother,' Karen assured her after she finished delivering the tenth or eleventh story to prove how well Bisente was going, 'and I'm looking forward to seeing Julian and the horses when the photographer is here, but, if you don't mind, I'm going to try and do some damage control with these picketers at Pilatos before the situation gets out of hand.'

'Not a good day to meet Lane, is it? You know, with him bringing his war to your gates, so to speak. Perhaps he won't be with Andrea today; he might be down at Pilatos Farm or somewhere else. It could be quite awkward for you if he does turn up.'

'Oh, he'll turn up,' Karen narrowed her eyes and tried to find the pattern in what was going on today. Her mind ran in many directions, with thoughts scurrying like mice in a maze. She considered the factors and possible outcomes, ran through alternatives, and tried to work out his objectives in initiating this demonstration today.

She thought over what she learned about him and his past campaigns during her late-night study sessions that week. Her mother was correct in her terminology – he was bringing the war to her, and the picketing today was the equivalent of some of his soldiers shaking spears at her. She and the other Pilatos executives were on one side, he was on the other, and the issue they fought over was the welfare of the Stablex horses, which wasn't a real issue as she knew beyond doubt that they were superbly cared for and were in no way suffering. Science and logic were on her side, but she knew that people were moved by emotions, not logic.

She could take a drive anywhere in rural America, or any other country, and she would find horses that really were suffering, ones that were not receiving enough food or veterinary care or farrier work, she would find horses hungry and in pain, horses treated and trained in cruel, barbaric ways. There was so much that was wrong with how horses were looked after in her country and around the world, but not at Pilatos Farm. Of course, activists liked the right target, so it would suit them to ignore all the horses owned by individuals, horses that did need their help, and focus on the Stablex horses owned by a multinational company because that would bring a lot of media attention if they could get the war underway.

And today, she thought as she started to see the pattern when viewed as war games, today, the leader of the activists was going to meet with one of the generals of Pilatos to assess her, just as she wanted to evaluate him. So, he created a skirmish to see how she would react. Yes, that made sense. He had already made his ultimate objective clear to Joe when Matt told him that the facility would shut. That was what they wanted – no Stablex - and today was a way of weighing her up, and tomorrow would be a way for them to have an inside look at the horses.

There was nothing to hide, though, she told herself. The facilities weren't kept locked away from the world because they were hiding what was being done to the horses; it was to stop industrial espionage as they had billions of dollars at stake with Stablex. Also, they had to ensure the highest quarantine conditions for the horses - they had to be kept safe from equine illnesses and disease. Tomorrow, security would be watching Lane and his friends to ensure they did not damage anything, so having them take photographs of the horses should not do any harm. After all, Lane had claimed to have already seen the facility, so he either entered as one of the members of a work team or had an employee secretly video the facility for him.

Yes, she wanted to meet them today and show them that she was not upset by the demonstration at the farm gates, and she wanted them to see the horses tomorrow and realize that their welfare concerns were groundless. She would produce some facts and figures that Sandy had found, showing how many horses in the U.S. were suffering from neglect and starvation, and try to convince them to turn their attention to horses that genuinely needed assistance.

'Earth to Karen,' Isabella repeated for the third time before her daughter came out of the maze of thoughts, 'glad to have you back. I do find it unsettling when you disappear into your thoughts like that.'

'Sorry, Mother, but sometimes I do need to block out everything outside of my head so I can focus on what's inside.'

'Yes, I know, and it allows you to come up with some remarkable ideas and solutions, but I still find it a little odd. Now, as I was saying when you were off in your head somewhere, go and use my office to do what you need to do, and I'll let you know when Andrea arrives. I do hope Lane is with her. You know, I follow him on Facebook and Twitter. I think he's an extraordinary man. And handsome. Very handsome. He makes me wish I was your age.'

'Really, Mother?' Karen arched her brows at Isabella. 'He's years younger than I am, and he seems decades younger in some ways from what I've seen and read. It's hard to imagine a man nearly my age living like he does.'

'Which is?'

'Like a gypsy, just traveling around staying with friends, no car, no more possessions than what he puts in a backpack. He lives like a teenager.'

'And is that so wrong?'

'Of course, it is,' she said as she made a move to leave the room because she knew she couldn't argue why it was wrong, only that she knew it was wrong. 'He should start taking responsibility for his life, like an adult. Like me.'

'So, focus on earning money for oneself rather than helping those who need help?'

'That is a ridiculous thing to say,' Karen said airily, hoping to end the disagreement with the sweeping statement that worked well when she was a teenager. 'I'll be in your office if you need me. Let me know when the photographer and the others arrive.'

Isabella watched her daughter march out of the room, and her lips twitched with amusement. There were many regrets she had in life, perhaps the greatest being that she had not been a good mother to Karen. She had been a wonderful society wife and an excellent businessman's partner, but she hadn't been the right mother for a child.

Now, her daughter was distant and restrained, in control and alone. It would be interesting when she met the absolute opposite of what she had become, someone who, instead of being cool and shadowed, was warm and filled with sunshine. I hope they fight like cat and dog, she smiled as she picked up Karen's empty glass and took it to the sink, it would be good for Karen to let some emotions out and lose control.

In the ninety minutes before her mother advised her that Andrea had presented at the security gates, Karen managed to accomplish a mountain of jobs that really should have been done by Phillip Reach. He was still of the mind that 'a mute boy from the outback' and his mystic-crystal followers posed no threat at all to them, but she had begun to see otherwise.

She had organized the spokespeople from several welfare organizations to be at the Pilatos Farm gates within two hours to speak to any media present. They would confirm that the facilities were carefully inspected and monitored and that the demonstrators were ill-advised if they believed there were any issues with the horses. Using her father's friendship network, she had contacted a number of the larger media outlets to ensure that they didn't pick up this non-story and turn it into a sensationalized falsehood that misled the public. Also, she had promised them a lot of advertising for the new product being developed, as well as free samples, which would be in short supply once people learned what it could achieve.

Pearce informed her that there had been about ninety people at the gates when he arrived, but more were coming every few minutes. A call had gone out, and they were picking up this horse-cause with relish without having any understanding of that cause; it was merely a chance to protest against a multinational company in what they saw as a glorious David and Goliath match. They wanted to hate the powerful, and this was their chance to show their own power.

In a move to try and decrease the crowd animosity towards Pilatos, Karen organized several food and coffee vans to go to the farm gates and offer free food and beverages financed by Pilatos, with serviettes and reusable cups all branded with the Pilatos logos. She smiled as she thought of people faced with turning down free refreshments from the company they envisioned as their enemy. Few would turn it down as she had faith in the greed of humans: people loved free stuff.

As she left the office to join her mother on the front lawn to greet the Dimity gang, as she was coming to think of them, she knew the protesters would now be enjoying free sample bags of Pilatos products with over five hundred dollars' worth of items in each.

There were pens, art pencils, notebooks, and other products from their office and art supply subsidiaries; drink bottles, cups, and reusable shopping bags from their environmental range designed to reduce wastage; vegetable seeds, organic certified plant fertilizer, and recycled plant pots from their agricultural lines; dog and cat care goods from their veterinary side of production, and a selection of their most popular skincare and non-prescription pharmaceutical products from the part of Pilatos that was most well-known.

The sample bags would serve as a reminder of how Pilatos improved lives and of their environmental sensitivity. While other companies remained resistant to the types of change that helped the environment, Pilatos was becoming a company that cared for the future of the planet.

A smile played around her lips as she strode towards Andrea and the three men as they alighted from a silver sedan. Although she was sure that there were some protesters so profoundly committed to Lane's cause that they might turn down the bags, she was even more convinced that there would be people trying to get several bags because humans were inherently greedy, and they would be desperate to get the free goodies. Perhaps he thought his move with the protesters might be a check, but it was an empty play that she was neutralizing. He would not win.

Isabella looked on with interest as her daughter, shoulders back and head high, stepped forward to meet her adversaries.

'Andrea,' Karen put her hand out and shook the steady hand of the photographer, meeting her dark brown eyes with a smile, 'thank you for coming to Bisente. Karen Lawford,' she nodded to indicate herself, 'and this is my mother, Isabella Lawford.'

'Karen, Isabella,' Andrea addressed them both, 'and I'm happy to be here. It was lucky I had that cancellation so we could fit you in.'

'Lucky, yes,' Karen agreed without any belief in her voice. She had wondered if she should feign ignorance of the identities of the others, but her gut told her to be upfront and honest. They would know that Pilatos had investigated them and that she was Pilatos, so there was no need to be coy at this stage. 'And I'm glad you've bought Lane, Matt, and Tom with you,' she smiled at each of them, her eyes cold. 'Welcome to Bisente.'

Four pairs of eyes regarded her, each with a different expression. Andrea's held an iota of warmth, as though she could be glad to be here, but her brother's eyes, so similar to hers in shape and color, were quite hostile. Tom wore a stern, inscrutable expression like a mask, and Lane looked at her with open curiosity as though he was examining something new and interesting. She met his soft brown gaze and shivered inwardly. He had such an open, guileless look to him, and she had the feeling that he was looking through all the layers of her life to her inner self that remained cloaked from the world. It was unsettling, and she pulled herself back from his gaze before she fell in and drowned.

With her eyes hooded, she held out her right arm to shake the hands of each of the men, finding it easy to stare into the hostile and the unfathomable faces of Matt and Tom, but refusing to raise her eyes to Lane's face.

Lane began to sign something, and she let her peripheral vision examine his movements, *find out if she can understand sign language*, and then Matt verbalized the message, 'Lane says he's pleased to meet you…or, do you understand sign language? Perhaps I don't need to translate.'

'I'm sorry, I've never had any reason to learn before this.' Karen said honestly, 'so please continue to interpret, if you don't mind.'

Matt and Lane shared a quick glance at each other, and Karen guessed that they were going to test her. She had an uncanny insight into what people were thinking at times, and it made sense that they would want to find out if she could interpret sign language.

*Tell her that the button on her chest front is undone,* signed Lane, glancing at her shirt, *she won't want to be in photos like that.*

'Lane said that you are younger than he expected,' said Matt.

Refraining from looking down or checking her buttons, Karen inclined her head to Lane, her eyes on his shapely lips, 'Thank you. Good genes and a great skincare range from our company.'

*See if she knows what is going on today at the stallion farm.*

Matt nodded and said, 'Lane said he hopes it will still be OK to go to Pilatos Farm tomorrow. He heard there was a bit of a disruption there today.'

An interesting modification to what was actually signed, thought Karen, glad she had learned several thousand words and expressions in sign language this past week. She would not be proficient in using sign language herself, but understanding it was easy, just as she'd found understanding any new language was easy after she learned the basics.

'I wouldn't call it a disruption,' she raised her eyes to Lane's inquisitive regard and smiled with what she hoped looked like a cat-with-the-cream smile and spoke in icy tones, 'it's more of a small distraction. I've made sure that the protesters are, shall we say, taken care of.'

She was rewarded with a flash of alarm. Lane, no doubt, thought her notion of 'taken care of' was likely to be something violent rather than caring for his followers with free food, drinks, and gifts. Good. Let him stew on that, she thought maliciously, and whatever round that he wants to call this has gone to me.

'Would you care for some refreshments before taking the photos?' Isabella interrupted, correctly interpreting her daughter's victorious look and keen to intervene before the hostility became unbearable. 'I have drinks on the balcony if you would care for some.'

'No, thank you, Isabella,' Andrea smiled warmly at her. 'When I'm in my creative mind space, I simply want to find my subjects and capture them. It's almost like a hunt, and I'm a little obsessive. I'd prefer to avoid any distractions as I'm seeing backgrounds and lighting and moods that I want to catch in my photos.'

'You sound as keen on your work as Karen is on hers,' laughed Isabella, taking her daughter's arm and forcibly leading her towards the stables. 'Julian is working some of the young horses down here if you'd like to come this way. I'm sure he'll want to be in some of the photos.'

Andrea took a single camera from a bag, one with a large, wide lens, and nodded to the men to bring her other equipment. With practiced movements, they gathered up various bags and a tripod and followed along.

From the corner of her eye, Karen noticed Lane sign something to Matt and take the tripod from him, so he had a hand free to use his phone and make a call. She had no doubt he was calling someone on-site at the Pilatos Farm gates to see what evil had befallen their followers at her orders. From his worried look and repeated dialing, it became apparent that the protesters were otherwise occupied, no doubt enjoying the bounty of their Pilatos gift bags, and weren't answering their phones. The men looked worried. Karen felt smug.

As they walked, Karen gave a brief narrative about Bisente and what the horses were achieving and expressed a hope that Andrea would do some portrait photos of her mother's favorite horses that could be enlarged and framed.

'That would be my birthday present to Mother,' Karen threw Isabella a smile. 'I'm sure she'd love to have the bragging rights of a wall covered with Andrea McLeay photos of her horses.'

'I hope I'll have some that will be suitable for that,' Andrea said as she turned her head left and right, evaluating the light, the trees, and the buildings. Looking in the main hallway of the stable block for the competition horses, she admired the natural timbers and the play of light and shadows as workers groomed horses, saddled them, and led them in or out of the large central hallway. 'I'd like to start in the stables if that is alright. The horses starting their work, their expressions, their eyes, their spirits - that's what I see now.'

Removing the lens cap and adjusting the camera to suit the darker interior of the main stable block, Andrea withdrew to a place where she saw the world through the lens, leaving Isabella and Karen standing with the three men.

'She'll only take so many without us,' Matt explained to Isabella, 'the natural photos that take her eye, then she'll get us to pose horses or work as ear-prickers, and she'll start using some of this equipment. When Andy goes into the zone, where she is now, we just stand back, and she goes for it.'

'Artists are like that,' Isabella nodded, 'it is to be expected.'

'You have an amazing set up here, Mrs. Lawford,' Matt waved a hand around him, 'it looks like heaven for competition horses.'

'Isabella, please,' she insisted, 'and, thank you. I believe our horses perform best when they are happy. Don't you agree?'

'Absolutely,' he nodded. 'These horses do look happy. Do you mind if we look at some of the horses in the stables? Perhaps you could run us through who they are and what they do.'

'It would be my pleasure. This way,' Isabella led them to the stables where Andrea was snapping images of dust-speckled beams of light touching the backs of horses and the laughter on the faces of riders who were saddling up their enormous mounts and chatting to them as though they were human. 'We have fifty-six stalls in this block, and they are almost all full, mostly with our own horses, but we do have outside horses here for training as well, and some of our riders have their horses here. The horses also have grazing paddocks where they spend time each day – the younger horses are often in together in large groups, but our top competition horses have their own paddocks which they do not share as we don't want to risk them injuring themselves with rough play or from a stray kick from another horse.'

As they passed under the eaves of the stable, a massive chestnut horse with a blaze stretched his head over his door and snorted gently at them. Isabella laughed and placed a hand on his neck, giving him a rub.

'This is Boo, though you might know him as Bisente Halloween, ranked as one of the best show jumpers in the country at present. He's one of my favorite characters.'

Boo nodded his head at the others, and for the first time, Tom's impenetrable mask cracked, and he smiled at the horse.

'I remember when he first started,' he said. 'I was competing on H.G. Phantasmagorical, and Julian came out on this enormous chestnut with all the bling and the patch on his rump that looked like a Halloween pumpkin. He went clear from the start, and it was obvious that he loved to jump.'

'Yes, he does,' Isabella said. 'I remember Phantasmagorical. Do you still have him?'

'My sister is riding him now. She hopes to get to some events this season.'

'I'll keep an eye out for her,' Isabella smiled at him. 'Let her know that she'll be welcome in the Bisente camp any time.'

One of the riders called Isabella, and she left to hold a horse while the girl mounted.

'I'm glad you like show jumping,' Karen said to the three men. 'So many animal liberationist and animal extremist people want to ban all horse riding, starting with sports like jumping, racing, and eventing. I find it interesting that you are fine with these sports, where horses face a high risk of injury, but you don't like seeing the Pilatos horses being cared for carefully, with almost no risk of injury, and under the constant and approving scrutiny of our leading welfare organizations.'

Lane's hands signaled to Matt, *She doesn't understand what spiritual suffering is. She only sees physical suffering. She doesn't know the difference between this stallion jumping with his rider in a partnership that makes his spirits soar and those stallions forced into miserable lives that kill their souls.*

'Lane has pointed out that we don't have an issue with riding horses,' Matt modified the message, 'as long as the horses enjoy what they do. We speak up against Rollkur, blue tongue, and any other barbaric method of forcing a horse to perform.'

Tom turned away from Boo and pointed to the horses in the show jump arena, working smoothly over jumps with pricked ears and pleased expressions, 'You can see these horses are not fighting their riders or being forced; they aren't scared or confused or worried. Sure, they might not jump six-foot obstacles by choice if they were free in paddocks, but they are happy to do it with their rider onboard. They trust their riders, and the riders don't betray that trust. I challenge you, Karen, to look into the eyes of your Stablex horses tomorrow and ask yourself if you have betrayed their trust.'

'How do you even know the name, Stablex?' Karen asked them, subtly side-stepping the challenge. 'I can understand you finding out about our horses as we have so many employees working with them, and horse people speak to each other, but the name Stablex has been tightly guarded. I guarantee most of the stablehands and horse handlers at Pilatos Farm have not heard the name.'

*Tell her anything but the truth.*

'Lane says it was a grape-vine thing,' Matt shrugged, 'he has friends everywhere.'

'I'm curious as to what else you know,' she said, 'I'm taking you there tomorrow as I'm assuming you have seen the facility before, but if you haven't, then I'm hoping you will be pleasantly surprised.'

*Unlikely.*

'He hopes so, too,' Matt nodded.

'I'd like to know,' Tom turned to her, his dark eyes hiding any emotions, 'why you think what is happening to those Stablex horses is OK. Look at these horses – you know what a horse's soul should feel, and it sure as hell isn't what your Stablex horses are feeling.'

'They are physically well cared for,' she stated in cool tones. 'I prefer science and facts to some airy-fairy notion of souls and spirits and whatever other mystical, magical, unprovable things you believe. You are trying to create trouble over an issue that doesn't exist.'

'It exists,' Tom looked down at her, emotions breaking through his mask, and he looked savage.

'No, it doesn't. I have seen those horses many times, and there is no issue.'

He glowered at her and looked, for an instant, as though he could hit her. 'Stablex will be stopped.'

'No, it won't,' she smiled infuriatingly at him, her eyes arctic. She would never be intimidated by any person who appeared to be giving in to anger.

'It will be stopped, and so will you,' he clenched his fists at his sides and seemed to tower over her with a rage that was bubbling to the surface.

Without any sign of being daunted by his height and simmering rage, Karen stepped closer to him and said softly, 'Don't ever try to stand over me. If I think for a second that you are about to hit me, I'll drop you like a rock. You think I'll be intimidated because I have a vagina, but let me remind you that you have testicles, and if I had brought my knee up into them hard and fast ten seconds ago when I stepped in close to you, you'd be on the ground now, wondering if you'll ever use what's between your legs again.'

For long seconds they stared at each other, then, to her surprise, he laughed, his eyes suddenly filling with genuine amusement and all traces of the anger evaporating. Stepping back and holding his hands up in surrender, he shook his head at her.

'I might have testicles,' he grinned, 'but you, Miss Lawford, have balls.'

'I wouldn't put it like that,' she shrugged, 'but I'm not easily intimidated.'

*I like her.*

'Lane asked to see some of the other horses,' said Matt, giving his mute friend a dry look.

Karen spent ten minutes introducing them to some of the horses in the stables while Andrea continued wandering around, taking candid photos of the people and horses at work and rest. Several riders and stable hands came up to talk to Lane, Matt, and Tom. They were keen fans, judging by their body language, thought Karen as she watched them all but throwing themselves at the visitors, fawning over Lane and pulling out phones to snap selfies with him. Julian, who knew Tom from the show jumping circuit, came over to give him a hug and a slap on the back, and they fell into deep conversation.

Standing back from the Australians and Tom, Karen examined them as they interacted with each other and the Bisente employees. Lane and Matt seemed to genuinely be excited with every new person they met, happy to hug and accept kisses, their faces split by grins almost all of the time. Even Tom seemed to have relaxed the cardboard expression and was enjoying catching up with Julian. Andrea was so focused on taking photos and finding all the special moments, angles, and arrangements of light that she didn't even glance over to see what her friends were doing.

At some stage, Matt took a phone call, listened intently, then cast a curious look at Karen. She met his gaze unblinkingly, realizing that he had just learned about the food vans and lavish sample bags. He gave her a short salute as he put his phone away and turned to speak to Lane. It was then Lane's turn to look at her with something akin to respect before he turned away and signed something she couldn't see. She hoped they were confused about the generosity of Pilatos towards the protesters - it's hard to hate something that gives you gifts instead of grief.

When Andrea had exhausted her candid shots, she organized Julian so she could take a series of photos of him grooming, saddling, mounting, warming up, and jumping one of the main Bisente stallions. Then she had the horses that Isabella wanted immortalized in portraits led out and stood in front of a large flowering hedge. The handler stood the horse up, and Andrea gave directions to Tom to move the horse's legs an inch or two forward or back to make the photo balanced. Then, she'd instruct the handler to position the head precisely as she wanted, and when the horse was standing perfectly, Matt squeaked a toy out in front of it, so the ears pricked alertly.

Karen noticed that Lane had wandered back to the stables while the photographs of the horses were being taken, and she followed him at a distance, curious to see what he was doing. There wasn't anything secret about the horses or set-up here, so he had nothing to gain from snooping around. But he didn't snoop, he walked to the first stall in the building she hadn't taken them to, and when the horse put its head out to say hello, he gently laid a hand on the horse's forehead and gazed into its eyes. The horse closed its eyes, lowered its head, and looked to be enjoying the touch of the Australian. Lane smiled at the horse and moved to the next one, repeating the action.

'What are you doing?' Karen asked as she approached.

Lane looked up at her and smiled, his right hand on the forehead of a bay mare that had seemed to go to sleep as soon as he touched her. Karen's breath caught in her throat as Lane looked at her, his eyes shining with the delight of a child. He seemed too innocent to be someone planning to damage her company, but she would not forget his intentions.

*I'm asking the horses how they feel,* he signed to her, *their souls are happy. It makes me happy.*

'I don't understand,' Karen lied.

Holding up a finger in an internationally understood signal of 'wait a moment,' Lane took out a small notepad and black pen and wrote the exact message he had signed. His writing was neat and quite beautiful to look at, something that Karen hadn't expected. He had the air of something wild and free, and she imagined his writing would be a wild and free scrawl to match.

'I think it's pretty obvious they're happy,' she looked around at the grand stables, 'they have the best of care, the best food, they are comfortable. You don't need to put your hand on their heads to know that - it is evident everywhere.'

Shaking his head to indicate that she didn't understand, he wrote, *You live in luxury, but your soul is sad. I live with little, but my soul soars. How we live doesn't always determine the state of our souls.*

Karen snorted derisively at the words, 'I am not sad. I don't have anything to be sad about, except, maybe, the trouble you and your friends are planning for my company.'

*Sad and alone*, he wrote, looking at her intently as she read the words.

With a dramatic sigh, Karen's face fell, revealing deep sorrow. She reached for Lane's notebook and pen, chewed on her lower lip as she considered the words she wanted to write about her feelings, then, in her bold and flowery script, wrote *absolute rubbish*. When Lane read it, he grinned at her, and she returned the smile in a shared moment of humor amongst the careful maneuvering of opponents.

'I'm telling you,' she insisted, amused that he was so wrong about her, 'I don't have a sad soul. In fact, I don't believe we do have souls. We live a physical life, and when that is over, we are over. I agree that these horses are happy because they have everything to keep them physically happy, and I don't think the Stablex horses are any different.'

*The souls of the Stablex horses are dying,* he wrote.

Rolling her eyes at his words, she said, 'No, that's an emotional, unscientific, and unprovable view – an anthropomorphic view. It's not *real* just because you say it or write it. They're animals that are well looked after. They're not human slaves or spiritual entities; they're not eternal souls or cartoon unicorns.'

He shrugged his disagreement, indicating with his eyes that he didn't want to get into an argument over their differing opinions. Well, not at the moment, anyway. Moving to the next stable, he laid his right hand on the horse's forehead and breathed in deeply, his smile fading. Looking intently at the horse as though listening to something the animal was saying to him, he withdrew his hand and looked at Karen, his eyes troubled.

'Something wrong?' she asked.

Lane pointed to the horse, then at his heart, and made a stabbing motion to indicate that the horse was sore of heart.

'As I said before, like all the other horses, he's well-fed, cared for, and has all his needs met. His heart isn't hurting.'

She didn't know what the man was up to, but she was surprised at how easily she accepted his inability to speak. With his intelligent eyes that probed her whenever she met their gaze and his expressive face, she almost forgot about expecting to hear spoken words. Communication was more than the sounds of words. It was strangely refreshing to engage in this form of conversation.

'Actually, his heart is hurting,' a young woman with almost a Cockney lilt to her English accent spoke from inside the stall and stepped out of the shadows to stand at the horse's shoulder to talk to them over the door, her big blue eyes devouring Lane. 'Sorry, I was trying to fix the automatic waterer in the corner and had a mouthful of screws, so couldn't speak up. I'm Julie, by the way.'

She held her hand over the door of the stall to shake, then realized it was smeared in grease, so withdrew it with a grin and nodded at them, her short blonde curls bobbing around her angel's face.

'Hi Julie,' Karen spoke in her smooth educated voice, 'I believe we've met before, I'm Isabella's daughter, Karen, and this is Lane Dimity.'

'I know,' Julie enthused, her eyes shining, her emotional voice the polar opposite of Karen's cool tones, 'I'm a huge fan, Lane. I can't tell you how exciting it is to actually meet you in person. I have all your books and read them over and over.'

Karen grimaced internally; this girl-child read his books repeatedly while she had just learned in the past week that her adversary wrote books. Admittedly, they were touchy-feely spiritual books about connecting with the souls of horses, so not real books in her view, at least, not the sort of books that she would ever have looked at if she wasn't trying to learn about her enemy. She had downloaded a couple to her phone and had glanced through but had yet to sit and read a chapter.

Barely refraining from the external grimace, Karen watched as Lane oozed interest in what Julie had to say, looking at her as though she was the only person in the entire world at that moment. A very effective tool when gathering cult followers, she thought dryly, because that was what this was beginning to look like: a cult of horse-mad people addicted to whatever this man was feeding them.

After Lane tilted his head at the horse and raised his brows enquiringly, Julie breathlessly launched into the horse's story, her desperation to please Lane clearly apparent as the words tumbled out of her.

'This is Benny - Bisente Nonpareil - and he was competing in Europe until a bit over a month ago when his rider, Sophie, had a car accident and was hospitalized for several weeks. It was a pretty bad accident. Sophie's been doing all Benny's riding for the last two years, and he's a tough horse for anyone else, but with Sophie, he's magic. He jumps his heart out for her. Anyway, Benny woke up one morning five weeks ago, and instead of Sophie turning up like every other morning to work with him, she's disappeared, well, disappeared from his perspective.'

Finally, she paused a moment for breath, glanced briefly at Karen, and then glued her baby blues back on Lane's face and continued Benny's story, 'Well, it's not like he's going to understand someone telling him that Sophie is in the hospital. No one else could ride him properly, he really is a tough horse, so there's no way he was going to be able to continue competing over there, so Isabella brought him home, and he's been depressed. I mean, really depressed. He's lost weight, doesn't show a lot of interest even when he's out in his paddock, he just mopes. Normally he's a total dick when you're in the stall with him, I mean, I used to cross-tie him to do anything as he'd be at you all the time, not nastily, mind you, just annoyingly, picking up things, poking you with his nose, swinging his butt around and knocking you over, that sort of thing, but now he just stands against a wall and looks sad.'

Julie sighed wistfully and laid a small, pale hand on the neck of the big horse, 'So, when I heard Karen say that you thought his heart was hurting, I was amazed. It is, it is really hurting, but I don't know how you could know by just touching him, yet you did, and it is incredible.'

Nodding at his enthusiastic fan, Lane laid his hand on the forehead of the horse once more, then looked to Karen, a smile tugging at the corners of his mouth when he saw the skeptical look on her face. To Karen, it was too easy to set this up. A devoted follower like Julie could have easily told him in advance of 'the sad horse,' and he simply worked that into his routine. She didn't trust him, and she didn't trust his cult-level devotees.

'It's...interesting,' Karen met his unsettling gaze and refused to be moved by the depths that beckoned her, 'but there are so many explanations that I'm unlikely to accept the least likely one.'

His handsome face broke into a grin, and he winked at her, amused by her answer, leaving her with the uncomfortable feeling that her words were telling him more about herself than she was learning of him. It was not something she enjoyed feeling, so she shored up her defenses and became cooler and more withdrawn.

'I think we should return,' she told him in a clipped voice, 'and I'd rather not leave you alone in my mother's stables, so please come along.'

Lane shook his head almost sadly at her and raised a hand to ask for a bit more time, motioning for her to come to the next stable with him. With an audible groan of impatience, Karen stepped after him as he approached the next horse, a tall grey gelding with a bold face and a forelock almost to his muzzle. As the horse put his nose towards them, Lane held the back of his hand out for the horse to sniff, then placed his hand on the forehead, smiling as though the horse was communicating with him. Removing his hand, he took the pen and wrote in his notebook *strong, confident, happy,* and showed it to her.

'It doesn't take a savant to see that,' Karen replied wryly, pointing at the horse's expression, 'his ears are forward, his eyes are bright, his head is held confidently. I don't pretend to be a horse whisperer, and I can see that.'

Shaking his head, Lane indicated that it was more than that and reached for her hand to place it on the horse's forehead. Instinctively, she withdrew her hand from his in a jerked movement. She didn't want him touching her. Instead of showing offense, he smiled softly at her and motioned that he was just going to put her hand on the horse.

'I can see what you want,' she said sharply, her hands held down at her side, 'but it serves no purpose.'

Once more, he asked for her hand, his expression so unthreatening and calm that she found herself reaching her right hand forward without even realizing, and looked into his eyes and felt herself falling, even though she stood unmoving on solid ground. When he took her hand gently in his, a tremor ran through her, and her eyes went wide with surprise, but she did not take her hand back from him. It wasn't an unpleasant feeling, quite the opposite, and she was curious about the source.

Softly, he placed her hand under the forelock of the horse and pressed it to the wide flat bone of his forehead, and with his free hand, touched his temple and shook his head slightly, then touched his heart and nodded, indicating she was to stop thinking and just feel with her heart. When she went to open her mouth to speak, he put a finger to his lips. A tiny spark of resentment flared in her chest – no one hushed her like that – but the warmth that seeped into her bones from his hand that covered hers pushed the feeling away, and she fell quiet.

Without wanting to, she stopped thinking about talking and

focused on the connection between her hand and the horse, and to Lane as he showed no sign of releasing her hand. For a moment, it seemed that nothing mattered except that connection between the three of them as they stood together, sharing life through their touch. Images of bright and golden colors started flashing in her mind, a feeling of freedom, of flying over grass and being one with the ground below and the sky above, of goodness and comfort and belief, and her heart seemed to swell in her chest as she took it all in, and she felt good and complete and...

Snatching her hand back, she snapped back to her usual self and stared at him, disconcerted with a touch of anger. 'I don't know how you did that,' she put a hand up between them as though to push everything about him away from her, 'and I don't care what mind trick you used, but don't do it again. Don't touch me, and don't spin your weird emotional tricks with me.'

He shook his head, indicating that he hadn't meant to upset her.

'I don't care what you meant to do,' she regained her calm voice and raised her chin. 'I'm not one of your gullible fan-girls who would believe anything you say or do. I am Pilatos Industries, and I know you mean to damage my company. We're not friends. We're here to evaluate each other like generals meeting before a battle. I know that, and so do you.'

A troubled expression shadowed his eyes as he regarded her, the usual smile that played near his mouth gone as the corners turned down in disappointment. Once more, resorting to the pen and paper, he wrote, *You are not Pilatos.*

'Yes, I am. When you threaten my company, you threaten me. I don't know what you are capable of, but I can see how blinded your followers are by your...' she waved a hand around airily, unable to decide on a word to encompass all that was Lane Dimity, '...your snake-oil, smoke-and-mirrors, illusions, and delusions of grandeur, so I do fear what they are capable of. I want to neutralize your threat, perhaps not as effectively as some of the Pilatos security would like, but I think, given a chance, I can convince you to keep your hounds leashed.'

*I will stop Stablex*, he signed, almost apologetically, and when Karen shrugged and shook her head to indicate that she didn't understand, he wrote it down for her.

'You won't,' she promised, 'you might cause us problems, but you won't stop us. Once people start using Stablex, it will change lives, and they won't give it up for any sob-story of dying souls inside healthy horses.'

*I have more than a sob story*, he looked up at her from under long lashes as he showed her the words.

'Maybe you do, but before you go ahead with your plans, I want you to look honestly at the stallions tomorrow. Don't go in with anthropomorphic views; just see how well we look after those stallions. I believe if you can truly understand that we are not a welfare issue, then maybe you can turn your attention elsewhere, to places where horses truly are suffering and really do need your help. I will even pay you as a consultant to ensure that we are doing the right thing by the stallions – and our consultants receive millions, so that is money that can go towards genuine welfare cases, and it could save many lives.'

*A bribe?* Lane wrote, arching his brows at her questioningly.

'A fee to ensure that we meet the highest welfare expectations, even yours,' she countered, 'I know you could cause us problems, certainly more than a few of your followers at our gates with placards…'

He grinned appreciatively at her and wrote, *The gifts – well played*

'Yes, I thought so.'

*Do you have enough for 10,000 protesters?*

Her eyes narrowed as she read that number, 'Is that your plan? Just swamp the farm with protesters? No, that's too simple. I'm sure it's more than that.'

Giving her a non-committal shrug, he led the way back to the others.

It wasn't long before Andrea had finished the photos and arranged with Isabella to get the proofs to her within a week. Isabella asked if they'd like to stay for the night as there were plenty of rooms at the farm, but, to Karen's relief, they declined and simply organized to meet Karen at the gates to Pilatos Farm the next morning. Andrea had agreed to take advertising photos of the Stablex horses for Karen at an exorbitant fee. Karen hoped that once they saw the stallions for themselves, they would realize that the welfare issues were unfounded, and that would put an end to any threat from the Dimity army of followers.

# CHAPTER FIVE

*It never ceases to amaze me that this beautiful animal could overpower me any time he wanted, and yet he is content to work with me, to follow my directions, to keep me safe, and carry me with trust in his heart. Some might think that the horse serves me, but it is so much more complicated than that. I honor and respect the horse, I strive to be worthy of his trust, and when we work together, my soul flies with his. He is my brother; she is my sister. They are my family.*

**From 'An Interview with Lane' published in Horse and Country Annual**

## Pilatos Farm - Kentucky

After a restless night, plagued with thoughts of the troublesome Australian man who spoke to horses, Karen woke before dawn, showered, and dressed in a dark-grey, calf-length skirt and jacket with a pale grey shirt and black accessories. Regarding herself in the mirror, she realized her grey theme had become her uniform - every day was grey. She shrugged, dismissing the observation as unimportant. It signified nothing; she just liked grey.

Breakfast was a quick affair where she adroitly avoided her mother's questions about Marcus and retreated emotionally from Isabella's ventures into being a caring, concerned, and loving mother. Perhaps, when she was six or seven, or even ten, it would have been appreciated to have a parent who cared about her rather than what she could achieve, but it was all a bit late for that now. Pearce watched the exchange with sad eyes, relieved that he had established a loving relationship with his children before they had grown up and erected the walls to protect themselves from any more hurt.

She said goodbye to Isabella, awkwardly accepting her hug, and had Pearce fly her to Pilatos Farm on the other side of Lexington. Before Lane and his three friends arrived, Karen wanted to inspect the stallions to ensure that she was right. She was positive that they were content and well cared for and that there were no welfare questions to be raised about their lives, but it didn't hurt to have another look before the Dimity people examined the horses.

The four-hundred-acre farm was a picturesque display of white panel fences, tree breaks, and green pastures dotted with well-fed horses. They were not the horses that Lane and his crew were upset about, though; the Stablex horses were stabled inside a forty-acre security compound that encompassed the stable complex, administration, and the laboratories. The compound was a hundred meters inside the Pilatos Farm boundary fence and could be seen from the main farm gates.

There was a security fence around the entire farm, but the one around the Stablex section was more like a prison fence than the usual industrial version, with lights, cameras, razor wire on top, and electric wires. Stablex promised to be a billion-dollar drug, so the precautions were reasonable protection of the future of Pilatos Industries. An extensive white security building provided access to the compound, and two similar smaller buildings were placed elsewhere in the fence for staff, while a fourth entrance was kept for deliveries of horse feed, equipment, and other supplies that had to undergo inspection and decontamination before entering.

The entrances to the compound were heavily guarded. All efforts were made to keep out contaminants that could harm the Stablex horses and keep in the industrial secrets that formed Stablex.

After walking from the helipad to the main entrance, Karen followed the usual biosecurity measures that were there for all to follow: remove everything in the first private change room, shower, blow-dry her hair, and change into on-site clothes in the second change room so that there was no chance of bringing in contaminants from outside the farm. She kept several of her outfits in her locker, so she emerged looking little different from how she entered.

Between the compound fence and the central hexagon of stable buildings was an expanse of lawn that formed part of the security. No one could cross that lawn anywhere in the compound without cameras tracking them and guards watching. Six huge stable blocks were arranged in a hexagon around a ten-acre green, and in the center of that sat the laboratories - a featureless white cube one hundred meters high, wide, and long. The laboratories had such stringent security that even Karen had only visited certain parts of it, and she had no inclination to return. There was something intimidating and unwelcoming about the white cube. Anyway, with hazardous materials, viral and bacterial research, and quarantined animals, it was not a building she wanted to explore.

Accompanied by several Pilatos employees who were giving her reports as they walked, she strode briskly to the stables. She went to Stable Block Three, which, like the other five, had the sprawling white front of a nineteenth-century Neoclassical mansion, complete with Corinthian columns and windows with grey shutters. The buildings looked like they had been there for well over one hundred years rather than a few decades.

Karen entered the building between two central columns in front of an imposing double door that opened on a corridor that had stalls on either side. Twenty sets of almost identical black ears turned towards her as the stallions regarded her entry, their expressions curious, their forelocks well-groomed. There was no whinnying or nickering, unlike in the Bisente stables, but perhaps because all the horses here were stallions rather than a mix of stallions, mares, and geldings, there was less fighting or need to call to each other.

Walking past the stalls, she looked in at the horses. Their stalls were clean, their coats were shiny, they were in excellent condition, their hooves were trimmed perfectly, and their expressions were intelligent as they watched her with neither fear nor trepidation. She compared their health to the starving horses she had seen in back yards around the country or the injured and suffering mustangs she had seen on the range. How could Lane think that there was something wrong with the way these horses were treated?

'Your visitors are at the main gates now,' one of the guards informed her. 'Joe is there talking with them.'

'Just hold them there until I arrive,' she indicated for him to relay her message. 'Apply the usual precautions, although I'm sure Joe will be ten steps ahead of me. Lane may need a pen and paper to communicate, so provide him with some of ours as he won't be allowed to take his in.'

The guard narrowed his eyes and asked, 'Are you concerned about them?'

'Absolutely. I know they organized the picket line, and I'm sure they will organize something much worse if we can't convince them that there is nothing here worth attacking.'

'Let's hope for that, then,' he nodded at her before turning aside to listen to more messages in his earpiece.

Pearce waited outside in an electric buggy. He, too, had showered and was now wearing a clean Pilatos Farm uniform.

'Are you sure this is a good idea?' he asked her as he drove the almost silent vehicle along the white cement pathway to the main gatehouse.

'No, I'm not sure,' she replied honestly, 'but I think it's a better idea than doing nothing and simply handling the storm he brews up with his followers. He said yesterday that he could have ten thousand here protesting… we don't want that. And I think he was underestimating. If he really galvanized his followers into action, we could be looking at millions around the world, and they could affect more than Stablex, though that will be enough to cripple us after all the money that has been sunk into it.'

'You know what Joe Kaiphas thinks we should do?' Pearce glanced sideways at her as he parked behind the main entrance to the compound.

'I haven't spoken directly to him about it,' she admitted, 'but I know how he might operate with his *people have accidents* mantra. I really would hate to think that he has ever undertaken any violence on behalf of Pilatos.'

'Don't be too naïve,' Pearce warned her, worried that she underestimated what Joe was capable of in his desire to protect the company he had worked for most of his life. 'Joe is a violent man. Your father, well, he doesn't like complications. This Lane Dimity might be a hell of a complication.'

'I know,' she sighed. 'I'm trying to protect the company and find a peaceful resolution.'

'If you like this Australian, and I've heard he's impossible to dislike, just do what you can to end the trouble before Joe steps in. There have been accidents before.'

'Thanks for the heads up,' she smiled at him. 'Hopefully, we'll be done here before lunch, and we'll be home by early this afternoon. I'd like to get this headache behind us.'

Stepping out of the buggy, she went in the back doors of the building, past the six guards who watched a bank of screens showing high definition images of every part of the external security fencing, the approaches to Pilatos Farm, and internal views of the compound. There was a second security center in the laboratories, which she had seen once, but it only monitored the cameras placed in that building and not the ones around the farm and stables.

In one of the waiting rooms, she found Lane, Matt, Tom, and Andrea standing with a stony-faced Joe and two security guards. Standing on the other side of the heavy glass of the viewing window, she watched their faces as various emotions played across their expressions, from Lane's mildly amused look to disbelief, anger, and resentment with Matt and Andrea, while Tom stood wearing his warrior's face, again.

As with all other visitors, they were assigned lockers for their belongings. They could keep the locker keys themselves, though, as Karen had often thought when she locked her belongings up, there were always more keys somewhere if someone wanted to go through the lockers. For now, their equipment, bags, and wallets were laid out on a table in the center of the room, with Joe looking over them as though he suspected they contained something dangerous.

'Is this really necessary?' Andrea asked her.

'It's standard,' Karen replied, with a nod of greeting to them. 'All phones, wallets, and any other devices or items, from laptops to pens, are removed from all visitors, including me. All the employees accept that they shower and change into company uniforms and leave all else behind when they enter the compound. We keep these horses in quarantine and can't risk any contaminants reaching them, accidentally or deliberately.'

'What about my cameras?' Andrea pointed to the two camera bags and the tripod on the table.

'They'll be inspected, which is standard procedure for anything that comes in here, and you'll take them in minus the bags. Sorry, but it's just how it has to be done. If there's anything you need from the camera bags, let Joe know, and he'll check them.'

'What do you think we might bring in?' asked Matt, frowning at the Pilatos guard who was waving a wand over them like airport security checking if they had recent contact with explosives.

'I don't think you'll be bringing anything in,' Karen replied smoothly, 'but high on our list of concerns are contagions – accidentally or deliberately introduced. We care about the welfare of our horses, but I know that there are extremists who would put their welfare second to causing us problems. Present company excepted, of course.' She gave them a serene smile.

'I think she called us extremists,' Matt chuckled to Lane, 'but not so extreme as to want to hurt the horses.'

*Extremists with a conscience*, Lane signed back to him, *I think she likes us.*

'You think?' Matt threw him a disbelieving look before casting a wary glance at Karen, who stood impassive in the viewing room. She showed no hint of having understood Lane. 'Not so sure on that one.'

'And we have to shower?' Andrea indicated the notice on the wall about all visitors having a decontamination shower and using company clothes on site.

Karen nodded, 'I've already done so. These clothes are my on-site clothes; I don't have anything that was on me before I showered. You'll find a range of company clothes in your dressing rooms along with hairdryers if you wish to use them. You were informed of all this in an email.'

'Yeah, like I'm going to read all my emails,' Andrea grumbled, 'especially when it's telling me I have to get naked and shower in hospital-grade disinfectant or whatever it is you use.' She suddenly flashed a dazzling smile at Lane and sang a few lines from a Spice Girls chorus in perfect pitch, 'Naked, nothing but a smile upon her face; naked, don't be afraid to stare she is only naked.'

Matt opened his mouth, pushed a couple of fingers past his teeth, and did an impressive gagging imitation. 'Sis, no. Just no. I'll need disinfectant for my brain – I do not want to think of my sister naked.'

'They might be communal showers,' she began, raising her brows teasingly at her twin, Lane, and Tom.

'No, they're not,' Karen cut her off curtly, impatient with their unbusinesslike attitudes. Typical Australians, she thought, disrespecting authority whenever possible. They should have been out the other side and headed towards the stables by now.

'Did you go through all this when you visited?' Matt asked Lane.

Karen tried not to stare, but she was interested in his reply as she wasn't sure how he had managed to access the stallions or even if he had at all. It was possible he'd been bluffing.

*I came in with a work crew*, he signed, his eyes sliding sideways to Karen as he noted her discreetly watching him, *same routine over at the workers' entrance.*

'I guess it keeps some germs out,' Matt shrugged, then snorted in wry amusement, 'but it didn't keep you out.'

'And it's not going to keep out air-borne illnesses like Equine Influenza,' Andrea pointed out, 'or even the mosquito-spread viruses.'

Tired of their slow pace, Karen told them she'd wait outside. Ten minutes later, they joined her, and she noted that, predictably, they'd avoided the Pilatos blue or khaki uniforms and, instead, had chosen jeans and t-shirts, all new and unworn, from the range of clothing provided for visitors.

'We'll start with Stable Block One,' Karen said as they walked towards the closest of the grand white buildings. 'I hope you'll find that the horses are extremely well adjusted here, and they want for nothing. As stated in the contract which you signed, Andrea, you are free to take as many photos as you wish, but we will retain the memory sticks here at Pilatos. If you wish to edit the photos yourself, you can use our computers here as we have most of the popular photo editing programs available; otherwise, the advertising company will use the raw images and edit accordingly, crediting you with the photos, of course.'

'You agreed to that, Andy?' Tom asked in surprise.

'I wanted to see the horses,' Andrea sighed and gave her head a half shake, 'I know I'd normally never give up my photos like this, but I'll do a quick edit on the ones Pilatos are buying for their advertising campaigns, and they'll have the rights to the raw images on the stick. I'll delete the crappy ones.'

Tom looked at her doubtfully.

'It was a lot of money,' she explained, squirming slightly under his gaze, 'and it gave us the chance to see them with our own eyes.'

He gave her a dissatisfied harrumph and continued to walk to the stables.

As they walked, Karen explained the layout of the buildings to them and listed some of the leading equine veterinarians who worked full time to ensure the stallions remained in the best of health. She gave them a summary of the other people employed to meet the highest welfare conditions of the horses, reminding them that several leading welfare organizations had approved everything.

'I am hoping that by being here today, you will realize that there are other horse-related welfare issues that are more pressing than this, and Pilatos Industries will be willing to sponsor several of your chosen programs as our way of saying thanks to the horses that are helping us.'

Karen finished as they came to a halt outside the main entrance doors of Stable Block One. She waited for a response, but they stared silently at her, unmoved by the thinly-veiled bribe.

'The budget for this year's sponsorship,' Karen continued after her pause was not filled by anyone else, 'is over ten million dollars. That is earmarked for equine-related charities and causes, and we'd certainly be interested in taking your advice as to which charities and causes are to benefit.'

'Yeah, we'll see,' Tom finally spoke, his hand pointing towards the door. 'So, can we see the horses now? Or are you going to continue to impress us with the money you're willing to throw around?'

With a calm expression to hide the annoyance she felt at his words, Karen nodded and swung open the doors to the stables. She was pleased that twenty sets of black ears immediately turned towards them as the inquisitive matching faces of the stallions regarded the visitors.

'The Stablex stallions,' Karen held out her left hand to indicate the horses, 'and, as you can see, there is no suffering here.'

She had almost hoped that the four visitors would show signs of disappointment in being proven wrong, but they stared silently with grim faces as they viewed the twenty horses in their twenty stalls. Did they see something she couldn't see? The air was a constant, comfortable temperature. The stables were impeccably clean as staff continually made rounds cleaning up the wood shavings in the stables, removing the manure and wet shavings so that everything smelled fresh. The horses had several small hard feeds a day and constant access to various forms of forage in their feed bins.

They are happy, she wanted to scream at the three Australians whose bleakness was fading to sadness as they stood and stared. Tom's face appeared fiercer than ever as he looked down the corridor of horses.

Lane broke rank and walked to the first horse, putting out his hand to be sniffed before placing his palm gently and respectfully on the forehead of the mighty black horse. With his back to his friends, his hand disappeared under the forelock that tumbled in waves down the front of the horse's noble face. As he stood there, the horse's ears relaxed back into thoughtfulness, and his head lowered, and Lane's shoulders hunched over as though he was suddenly bearing a huge weight.

Karen remained with Andrea, Matt, Tom, Joe, and the security guards as Lane walked to the next horse and repeated his forehead-touching trick that had the horse lowering his head and softening the set of his ears. He crossed the corridor and put his other hand to the forehead of the first horse there, still facing away from the people as his shoulders sagged lower.

A soft click brought Karen's attention back from Lane, and she realized that Andrea had raised her camera and was starting to take photos of Lane with the horses. The lighting was particularly soft and beautiful, so Karen imagined the photos would be quite ethereal, showing the connection between man and horse. Not that she wanted that for their promotions, she wanted images of happy horses to counter any claims from other extremists.

At the sixth horse, Lane stopped and leaned against the stall door as though he needed support. Karen felt it was a little overacted but held her tongue, curious to see what they would say about the well-cared-for Stablex stallions now that they could see how much expense had gone into ensuring the horses were happy.

'You OK, bro?' Matt asked with concern in his voice.

Lane shook his head and slowly turned towards them, his troubled eyes finding Karen, and he looked at her with accusation. She was surprised to see tears on his cheeks and felt that he was really overplaying the emotions, so she met his gaze dispassionately, wondering how he was going to play his hand.

*Their souls are dying*, he signed for Matt to interpret, *this is not living.*

'Lane said that their souls are dying,' Matt told her, 'and that this existence they have here is not living.'

'Nonsense,' she snapped, irritated that they couldn't see what was in front of their eyes, 'they are safe, they are well fed, they are cared for.'

*Why can't she see?* Lane shook his head, backing further down the passageway to lay his hand on the next stallion. *They are hurting. They are the silent tragedy of this company.*

'He doesn't understand why you can't see,' explained Matt. 'Lane says they are hurting.'

'I can see what he thinks; his acting isn't that bad,' Karen retorted, walking forward to pat the horse nearest her, his neck warm under her touch. 'This horse is not hurting. None of them are. You are operating from some fanciful, spiritual, new-age view of the world, where you imagine intangible and unprovable things like souls and spiritual connections exist, but we are living in this real world where food and water and shelter matter.'

Andrea walked forward to stand beside Karen. She pointed to the nearside neck of the horse, where a small tube extended from the jugular.

'What's this?'

'It's a catheter for collecting blood,' Karen explained. 'There's no pain associated with the site, and it's easier on the horse to have the vein permanently cannulated than to have a new needle every time blood is collected.'

'How often is blood collected?'

'Perhaps once a day. The blood can be tested to confirm that the horses are maintaining healthy levels of electrolytes, proteins, and enzymes and that their red and white blood cell counts are within desirable parameters. If any horse is coming down with any illness, the blood tests will alert us well before the horse shows signs of illness. I assure you, there is no discomfort to the horses.'

'So, they're all cannulated?' Matt asked, coming to look at the stallion's neck then walking to the next one to examine it.

'Yes,' Karen nodded. 'If you understand veterinary medicine, you'll know that this isn't a cruelty issue. Even so, I would prefer,

Andrea, if you photographed the horses from the sides where they are not cannulated, although we'll have them digitally removed if they show in any photos.'

'I don't know if I can do this,' Andrea's eyes filled with sadness as she looked at the stallions around her, 'they're so... so unfree.'

'You're not seeing this logically,' Karen's lips narrowed as she tried to make her understand. 'Do you actually see any horse suffering?'

'And you're not seeing this with your heart,' Andrea fired back, 'suffering isn't always about being well-fed and cared for.'

The movement of Lane's hands caught their eyes. *She's not going to understand. She's the same as the horses. Well-fed and cared for, but her soul is dying, and she doesn't know it.*

'Lane realizes you're not going to understand,' Andrea shortened his message, 'so I guess I'll just take these photos, and we can get out of here. I'd rather not spend more time than necessary amongst this...' she waved her hand at the clinically clean stable complex, unable to find a word to describe how she felt about the facility.

Gritting her teeth, Karen forced herself to maintain an utterly calm exterior. She needed to try and win these people over, and getting upset about the ridiculous boloney Lane thought about her when she wasn't supposed to know sign language would be a wrong move. It didn't matter if he thought her soul was dying or taking a trip to Saturn because it wasn't a real concept; it was merely the sort of mystical garbage that these cosmic gypsies dabbled in.

'We still aren't seeing eye to eye on the welfare matter, obviously,' Karen inclined her head at Lane, who observed her from several stalls away, 'but I trust we will come to some sort of an understanding by the end of this visit.'

'An understanding?' Matt looked at her in askance. 'You're kidding, right? All these stallions living in their clean cages like lab rats, and you think we'll see your point of view?'

Raising her brows at her twin, Andrea lifted her camera and began viewing the world through her lens, capturing images of the twenty horses, their eyes, their forelocks, the light playing on their long flowing manes, the way they stretched their noses out to anyone who passed. Karen watched her carefully; she wanted to make sure that she focused on positive images and didn't try to capture a fleeting ears-back or ears-down moment that could make a horse look savage or hopeless.

'Do you agree that the horses show clear signs of being well cared for?' Karen asked Matt, though her eyes flicked to Tom and Lane to include them. 'Do you agree that they are well fed, their hooves are cared for, and they appear healthy? That they have suitable food and water and can see other horses so aren't in isolation?'

'That isn't all a horse needs,' said Matt.

'But you do agree they have those things?'

'Yes, but we're not upset about what they have; we're fighting for what they don't have.'

'Which is?'

'Freedom,' Matt rattled a stable door to emphasize the word. 'Stallions need more than food, water, and shelter – they also need freedom.'

'They don't have a concept of freedom, as that requires an imagination of things they don't know. You're anthropomorphizing them, again, and thinking that they want what you want. They have good lives here.'

'Do they ever get to run in fields?' Matt grilled her. 'Do they get to touch other horses, or can they only look at them across the passage, day after day? Do they get to run and buck and play, snort and strut and explode into action?'

'They are too valuable to risk injuring themselves galloping around in paddocks,' Karen replied reasonably, 'and protecting them from possible injury is not a welfare issue.'

As Andrea took photos, Lane neared the end of the two rows of ten stalls, touching each horse as he passed, and Joe followed him, not willing to let him out of sight. There was a wide, well-lit walkway that ran at right angles to the corridor in which they were standing, and Lane stopped there and looked left and right along the length of it.

*Ask her how many horses there are in this stable block,* he signed to Matt.

'How many horses altogether in this stable block?' Matt asked her.

'There are ten sets of stables like this one,' Karen replied.

Tom stepped towards her, his face chiseled into hard angles of ferocity. 'So, two hundred horses in this building?'

Karen nodded, 'That's correct, all constantly under supervision and care.'

'And six other buildings like this?' Tom quizzed her.

She nodded.

'So, you have one thousand, two hundred stallions standing in stables, twenty-four hours a day, with needles mounted permanently in their jugulars so that you can draw blood whenever you need to? Is that what this is all about? Their blood?'

'One thousand, two hundred well cared for stallions,' Karen managed to remain non-confrontational despite her desire to tell these bleeding-heart animal lovers that they had no understanding of the real world, that horses don't have souls, that people's lives were supported by these horses, that the world wasn't a fantasy movie where animals had human feelings. It was only her fear of what might be unleashed by Lane Dimity's followers if his views on the Stablex horses could not be assuaged that kept her from saying what she really thought.

'And you really can't see what's wrong with this?' Tom looked genuinely puzzled that she did not share their view of the situation.

'I see horses that are well cared for.'

Matt waved his hand at the stables, 'Horses are not meant to live their lives standing in a stall without being able to move around and trot and canter.'

'They get to trot and canter,' Karen informed him, 'every horse gets time every day on an equine treadmill where they can trot, canter, or even gallop in relative safety. We have teams of experienced handlers in each block which ensure every horse is safely exercised. They don't stand in their stables all day.'

'Oh, sorry,' Matt's voice dripped with mockery, 'they only stand in the stables for twenty-three and a half hours a day, then spend some time on a treadmill, rather like one thousand, two hundred lab rats.'

'What's it all for?' Andrea lowered her camera to query Karen. 'Stablex, what does it actually do? Is it going to save the lives of children? What disease is it going to cure? What is so important that all these horses have to live like this?'

Shaking her head, Karen replied, 'Our official unveiling of Stablex is a few weeks away, and I'm not at liberty before then to disclose any information about it. You do need to appreciate that success in the pharmaceutical world is dependent on being one jump ahead, and at least a year ahead, of the opposition, which is one of the main reasons for such security surrounding this facility. I don't believe you see anything here that some of the workers haven't already spoken about, even though they were contractually obliged not to discuss anything here outside of this compound. If you don't know the nature of Stablex, then our security measures are working to some extent, although we were alarmed that you even knew the name. In two weeks, the world will become aware of Stablex and how it will improve life for many.'

Andrea patted the nose of the horse nearest her and murmured, 'Are our lives so important that we need to make noble animals like these stallions live like this so that our lives are improved?'

Since it seemed a rhetorical question, Karen did not reply; she merely shrugged.

'They're all Friesians, aren't they?' Andrea asked, looking around at the twenty horses that were virtually indistinguishable from each other. 'Why is that?'

Not seeing any harm in giving a basic explanation about this point, Karen patted the horse nearest her and said, 'It's not because we like black horses above all others, it's because a certain property was found in the blood of this line of Friesians that we didn't find in any others we've tested. It's that property that forms the basis of Stablex. So, all the horses here have a common ancestor and carry something we need.'

'Want,' corrected Andy with a sideways glance at Karen, 'I'm sure you don't need what they have; you just want it.'

Rather than entering into an argument, Karen simply smiled at her and moved away to see what Lane was doing. He had walked out of sight with Joe tagging along behind him, and she was curious about his whereabouts. Leaving the three visitors to continue the photography under the scrutiny of two security men who stood nearby, she strode down the passage to look for the Australian. Looking left and right, she only saw the occasional worker wheeling a barrow or carrying feed - there was no sign of Lane or Joe.

It didn't alarm her in any way as she trusted Joe completely; he would watch Lane closely so that he didn't do anything harmful, like let some stallions out. She walked to the right first, looking down the corridors of stables, but she only saw horses and Pilatos workers. Turning, she went the other way and found them two passageways along from where Andrea was still taking photos. Joe stood at the furthest stall almost shoulder to shoulder with Lane, who had his face buried in the cascading waves of a stallion's mane.

Barely concealing a scowl at his dramatic ways that were far removed from her restraint, she walked towards them. Joe looked up at her and nodded as she approached.

'Smelling the horse, Lane?' she asked, not trying to hide the cynicism in her voice at his display of equine love. The man was thirty-two, not an over-emotional horse-mad teenager who had to hug pretty horses.

He turned to look at her with a mixture of pain and anger in his eyes that hit her like a physical blow, stopping her dead and almost making her take a step back. What had upset him this time? If he could talk, she was sure he would be yelling at her. Instead, he glared as though she was responsible for the death of children and the end of Christmas.

The chiseled lines of his face were tight, and he clenched his jaw muscles as though he was about to speak; instead, his hands moved.

*They are quiet*, he signed furiously at her.

Karen shrugged her lack of understanding and didn't have to act as she had no idea what he meant by them being quiet.

Taking out the pen and paper with which he had been supplied, he wrote, *They are silent. You have silenced them.*

'I don't train them, Lane,' she said defensively, 'I haven't done anything to them – I certainly haven't silenced them, I don't even know what that means.'

He took several steps to reach her, and Joe moved to intercept, but Karen raised a hand to let him know that it was alright. She had confidence that Lane meant her no harm, despite the rage that danced in his eyes alongside a grief that she couldn't comprehend. Anyway, she had seen Joe fight and knew that even if Lane did raise a hand to her, it would be caught in Joe's lightning-fast grip before it got anywhere near her.

Standing over her, his eyes wild with feelings she couldn't grasp, he pointed at his own throat and shook his writing pad at her, then circled the word *silent* and touched his throat again.

'Like you? Silent like you?' she asked, looking into his eyes to see if that is what he meant.

Her heart accelerated disturbingly with him so close that she could have reached up to smooth the ends of his sun-bleached hair away from his forehead, and that thought was quickly followed by mild self-disgust that she would think of such a thing. She didn't want to touch his hair or his forehead, he was merely close and very distracting, that was all. When Marcus had stood this close to her, she had reacted as if he were a rather pleasant hardwood fence post, but there was nothing as inanimate about this outback man who radiated power and passion.

He nodded, the rage in his eyes dimming as he realized that she genuinely had no idea of what he was referring to. He searched her eyes as though he'd find a truth there that meant something to him, and she found she couldn't look away. Slowly, he raised a hand and gently, so very gently, touched her right ear and then pointed around them, telling her to listen. Then he pointed at the horses. *Listen for the horses*, was his meaning.

'They're silent,' she said, perplexed by the significance of that fact.

Lane then tapped his temple to tell her to think about it.

She narrowed her eyes and concentrated, letting thoughts run through her mind. Silent stallions. No whinnying or calling out. She thought of the frequent noises made by the horses at Bisente. She thought of the Bisente stallions that regularly trumpeted their challenges or screamed out their territorial claims. One thousand, two hundred stallions, and no calling out. She looked past Lane and saw a horse move his head as though he was neighing, but there was silence. She swiveled and looked down at the other heads and saw another horse's nostrils and lips quiver as though he was nickering. Silence.

The shock on her face as she turned back to Lane was sincere, and, for a brief instant, her unguarded eyes revealed the child she had once been, a child who loved horses and dreamed of riding her own wild horse; a little girl who could not bear to see a horse suffer. He saw that moment and knew that her soul wasn't dead - like the stallions, she could be saved.

Dropping the mask of the professional and efficient businesswoman over the imprudent display of emotions, Karen took a step back from Lane and said coolly, 'I don't know what this means, but I will look into it.'

*Vocal cords removed*, he wrote, and showed her, searching her face for a reaction that she refused to give this time.

'I have no knowledge of that,' her voice was tightly controlled so that she would not reveal her shock at those three words. Surely that hadn't been done to these beautiful animals...but she knew Lane was right. 'I agree it is unusual that there is silence from so many stallions.'

Lane motioned for her to walk to the stallion he had been hugging, and she realized that he hadn't been playing an over-emotional role for her benefit; he had been inspecting the horse's throat. He pulled back the mane and turned the horse's head slightly away so that she could see a scar under the horse's jaw; he then pointed to all the other horses in that section to indicate they all had the same scar.

Angry at herself that she had visited here so often but had always been so busy or preoccupied that she hadn't noticed the implication of noiseless horses, Karen looked and nodded, her lips pinched together. In her mind, she could already hear the reasons for this: there would be too much racket if all the stallions could call out, whinny, squeal, nicker, and scream at each other whenever they wanted. It was easy and painless surgery that posed little risk to the horses. They would be happier if they didn't hear other stallions calling out. It made sense, yes, it was logical, it was practical ...but still, the horror of over a thousand silenced stallions had shaken her. It had also given Lane proof that these horses weren't as happy as she had claimed - they were surgical mutes.

'I believe it's time to get back to the others,' she turned away from Lane and Joe, who had remained as expressionless as a rock through this. 'I will find out why this procedure has been performed, and I'll get back to you.'

By not looking at him as she led the way back to Andrea and the others, she was able to focus on the task at hand - completing the photography and having these four cordially removed from Pilatos Farm with a generous payment for the work done so far and a promise of more to come if they wished to act as advisors. They had shown little indication of being motivated by money, but she had witnessed the powerful and corruptive nature of mammon too many times to dismiss the notion that they were above its influence. She looked straight ahead as she walked. She didn't want to look at him as he was far too unsettling and astute, and it made her uneasy to realize how much she understood without words spoken aloud.

Sensing that Lane was no longer following, Karen stopped near the corridor where they'd begun. Looking behind, she saw that he had paused to write something, an expression of concentration on his face as he wrote. He looked up at her, and, again, she felt that almost intimate touch to her insides as she met his eyes. It was decidedly disagreeable, she told herself, not at all pleasant. It was unnerving. Unpredictable. Unacceptable.

Ripping the page out, he handed it to her. *I'll keep quiet about the vocal cords – for now – but I want you to find out why it was done and tell me.* His phone number was written at the bottom of the sheet.

'I'm fairly sure I can tell you now,' she said grimly, trying to sound confident in her words, 'and I am sure it isn't considered a welfare issue as it would have been performed by equine vets who care about the horses. If you think about it, it's possible that hearing so many other stallions could be very unsettling for the horses, so it improves their standard of living here.'

Tucking up one side of his mouth in clear disbelief at her words, he raised his brows questioningly at her with an expression of, *Are you really going with that?*

Why hadn't someone informed her that the damned vocal cords had been cut out of these horses? She mentally cursed the decision that seemed barbaric, even to her. It was going to be a public relations nightmare once it got out. She would have to find welfare experts, veterinarians, and respected horse-riding heroes to go on record as supporting the surgery and stating that it made their lives better. What a freaking headache to be hit with a few weeks out from launching the information about Stablex and months from releasing the drug.

*They need a voice.* He handed her the piece of paper, looking at her intently as though he could see things in her that she knew weren't there, like heart and soul.

'You seem to have done quite well without one,' she muttered, immediately regretting the words. Damn him. He had her so rattled that she was speaking without thinking. 'Sorry, I apologize for that.'

Lane shook his head and smiled to show there was no need for an apology. He'd lost his voice the day his father told him to stop talking, the hour he realized that his spoken words could not alter what happened that day, but he'd found other ways to communicate and change what needed to be changed. He had become used to many attitudes about his silence, from those who spoke loudly as though he was deaf to those who ignored his presence altogether, referring to him as 'the mute' as though he was a plant in the corner. The words Karen spoke were more of a compliment than anything else, but he could see she was embarrassed by mentioning what she saw as his disability.

When they turned the corner, Andrea was kneeling on the ground aiming the camera up at one of the black stallions while Matt stood in front of the horse and slightly to the side, snapping his fingers and making kissing noises to get the horse to look in his direction.

'Beautiful,' Andrea murmured, lost in the world of her lens as she captured the beauty of the horse. 'Get his head up a bit more, no a bit to the right, more, more…that's it.'

'Lane wants to know if you've finished yet,' Matt said to his sister, 'seems it's about time we shook a leg. You'll still want to edit a few of those on the computer before handing them over.'

Andrea blinked as she came back to life through her eyes rather than through the lens, glanced at Karen, who stood tight-lipped nearby, and at Lane, who was leaning into one of the horses as though whispering a secret into its ear. Quickly lifting the camera, she took some shots of Lane with the stallion, noting the perfect lighting that reflected from their eyes and framed their heads in a halo.

'Sure thing, just a few more shots. Do you want some photos of the people tending the horses?' she asked Karen, hoping for the opportunity to see more of the facility. 'Perhaps showing some of the workers feeding or grooming the horses to highlight their care.'

Even though she realized that Andrea was more concerned with seeing what else there was in the complex than in taking images of the positive side of Pilatos Farm, Karen agreed. Last night, she had organized with the stable managers to have best looking, youngest, and freshest-faced workers assigned to Stable Block One, and she could hear the voices and clatter of equipment a few corridors over as they cleaned stables and groomed horses. Leading the way to the activity, she was pleased to see the sort of young men and women who you could expect to see modeling clothes in horse magazines and swimsuits in sporting journals. There were no evil-looking, hard-eyed scientists to be seen, just young, keen horse people who enjoyed working with horses.

As Andrea photographed them, Tom stood next to her holding her tripod and second camera, and Lane and Matt walked over to meet the Pilatos employees. Karen stood back and watched, trying not to roll her eyes at the youthful exuberance that greeted the Australian men. To anyone interested in horses, Lane seemed the equivalent of the world's most popular rock star, and it wouldn't surprise her if his fans would do anything for him. Unfortunately, these fans worked with the Stablex horses, and that was a very concerning thought.

Smiles, shining eyes, and infatuated expressions were aimed at Lane as he shook hands and returned hugs. Karen was glad of the no-phone policy; otherwise, she knew that she'd have to suffer through endless selfies as everyone wanted to prove to the world that they had met Lane Dimity in person. Honestly, last month, the man hadn't even blipped on her radar, and now he was an overwhelming presence with the potential to damage her company. Damn him.

Refraining from telling them to get back to work, Karen stepped forward and asked them to explain to Lane and Matt what their work involved. Luckily, they genuinely liked horses and admired these black stallions, so their accounts of grooming, cleaning, and keeping the stallions happy were testimony to the fact that these horses were genuinely well cared for.

By the time Karen had ushered the Dimity gang back to the main office of Stable Block One, she had hoped they had seen enough to convince them that Pilatos did have the welfare of the horses at heart. Of course, cutting out their vocal cords was going to be a tough obstacle to overcome in the public perception of Stablex, but she had hopes that it was not insurmountable.

In the office, a modern, minimalistic mix of white and chrome, Andrea was given a laptop with several of the most popular photo editing programs on it, and, after downloading all the photos from both cameras, she started selecting the ones that would fit into the parameters of the contract: beautiful horses, clean stables, happy workers, and everything else the company would want to promote. Andrea knew if she hadn't taken the photos, any other equine photographer would have, so the images were always going to be produced, but at least this way, she had seen for herself what was going on in the production of Stablex.

After organizing morning tea for them, Karen left the four under the hawk eyes of Joe and his men and removed herself to a private office where she could catch up on emails. There was too much to be done to waste time standing around watching a photographer edit photos, no matter how talented she was. She checked over the plans for the Stablex launch, changing some details but approving all other arrangements. There were some more business matters, and then she checked her personal emails. There were two messages from Marcus, one written in sadness over the end of their relationship, the other written in anger that she had shown so little reaction to the break-up. She ignored them both.

A piece of paper landed on her keyboard, and she spun around to see Lane standing over her, with Joe a couple of steps behind him.

*Call me about their voices.*

'I assume you have text-to-voice on your phone,' she looked at him quizzically, 'it's going to be a fairly one-sided phone call otherwise.'

His face split into a grin that could set anyone's heart aflutter, but not hers. No, the rapid response from her heart was due to being surprised by him being there, not because of him. She assured herself that it could have been anyone who snuck up behind her like that, and her heart would be doing the same tap-dance in her chest.

With a mischievous wink and a nod, he let her know that she was correct about his text-to-voice. Then he pointed at his friends, motioned a 'yak yak' signal with his hand, and held his hand to his ear like a phone to indicate that one of them could talk for him.

'I'm sure they'll be looking forward to talking to me,' she said with an acerbic tone to her voice that made him smile at her. She frowned back. It was not her intention to amuse this man; she simply wanted to minimize his damage to Stablex and Pilatos.

The photos Andrea showed her were perfect for promoting a positive image of both Pilatos and Stablex, and Karen knew the advertising section would make good use of them over the next year or so. Joe oversaw the removal of the photo sticks from both cameras and handed them to Karen before giving the cameras back to Tom, who scowled at him.

'Thank you again for your work,' Karen addressed Andrea. 'We've transferred the payment to your account, and, as agreed, there will be ongoing royalties on any images that are repeatedly used.'

'All good,' Andrea shrugged. 'I'll get those portraits for your mother printed off and to her within the next few weeks and send through copies of photos to the magazines doing articles on Bisente.'

'I do hope you'll consider changing your mind about action against us now that you've seen the facilities here.'

'Do you think that's going to happen?' Andrea snorted and shook her head. 'It's like you and I are looking at totally different things. You think we should see happy horses, and we can't believe that you can't see what is in front of your eyes.'

'I'm sorry about that,' said Karen, surprised to find that she actually did feel something akin to regret about them not agreeing on this. She had tried the gentle approach to solve this problem, and since it didn't work, then it would be up to Pilatos security to try and control it. Looking at the hard face of Joe Kaiphas, she felt another stab of regret that it would be up to him and his team.

As Lane and his friends drove away from Pilatos Farm, Andrea sat in the front seat next to her brother, who was driving, fiddling with the undersides of her cameras. Using a tiny screwdriver, she removed a small panel in the space where the photo stick was inserted, revealing another photo stick.

She held the first one up and grinned triumphantly at the men, 'I have all the photos stored on these, along with a few hundred that Karen doesn't have. I love my little spy modifications.'

'Looking forward to seeing them,' said Tom from the back seat, 'and Lane says to remind you to tell the buses to move on in.'

'Yep, on to that right now,' she replied, taking out her phone and pressing in a number, 'Jed? Hi, Andrea here. We've finished at the farm now if you want to get your people on site. Thanks. Talk to you later.'

Fifteen minutes later, as they approached Lexington, they passed a convoy of twenty-two buses, all loaded with protesters heading out to Pilatos Farm.

'That should ramp things up a bit,' Matt watched the seemingly endless line of buses flash past, 'and catch some more media attention.'

'Where should we go?' Andrea asked. 'You don't want to go back and join the protest?'

'Not on your Nellie,' Matt glanced sideways at his sister, shaking his head. 'We're going to be walking a dangerous road from here on in, and I want to be far away from that Joe Kaiphas and his thugs when John Lawford unleashes them on us. And he will.'

'We're going to stop them,' vowed Tom. 'We will bring them down, and we will get freedom for those horses.'

Lane stared out the window at the farms, businesses and houses that they passed as they headed into Lexington. Every part of his being cried out to save those stallions, but a second cry was forming: save Karen Lawford. She was trapped every bit as much as those horses, and just as they had no concept of cantering free over paddocks of grass, she had no concept of what her life could be like without the shackles of corporate life crippling her. He needed to expand his plan.

# CHAPTER SIX

*Every time I ride a horse, I connect with all those who have ever ridden a horse with love in their hearts, respect in their hands, and understanding in their minds. Stretching back through the decades, centuries, and millennia, the people who ride horses are connected to each other and connected to me. Within all of us lives the child who once looked at horses with wonder, who dreamed of flying horses, wild stallions, and adventures with a horse we loved. We are the riders of horses. Having this in common should overcome all our other differences.*

**Lane Dimity – at the World Equestrian Games opening ceremony.**

## Lake Junaluska - North Carolina.

'I've got it,' Matt announced, holding up a page that had emerged from the printer, 'and I don't know who our contact is, but all the information is here, and it looks genuine.'

The printer zipped out a few more copies, and he brought them over to the table for his sister, Lane, and Tom to read. The table was an enormous slab of timber that fitted in with the rustic look of the exposed beams, floors, and stairs of the expansive home overlooking Lake Junaluska in North Carolina, where they'd been staying since leaving Pilatos Farm.

When they realized that they could be in danger from Pilatos security, they asked for help from their network of horse friends, putting out a word-of-mouth call for a quiet place to stay for a week or so. A cosmetic surgeon who bred Gypsy Cobs offered them his house at the lake while he was overseas. There were no horses at his lake property, but there were plenty of photos of them along with rosettes on the walls and a full-size fiberglass Gypsy Cob in the corner of the main room, complete with synthetic mane, forelock, and tail that cascaded in great hair-falls as impressively as a real cob.

To reach the house, they'd left their car at a friend's horse stud outside Lexington and hitched a ride on a horse truck to a show at Columbus. Then, they caught a bus to Wheeling, had one of Tom's cousins drive them down to Charlotte, where they borrowed a spare car from an Australian friend who was training dressage horses there and drove over to Lake Junaluska. It was a convoluted journey taken over two days, but they suspected they needed to go to ground and not make it easy for Joe Kaiphas's men to follow or find them. They had been warned that it was dangerous to go up against Pilatos, and once those demonstrations had started, they knew they needed to make themselves impossible to find.

It was easy to keep up pressure on Pilatos using social media platforms. Tom, who enjoyed the intricacies of information technology, used VPNs to ensure that no matter where they were located when they accessed the internet, their location was lost in the Virtual Private Network. Lane's social media posts questioned what everyone knew of the stallions at Pilatos Farm, raising awareness and curiosity. All around the world, people began to ask why so many stallions were continuously stabled for a pharmaceutical company.

No claims or statements were made; Lane merely asked questions, often with images of horses cantering or galloping over various landscapes to remind followers that horses were meant to move freely, not be locked in stables all their lives. He knew Karen would be watching the campaign closely, and he found himself composing sentences that he hoped would reach her and make her think about her life and her choices and about what else might be out there for her. A grey life of work for a company that imprisoned those horses was not for her; only she didn't know that yet.

'So, the launch to the pharmaceutical and medical community is next month,' Matt read the details their informant from Pilatos had sent them. 'It's a few weeks away at the Pilatos Centre in Lexington.'

'Who do we know there?' Andrea asked, collapsing back into the leather sofa next to Tom.

'I have a cousin there,' said Tom.

'You have cousins everywhere,' laughed Matt, 'I swear, man, every town we go to, you seem to have a cousin.'

Tom shrugged and grinned at him, 'Sometimes they're second and third cousins. Don't blame me for keeping track of my family.'

'Tom's cousin,' Andrea brought them back on task, 'and I'm pretty sure that Jemmah from Rosewood is based at an equestrian center just south of Lexington – she'll have plenty of contacts. And that Irish guy we met in Athens a few months back said he was doing trackwork somewhere in Kentucky. I liked him.'

'We'll start with them,' nodded Matt. Giving his sister a cheeky smile, he added in an Irish accent, 'You can have the job of contacting Michael of Kilkenny – I got the feeling he liked you, too.'

Andrea threw a pencil at him.

Matt turned to Lane, who was sitting in an oversized armchair nursing his chin in his hands. 'Will you want protesters at the launch? Should we ask these people to start reaching out to friends who'll come along on the night?'

Lane shook his head, his eyes closed as he let rivers of thought flow through his mind. It would be a big night with people from every part of the medical and pharmaceutical industry there, as well as politicians and anyone who might be beneficial to the promotion of Stablex. A protest might inconvenience people as they arrived and left and could get some media attention, so it probably was a good idea. It could also provide a distraction for an even better plan to upset the launch.

*Maybe call them tomorrow,* he signed to them as he raised his dark eyes to meet theirs, *we need to come up with something that will stay in the minds of the people at the launch, something bigger than a protest.*

'Don't do anything that could get you arrested,' Andrea warned him, 'or us. I don't want to get arrested either. It's a wonder we've managed to stay out of jail so far, all things considered. We've really pushed our luck at times.'

'I'm less worried about jail than I am about that security bloke, Joe,' Matt grimaced at the thought of Joe's cold eyes. 'I get the feeling that he could make any of us disappear, and it would only be thought of as an accident. I don't want to cross him.'

'I think we already have,' said Tom, 'the way he looked at us the other day made me think he could kill any of us and not lose any sleep about it.'

'Hence,' Andrea waved a hand around the house, 'we went to ground like foxes.'

'Cunning like a fox,' Matt smiled, waggling his eyebrows.

'As long as we don't end up dead like a fox,' Andrea sniffed.

Lane's phone vibrated in his pocket, and he took it out and looked at the message as the others continued to talk.

*I've spoken to our vets. The throat procedure was performed humanely. It was done after consulting with ADOR. Our vets and the ADOR inspectors assure me that there is no issue.*

Animals Deserving Our Respect was an outspoken group of animal activists that worked to close down the horse meat industry and campaigned to end the suffering of livestock, from the shearing of sheep to the castration of cattle. They also wanted to ban horse racing, so it should have been surprising that they'd support what was happening with the Stablex stallions. Of course, he was well aware of how they worked and knew that, like too many other charities that pulled in big donations, some of their decisions seemed influenced by the donations, not the welfare of the animals.

*How much did Pilatos pay ADOR for their consent?* He texted back, imagining the look of fury on her face as she read that, and he smiled to himself as he thought of how her stormy blue eyes would flash. It was fun to poke the tiger with a stick.

*Donations are not payments*, came the quick reply.

Lane smiled and fired back, *The ADOR heads all drive 100k cars and fly business. Donations are always needed to fund that lifestyle.*

*I don't care about their lifestyle. They are a respected welfare group, and they approved the throat surgery. I have documents from them if you need proof.*

He changed tack and texted, *Silent stallions. Don't you feel anything at all for the horses with no voices? Unable to call to friends or ask for feed, or simply be a stallion and make stallion noises?*

*My concern is that they are well cared for, and it's all approved by vets, ADOR, and other welfare groups. You need to focus on horses that really do need your help, or are you chasing donations?*

He chuckled at that, and Andrea asked him who he was texting, so he signed, *Our nemesis.* Pointing to her laptop, he continued, *Look for a scar on the necks of the horses in your photos.*

Andrea quickly clicked through her files to open up the photos of the stallions and soon found one that she zoomed in on, revealing a scar.

'What the actual...?' Tom squinted at the image, trying to work out what it was.

Moving to photos of another horse, they found an identical scar, and another on a third horse.

'They've silenced them,' Matt whispered, his face shocked, 'they've cut their vocal cords, haven't they? That's why they were so quiet – they can't communicate.'

Tears filled Andrea's eyes as she looked at the scars, apparent in quite a few of her photos now that she knew what to look for. All her life, she had heard the great range of vocalizations that horses make, particularly stallions, and it was appalling to think of those horses silenced by surgery, unable to call or protest or connect with the other horses around them.

'Did she know?' Andrea asked Lane, her face turning rigid with fury. 'Did that cold grey bitch know that the stallions had been silenced?'

Lane held up a hand to calm her outburst and shook his head, *I showed her. She seemed shocked. She's now saying that ADOR approved it.*

'ADOR would approve anything if you paid them enough,' Tom spat the words in disgust. 'Get on the net and tell the world about this. It will bring them down.'

'Every person on the planet,' said Matt, 'who in any way likes horses or any animals is going to be outraged by this. We pull on this, and the whole house of Stablex will come tumbling down.'

Seeing the hesitation on Lane's face as he sorted through his ideas and possible actions, Andrea shook her head, 'No, I don't think we're going to put this out there yet, are we?'

Lane tweaked an eyebrow at her, his dark eyes still deep in thought.

Andrea continued, trying to think like Lane, 'We don't even know what Stablex is yet, do we? So, we need to find that out and use the silencing of the stallions in a direct attack on the people Stablex will benefit... is that right?'

*You know me well,* Lane grinned at her, *if it's a drug that saves the lives of children, we will have to be careful. If it is a drug for cosmetic surgery or vanity, then we can come up with an attack that will rip the throat out of Pilatos.*

'The launch isn't that far away,' Tom tapped the piece of paper that Matt had printed off for him, 'so we need to find out what Stablex is, shape our protest according to that, and still try and save those stallions. I'm sorry, even if it is a miracle cancer drug for children, there is no excuse for doing what amounts to putting those stallions in battery-hen conditions. I stabled my competition horses, but they spent a lot of time out of their stables, galloping over the ground the way a horse is meant to. I don't want to stop animals and people working together, and I don't want to stop horses working in partnership with riders, but what they've done to those stallions...'

'And she can't see that, can she?' Andrea asked Lane, continuing once he shook his head. 'I thought she had been raised around horses. We looked up her history – she used to compete and looked like she had a great natural seat on a horse; she looked like she was one with her horses. So, how can she go from that to thinking what is happening to those stallions is OK?'

Lane shrugged and texted a reply to Karen's last message. *Ouch. No, I'm not after donations. I want you to see what is happening with those stallions. I want you to understand horses like you did when you were a child.*

Holding up fingers to count off points, Matt said, 'One – we find out what Stablex is. Two – we reach out to our contacts to mobilize a protest army for the launch. Three – we see what Lane has in mind for sabotaging that launch and showing everyone the horror of what is happening to those horses.'

*I have a few ideas,* Lane paused to rub his forehead with one hand, closing his eyes as he tried to imagine what would happen at the launch, picturing the crowd, the presentations, the movie screens, the security, the speeches, the handouts…they would be bombarding the audience in as many ways as possible with the hard sell of Stablex. *I think they'll have videos running.*

'Like a promotional video?' asked Tom. 'One that shows happy horses linked to Stablex to try and counteract us linking sad horses to Stablex?'

*Exactly,* Lane pointed at him, *with the name linked to positive images. We can work with that.*

Leaning over to the table where Andrea's laptop sat, Lane asked to use it by giving his friend a questioning glance with one hand poised over the device. Andrea nodded consent, and he turned it around and flicked through the images until he found a close-up of a stallion's eye that looked as though tears were gathering.

*We will find the negative images. We will make everyone remember our images.*

'Are we punching above our weight with this?' asked Andrea. 'We're just four people, and this is Pilatos. It's a billion-dollar monster that could squash us, and we're squashable.'

*Probably,* Lane grinned at her, a glint of battle-lust in his eyes, *but we have millions of people who think I'm worth listening to,* he gave a self-deprecating grimace at that notion, *millions who want to change the world with us. It's not just the four of us – we have an army.*

He glanced at his phone, but Karen had gone silent. She was going to hate what he had planned for the launch, but he had seen those photos that Andrea had found when she was researching the Lawford family, photos showing Karen as a child with her horses. There were shots of her riding bareback, jumping, racing across green fields bent low over her horse's neck, and standing hugging her horse. She had been connected to her horses on a spiritual level, he knew it in his heart, and he believed that if she could remember that connection, she would see what he saw when he looked at the Stablex stallions.

*We have a lot to do,* he sighed and shook off his touch of melancholy, clenching his jaw in determination: he would overcome all obstacles in his quest to help those stallions. *Keep the protests up at the farm gates.*

*Keep social media active. Start reaching out quietly to our friends in Kentucky. We have a big show to put on when they have their product launch.*

He went to spell Stablex on his fingers to start another sentence and paused, suddenly realizing what the name meant. It was so obvious; he couldn't believe he hadn't thought of it earlier. The stallions. The blood. Taking a piece of paper from the center of the table, he picked up a pen and wrote in large letters across the page.

**STAllion BLood EXtract**

'Of course!' exclaimed Andrea. 'Damn, it's so obvious. There's something in the stallion blood that they're extracting for this drug.'

'Testosterone,' suggested Matt, thinking that if it was anything else, they could get it from mares or geldings, but they needed stallions.

'Maybe,' said Tom, 'but if it was only testosterone, they could make that artificially.'

Andrea nodded agreement, 'Karen said that there was something unique about these stallions; maybe it's a hormone, like when they use pregnant mare urine to make hormone replacement drugs for women rather than a synthetic equivalent. I want to know what it is about this stallion blood extract that makes it the base for a wonder drug.'

*They steal the souls of the stallions with the blood,* Lane looked at his three friends, hoping they could understand his beliefs about the life force of all living things. Of course, they did, he reminded himself – they were each born of their land and connected to all life through their beliefs. *They might not know what makes this extract so successful at what it does, but it is taking the spirits of the stallions to give to humans. We have no right to do that.*

His friends nodded solemnly.

*We will stop them.*

# CHAPTER SEVEN

*Give yourself permission to let go of your worries, your fears, your stresses, and your concerns, and just be. It is OK to just be.*
**Lane Dimity. Twitter post. Over ten million shares.**

### The Pilatos Building - New York

After reading Lane's text about wanting her to understand horses like she did when she was a child, Karen snorted in disgust at the nonsense and dropped her phone into her desk drawer. She didn't need to respond to his idiotic ideas; he just wanted to bring his unique form of new-age drivel into her life to damage her family's company. It was just unfortunate that he had so many followers that he might succeed in making a negative impact on Stablex, and so she had to deal with him.

Well, she didn't have to do it personally, she told herself, her father had faith that Joe and his team could take care of Lane and his troublesome friends, but she knew that Joe had no idea where they had gone. He was still posting on social media and actively increasing the pressure on Pilatos through his followers, and even Joe's best IT specialists were unable to pinpoint where the man was based. At least she had a direct line to him, though she didn't feel inclined to pass on his phone number to Joe at this stage. It wouldn't achieve anything, anyway. It wouldn't help Joe locate him.

Eyeing the stack of contracts that she needed to work through before heading up to her apartment, she found her thoughts circling back to Lane Dimity. She was surprised he hadn't made the vocal cordectomy details public, and she hoped that he might see reason about it. Maybe, he would understand that the stallions' lives were improved by not being able to roar and scream at each other. Their lives were more peaceful with their silence, and that was a good thing. Perhaps he would see that.

Unlikely, she sniffed; he anthropomorphized horses and was not going to see reason. Perhaps she would have been the same when she'd been a child. Images of the ponies and horses she'd had when she was young trotted into her mind, and she smiled for a moment, a fleeting memory of the emotions from those times shying into her thoughts. I was a child, she reminded herself sharply, and my father forced me to grow beyond childhood make-believe, but this Australian is still stuck in that youthful fantasy. He needs to grow up.

Sighing, she took the top contract and placed it in front of her, forcing thoughts of horses, emotions, and Lane to the recesses of her mind. This was real. Work, contracts, making profits. This was what was important.

When she made her way up to her apartment late in the evening, she ran a bath and relaxed in the hot water with opera playing loudly, drowning out wayward thoughts. It was good to be alone. After drying, she slipped into grey silk pajamas, tidied the bathroom, and went to bed. She had eaten in the office, so she didn't need anything else to eat, just sleep. She needed sleep.

For an hour, she lay quietly, willing herself to sleep, but the gentle arms of slumber didn't reach for her. Taking up her phone from the bedside table, she flicked through the phone calls and messages she'd received that day. Stopping at the texts from Lane, she reread them, wondering if he was awake at this hour. Midnight. Did he sleep or plot against her? Did he even think of her at all, or just of Pilatos?

A smile played at the sides of her mouth as she imagined sending him a text now and waking him if he'd managed to drift away to dreamland. Maybe she could ring him for a chat and see how his text-to-voice function worked at midnight. It would be good to annoy the man. If she knew he was asleep, she'd do it, just to have the satisfaction of disturbing him.

She wondered if he ever got angry at that sort of thing. Marcus was always alarmingly annoyed at anyone ringing him at night. Somehow, she couldn't imagine Lane being upset by it. He was upset by the ill done to others, not to himself. Lane seemed so much gentler than Marcus, yet stronger at the same time. How could that be?

Her mind wandered, and she had no knowledge of drifting down over the borderlands into sleep.

The following day was filled with work, from perusing more contracts to making phone calls and helping her father at a couple of meetings. The crowds were growing at the Pilatos Farm gates, and the media were starting to report on the demonstration, as well as the comments being made by Lane.

After listening to her father shout at Joe for ten minutes about damage control and stopping *the mute*, as he called Lane, Karen became aware of a dull ache starting at her temples. There were too many balls in the air to be juggled to allow for a headache, so she took painkillers and soldiered on, taking care of issue after issue through the afternoon, before giving in to the growing migraine and heading to her apartment before five, an unusually early finish time for her.

It's just one of those mini-migraines, she told herself as she rested her imploding head against the mirror in the bathroom, her eyes shut against the small amount of light because light equaled pain. I'll get sick soon, and then it will pass, like always. It will pass.

Half an hour later, she was on her knees at the toilet bowl, dry-retching as agony bombed her brain. She sobbed from the pain, curling up on the tiles until the next bout of retching consumed her. Then, two hours after she'd left her office, it began to recede, and she crawled, fully dressed, into bed and slept.

It was almost midnight when she woke, her head in a peaceful haze once the battle had passed. After a quick shower, she returned to bed with a bottle of mineral water and started doing some more research into that thorn in her foot, Lane. Research, she insisted to herself, this is research, as I must know my enemy.

There seemed to be hundreds of YouTube videos of the man, many taken on phones by fans at some of his Spiritual Horse clinics and Horse Harmony demonstrations, others looking more professional. He sure could ride, she thought as she watched a clip of him galloping a white horse bareback and bridle-less along a beach, sitting on the horse as though he was an extension of it and not a separate body. Another video showed him resting his forehead against a tall Palomino's neck before vaulting onto its back and performing Grand Prix dressage movements worthy of an international event, all without a bridle or saddle or even a rope around the horse's neck. It was as though they were one.

She found herself staring at photos of the man, admiring his movie-star features that so often melted into an infectious smile. His shirt was often removed to reveal a tanned and defined torso that could have starred on billboards for underwear. It was interesting that, as good-looking and popular as he was, he was rarely romantically linked with anyone. She suspected that he and Andrea were an item, but then she was often photographed with a partner, so perhaps it was merely friendship between them.

There was a feast of information about him over the past ten or fifteen years, but not much about his childhood apart from the fact that he was orphaned at the age of eight when both his parents died and the couple who lived on the next-door property raised him. It must have been hard to lose parents at that age. She felt an alien welling of emotion as she thought of eight-year-old Lane alone in the world, but maybe it was almost as sad having parents who may as well have been lost to her.

The following night, after another long day working tirelessly for Pilatos, she spent another couple of hours in bed learning more about this horse-hippie, as her father had referred to Lane that day. She almost felt as though she was coming to know him, and though his world was far removed from her own, she thought she could start to see what motivated him. He wasn't evil, perhaps misguided, and he certainly did seem to love horses.

It annoyed her that there hadn't been any direct contact from him since messaging him about the stallion's throat surgery. She would have expected he'd want to keep needling her. Maybe he didn't care about her one way or another, and she was inconsequential to his plans. All that mattered to him was stopping Pilatos. Well, she smirked to herself, maybe he'd better learn that he ought to care about her, as she was anything but inconsequential when it came to Pilatos.

'Let's see if you're sleeping,' she murmured maliciously as she picked up her phone and started formulating a message. 'I think it's time to engage you in some after-midnight aggravation.'

After eight attempts at writing something challenging, confrontational, or argumentative, Karen deleted the final effort and stared at his words from days ago. Why couldn't she write something? Maybe she should leave him alone and let Joe deal with him. But an attack on Pilatos was an attack on her, and she felt bound to engage the enemy, or so she justified it in her mind.

Tapping her fingers on the covers of her bed, she spoke aloud to her room, 'Maybe if I can involve him in a conversation, I might be able to influence him or learn something about his plans. Friends close and enemies closer sort of thing.'

Realizing she was speaking to her empty bedroom, she snapped her mouth shut and tapped the phone off. I'm being totally and unbelievably ridiculous, she snorted at her behavior and rolled over in her bed, determined to go to sleep and forget about Lane. He was an irritation, an anomaly in her organized world. He was jarring color against her preferred neutral tones. He was something Joe could handle, not her.

Twenty minutes later, she sat up, the phrase, 'friends close and enemies closer,' running on a loop in her mind. Like being hit in the face with a bucket of iced water, she realized she didn't have any friends. She had acquaintances. There were people like Pearce and Sandy who were there because they were paid to be there. She had memories of school friends who had gone their own way. Colleagues. But no friends.

No one she could ring in the middle of the night if she were lonely. No one who would even suspect she suffered moments of loneliness. She thought of the looks Lane and his friends threw to each other and the smiles and laughs she'd seen them share on the videos. They were there for each other, but no one was there for her. No one had ever been there.

Her quiet apartment suddenly and overwhelmingly seemed like the loneliest place in the world.

*Are you there?* She typed and sent without thinking, then gawked at her words in mortification, a sick feeling in her stomach.

What was she thinking? How could she take those words back? It was so stupid, stupid, stupid…

*Always.*

As she read the single word over several times, she felt a rising of emotion in her chest, tightening her heart and burning her eyes. It was just a word. A word tossed away without meaning. It meant nothing. But it seemed so perfect. It seemed as though she'd reached out when drowning, and he'd taken her hand. It seemed like a promise, not a word.

She was illogical and fanciful, and she scolded herself, just as her father used to chastise her for whimsical childhood nonsense until she learned to abandon it.

*I'm sorry, I didn't mean to send that. It's nearly 2 a.m.*

*The lonely hour,* his words popped up on her screen, *there's something about two in the morning that makes you feel lonely.*

*I'm usually asleep at this hour,* she replied, *I don't get time to feel lonely – work and sleep.*

*Can you see the night sky there? The stars are blazing here.*

Karen looked at her drawn curtains, blocking the light of the city out of her room. She doubted she'd see any stars even if she looked outside.

*Black-out curtains. I don't think I ever see stars from my window.*

*Really? That is sad – and lonely. I'd feel lonely at night if I couldn't see the stars or the clouds that moved in front of them.*

Karen smiled at that, he was such a cowboy, and she was such a city slicker. They could never be friends because their worlds were so far apart. Still, it was entertaining communicating with him, and there was something comfortable about written words without facial expressions or tones to define their meaning. She was amused by the fact that she read his words with a drawling Australian accent.

*You obviously don't spend a lot of time in cities.*

*Not if I can help it,* he replied, *you disconnect from Earth too much in cities, always wearing shoes and walking on concrete and bitumen. You need to walk barefoot on grass and sand and dirt so that your body can connect directly with the Earth. When did you last walk barefoot on grass?*

*Like, when I was ten,* she added laughing emojis along with some high heel shoes, *if God didn't want us to wear shoes, He wouldn't have invented cobblers all those years ago.*

*God has a lot to answer for, then, all those sore feet, backs, and legs from high heels. He should have just given us hooves, then we wouldn't need shoes.*

*We'd still nail the shoes on like we do with horses.*

*Good point,* he included a couple of laughing faces, *and it'd probably be harder walking in six-inch heels that were nailed to your hooves.*

Karen laughed at that comment and found that the smile stayed on her face as she replied to his banter, *It wouldn't work for me as it'd take too much time changing shoes to match outfits – all those nails in and out would be a nightmare.*

*I agree - you'd have to use a barefoot farrier and some of those clip-on hoof-boots that you could change when you changed outfits.*

Again, she laughed, glad that she had grown up around horses so that she knew what he was referring to, *Then I'd get on Facebook and attack everyone who dares to nail shoes to their hooves instead of doing what I do because my barefoot shoeing is the only way to treat our hooves.*

*And when someone said hoof-boots looked clunky, you'd show them your range of newly-released elegant hoof-wear for work and evening.*

*Don't forget my gym boots – they would be far better than the nailed-on ones.*

*Even in the alternate universe of humans-with-hooves, you would be a mogul.*

*And you'd be a cowboy, bare-hoofed on the range under your stars.*

She imagined him laughing at that, then pulled herself up. How did she know that he was at all amused by her words? He could be playing her for a fool, and here she was nattering away like a silly teenager. It might not even be him, it could be one of his friends reeling her in, and she was hooked on the words like that drowning person holding on to the outstretched hand.

Idiot. Idiot. Idiot. Her laughter died, and the warmth in her chest receded into a dark corner surrounded by the cold reality of life as she knew it. It was a hard world, where profits counted for more than laughter because profits were real, and laughter could be faked.

*I might slip on a pair of hoof-crocs now and then*, he replied.

A minute ago, that would have made her laugh; now, she wondered who had written it. She was being catfished, and she was stupid enough to fall for it, laughing and feeling warm and fuzzy about text messages that could have been from a group of people sitting at a table mocking her.

I'm a bona fide moron with a law degree; she shook her head at herself and tapped the phone screen off. I should know not to let my guard down. No good ever comes of it.

After several minutes, her phone chirped the arrival of another message. She wanted to ignore it, but her resolve only lasted a few seconds. It wouldn't hurt to look.

*Are you there?*

Seeing her first rash words to him thrown back at her undid the stitching of her composure, and a sob shook her as tears filled her eyes. Damn, it was the middle of the night, and she was weak and alone, and she wanted to believe this was a person reaching out to her, but she could not allow herself to trust or believe. It wasn't safe. It was a game she would lose.

After a few more minutes, the phone lit up again.

*I'm still here.*

 Karen's lips narrowed at the message. Sure, someone was there texting to her, or maybe several people were, and she couldn't trust them. For some reason, that hurt.

*I don't even know who you are,* she texted, feeling some need to be honest and explain herself rather than ending the conversation with silence, *for all I know, you could be a group of people having a laugh at my expense.*

*No! No! Don't think that.*

She looked at the words, unable to stop a cynical twist to her lips as she thought how words could lie.

Her phone vibrated with an incoming call. It was a video call from Lane's number. She looked at it until she was sure he would stop ringing, but it continued. Running a hand through her tousled hair, she answered.

Damn, he was ridiculously good-looking. Even in the middle of the night, when he had an excuse to look disheveled and less like a movie star, he managed to make disheveled hair and a Star Wars t-shirt look like a commercial for clean living.

She assumed he placed the phone between his knees so that he could use both his hands, and he signed to her, *It's me. No one else here.*

Continuing her charade of pretending to not understand sign language, she replied aloud, 'I'm assuming you said you're alone.'

His hand reached towards the camera, and he turned the phone around to scan the empty room. He was sitting up in a hewn-timber bed in a room decorated in a frontier-style, the walls covered with Native American tapestries and black and white photos from the west of long ago. The video returned to him, and he placed the phone back between his knees so that she could see his face, arms, and upper torso.

He picked up a pen and paper from next to his bed and wrote a message, holding it up for her to see. *I wouldn't trick you like that. Please believe me.*

'We're not friends,' she spoke regretfully to her phone, unaware that Lane could see the fear, mistrust, and loneliness in her eyes in the same way that he could read it in the eyes of horses. 'I'm sorry I texted you. I shouldn't have. It was 2 a.m., and I couldn't sleep, and, obviously, I couldn't think straight. It was…it was a mistake to contact you.'

He shook his head, his eyes full of warmth and understanding, and God damn it, she could *feel* his empathy and kindness as he regarded her. Pointing to his heart, he squeezed his hand and shut his eyes, and she knew he was telling her that it was OK if her heart hurt. He wasn't even using proper sign language, and she knew what he was saying.

'It might be OK to have heartache in your world, but there's not a lot of room for it in mine,' she nodded at her own words, knowing them to be true. 'You get up each day, you do your work to the best of your ability, and you go to bed at night.'

Lane held up a finger to indicate for her to wait for a second or two, and he reached into his bedside drawer to bring out a small text-to-speech device with a screen of predictive text, which he touched to create sentences at a normal speaking pace. An educated and only slightly robotic male Australian voice addressed her.

'That's not living, Karen, that's like slavery to your work. You need to live.'

'That is so good!' she exclaimed at the almost natural sound of the artificial voice. 'You should use it all the time. I was expecting a Stephen Hawking sort of voice, but that sounds pretty much like I'd expect you to sound.'

'Really?' the voice asked, matching Lane's amused look, and she wondered if there were icons to indicate emotion so that the voice was more colorful than monotone. 'I'm not sure it's a compliment to say you thought I'd sound like an artificial voice.'

'Do you ever talk? Use your own voice?' she looked at his image intently, wondering what his voice would sound like if he used it. 'From what I've read about you, there's no physical reason for you being unable to talk; they say it's selective mutism.'

'I don't seem to be able to select it,' he smiled wryly at her, 'but, you're right, it is selective mutism.'

'Do you ever talk? Or shouldn't I ask that? Sorry, I don't mean to pry.'

'You do mean to pry,' he raised one brow at her, then smiled, 'but that's OK. Not many know this, but I can speak to horses when they need to hear something. Other than that, I don't speak. I know the ability is there, but there's a line drawn in the sand between me and my voice, and I don't think of crossing it. It's hard to explain. I'm OK on this side of the line.'

'Was it the death of your parents that started it?'

She immediately regretted the question when she saw the wounded expression that dropped over his face. It passed quickly, but she'd seen it, and it hinted at a hurt so deep that she couldn't begin to understand it. She knew she had no place trying to enter that part of his life.

'Sorry, forget I asked that – I had no right. It's none of my business.'

'Don't apologize,' he offered her one of his heart-melting smiles, his eyes looking directly at her before they dropped so he could select the words on his screen. 'I'll tell you one day, but not like this.'

'I should let you go,' she said, surprised that she sounded rueful about ending their chat and even more surprised that it was genuine. 'We both need sleep. I have lots to do tomorrow, and, no doubt, so do you.'

He tilted his head with a look of resignation as he faced what that meant, 'Back to war tomorrow. I wish we were on the same side.'

'I'm sure I'm going to regret speaking to you under the white flag of 2 a.m. sleeplessness,' she smiled at him and shook her head slightly, 'but I'm glad it was you. When I thought it could have been a group of you catfishing me, I felt like a fool. Of course, I guess you could still have friends under the bed or outside the door…I hope not.'

'Has anything you've read about me led you to believe that I would do something like that?' He looked at her intently, trying to will her to see him for who he really was. He might fight hard over the welfare of horses, but he was honorable. He did not believe in hurting people. The end did not justify the means if damaged people were left in the wake of his actions. He wanted them to grow and learn and understand, not get traumatized. 'I'm not fighting you; I'm fighting what is being done to those stallions. Remember that.'

'You're fighting Pilatos, and I am Pilatos,' she pointed out.

'No, you're not. Your grandfather started the company, and your father runs it. Pilatos is an entity run by people, employing people. It is not you.'

'We can disagree on that.'

'Perhaps we can talk about it more tomorrow night,' he gave her a questioning look, indicating that he wanted to talk again.

'I don't think this,' she waved her hand around to indicate the whole experience of talking to each other while they lay in bed, 'is such a good idea. I know you are plotting against Pilatos, so this is almost like treason for me.'

'It's you learning more about your enemy,' he pointed out, giving her a good reason to repeat their communication. 'Surely, that's a good thing.'

'Hmm,' she frowned, 'I could justify it with that, but what about you? What's in it for you?'

'Enjoyment,' he grinned at her. 'Talking to a beautiful woman at two in the morning when I'm alone in bed far from home seems like a good deal to me.'

Her cheeks warmed from being called beautiful by this younger man who was, perhaps, the most attractive creature she had ever seen, and she deflected the compliment with a question. 'Did that artificial voice actually sound flirty then? I never heard Stephen Hawking's voice sound like that.'

Lane laughed, 'His voice was a trademark part of his package and stuck in the Twentieth Century. This voice is an advanced program and is very flexible.' He grinned at her, tapped something on the screen, and a voice with a distinct Scottish accent spoke, 'This is the Glaswegian male voice; please select if you wish to change to this voice.' He pulled a face at the voice and shook his head, returning it to the flatter Australian tones. 'It also does female voices if you want to see me speak in the Queen's English in a voice not far removed from the Queen.'

'No, this one is fine, thanks,' she stifled a giggle. Giggles were for teens, not her.

'Call me anytime you want. In the middle of the night is good,' he looked at her encouragingly, 'we can avoid talking about work. There are a million other things to talk about. More than a million.'

'We'll see,' she was non-committal. In her heart, she knew this was not a smart move, yet her heart also told her it was wonderful. Fickle heart. 'I guess I'll see you on the battlefield. You're not going to win;

you know that, don't you?'

He shrugged, 'Rule Number One – call or text me anytime. Rule Number Two - no talk of work here. Let's keep this separate.'

It seemed a sensible idea, though she was sure they wouldn't be able to keep the stallions out of their conversations, assuming there were any future conversations.

'Thanks for talking, Lane.'

He signed, *goodnight, sleep tight,* and the connection ended.

Karen didn't expect to get back to sleep after such an interesting - or perhaps invigorating, or maybe unusual - call like that in the early hours of the morning, but she drifted swiftly down the halls of sleep, a smile touching her lips from the warmth of having someone there for her in the middle of the night.

# CHAPTER EIGHT

*Understand your horse. Connect with your horse. Feel his fears and thoughts and emotions. Send him your confidence and your belief that you will protect him. Do not underestimate the power of your thoughts to influence him. Your fear, your lack of confidence, your unhappiness - they will touch him as surely as he can feel the tiniest of insects land on a single hair, not because he can read your mind, but because your emotions change your body language, and that is what he reads. Look to all horizons and tell your horse that you will protect him, that he is safe, and that you are the one who will keep the wolves of his imagination away from him. You are connected to him already; you just need to understand that your thoughts and your visualizations are more powerful than you realized.*

**'Horse Dreaming' by Lane Dimity, p.148**
**International bestseller**

### The Pilatos Building - New York
In the four days after her phone call with Lane, Karen had thrown herself into work, spending more hours than usual at the office and only retiring to her apartment late in the evening to sleep. The imaginative nonsense of talking to the Australian in the middle of the night was something she wanted to put behind her, an aberration in her ordered life, caused, no doubt, by her break up with Marcus. It wouldn't happen again. Lane and his people were the enemies of Pilatos, and it was a dangerous game to engage any of them on a personal level. She accepted that, and would not err again.

The crowds picketing the Pilatos Farm gates had grown to several thousand, and their protest was making newspapers and news broadcasts on a daily basis. Their *Free the stallions!* chant echoed in her head whenever silence surrounded her, and her anger at their ignorance was growing by the hour. The stallions were well cared for, and everyone was shown clear evidence of this, but the protests grew and spread to other subsidiaries of Pilatos, with demonstrators setting up camp outside buildings and disrupting the flow of traffic in and out of the Pilatos companies.

'I want this stopped!' her father shouted at her and Joe in his office one afternoon as the Pilatos demonstrations once more made the news. 'I know that damned Australian is behind this, but where's the evidence? I want something that can prove in a court of law that he is maliciously damaging our reputation when we have absolute proof that there is nothing damned well wrong with those horses.'

'I've been over every public post or tweet from him,' Karen rubbed her temples as she spoke, looking out the window at another overcast day, the grey clouds matching her grey linen pants suit. 'He has not crossed any line as far as defamation is concerned. If we could get one person to give evidence that he spoke in a defamatory manner about Pilatos or Stablex, we could run with that, but no one will say a word against him. If he has slandered us, no one will repeat what he said.'

'Said?' John looked at her and thumped his fists down on the solid oak desk, raising his voice to a shout, 'Said? The boy doesn't say a thing – he's a mute. We can't get him on slanderous signing, for God's sake.'

'Actually, we could,' Karen pointed out, 'but his followers wouldn't speak against him.'

'His followers?' John roared. 'He's not the Second Coming with Disciples; he's a two-bit con-artist, convincing gullible idiots that our horses need saving. I'll show you something that needs saving: mustangs starving on the range need saving. Unwanted horses dumped in national parks to die need saving. Horses owned by idiots who can't afford to feed them or give them vet care need saving. Our stallions do not need saving.'

'I know, Dad,' Karen pressed the fingers of her right hand to her temple in an attempt to alleviate the throbbing pain. 'I thought he'd back away from the issue when he saw the stallions in person, but he picked up on the vocal cordectomies that they've all had. All of them.'

Stepping away from the window, she met her father's cold gaze with an arctic one and continued, 'I didn't know they'd all been surgically silenced. If I'd known, I wouldn't have taken him there as, I gather, when he was on-site before, he hadn't seen the scars from that particular surgery. Now, of course, we have a mute man dealing with twelve hundred muted stallions, and though he hasn't released that information to his followers, I know it's going to hit the fan before too long. He's not going to sit on that.'

'So, your attempt to make things better only made them worse; well done,' John's voice dripped with acerbic sarcasm. 'It seems your soft approach is not what is needed.'

'It *could* have worked,' she retaliated with heat, 'if you had informed me of what was done to those stallions. I know the surgery hasn't hurt them, but can you imagine what the public will say when that little gem gets thrown at them by this man? He doesn't have to put much of a spin on that to make every bleeding-heart animal lover around the world weep for these horses.'

'Then we get in first and prove that as part of our considerate and caring ownership, we improved the lives of these stallions by giving them minor and painless surgery. Find examples of other horses where this has been done for their own good.'

'I have all that,' Karen sighed and pointed at her laptop, 'I have statements from vets and our welfare groups supporting this surgery, though it won't be enough if he uses it against us. Also, we can't release the information first in case he isn't going to use it, and we shoot ourselves in the foot by telling everyone what we've done.'

'We're going to need you, Joe,' John turned his attention to his long-time employee. 'Don't you disappoint me, too.'

Karen tried not to wince at that jab. She was used to those comments after a life of striving not to disappoint her father. His approval was often silent, but his disapproval was always sharp and painful.

'I'll try not to, sir,' Joe inclined his head, his face devoid of emotion. 'Unfortunately, I still don't have much to report. No one has been able to locate him or his three friends. We're only assuming that he is the force rallying these protesters, but there's no evidence of a directive or request to his followers to demonstrate. I have a couple of people amongst the crowd at the Pilatos gates, and the sentiment seems to be that they are there because Lane Dimity wants them there, but no one can say that they've heard him tell them to be there.'

'If you can find where he is,' John leaned forward, his eyes narrowed, 'what can you do to end this problem? He can't be bought off, and he can't see sense – what can you do, Joe, to protect Pilatos from him?'

Karen found herself holding her breath, waiting for the answer. Joe had been in the military before joining Pilatos, and with the cold-blooded way he approached life, she had no doubt that he could have a violent solution to the Dimity problem. Would he openly admit to an intent to harm Lane and his friends, or would it simply be implied?

How would she feel if she knew that Lane would be harmed by Pilatos?

'He's Australian,' Joe gave a slight shrug, 'he can be deported. Same with the McLeay twins. The police could easily find evidence of any number of felonies that result in deportation. Once he's off U.S. soil, if some accident should occur, it's not likely to be connected to us.'

'Whatever it takes, Joe,' John sent a withering look to his daughter, implying she wasn't prepared to do *whatever it takes* to achieve their ends. 'Just get it done. And, in the meantime, we keep up the pretense of trying to work with them using Karen's approach. At least we can feed them information we want them to consider, such as our vet and welfare reports that dispute their idiocy. Obviously, it would be helpful to know where they are based at present, but I'm sure the evidence you mentioned can surface at places they've already been.'

'Naturally,' Joe said flatly.

'Enough with these horse people,' John flicked a hand as though swatting a fly away, 'we're spending too much time discussing them. The security breach at Pilatos Agricultural Chemicals. Tell me about that.'

While Joe gave her father the details of missing chemicals, Karen listened with an expression of intent interest while her mind wandered elsewhere. The chemicals could not be used in the manufacture of bombs or illicit drugs, and Joe doubted there were any missing. It was his belief that accounts and figures had been created for non-existent products, and money was being channeled through other Pilatos accounts, possibly by an embezzling employee or even an outside hacker who had accessed their systems. The money needed to be tracked to discover where it ended up. He was moving the investigation to his cyber-detectives - the same ones who could not locate where the messages and phone calls from the Dimity gang were originating.

'I'll handle that,' John made a note on his phone. 'If we have someone guilty of embezzlement, I want to deal with them.'

The two men moved to security arrangements surrounding the upcoming Stablex launch in Lexington, discussing how Joe's people were screening everyone employed at the event, as well as the measures in place to keep everyone, from protesters to terrorists, away from the facility. They also covered various backup plans for all parts of the evening.

The half-ear that Karen was lending their discussion tuned out as she flicked her laptop screen to the images they were using at the Stablex launch. Andrea's photography was emotionally moving, with the magnificent stallions carved from ebony, with light reflecting from their features and diamonds sparkling in their eyes. Words about the power and virility of mighty stallions flashed over photographs of these beautiful black horses. There were posters for the walls, videos for the various screens, and no-expense-spared promotional products featuring Andrea's photos that would be given out freely on the night. She couldn't remember seeing any promotional event that had better or more memorable images than this: people would remember Stablex - it would brand itself in their memory from that first moment.

But what had Lane planned for that night? Karen wondered about his intentions. There were security teams to keep protesters far from the center, there were in-depth security checks to ensure all employees were genuine, there were measures and counter-measures to cover every possibility, but she knew he would try something.

Unless, of course, Joe had him removed from the game first. Would his army of followers keep up the fight if their idol was charged with drug offenses, or possession of child porn, or some other charge that Joe's men could fake? Would they be so shocked to see their hero revealed as a criminal that the fight would be over, or would they believe it was a conspiracy to silence him?

She wasn't sure her father or Joe had any idea of the standing of this outback man in the world outside Pilatos. They hadn't heard of him until recently or hadn't taken notice if his name had come up, but he was respected and loved by his followers, and they believed in him. What would happen when their champion was smeared by criminal charges that Pilatos invented? He was just one man who didn't speak, and they were a multinational giant who could destroy lives. A distant memory bubbled to the surface of her thoughts, of a puppy she had carried home when she was eight. Her father had called it a mongrel and pulled it from her arms. The puppy yelped once, then went silent, and her father took it away. He made things disappear.

There was something of the puppy about Lane: the innocence, the tail-wagging joy, the bounding energy. If her father made him disappear as he had the pup all those years ago, would it make a difference to her life? Was she so committed to Pilatos that nothing else mattered?

'You know I don't like to repeat myself, Karen,' John spoke sharply, his voice cutting into her daydreaming.

She looked up to see a disapproving expression on his face. As usual, Joe's face showed no emotion. He was a rock of a man.

'I was thinking about the images we're using at the launch,' she murmured.

'I thought that was taken care of,' John frowned, 'but we've moved on from that. I want you to examine the land sale contracts for the timbered areas we're buying in Maine. Those self-styled wildlife warriors down there are trying to have the landowners renege on the contracts, and I want to make sure they can't back out.'

'Is that the area where there's a high concentration of black bear, moose, whitetail deer, and beaver?' she asked, her brow pinched against the approaching migraine as she tried to bring up the information in her mind about these purchases by the timber industry arm of Pilatos.

Joe gave a short, curt nod.

'Any chance we can set some of the land aside as wilderness for the animals to appease those who want to protect the wildlife?' she asked, aware as soon as she spoke that her idea would be considered a compromise, and her father did not compromise.

'We don't negotiate, and we don't back down,' he said fiercely, standing to his full height, his shoulders held back and arms akimbo, in what she thought of as his Superman pose. 'We are buying that land for the timber: the timber makes money, the animals don't. They can go elsewhere, but we need that timber to fill orders.'

'I'll go over the contracts tonight,' she reached over the table towards Joe, her hand hovering near the piles of paperwork in front of him. 'These ones, Joe?'

With impassive eyes, he looked at her for a moment before pushing a couple of files towards her.

'Thanks,' she nodded at him, wondering what lay behind that mask that never seemed to drop. Did he show emotion towards his daughter, Karina, or was he this distant android character with her, too?

'Do what it takes, Karen,' her father told her, repeating his oft-used phrase that meant anything was acceptable in order for him to get what he wanted. 'I don't want to think that you're starting to go soft. This,' he waved a hand around to indicate the room and the building, 'is our kingdom, and we hold it by force, not by kindness. What are our weapons?'

'Wealth, power, and knowledge,' she supplied automatically, having been drilled on this for all of her life.

'And we use those tools to hold what is ours,' he looked out the window at the landscape of buildings, swinging an arm wide at all that lay before him. 'We go to battle every day with all the other kings and barons and their knights who challenge us, and we don't let the horde threaten us or make us yield on points like wildlife, old-growth forests, or stallions in stables. The way of the powerful has always been war, and we continue the war, only not with swords, spears, or guns – we win through commerce.'

'I know, Dad,' she said, trying to keep the weariness out of her voice. He had trained her well, and she did not need to hear his kingdom lecture again.

'It's not a world where you win by going soft, and in this place, winning is everything. Out there,' he pointed at the other buildings, 'are those who watch us and who would move in on Pilatos at the first sign of weakness, so don't go soft on me. I don't care about beaver dams and moose grounds when it comes to that land in Maine – I want the timber. Don't let me down. Make sure you get those contracts upheld.'

'Of course,' she assented.

'If that is sorted,' he gave her one last look as though he was beginning to doubt her ability to hold her place in his kingdom, empire, realm, or whatever metaphor he was using to remind her that they fought for their position and fought to maintain it, 'we'll move on to the take-over of Mundros Pharmaceuticals. Joe, have you taken care of the Director who was refusing to move on her stance?'

Half an hour later, after John dismissed them both, they walked into the large reception area outside his office. The two assistants were busy at their desks and only gave Joe and Karen a brief look before returning to their work.

'Joe,' she started, her gaze roaming the walls with several million dollars worth of art on display, before she met his flat stare, 'how is your daughter, Karina? I haven't seen her since she was three or four, and she must be, what, twelve now?'

'Thirteen this week,' he replied in his cool tones, 'and she's doing well.'

'Perhaps you could bring her into the office one day,' she continued, finding that she was genuinely interested in learning more about the daughter of this hard man, 'and she could spend some time with me to see if she has an interest in being a lawyer or working for Pilatos.'

'I don't think so,' he gave an almost imperceptible shake of his head.

Surprised, Karen looked closely at him, but there was no hint of what he meant by turning down her offer, 'I'm happy to show her around if you like, but maybe this would be too boring for her. Thirteen-year-old girls can be quite uninterested in the world of business.'

'Whether or not she's interested in business is irrelevant. I don't want her to have anything to do with you.'

The words hit her like an ice-water challenge, and she froze for an instant. She'd known this man most of her life, and she had an instinctive trust in him, so this was a total shock to her. He didn't want his daughter to have anything to do with her? That was… that was a puzzle, to say the least.

'Because I'm one of your employers?' she asked, grabbing for a possible reason even though some part of her told her to leave this stone unturned.

'No, it's because of what you have become,' he informed her.

Taking a step back so she could stare at him, really stare at him, all of him, from head to toe, she frowned and shook her head in confusion, 'I have no idea what you are talking about, Joe. I would think I was an excellent role model for a young woman: a powerful, independent, and intelligent woman.'

'I have no issue with those qualities,' he provided, 'in fact, when you were a youngster, I thought if I could have a daughter like you, I would be the happiest man on earth. It's why we named her Karina, you know, so we could have our own little Karen.'

She'd never heard Joe talk about his personal life and hadn't realized that his daughter was named after her. On the one hand, she was very touched that he had thought so much of her, and on the other, she could not understand why his admiration appeared to have vanished.

'I hadn't realized,' she murmured, curious about his opinion but not prepared to invest any worth in it.

'It was because you were strong-minded, independent, intelligent, and outspoken,' he continued. 'You were everything a young woman needed to be to do well in life.'

'So, according to you, where did I go wrong?'

'You came into this man's world, your father's so-called kingdom, and instead of bringing everything that made you an amazing woman and making this man's domain bend to you, you bowed to it. You felt you had to out-man the men. You copied the hardness that made the men successful in a man's world instead of being true to yourself and bringing what was unique about yourself and changing it to suit you. The men around you compromised nothing; you compromised everything.'

He shook his head sadly at her, and the emotion in his eyes jarred her. Joe was not one to ever show emotions.

'I don't want my daughter believing she has to sell her soul and her femaleness to succeed. If that is what she wants, I am fine with it. I am happy to support her in whatever she does. If she is gay or transgender, I will support her. If she struggles to overcome life's obstacles, I will support her. But I don't want her believing that she has to think and act and behave like a man in order to succeed.'

He took a step closer to her, his voice a raspy whisper, 'Once, long ago, you cared for the wildlife and the horses and the people who needed help. You could have changed Pilatos to your way of thinking, but you gave up on yourself and became the son your father wanted, carrying on the work the way he expected. You are not the role model I want for my daughter.'

Karen had never heard Joe utter such a large number of words together, so it took her a moment to digest his message and find her own words. 'This is who I am,' she defended herself, though she knew she shouldn't have to. 'I'm a lawyer who peruses company contracts and who works for the company as best I can.'

'You might be that now,' he scowled sourly and gave a slight shrug, 'but I remember you as a girl riding those horses at Bisente. That was who you were, and you gave that up.'

'We all give childhood up, Joe, that is called growing up,' Karen closed her eyes for a moment against the light of the room that was making the pain in her head grow exponentially. *Trust no one*, she heard her father's voice repeating his life's commandments in her mind, *always suspect the trap, paranoia is your friend, consider all possibilities.*

Like a flash of lightning across her synapses, it occurred to her that Joe didn't mean a word he said; it was merely a way of checking her loyalty to Pilatos. He was her father's man through and through; he always had been and always would be. He would put himself in front of a gun for John Lawford. Her father thought she was getting soft, and Joe was playing his hand to try and bluff her into revealing her cards. Too bad, she thought, mentally shoring up her mind against Joe's uncharacteristic display of empathy that she now saw as fake; I'm not playing this game with a pair of twos in my hand.

'Also,' she straightened her shoulders, ignored the throbbing behind her eyes and met his gaze dispassionately, 'I take it as a compliment that I'm *out-manning the men*, as you put it, and your daughter would do well to learn from my example if she wants to get ahead in this life. This isn't about being feminine or masculine or what's hiding in our underwear; it's about winning. I'm winning.'

With that, she turned away and left, her head held high, but, damn, she thought to herself, she had nearly fallen for the line about his daughter and had almost doubted herself, her life, and her actions. For a brief instant, she had nearly believed that the child who had run wild on the horses at Bisente deserved a different life from this. She almost imagined what might have been if she hadn't worked so hard to be everything her father wanted, but it had been a clever snare set up by Joe. It was his job to find the weak points in Pilatos, and she was not one of those.

She spent the rest of the afternoon and early evening going through contracts. The Maine contracts were watertight, so there was no way the animals of the area could hope to find refuge there once Pilatos took over the farms. Luckily, the government had been backing away from protecting wildlife in favor of profits, so the activists who hoped to keep the land for the animals didn't have a chance against them. The trees would be milled. The other contracts she perused came from various parts of Pilatos, and all were in order. Their legal team was exceptional, and, truth be told, there was little need for her to check them, but her father liked to have someone he trusted doing this.

Almost everyone else had left the offices by the time she went up to her apartment. The final stage of the mini-migraine was almost on her. She sought the dark and the silence as the pain enveloped her mind, and, finally, she spent a half-hour on the floor of the bathroom vomiting from the pain before it receded. Slowly, the haze of relief moved in. She washed her face, stripped to her underwear, and crawled into bed, huddling into the fetal position as she drifted away in sleep.

It was after midnight when the vibration of her phone on the table next to her bed woke her. Straightening in the bed, she banished the dreams that had plagued her and reached out for the phone.

*Are you awake?* Lane's text caused her to take a sudden intake of air.

Rude and ignorant, she thought, putting the phone down and conveniently forgetting that, previously, she had messaged him in the middle of the night. He shouldn't message me at this time of night as though we are friends.

She would ignore him and perhaps get back to him tomorrow. Or maybe not at all. Her heart pounded. Of course, it would be good for Pilatos to try and keep channels of communication open with this man who seemed to pose such a threat to the company. She felt a little light-headed, no doubt the remains from the migraine, she told herself, and her racing heart was left over from whatever dream retreated from her memory. It was probably best to try and form some sort of relationship with the man. Keep your enemies close, she nodded to herself as she picked up the phone.

*I am now*, she texted, smiling as she added, *thanks for waking me.*

*Sorry about that. I couldn't sleep. I assumed the rest of the world was awake too.*

*That's a fairly big assumption.*

*Five billion people awake because I am?*

*Yes, but it's closer to 7.6 billion and climbing fast.*

*Too many people. Not enough planet.*

*Is that what's keeping you awake?* she asked, sitting up in bed and putting pillows behind her back so she could be more comfortable for this chat session.

*Partly.*

*Not a lot you can do about it. Worry about the things you can change.*

*Wise advice. What do you worry about?*

Karen stared at the words, wondering how to phrase an answer to them. She didn't want to dig too deep for an answer and reveal any weaknesses; she wanted to give an answer that skimmed across the surface of her life. Perhaps something that would lull him into believing they were sharing confidences when she knew not to trust him or anyone.

*I worry about doing my job properly and being on time. I worry about keeping our employees in jobs. I worry about the things I can change.*

*What about the planet? Global warming? The disappearing species? Increased activity at Yellowstone?*

*No wonder you can't sleep,* she added a shocked-face emoji, *that's a lot to worry about. There really isn't much point in worrying about all those things.*

*And yet, I do. And you. I worry about you.*

The words caused a flush of warmth in her chest, as though he really did care about her, but the flicker of heat passed quickly, and cold reality reasserted itself. She was one of the heads of Pilatos, and he was an animal extremist who threatened her company. He didn't worry about her, and, anyway, his concern meant nothing to her.

*You'd do better worrying about the volcanic activity in Yellowstone.*

*No chance of changing you?*

*No chance,* Karen chuckled to herself and added, *and no need.*

*And yet, I feel compelled.*

*How very narcissistic of you.*

*Is it narcissistic to want to make your life better?*

*Yes. It implies you believe you have the power to manipulate and change my life to suit your notion of what is better. Borderline sociopathic, really.* She grinned at her last comment, enjoying the insult and confident he wouldn't take offense.

*Interesting point. So, if I see someone who is unhappy, and I know I can do something to make them happy, I should leave them alone because making them happy would make me a sociopathic narcissist?*

*I'm not unhappy. I don't need to change. You're the sociopathic narcissist...*
*so who's the one who needs to change?*

His next message was a photo of a girl and a horse. A smiling girl with shining eyes and joy on her face as she hugged a grey pony and held up a rosette to the camera. She remembered that day. She was ten, she had just won a junior show jumping competition with Bisente Casper, and had qualified for the state show. The world had been perfect that day. The photo had appeared in a magazine, and it seemed that Lane had been Googling and had found it.

A second photo appeared. A laughing girl cantered bareback and bridle-less on a black horse across a green paddock with the brilliant blue sky of summer behind them. She wore her favorite rainbow t-shirt and bright red jeans. So much color. The sensation of freedom as she raised her arms and laughed into the wind came flooding back, moving as one with her horse as they raced together. It was a good moment.

The third photo was a copy of her official Pilatos portrait that appeared in the company media. She was dressed in grey, and she looked somber and stern and still. There was no color, no action, no laughter, no shining eyes. Karen Lawford. Successful lawyer. Heir to Pilatos. Colorless. Dispassionate.

*You looked so happy when you were young with your horses. Sorry to be the sociopathic narcissist who wants to see you smile like that again.*

Tears welled in her eyes as she looked at her childhood self on two of her favorite horses. It was all so long ago, but she remembered the passion and the love for those four-legged friends. She almost wanted to tell him that it had nearly broken her the morning when she ran to the stables to get Casper ready for the state show, and she found his stall empty. She wanted to confide that she had cried for a week after her father had told her that he'd sold her pony to the family of the girl who had come second to her all season. She wanted to share the pain of watching that girl win at the state show on Casper as she stood on the sidelines in the shadows. She wanted to tell him that she never found out where her black horse had gone – she came home from school, and he was sold, and her father told her to stop getting so attached to animals. They were just animals, he said; they were there to be bought and sold.

*I grew up*, she wrote, forcing away the thoughts of the horses she once loved, *childhood is a distant place.*

*We are meant to grow*, he told her, *but we should hold our childhood close in our hearts. All that we become grows from that place. Where is that child who loved her horses?*

She died, bit by bit, Karen thought to herself. Every time she fell in love with a horse, and her father sold that horse, she died a little more. She made the mistake of loving them, and that meant they had to leave.

*She's too young to be a lawyer,* Karen smiled at her words and patted herself on her back for the neat side-step to avoid her emotions, *they wouldn't take her seriously in meetings. What about you? What happened in your childhood to cause the selective mutism? Or aren't you ready to tell me yet?*

*Simple, really. I was told not to talk, so I stopped talking.*

It seemed he could side-step issues as neatly as she.

*So, I'm expected to talk about what happened to my childhood, but you won't share yours?*

*Seriously, I was told not to talk. I'll tell you the full story one day. Maybe next time we chat.*

*Will there be a next time?*

*There will be if you want to know the story.*

Touché, she chuckled in amusement before tapping in her next comments. *I did some research on you. No one seems to know what the story is, only that it probably took place when your parents died. Why would you tell me if no one else knows?*

*There are those who know, but they choose not to make it public. I'll tell you, and then you can decide if you want the world to know.*

*Do you trust me?* she asked.

*I trust you to be you.*

She snorted and wrote, *Slick.*

*I thought so.*

This is dangerous, the logical voice in her head spoke up when she smiled at his comment, you are meant to be learning about your enemy, not opening yourself up to emotions that cannot be trusted. Back away. You have kept the communication channels open, and you have allowed him to see you as a person and not a company, so back away now.

An image of Black Beauty balking at the bridge that was unsafe to cross flashed through her mind. Forming any sort of a relationship with this man was like that bridge, and it would collapse if she tried to step on it, she must only walk on safe ground. Her emotions urged her to step onto the bridge, but she knew that they could not be trusted.

*I need to get back to sleep,* she wrote, withdrawing from the friendly banter.

*Big day tomorrow?*

*Big day every day. There's this annoying Australian trying to damage my company.*

*That's no good. Can't be me. I'm just trying to make life better for some horses.*

*I don't want to fight. S*he rubbed her eyes after sending the words. She didn't want the tension of conflict creeping back into her mind. She didn't want the feelings.

*Neither do I.*

*Goodnight.*

*Sleep tight. Don't let the bedbugs bite.*

Karen snorted. It was silly nonsense, and yet it was amusing. And strangely warming.

She stared at his words until the power-saving mode darkened her phone. Putting it back on the side table, she tucked pillows around her so that she had a safe nest under the covers and curled over onto her right side. Childhood memories flitted into the muted tones of her mind, and she remembered what it was like to be young. The world was full of color then; there were hopes and magic and laughter, spiderwebs were made of dawn gold, every day was an adventure, and horses were her friends.

A smile touched her mouth. The memories were alluring, and his messages were entrancing. No wonder the Australian seemed to have as many followers and supporters as Jesus. But it's all just smoke and mirrors, she sighed, her smile fading, and he's the carnival man promising that the magic is real when it was all sleight of hand. Pilatos depended on the success of Stablex, while Lane needed it to fail. He was the carnival man who tempted her to leave what was important and run away with him to the land of make-believe.

She could not trust him. She couldn't trust herself when it came to dealing with him. She had to focus on her usual work at Pilatos and on introducing Stablex to the pharmaceutical and medical community in Lexington. Then her attention had to move to having it released onto the market as scheduled so that their massive investment in developing the drug would be repaid tenfold from sales. It was a revolutionary drug, and she knew the demand worldwide would be enormous…as long as this Australian and his legion of followers could be controlled. Clearly, she was not fit to be the one to control him.

# CHAPTER NINE

*We are the stuff of stars. The atoms in you and me, in the air around us, the trees and hills beyond, in the dogs, cats, and horses who share our lives, the water that we drink, and the bed where we sleep - these atoms were made long ago in stars, so very far away. The stars died, and the atoms were released to start new solar systems, and in ours, Earth was formed, and Life arose, and all the atoms here in every rock, liquid, animal, or plant have come from those stars. We are the children of the universe. We are all connected. Reach out and connect.*

**'Connecting with Your Horse' by Lane Dimity, p. 165**

### The Pilatos Building - New York
### John and Joe

'She's been communicating with him,' John Lawford sat at his desk, eyeing Joe, who stood at ease facing him. 'How do you judge her loyalty?'

'I don't believe there's any cause for concern, John,' Joe spoke in his flat voice, his face a mask of neutrality. 'I've spoken to her, and she puts Pilatos above all.'

'So, this texting back and forth last night, what is that?' John held up a phone log that detailed the times of dozens of messages between his daughter's phone and Lane's, though there was no hint at the content of those messages, just that they had taken place.

'I imagine she is trying to get to know the enemy. That's something you have always drilled into her: don't underestimate the enemy; learn all you can about the enemy.'

John dropped the paper to his desk and shrugged, 'That could be it, but I have a bad feeling about this.'

'Karen also knows not to trust feelings,' Joe's dark eyes stared unblinkingly at his employer, 'as you've taught her. Perhaps you should take your own advice on that.'

'Perhaps,' John leaned back in his chair and swiveled it around to look out his window. 'Have we underestimated this horse guru?'

'I believe so,' Joe nodded, walking forward and taking the liberty of sitting on the edge of John's desk, facing out over the New York skyline. Their many years together had led to a camaraderie that was not shared by anyone else in John's employ, not even his daughter. 'We were thinking of him as a man with a mission, but he's more of an entire movement that is religious or cult-like. Their allegiance to him is unwavering, and no matter who we have spoken to, if they are believers in Lane Dimity, they will not hear a word against him.'

'If you frame him for drugs, theft, or something else, will that shake their belief?'

Joe narrowed his eyes imperceptibly as he considered the question. He had been studying Lane, his writings, and his followers and was learning more each day about the power the man wielded with a single social media post. People had complete faith in him, bordering on worship. He tried to find a way to make John understand the level of commitment.

'Your mother loves the President,' he knew how patriotic Mrs. Lawford was when it came to her political party, 'but if he told her that Jesus was fake, would that shake her religious belief?'

Thinking of his mass-twice-a-week mother and her overwhelming dedication to her Lord, John could see Joe's point. If Lane's followers had a fraction of the blind faith displayed by his mother, nothing would convince them of a flaw in their messiah.

'Then, we're not going ahead with an attempt to damage his reputation?'

'We will,' Joe nodded, 'but not because we expect it will sway his followers. We want him deported.'

'Are you prepared for a more extreme action if needed?'

'If the opportunity arises,' Joe's voice remained cool as he discussed the option of killing Lane, 'but we'd have to be able to locate him if there was to be an accident, and he has disappeared.'

'He can still text my daughter in the middle of the night,' John spoke with disgust, 'so why can't he be found?'

'Every communication is routed around the world,' Joe explained, leaving it at that.

He had learned that four years earlier, Lane had criticized an extremist religious group for their treatment of women, children, horses, and other animals, and his words had led to change. As a result, some of the more fanatical of the group wanted Lane killed, leading to the current security measures that meant Lane was virtually impossible to locate when he chose to go to ground. It seemed he had followers in all sorts of places, including IT specialists, who helped him to hide digitally when required. Obviously, he suspected that Pilatos would be trying to locate him, and his concealment was more than adequate to keep him hidden from Joe's team.

'Will he be at Lexington for the launch?' John asked.

'Perhaps,' Joe was non-committal. 'I imagine he'll have protesters there, and we're doing all we can to secure the evening and minimize the Dimity Effect.'

'*The Dimity Effect*,' John scowled. 'How can we go from a clear run between developing Stablex and marketing it, to talking about this man as *an effect* that can damage us?'

Joe treated the question as rhetorical and remained silent.

'Keep an eye on Karen,' John continued after the pause that Joe had avoided. 'I want to think that she's only talking to him to keep on top of the situation, but I don't trust women – they get too emotional.'

'I don't believe she falls into that category,' said Joe.

John grunted, 'We'll see.'

### Lake Junaluska, North Carolina
### Lane, Andy, Matt, and Tom

'Cabin fever,' Matt said as he paced across the wooden floor of the house overlooking Lake Junaluska, 'I'm telling you, I'm getting cabin fever. I want to get out of here.'

'Just another few days,' his twin assured him as she worked through the emails to Lane. Thousands came in every day, and a team of volunteers from around the world sorted through them, replying to most and forwarding any of particular interest through to Lane's inner circle for consideration. 'Jodie and Abram have totaled at least a hundred marriage proposals for Lane this week – thank goodness they didn't send them through.'

'I'm hoping they politely declined on his behalf,' chuckled Tom from where he lounged on the sofa. 'Unless you're ready for marriage, Lane.' He rolled over onto his side and threw a cushion at his friend who lay on his back on the floor rug, staring at the ceiling, 'Maybe some elderly London socialite would be right up your alley.'

*You'd like that*, Lane cocked an eyebrow at Tom as his hands talked, *then you could marry her mother.*

'Good one,' laughed Matt, 'then, when we asked, *who's your Daddy,* you could point to Tom.'

'You really do need to get out,' Tom said dryly, a pitying look on his face as he regarded Matt's laughing countenance, 'your humor is imploding.'

'I do, I do need to get out,' Matt strode to the door, opened it, stared out for a moment, then closed it behind him and returned to the main room where the other three were relaxing. 'I can't imagine Pilatos having people looking for us in every town. Perhaps we can have a meal out later instead of eating in again.'

'They don't have to have someone in every town,' Tom pointed out, spinning a cushion in the air above his face, 'it only takes one of the Dimity fans to see us in town and tweet about it, then someone from Pilatos finds the tweet while searching for our names, and they have us.'

'Yeah, I know,' Matt grumbled, collapsing into an oversized armchair and leaning back, his dark eyes on Tom and Lane. 'Sometimes, I hate this digital age. I just want a simple life in the outback with family and friends and no public life at all.'

*You and me both*, Lane exhaled heavily, *I want to disconnect from this crazy world where people cut the vocal cords of stallions to keep them silent so that they can house them together without noise in order to make some vanity drug. I want to unplug from this sick world and go home. Sometimes, I feel like I've done enough, and I want to walk away.*

'Do it,' said Tom, placing the cushion back on the sofa and sitting up. 'Forget about the Stablex horses and just go. You can leave a few messages for your followers, and they will try to derail the Stablex train for you. You can go.'

*I need to do it myself*, Lane shrugged, *I need to see those stallions run free. I want to see them gallop over the grass and challenge each other and play.*

'I know where you're coming from,' agreed Matt, 'seeing them locked up in those stables, day after day, week after week…well-fed and cared for but never experiencing what it's like to be a stallion. My soul hurts thinking of them.'

*Maybe we'll go home once we've freed them.*

'Maybe,' Matt nodded, his eyes going dreamy as his thoughts wandered to a possible future. 'Maybe I'll take you up on the offer to stay at Ellamanga. I could live in the cottage there and connect back to the land. I'm missing Australia.'

'Same here,' Andy looked up from her laptop. 'I want to ride to the top of those Ellamanga hills and look out over the outback and scream out to the world with no one to hear me. I want to be far away from people.'

*Soon*, Lane closed his eyes, picturing the home of his heart, Ellamanga, *I go there in my dreams. If I should die, that is where you will find me.*

'Don't go dying,' Tom nudged him with a foot, 'and don't go talking about it. It's bad luck to invite Death in by talking about him.'

'Let's talk about the night in Lexington,' Matt changed the subject, uncomfortable with any talk of death. His deep instinct was to avoid the Kadaitcha man who brought death, and talking about dying was one way to bring him to your door. 'Do we have an in, or are we just going with demonstrators on the outside?'

Tom threw him a lazy grin feeling pleased with himself, 'Pilatos would be amazed at how many of their employees love horses and think Lane is wise beyond belief. Yes, the plan I was working on is a go as of an hour ago.'

'Really?' Andy looked at him, frowning, 'So when were you going to tell us?'

'About now,' he replied with a wink. 'I wasn't sitting on the plan; I was sorting things out in my head as I lay here looking like I was doing nothing.'

'You still look like you're doing nothing,' Matt grumbled.

'Back at ya,' Tom chuckled.

'So, my photos? The videos? The pamphlets?' Andy fired questions at Tom.

'Yes, yes, and yes,' Tom nodded, 'I was trying to think up the right music to go behind it. Perhaps something from The Man from Snowy River, maybe Spirit.'

*Snowy River*, Lane closed his eyes, hearing the music swell in his mind, filling him with images of horses running free in the Australian high country, *and Pegasus.*

'Pegasus?' Tom shook his head to indicate he didn't know that song.

'I Am Pegasus,' Matt informed him, 'by Ross Ryan. An Aussie song that was before our time, but it's a good one.'

'I'll find it and add it to the playlist,' Tom made a mental note to remember the name of the song. 'Once I hear it, I'll know where it belongs on the night's entertainment.'

'Entertainment?' Andy snorted. 'I don't think Karen Lawford and her father are going to see it that way. They'll see it as a terrorist act.'

'There's no violence,' Tom assured her, 'so maybe sabotage of their night, or even a reprogramming of events, but it's not terrorism.'

'Would we be prepared to go that far for our beliefs?' Andy asked, worried that they would step over the blurred line between trying to change people's attitudes about animals like these stallions and bringing destruction in order to force change. 'If one of Lane's followers decided to blow up one of the Pilatos factories, what would we do? We want people to act, but the world is filled with people who have no brakes on their behavior, so what if one of them tried to kill John Lawford to help us? How do we make sure that doesn't happen?'

Sadness sat heavily on Lane as he considered her words. It was something he worried about. He had wanted change through kindness to others and an appreciation of the value of all life, but he knew that any movement that wanted change attracted extremists who wanted it at all costs, even the cost of human life.

*I don't know,* he signed, *but I'm working on it. Kindness, understanding, gentleness, peacefulness, love, making the lives around us better, not worse, respect for all life…I try to push those ideals every day, but I know it's not enough.*

'We could stay away from Pilatos Farm,' suggested Andy. 'Just leave it and walk away now.'

'We could,' Tom began hesitantly, his tone making it clear that he didn't agree with that for a moment, 'but I've worked hard to find people on the inside of Pilatos, and as I've often said, everyone has a doppelganger, and guess what? Lane's doppelganger is called Sean, and he's on the security team at Pilatos Farm. Coincidence? Or opportunity?'

*Coincidence if he wants nothing to do with us,* Lane signed, *opportunity if he understands what we want to achieve and is prepared to help us.*

'Opportunity it is, then,' Tom grinned at him, tapping the screen of his phone, 'I reached out, and he responded – we're communicating.'

Andy wrinkled her nose skeptically, 'So, how do we know he wants to dance with us, and he isn't going to play us for the fool while staying loyal to Pilatos?'

'Because I'm not as stupid as you think I am,' he threw another cushion at Andy, who caught it in one hand and threw it back twice as hard. 'Sean grew up on a ranch in Wyoming. His family breeds Quarter Horses, and he did cutting through his teens, going all the way to the nationals several times. After school, he joined the military, served for six years before puncturing a lung and getting a medical discharge, then went into security. He's a horseman. Most of the farm security are – they have to be in case they have to handle the stallions.'

'So, he's a horseman,' Andy shrugged, 'most of the people working at Pilatos Farm are horse people, and they seem quite happy with what's happening to those stallions. How do we know Sean wants to help us and not trick us?'

'I met his sister first,' Tom explained, giving her a slightly exasperated look, to which she responded by poking her tongue out. 'She was the one who told me how her brother didn't like what was happening to the horses he was working with, though she didn't know the details, just that he'd come home and say he wanted to wash away the things he saw at work. She told me he wanted to leave his job and go home. I've done the research, and it all checks out: Sean has a lifetime of caring about horses. He is our opportunity.'

'I have such a bad feeling about this,' Matt shuddered, sensing the patter of feet on a grave. 'We're too small. Pilatos is too big. We care too much. The Lawfords care only about profits. I'm like Sean – I want to go home.'

*So do I,* Lane signed, *it's all too big. I am just an outback horseman who wants people to treat each other and their animals better, but it's like I began rolling a snowball that was the size of an orange, and I controlled it. Now, it's the size of a mountain, and I can't control it anymore. People confuse me with the mountain, but I'm the silent man behind the rolling mountain, wishing I could go home to the plains of outback Queensland.'*

'We'll finish what we started with Pilatos,' Tom nodded at him supportively, understanding that his friend disliked being treated like a hero, an idol, or even a god with some of his obsessed believers when he merely wanted people to read his words and take a step towards kindness. 'And then you go home. You were never meant to be a warrior, and this has become a war - a war between those who respect life and those who put personal greed above respecting life. People like me love the battle, but for you...for you, it's soul-destroying. You want to inspire and create, not fight and destroy.'

*Do you want to destroy?* Lane asked him.

'I want to destroy greed,' Tom's eyes looked beyond the room to the past centuries of greed, an insatiable hunger for wealth and power that had done so much harm to his people, his land, the animals he loved, and the world that was his home. 'Pharmaceutical companies like Pilatos are multi-headed monsters that engulf us to make more money for the wealthy who own them. There are the medications and vaccinations that save lives, and those are great, but there are so many products pushed on to people that are more about profits for the companies than helping the people or the animals that use the products.'

'You're preaching to the converted,' Andy reminded him. 'How many times have we gone over this same ground? I thought we could make a difference, but I'm beginning to agree with Matt – we're too small, and they're too big. They're carrying on as usual, and we're hiding out without even knowing if we need to hide – we're rabbits going up against an army of hunters.'

'But rabbits multiply,' Tom spoke enthusiastically, playing out Andy's metaphor to an end that suited his vision. 'We four rabbits might not be able to take on the hounds that are Pilatos by ourselves, but our message is spreading. We're not four rabbits hiding in fear; we're staying safe as we incite a million rabbits to rise up. The numbers outside Pilatos are growing, and after the launch in Lexington, they'll grow exponentially, I promise you. Then Sean and all the others like him inside Pilatos will turn on the hounds, as well. We're not too small, and they're not too big. Change is coming.'

'I'll tell you who else is coming,' Matt stood and stretched, feeling invigorated by Tom's belief in their crusade, 'that journalist from New York who wrote the exposé on animal charities. The one who brought down those three senators after she proved their involvement with that big lick riding and its shocking animal cruelty.'

'Vicki Marshall?' asked Tom, asked Tom, remembering that Matt had been tasked with contacting her.

'Yep. We're meant to meet her in just over an hour at a park just under an hour from here. Do the math.'

'Do you think she'll see our side or the corporate side?' Andy asked, packing up her things.

'Once she meets Lane,' Matt grinned and winked at his sister, 'she'll see our side. Who can meet the Second Coming and not be hypnotized by his god-like charm?'

Another cushion went flying through the air, hitting Matt squarely on the jaw, and he pointed at Lane, whose aim had been so accurate. 'And here we were thinking that you don't like violence,' he shook his head with mock sadness, 'but you don't seem to have a problem with friendly fire.'

*No problem at all,* Lane smiled, picking up another cushion and bouncing it threateningly in his hands.

'I give up,' Matt held up his hands in surrender, 'no more cruise missile cushions. I take back my god comments. Forget the cult-leader religious fervor - you'll have to use your outback charm to win her over.'

*It's not working that well with Karen Lawford,* Lane grimaced. *I thought I could reach her, but I'm the enemy, not the bringer of light.*

'Of course, you're not the bringer of light,' Andy snorted, picturing the calm, unsmiling face of the Pilatos lawyer. 'That woman lives in that corporate world where profits rule and feelings aren't cool. She's a lost cause, Lane. She's not a wild horse that will learn to trust you -

she's the heir to Pilatos, and we are the enemy. Forget about her and focus on winning over the journalist. Does anyone know if she likes horses?'

'She competes at dressage,' said Tom, who believed in researching the backgrounds of everyone they met, especially ones as good-looking as Vicki. 'Interestingly, on a Bisente horse. I believe that she will be on our side, which is why we're meeting with her. She's going to be at the launch in Lexington, too.'

'That promises to be a big night,' said Matt as he exited the room, heading towards the garage where there was a car the cabin's owner had told them to use.

'You have no idea,' Tom followed him, speaking loudly so all three could hear. 'I've received emails from some Pilatos employees, including someone whose team is vital to the launch. I'll fill you in on the way.'

### Nicholasville, Kentucky
### Jacinta and Nia

The usual queasiness churned in Jacinta's abdomen as she sat at the breakfast table, looking at her toast and coffee. Like every other workday for the past two years, she was ready to leave for work early, as being late earned demerit points, and they ate into the generous Christmas bonus which she needed.

There was no doubt, working for Pilatos had its rewards if you played by their rules. Last year, she had a mere twenty demerit points for minor things, like not having her hair contained according to guidelines and having some errors on the daily paperwork, and her Christmas bonus had been enough to buy her parents the overseas vacation they had been planning for thirty years.

Working for Pilatos was lucrative, even when you cleaned stables and groomed horses. It had started as her ideal job: working with horses, working alongside veterinary surgeons from whom she could learn, an income above anything else she could legally earn, and the chance to save for her dream of studying to become an equine vet. There was even shared accommodation in a new three-bedroom house in Nicholasville, only twenty minutes from Pilatos Farm, with courtesy buses to and from work, so she didn't have the expense of rent or a car. Her bank account was swelling, and not only would she be able to pay for the college course, she would also be able to buy her own house.

Pilatos was generous. The income, the bonuses, the accommodation, and other benefits. Just the other day, one of her supervisors mentioned that she could apply to Pilatos for a scholarship to study veterinary science, and it was likely that they would pay all her fees. The idea of an employer paying for her to become a vet was exciting, and she should have been over the moon about the opportunity, and yet the queasiness before work continued. She blamed Lane Dimity.

For most of the first year of working with the Stablex stallions, she had gone to work in a happy frame of mind. The horses lived in luxury; even the ADOR people, who had shut down so many animal-related industries, had commended Pilatos for its care of the stallions. She had her allotted twenty stallions, and she enjoyed working around them, getting to know them as she cleaned their stalls, cleaned their hooves, and groomed them. Each day, she would give them exercise time on the two treadmills assigned to her group, and they seemed to enjoy the chance to trot and canter on the treadmill outside their stalls. The stallions were kind and gentle and not at all savage like some stallions she had read about.

There were the occasional deaths, she was told, but nothing to be alarmed about, no more than if they were out on the range galloping around and risking breaking a leg or colicking or succumbing to some other accident. Sometimes, she suspected a horse had been exchanged for another during the night, but she couldn't be sure as they were almost identical.

It was clear they were happy. Everyone said so. Until she started following Lane Dimity and looked deeper. That was when she noticed their eyes, really noticed them. There was no joy there, merely acceptance. And then, Max died.

She didn't like calling them by numbers, so gave each of her stallions a nickname, a practice that had spread across the entire stable complex, though the stablehands were careful to avoid using the names in front of any supervisors. It was a rule that the stallions were to be known by their numbers and not personalized with names.

Max had been the gentlest of Jacinta's charges, with a forelock that extended past his nostrils and a mane that fell below his neckline and a way of breathing gently on her as she cleaned his stable, as though he liked being with her.

She used to chat to him as she brushed him, telling him how he should be charging into battle carrying a knight in shining armor, or that he could be dancing for princesses in European castles, or competing at the Friesian National Championships as he was clearly one of the best Friesian stallions in all of America. She loved Max. If she could have climbed on any horse and ridden away into the sunset, she would have chosen Max.

Then Lane Dimity's writings entered her life. He asked people to connect with the souls of their animals and care for what was there, not just their physical needs. He wrote as though he was addressing her and no one else, asking her to look into the eyes of her horses and recognize what was there. So, she looked into Max's eyes and saw a sadness so deep that it almost broke her heart when she recognized it. He was healthy, well-fed, under the best veterinary care, and he was well behaved, compliant, and gentle, but he was sad - desperately, agonizingly sad.

When he started to go off his feed, the vets looked for an illness but found none. When he hung his head low, they looked for pain or injury in his neck but found none. When he lay down and didn't want to get up, they scanned for blockages and growths, but there were none.

Jacinta spent his last two nights with him, even though other workers like herself were always present with the group of twenty stallions. She worked for all the stallions during her shift, then stayed with Max in his stall after her work, risking the ire of her supervisors for becoming so emotionally attached to the horse. Jacinta justified it to them by pointing out that any checks by welfare organizations would show that the sick horse had full-time care during his illness, which was a positive for Pilatos.

She stroked his noble face as he lay dying, his illness a veterinary mystery, but she knew. She knew and couldn't tell anyone as they wouldn't understand, and she'd risk losing her job if a supervisor overheard her talking about Max's sadness because they only dealt in physical causes of issues. She knew that, with Max, there was no physical cause for his illness: his soul had died, and his body was going to join it.

It wasn't anything she could discuss with anyone else as Pilatos had strict guidelines about avoiding any talk in relation to the stallions regarding religion, spirituality, emotions, or non-science-based conjecture. There was the exception of being able to state that the stallions were 'happy' because all physical needs were taken care of, but she risked losing her job if she tried to tell anyone that Max was so sad and depressed that he was dying.

He didn't need medication or scans or food; he needed to call out to friends, gallop across paddocks, stand in the rain, and race the wind. He needed to be a stallion, not a pampered laboratory animal. She knew that, and she remained silent, muted by her desire to keep her job, keep the income, keep the accommodation, and keep her plans for her future. She remained silent as Max died.

On that final night in his final hour, his great head lay on her lap as her tears soaked into his forelock. Five other workers came and stood guard at the door, men and women who cried silently as Jacinta sat on the floor cradling Max's head as he died. In that final moment when his soul flew free, she *felt* him. His kindness, strength, and forgiveness shot through her like a light in a dark cave, and, for that brief instant, his joy at being free illuminated her soul, and she understood all that Lane had been saying.

As she felt Max's spirit race away into the night, calling his joy to all who had gone before, she realized that her ideal job at Pilatos was an illusion. She was not caring for these horses; she was merely looking after their bodies as their souls withered and died so that she could collect the financial rewards. It made her sick.

When Max's last breath escaped his stilled body, she looked up at the five who watched over her and the stallion, seeing the grief in their eyes and recognizing her own feelings in their hearts.

'He's free,' she nodded at them, trying to control the sob that tore at her insides.

'Run free, Max,' whispered the youth from New York who wanted to use his Pilatos wages to fund a no-kill dog rescue.

'Follow the light,' murmured the Irish girl who dreamed of owning a horse stud one day.

'You're home, big fella,' drawled Carl, who had grown up on his grandfather's ranch in Texas, riding horses before he could walk, and who had come to Pilatos Farm because all he'd wanted was a job working with horses.

'I loved you, Max,' sniffed the young woman who had lived her whole life in Lexington and had never been able to afford a horse, so she was saving to buy a small farm and a horse.

'Forgive me, I'm so sorry,' sobbed Tina, who had been training to be a jockey before a fall had caused permanent weakness to her left arm. She'd been thankful that Pilatos had hired her for her ability to handle horses and had overlooked her medical issue.

Jacinta had seen it in all of them: that realization that they were failing these stallions. It didn't matter how well they cared for them; they lived silent lives in stalls without sunlight and rain, protected from the world where they should have been running, locked away from the grasses on which they should have been grazing, deprived of what it meant to be a stallion. But they didn't talk about it. They looked at each other in shared understanding, dried their tears, and moved away so that Jacinta could notify a supervisor that Max had died.

Within the hour, a forklift had arrived, and the front of the stall had been unclipped so that Max's eight hundred kilo body could be moved to the autopsy room. His cause of death remained unknown, but industrial disinfectants were used to clean his stall, and swabs were taken from all other stallions in the block to see if any virus grew in the agar.

A day after Max had died, another sad-eyed stallion with a scar on his throat arrived. He had been allotted a number nearly a thousand higher than Max's number, but Jacinta called him Echo. He still carried faint traces of hope in his eyes and moved his mouth as he attempted to communicate with the stallions around him, but she knew the last of the hope would soon die. Like the others. Like Max.

And so, every day before work, she felt queasy with guilt about taking part in what was happening to the stallions at Pilatos Farm. She didn't even know what the blood extract was being used for, but she didn't care - nothing was worth the price the horses were paying. The only things that kept her going were Lane's words. They seemed to speak directly to her.

Last night, before going to bed, she read his latest message, and they resonated within her. *Forgive yourself. If you have contributed to the suffering of an animal before you understood what that suffering was, then forgive yourself. Move forward and learn, and don't repeat the mistake. Endeavor to make the lives of other animals better so that you bring balance back to how you have treated them in the past. Now that you know, you can't be forgiven if you continue to contribute to the suffering. Change is coming.*

She wanted to be part of the change.

Nia, her housemate, walked into the kitchen, dressed and ready for work. She was a mechanic at the stables, working on any machinery that needed maintenance or repairs. When she had started at the farm, she had been a robust young woman who towered over Jacinta, but, in the last few months, she had been losing weight and now appeared tall and fragile. Her face was solemn, and her dark eyes that had once danced with laughter were shadowed by sadness.

'Sleep well?' Jacinta asked her.

'No,' Nia shook her head. 'You?'

'No. I...' Jacinta stopped and played with her toast. Pilatos had spies all over the place to discourage workers from becoming too friendly with other workers and to generate an atmosphere of distrust between employees. One never knew if they were talking to someone who would hold their confidence or someone who would take the information back to a supervisor. Also, in the shared houses, people were moved every three months to discourage friendship bonds that might infringe on loyalty bonds to their employer.

Jacinta longed to speak to someone about Lane Dimity, but specific warnings had come from above about the man and his intent to damage Pilatos. If she spoke to Nia about her belief in Lane's messages, it might go straight back to her supervisor, and if she lost her job, she would no longer be on site to help the stallions if the opportunity arose.

'I haven't felt well since Max died,' she confided, thinking that there wasn't much in those words that Nia could report.

Nodding, Nia replied, 'Don't worry. Change is coming.'

Jacinta's head snapped up at the words. Did Nia read Lane's writings? Was she worried that Jacinta might be the one to run back to Pilatos if Nia spoke of her beliefs?

'I read that somewhere last night,' said Jacinta vaguely, as though she wasn't sure where she had read the words.

'Same here,' Nia sat down opposite Jacinta, looking at her intently as though willing her to say more, then she looked from side to side and put a finger to her lips.

Frowning, Jacinta looked around, then silently asked Nia what was wrong.

Tapping one ear with a finger, then pointing around the kitchen, Nia raised her brows at Jacinta questioningly. It was clear she was asking if Jacinta thought the apartment was bugged. It was something Jacinta had thought about in the past, given how paranoid Pilatos had become about security concerning the drug they were making, but since nothing was ever spoken that could in any way contravene the guidelines given to employees, she hadn't dwelled on the possibility.

*Maybe,* she mouthed silently to Nia, who continued to regard her earnestly as though trying to solve a puzzle.

Taking a small notepad and pencil from her jeans pocket, Nia scribbled something and pushed the pad across the table. *I want to be part of the change,* she had written.

*Me too,* Jacinta wrote underneath her words.

For the first time in the two months that they'd lived together, Nia smiled broadly at her housemate, the shadows slipping slightly from her eyes. Taking the notepad, she wrote something else and pushed it back.

The letters *L.D.* were written inside a heart. Jacinta grinned at her and wrote *4EVA* underneath the heart. They smiled warmly at each other, not fully trusting, but heading down the path towards it.

**Pilatos Farm**
**Noah and Abhirka**

'That's the third this week, isn't it, doctor?' the forklift driver asked Noah as he delivered the body of the horse to the autopsy room.

Pushing a hand through the thick brown waves of his hair, Noah nodded and sighed. His instructions were to downplay any deaths and ensure the statistics proved that the Stablex stallions were better cared for than any other horses in the country. Their level of care was exceptional, he didn't have to fabricate anything about that, but he was beginning to feel that something was missing.

'You have to expect losses with this number of horses,' his rich Kentucky voice rolled out the words, easily hiding any doubts he secretly carried. 'Anywhere that twelve hundred horses are together, you're going to have deaths as horses have so many things that can go wrong with them, including various forms of colic, breaks, tumors, nerve damage, and pre-existing conditions.'

The driver's mouth tucked up at one corner, and he gave the vet an unconvinced look, but he knew the routine around the farm. You always spoke in favor of whatever Pilatos was doing, and you never implied that anything was wrong with the horses.

'Yeah, well, you're the expert,' he undid the chains attaching the horse's body to the forks and patted the sleek black rump of the deceased animal, 'but this don't look like colic or a break, so maybe you'll open him up and find a tumor. Is that what the others had?'

Noah threw the driver a dark look as he really did not want to talk about the deaths of these horses. 'I'm not at liberty to discuss,' he said shortly.

'None of us are, doc,' the driver shrugged, repeating softly, 'None of us are.'

He tipped the chains back into the toolbox at the side of the forklift and climbed aboard to back out of the room, leaving the loud bleep-bleep-bleep of the reversing machine behind as he continued back down the corridor.

For the next five minutes, Noah stood over the stallion, staring blindly down at the body that had been so magnificent only a few days ago. He had been one of the leading equine vets in the country, working with horses that were competing at international level. His move to Pilatos five years ago had seemed like a career advancement with a doubling of his income. When did the joy of working with horses become this cold, dead feeling in the pit of his stomach? Years ago, when he'd worked in competition stables, he had walked down the rows of horses, patting them and talking to them, proud of keeping them in the peak of health and fitness for competition. Now, he walked past the beautiful black heads of the Stablex stallions and apologized silently to them. Why was that?

Lost in introspection, he didn't hear Abhirka, the vet nurse, approach from behind. He wasn't aware of her standing there for a minute, observing his hunched shoulders as he gazed down at the horse, like a wounded wolf grieving over a cub he'd failed to save.

'Are you well, Doctor?' the lilt of her accented voice broke into his thoughts.

'Uh, sorry, Abhirka, I didn't hear you,' he looked around at her and smiled, the warmth in his eyes for her looking out of place on a weathered face that was lined with sadness. 'I'm not doing my job properly, am I? I became a vet to save animals, but I seem to be failing at that.'

'You cannot blame yourself, doctor,' Abhirka spoke gently, 'you do what you can.'

'It's not enough,' he shook his head and told her for the tenth time that week, 'and call me Noah.'

'Yes, Noah,' she paused, seeking to find words to help him. 'Noah is a good name. The name of a man who saved the animals.'

A brief laugh burst from Noah as he compared his role at Pilatos to the character of Noah who built the Ark. 'I'm certainly not living up to my name, then.'

'Names are very powerful things,' she continued, 'do you know what my name means?'

'Absolutely no idea,' he smiled down at her, his eyes kindly as he considered the diminutive woman who was the best assistant he'd had the pleasure of working with. Of course, she had been a qualified vet in her home country of India and was waiting for her qualifications to be recognized here before she could practice, so it made sense that she was excellent at her work.

'It means wife of a cowherd,' she smiled up at him, her brown eyes twinkling.

Once more, Noah laughed, 'Really? I thought you were going to say it meant savior of souls or universal love. Wife of a cowherd? That, uh, that is an interesting meaning.'

'It reminds me of what is important,' she explained, hoping something in her words would reach him. 'We sometimes focus on the big seemingly important roles in life, such as *savior of souls*, which would be a very grand thing to be, but every role has its own importance. A billionaire in India still has to respect the sacredness of the cows and, in fact, the sacredness of all animals, but the cow is especially honored for giving more than she takes. As such, he should also respect the role of the cowherd who tends those cows, and by association, the wife who cares for the cowherd who cares for the cows who are respected by all.'

Her gentle voice almost sang the words, and Noah found they soothed the tension he had been feeling at the thought of another autopsy. He wasn't even sure that her story had great meaning for him, but there was something in the message that was a balm for his pain.

Abhirka continued, 'You do not have to be the most important person in India to be important, just as you do not have to be the most powerful person in Pilatos to count for something. You cannot save all the horses, Noah, but you can ensure that you give them the best chance. Noah of the Ark did not save all the animals, but he is remembered kindly for saving those he could.'

'I doubt I'll be remembered kindly for anything to do with these stallions,' he admitted, adding a sigh as he looked down at the body that he was about to dissect. 'I work with a lot of other staff to try and keep the horses happy, and I'm the one given the job of cutting up the bodies to try and work out why they died. The second part seems to prove the failure of the first.'

'Do you believe the horses are happy here, Noah?' Abhirka asked, looking at him inquisitively.

'They're well-fed; they have the best of care. They want for nothing.'

'Are you not also well fed and cared for? And yet you do not seem to be happy.'

'I'm a man – we're never meant to be happy, except for fleeting moments.'

'Ah!' Abhirka nodded as though he had made an astounding revelation, 'So, happiness for you is not a state, it is a moment?'

'I suspect you are about to trap me in one of your word games that make me feel foolish,' he gave her a lopsided grin, 'but continue. Perhaps if I feel foolish, I'll worry less about being a failure.'

'If happiness is in the moments,' she went on, 'then what moments do these horses have to be happy about? Describe the moments that make horses out on the range happy, or horses in a paddock, or in a herd. What makes them happy?'

'A full belly, comfort, a safe place – and they have all that here.'

'Their bodies are happy here, then. What of their souls?'

'What if they don't have souls?'

'What if they do?' she countered. 'For thousands of years, Hindus have believed in the sacredness of all life, and it is assumed that our life force will come back, again and again, to learn what is needed to be learned. So, you can return as a male or female, a poor person or rich, a cow or horse or bird or worm, depending on what it is you need to learn.'

'And for thousands of years, my people have believed animals don't have souls; they are to be dominated by humans,' Noah said almost sadly, realizing that the Hindu beliefs appealed to him more than the Christian ones.

'So, Noah, how have your beliefs worked out for the animals? Is this how you want to see the great stallions live their lives?' She poked the body with the toe of her shoe. 'And end their lives?'

'Of course not,' he muttered savagely, feeling impotent in the face of these mysterious deaths that had no clear scientific cause, 'but I am powerless to do anything except try and help them live for as long as possible.'

'If you could grant this horse one happy moment before he died,' she pressed him, wanting to see where his empathy and intelligence and instinct would take him when he thought about the lives of these horses, 'what would that be? What would you want him to experience before he left this earth?'

Looking down at the dull surface of the open eyes that saw nothing, Noah imagined this great horse once more on his feet and galloping, his mane and tail billowing around him in the wind as he strode over a field, his hooves sounding like thunder on the ground. For a million years and more, the ancestors of this horse had felt the wind in their faces as they charged over the land, running because it was good to be alive, flying over the grass because they had evolved to outrun their predators. And he lay here, dead, after two or three years of living within the walls of a windowless building, never feeling the wind while cantering on a treadmill, only the slight never changing breeze from the air conditioners that maintained a constant temperature throughout the complex.

'I'd want him to run free,' he whispered to Abhirka, or perhaps to himself, or to the horse, he wasn't sure which. 'I've seen horses in those moments when they are galloping loose on the range, and at that point, then, when the sky and the earth blur into one, in that moment, the horses know happiness.'

'Yes!' Abhirka exclaimed, pleased he could see that. 'Their souls sing in those moments, as do ours when we watch them. When you know the life force that is a mighty stallion, you know their souls are not for *this* life,' she waved her hand around at the white walls and disinfected floors. 'Lane Dimity is right. This kills their souls, and it is killing yours, too, Noah. You are sad too often. This weighs heavy on you, and I believe you are drinking, too, in order to escape what you sense here. It is time for a change.'

He was surprised she would even mention Lane's name since there had been clear directives from Pilatos that the man was considered dangerous to the company, and there was to be no communication between any employee and Lane. Even discussing him with other employees was prohibited.

'Isn't that grounds for dismissal?' he asked her, raising his brows and glancing around as though expecting to see a microphone poking out from the walls to catch their every word.

'Pwah!' she snorted derisively. 'What do I fear from someone who locks horses up like battery hens? That I am sent back to India, where I am a vet rather than a vet nurse? That does not scare me. That I lose my job? I look at this horse and wonder why I want to work here anyway. Have you read any of his books?'

Noah shook his head. He didn't have time to waste on spiritual matters while he needed to work with the science of keeping these horses alive.

'Then read them, Noah. Read them.' Abhirka patted his arm and smiled at him. 'He is a sensible man, not an extremist. He understands animals, and he recognizes that humans eat meat and hunt. He just asks for us to respect the animals and treat them with dignity in life and in death. I do not think we offer these horses the dignity they deserve. Also, I think, as a vet, you will find much to love in his words.'

'Maybe, maybe not,' he shrugged as he walked towards the wall where his personal protective equipment hung. It was time to do his job and stop talking. All staff taking part in autopsies had to wear full protective equipment just in case a virus, bacteria, or chemical that could endanger a human was present. 'Suit up. It's time to cut.'

When his shift ended that afternoon, he returned to his car and found three of Lane's books in a bag on his back seat, placed there, no doubt, by Abhirka. They'd be considered as bad as dealing drugs here, he mused to himself as he reached into the bag and read the titles, careful not to expose them to the view of the security cameras in the car park. It wouldn't hurt to have a look at what the man wrote. He would need something to help him sleep tonight, he smiled to himself as he dismissed the books, though Lane did seem to have the attention of many, including Abhirka, so perhaps it was time to learn what all the fuss was about.

## The Pilatos Building, New York
## Karen

At the end of another long day working in her office and attending meetings, Karen dragged herself up to her apartment and collapsed fully dressed on her bed, staring at the ceiling. Her ashen dress with the narrow black belt and black collar had survived the day unscathed, finishing as fresh as it had started, but she felt scrunched, creased, and wrinkled inside it. Kicking off her Jimmy Choos so that they tumbled through the air and landed with a soft whoomph on the carpet, she spread her arms wide and lay still, enjoying the quiet and the cessation of work which had pecked at her all day like Prometheus' vulture.

It took a lot of energy to always appear calm and in control, she mused, keeping the cool façade in place and free from cracks or distortions. She occasionally overheard the derisive remarks about her ice-queen persona, but when those same people made errors and hit panic buttons and fell to pieces, she was often the one they relied on to fix everything. Who was there to fix her? She wrinkled her nose as she asked herself questions. When she spent so much effort to keep her cool façade flawless, who even suspected that life lay beneath the ice?

She hadn't had to deal with any Stablex issues that day, which had been a huge relief, as the day had been filled with other problems. There had been more difficulties with the purchase of the Maine land. Some complications had arisen concerning the take-over of a small, family-owned pharmaceutical company after one of the owners committed suicide. Tensions had been high in several meetings with her father and various heads of Pilatos subsidiaries. The backlog of contracts needing her approval seemed to have doubled in size, even though she had spent every spare minute working through them.

The work had been relentless, and she hadn't even had the time or energy to do her usual gym workout to finish the day. She felt empty of spirit as she lay, still and alone, in her apartment.

That suicide niggled at her. It had been easy to shrug it off during the meeting about the take-over as it wasn't her fault that the man had made poor business decisions about his family's company and ended up in the position of having to sell it. It wasn't her fault that her father had refused to negotiate on the deal once the target company was in an untenable position and had to accept the Pilatos terms. It wasn't her fault that the man had used the gun in his desk drawer to end his life in his office. And yet…and yet…it felt as though the man's blood was dripping beneath her icy surface, tainting her life below.

She had stared, unblinking, at the man's daughter, a woman the same age as herself, as she'd raged at them four hours earlier. Then, after Joe and a female security guard had removed the daughter from the building, she had returned to work as though nothing had happened. If her father had made similar errors of judgment and caused Pilatos to fall to a hostile take-over, would she blame the generals of the conquering force, or would she blame her father for making the mistakes? Wherever she placed the blame, she could not imagine beating her chest and wailing at those generals for the actions of her father, although, she conceded, she couldn't imagine her father using a gun on himself; he was more likely to use it on everyone else.

Now, in the peace of a silent night, she felt remorse for her handling of the daughter, or, rather, her refusal to handle the daughter. She wondered where the woman had gone to school. Her name was vaguely familiar. How odd if it turned out they had been at school together, and life had brought them to this point to meet again. She rubbed at her aching temples, refusing to go any further down that path of thought.

If Marcus had been there, he might have rubbed her feet or fetched her a glass of wine, but she was glad he was gone. She hadn't missed him yet, though this should be the time when she'd be desperate for him to be there so she could talk about her day and ease her tension away. He had called a few times, and they'd spoken civilly, rather like business acquaintances who may have spent time at the same school long ago. The most upsetting thing about breaking up with Marcus was the fact that she felt nothing, and her absence of feeling concerned her. Had she become like her father? Capable of leaving his wife at Bisente and carrying on as though she no longer existed? She used to have feelings, but they seemed to have migrated elsewhere, like birds escaping winter.

Was this the pattern for the rest of her life? Work until exhausted and fall into bed, too tired to eat? Alone? Was this all there was?

Images of Lane and his friends flashed into her mind, their color and their laughter, their bright smiles, and the intensity of their feelings. There was a vibrancy to them that was alien to the world in which she lived, but she seemed to remember childhood having that level of enthusiasm and vitality. Closing her eyes, she recalled vaulting bareback onto a favorite horse as a child and riding wild and free across Bisente, her hair streaming out behind her as they raced the friends of her imagination.

She didn't miss Marcus, but she felt a sudden aching need to ride a horse again. That was something her father never understood and never would, but she knew her mother would know what she meant if she turned up at Bisente and said she had to ride. Isabella had always told her that horses were in her DNA, and anyone genetically coded to need horses could not be whole without them. Isabella said a lot of things that had no place in Karen's life, but maybe she should visit

Bisente again sometime soon and take the time to go riding with her mother. She had been so busy trying to be her father's daughter that she hadn't given much thought to what she missed about her mother.

The chirp of her phone interrupted her musings, and she rolled over to pick it up from the edge of the bed. Fingerprinting it on, she saw that Lane had sent her a message. Without reading it, she turned off the phone. It had been enjoyable texting him, but it was fraught with problems, like walking-across-a-minefield sort of problems. Although she had been lamenting that she didn't seem to feel emotions anymore, she was scared of the emotions she *might* feel if she continued communications with the Australian. Perhaps tomorrow, when she wasn't weakened by exhaustion, she would deal with his message, but not now. She wasn't strong enough to behave rationally, and her father had drilled her well on always being rational. Emotions weren't rational.

She sniffed at her mixed-up, jumbled mess of thoughts and told herself to get up and have a shower to clear her head and wash away the day. With a sigh, she rose from the bed, stripped off her clothes, and showered. After donning a silken sheath of a nightgown, she walked to the main window in her living area and looked out over the city. A million lights from a million people blinked back at her, and she felt the loneliness creep in. She had everything, and yet she had nothing.

A small brown paper package on the dining table caught her eye. She hadn't even noticed that Sammy had left the mail there for her when she'd cleaned that day. A spark of curiosity lit up as she looked at the package. Work-related items would have gone to her office, so what was this?

It was not much bigger than a DVD case, but it was soft like something made of fabric. Turning it over, her eyes narrowed when she saw the initials L.D. on the back, with the address of his station in the outback written there. Damn the man. What was he doing sending her something that looked like a gift? She had no fear that it was anything dangerous as all mail that entered the building passed through scans, x-rays, and devices designed to detect any hazardous substances.

Sitting at the table, she carefully opened it to reveal a silk scarf which she pulled out to inspect. There was no note, just the scarf. It had been hand-painted in the colors of the outback, a long landscape of the seasons running the length of the scarf, from the green grass, white thunderheads, and blue skies of the outback wet season to the red soil, brown grasses, and clear blue heavens of the dry season. The colors were achingly brilliant, and along the length of it galloped black horses, small as though seen from a distance, as they raced across the Australian outback, their manes and tails flowing out behind them.

It was beautiful. It was the most colorful item in her apartment. It was unnecessary, and she wished he had not sent it to her. It was not something she would even wear because she had changed her entire wardrobe to neutral tones years ago. Still, it was so pretty. Karen held it up, enjoying the soft caress of the silk as it draped across her hands. She wrapped it around her neck and looked at her reflection in the mirror. It had been years since she had worn bright colors, and it was strangely unsettling to see the intense outback hues against her skin.

Turning away from what she saw in the mirror, she switched off the lights and went back to her bedroom. For a few seconds, she considered turning her phone on and reading his message, perhaps answering him. Her father had ordered her to get close to the man, but not tonight, not now. He was dangerous to Pilatos, but he was also dangerous to her, especially when her defenses were down from sheer tiredness. As she climbed under the covers, rolling onto her side and curling up to sleep, she took the silk scarf from around her neck and held it nestled against her chest.

It was one in the morning when she woke to find the scarf still in her hands. For a minute, she tried to catch the receding dreams that beckoned from the mists of her mind, but they vanished like a mirage as she approached, and she gave up. She was not one to pursue fading dreams.

After some consideration, she took her phone, turned it on, and looked at Lane's text. With a few hours' sleep behind her, she was in a much better place mentally to cope with the cerebral dance of words and meaning with him. Or so she told herself. Perhaps, deeper down was the simple desire to reach out and connect with someone so that she wasn't so alone, but she didn't want to dig that far beneath the surface of her actions. This was for Pilatos, she told herself, almost convincingly.

*Don't work too hard. Take some time for yourself. Call me or text sometime. Any time is OK. Now would be fine, whatever the time is now. Go on, do it now.*

Karen lay on her back, nestled into her pillows, the phone held above her face so she could read his words. She smiled. It would serve him right if she called him now, in the middle of the night. He was impetuous like a teenager, and she felt old and sensible. When did that happen? She asked herself in surprise. When did I start thinking like I'm old and that a man only a few years my junior is young? Was I ever young and enthusiastic like Lane, or did I go from childhood straight to being old?

Part of her mind answered that she had grown out of childhood to become reliable, dependable, and sensible, but it wasn't really her fault. She had always been under pressure from her father to become the person he wanted her to be: the lawyer, the businesswoman, the person who could run Pilatos when his time was up. But would it ever be up? He looked like he'd live for another forty or fifty years without aging anymore and without loosening his hold on the company. With his father's share of the company along with Isabella's share, he controlled ninety percent, while she had ten. It wasn't likely her father would allow her ten percent to have much of a say in the running of the company while he controlled the rest. And was she going to hang around doing what he wanted for the rest of his life?

Maybe. She looked at her phone. He wanted her to get to know Lane Dimity. She smiled, and her face took on the look of someone much younger than she felt. She would be reliable and dependable and do what her father wished.

*It's now*, she wrote and sent before she could overthink her actions.

Within seconds the phone chirped in her hand, and she read, *It's always now.*

Did the man never sleep? Or did he just wake instantly and put his brain into top gear without a break?

*Not always,* she replied. *Yesterday isn't now. Tomorrow isn't now.*

*Somewhere in the continuum, they are both now.*

A laugh bubbled out of her as she read his words. He was incorrigible and so typical of a man to use any logic possible to avoid being wrong. Of course, two could play at that game; she smiled to herself as her fingers blurred over the keys.

*Any reasonable and rational person would assume that the use of the word 'now' between two people always referred to their place in the space-time continuum, not some other randomly chosen spot where 'now' might be a billion years ago or three days ahead of their place in the STC. For you and me, it isn't always 'now' – yesterday has gone, and tomorrow is yet to arrive. Neither is now.*

*Ouch,* he messaged, then a few seconds later, he added, *I got burned.* A third message popped up before she could reply. *But that was then; this is now.*

*Smartarse.*

She half-expected him to reply with a puerile 'I know you are, but what am I?' and she was glad her teenage expectations missed the mark.

*You're right. For now.*

*Thanks for the scarf. It was very unexpected but appreciated.*

*I thought you could do with some outback color.*

*It's quite the artwork and is definitely the most colorful item in my wardrobe.*

*It should go well with grey.*

She shouldn't have been surprised that he noticed her color choice, but there was something quite personal in that observation. Marcus had lived with her for over a month before he realized everything she wore was gray, white, or cream with occasional colored accessories. Was his comment derogatory or sarcastic? Written words were so difficult to analyze in regards to tone. She would have to rely on his general kindness and assume that there was no sharp edge to the comment.

*I'm reading your book, Ride With Heart. It's good.* She hadn't had much time to read it but had downloaded it to her phone and skimmed through to the fourth chapter. It was well written, and she could see why many found his views so alluring. The notion that riders and horses had souls that could communicate at a level beyond what they realized was a tempting idea. It was nonsense, of course, but she could understand that many found it appealing.

*You think it's crap, don't you?*

Karen snorted and covered her mouth to smother a laugh as though there was a risk he might hear her amusement at his blunt accuracy.

*No, it's good. Really good. Probably not within my belief system, but I quite like the Buddhist religion without following it.*

*Tactful. And I repeat my last message as a statement, not a question.*

Shaking her head at him, she messaged, *You really should learn to accept a compliment without questioning it.*

*You are beautiful, funny, intelligent, and one of the most fascinating women I've ever met.*

The words jumped out at her and seemed to drill through her eyes and down into her chest region, where they swirled around erratically. That was unexpected, and she didn't know how to respond, so she read the message eight times, her mind racing in all directions.

The phone chirped again. *Not so easy to accept without question, is it?*

*Unfair,* she replied shortly.

*Is the truth ever unfair?*

*It is if you tell someone their haircut is abysmal, or they look fat in those pants or that you never liked them at school. Those truths would be unfair.*

*OK, I'll give you that, but what about a positive, constructive truth? Like telling you how amazing you are. Is that unfair?*

*It is when you know that I don't know how to answer it. I don't know if it's a truth or blarney. I don't even know if that's you or one of your friends.*

In twenty seconds, her phone was buzzing to signify a video call. Damn, she thought as she quickly ran her hand through her sleep-messed hair and hitched up her nightgown so that it looked more decorous and less porn-star. Accepting the call, she saw that it was, indeed, Lane who was messaging her. Like her, he was in bed, and he turned his phone around so that she could see his room was empty apart from him, and he'd clearly been asleep judging by his hair, pillows, and bedcovers. He slept without a shirt on, and she found her eyes drawn to his muscular torso. Of course, she told herself, he could have been wearing a tatty old pajama top and removed it to look sexy just for her. And he was sexy. Ridiculously so. He had to know that and, perhaps, was deliberately messing with her head. It was working.

'Hi there. I see it is you and not one of your friends,' she smiled up at her phone, hoping she looked even a fraction as delicious as he did. 'I'm alone, too.' She turned the phone around so that he could see a three-sixty of her room.

*That's a relief,* the words appeared on the screen under his image.

'Yes,' she grimaced comically and spoke to her phone, which she held at arm's length so that he didn't have an extreme close up of her face, 'it would be a tad tacky to have someone sleeping next to me while we were having this middle-of-the-night conversation.'

For several seconds he gazed at the screen, looking at her image, and she stared back at him silently.

His eyes dipped downwards momentarily as he tapped the keys, and then he continued to look at her as the words, *What are we doing?* appeared under his face.

'I don't know,' she murmured, caught by the earnestness of his eyes. 'I think you're trying to con me into trusting you and revealing things about Pilatos, and I'm trying to convince you we're friends so that you will back away from Pilatos.'

He shook his head at her and smiled with some sadness. *You won't betray Pilatos. I won't back away. We both know that.*

'Then we're just two people passing time in the night until your world or my world comes crashing down because of the other,' she paused and wriggled uncomfortably, feeling pinned by the question about what they were doing. 'I don't want to examine it too closely.'

*I do, and I don't.* He gave a confused shake of his head and grinned, tipping his spare hand outwards in a *whatever* gesture.

'Are you writing another book?'

Lane pointed at her and nodded to show he admired her change of subject before glancing down to tap out an answer. *Yes. It's about the connections some of the world's best horse people have with their horses.*

'Do they see it as spiritual like you? Or do some see it as them training an animal without any of the spiritual soul-connection stuff going on?'

*Most sense the connection. Did you?*

'I haven't ridden for ages now. I suppose, when I was a child, I thought of my horses as my friends, so maybe that was part of my childhood, like Tinkerbelle and Simba, but that didn't make any of them real.'

*We should go riding together.*

Raising her brows at the suggestion, she pretended to see it as a sexually loaded comment and replied with a flirtatious, 'Why, Mr. Dimity, that would be moving our relationship along rather quickly, wouldn't it?'

Then she felt ridiculously awkward when he rolled his eyes and shook his head at her. What had she been thinking? Flirting was something she had never mastered. She floundered like an albatross landing on uneven ground. It wasn't pretty. It certainly wasn't flirtatious.

'Yeah, sorry,' she snorted in disparagement at her poor attempt at being coquettish. 'Forget I even said that. I don't get many men asking me to go riding with them these days. It probably won't happen, though. There's no time anymore for horse riding.'

*Make time for what's important,* he narrowed his eyes at her as though demanding she take note of his comment.

'Is it important, though?' she tilted her head to one side, thinking about it. 'I'm not seeing it, myself. I barely have enough time to get my work done and really can't justify taking the time to ride a horse.'

*You used to be a good rider. I've seen lots of photos.* As soon as he'd tapped in the words, he was looking at her attentively again, as though the expressions on her face were the most important things in the world to him at that time.

'Thanks. That's a compliment I can accept graciously. I was good,' she ducked her head, accepting his praise, 'but it's in the past. I'm a city girl now, and I work and live in this office building.'

Seeing the horrified expression on his face, she laughed, 'No! It's not that bad. Really. I have a great office, and there's a gym, and instead of having to commute home, I walk upstairs. It's convenient and sensible.'

Lane screwed up his face at her as though he simply couldn't stomach what she was saying. *Sure. And that's what life is all about.*

'I don't know what life's all about,' she said, feeling slightly annoyed at his needling, 'but I know I have a job to do, and I know there are people whose jobs depend on me doing my job properly.'

*Then look after yourself and give yourself time to do something that helps your life - like riding a horse.*

'That won't help, it will just be time away from things that need to be done, and I'll feel guilty about not doing them.'

*So, you couldn't walk away from your life? Get on a horse and ride off into the sunset?*

'Of course not!' she exclaimed without even thinking. It was an instinctive reaction to be abhorred by the notion of doing something as irresponsible as leaving Pilatos when she was needed. 'This is my life. It always has been and always will be. I am Pilatos.'

For a long minute, Lane looked out at her as he processed what she had told him. There was more to it than the words. Her immediate reaction was to tie herself to Pilatos in the same way that someone might align themselves with their own family against the rest of the world. It was a response that told him more about her than she had intended, and he realized that it was almost impossible to imagine a situation where she'd choose a cause, or a person, over her loyalty to Pilatos. She certainly wouldn't choose him, or the life of those stallions, over Pilatos. Not at this point, anyway. He wondered if she ever would.

'Could you walk away from your life?' she asked when he didn't type any words into the lengthening pause. 'You spend a lot of your time helping others and helping animals – could you just leave it?'

*Absolutely*, he responded instantly, *the world would continue quite well without me. How long would people really grieve if I was gone? Not long. How long would Pilatos suffer if you walked away? Others would step up, and it would go on.*

'I accept that I might be replaceable, but you certainly aren't,' she said with feeling. 'Your followers adore you. You are like a religion to them, not a human being.'

Lane scowled at that thought, *Yeah, that makes me feel great. Not.*

'But think of all your power. You tell your followers to do something, and they do it. People would kill to have power like that.

*Which is one reason I don't want it. I'm a man who makes mistakes and who wants the world to be a kinder place. I hate that people think I'm more than I am.*

Seeing that he was genuinely distressed by the pedestal he'd been placed on, she felt an unusual desire to comfort him. When was the last time she had felt moved to comfort someone? But then, when was the last time she had met a man who didn't want more and more power to the point of absolute power?

'Maybe you are more than you think you are. Anyway, what the rest of the world sees, or needs to see, doesn't have to be the person you are; it just has to be the person they need in their life. They need you.'

*What do you need?*

She was reminded of the conversation with Marcus about her not needing him. He was right on that; she didn't need Marcus. But what did she need?

'I don't know,' she replied softly and honestly. 'How do you work out what it is you need?'

*By losing it.*

What would she have to lose before she recognized that she needed it?

# CHAPTER TEN

*It never ceases to amaze me that this beautiful animal could overpower me any time he wanted, and yet he is content to work with me, to follow my directions, to keep me safe, and carry me with trust in his heart. Some might think that the horse serves me, but it so much more complicated than that – I honor and respect the horse, I strive to be worthy of his trust, and when we work together, my soul flies with his. He is my brother; she is my sister. They are my family.*

**'Ride With Heart,' by Lane Dimity. P. 125**

### The Pilatos Centre - Lexington

John Lawford stood on the stage at the main hall of The Pilatos Centre, glaring out at the two hundred lavishly decorated tables, each with ten empty seats around it. Eight thousand crystal glasses glittered richly in the settings: one for water, white wine, red wine, and champagne for each of the two thousand guests. The silver shone, and the room smelled like fresh forest and rose gardens as the staff fussed over the last of the details to prepare the room for the evening.

The theme colors were black, sky blue, and grass green. The hall was exploding in those colors, from elaborate table centerpieces of dyed and artificially scented roses to the chandeliers of jeweled black, blue, and green. There were framed posters of black horses all around the walls silhouetted on blue-over-green backgrounds: horses galloping, rearing, jumping, trotting, and standing proud.

Blue sky, green grass, and black horses, he nodded almost imperceptibly as he looked at the framed prints, it made a remarkable statement, and it was memorable. People would remember these colors and images in relation to Stablex.

The name *Stablex* was featured everywhere, with its black lettering on green and blue, on drink coasters and branded on the chair covers, on serviettes, and hanging on silken banners from the ceiling. His eye kept being drawn back to the black horse images. He liked the connection that was being made between the brand name and the vigor and energy of the horses.

The photos by Andy McLeay had been enlarged and were treated like artworks around the walls, in antique frames with individual lighting. Magnificent Friesian stallions with bold faces and arched necks, everything about them was masculine and dominating and virile - they encapsulated all that he wanted men to associate with Stablex. Karen had done well in choosing the Australian photographer, and he knew these pictures would be reproduced around the world for their beauty, and it would be free advertising for Stablex.

'Anything you want me to change?' asked Phillip Reach, his tongue darting out busily to lick his lips. 'Or are you happy with what we've achieved here?'

John's cool gaze swept over the room, ready for the two thousand guests that evening. He didn't miss the fact that Phillip implied that he was at least partly responsible for the décor when he knew that Karen had been the one to organize the decorating company and had approved the finer details, such as the framed McLeay photographs. Still, it suited him to have weak men like Phillip working under him. Strong and powerful men would challenge him, so he preferred to have the reptiles around him, not the lions. Except for Joe. He was an exception. He was a lion, but he didn't want to take over the pride or the range; he just liked to hunt and be left alone.

'It'll do,' John's gruff voice barked the words. 'Now, keep those do-gooders out of here.'

'Taken care of,' nodded Phillip self-importantly, once more implying that he was responsible for a task someone else had managed. 'Security will be checking everyone who arrives. The demonstrators, who are already causing a problem, can't get any closer than the main gate, hundreds of meters away, so we won't even hear them. Once the guests pass through the gates, they'll forget the troublemakers.'

'You think?' John narrowed his eyes and stared down at Phillip, who wilted noticeably under his gaze. It wouldn't have surprised John if the man had peed himself like a cowed dog.

'Yes, John. Yes. They'll be out there far from here. No problems. We have security and police to keep them back from the road so the guests can drive through them. It's just the usual run-of-the-mill protest.'

John grunted with a measure of disbelief and was pleased when Joe joined them. In Joe, he trusted.

'Everything taken care of?' Phillip asked Joe as though the head of security reported to him.

Instead of answering, Joe regarded him silently. Phillip's spine became flaccid under Joe's look, and he coughed, licked his lips frantically, and threw out some words about needing to check on the video show for the night before scuttling away.

'And?' John asked after Phillip had retreated.

'I've done what I can,' Joe shrugged. 'We got rid of two staff yesterday because they were overheard wanting to do something to help Lane. I don't know who else is turning, John, they work in this sector of Pilatos because they like horses, and the man is a horse guru. It's hard to deal with horse people when they believe they are on a quest to save horses.'

'Damned lunatics!' John spat the words with ire. 'I don't know how we can prove to them that there is no need to save the horses. We've saved them. Go save the starving and the abused, and leave these horses alone.'

'My men are loyal,' Joe nodded, quietly confident that no one on his team would betray him. He had men who had served alongside him in the forces, not horse people. 'We'll keep the place safe tonight. No protesters will get in, though if any of your people have turned and we've missed the signs, I don't know what they'll be capable of from the inside. We are prepared to neutralize any danger.'

'You'd better,' growled John, 'there'll be a lot of important people here tonight, and we need them buying and promoting Stablex, not having their pieces picked up from a bombed building.'

'There'll be no explosives,' Joe shook his head at John's uncharacteristic lack of logic. 'The place has been checked multiple times from top to bottom, and every worker and guest arriving is checked. Lane disapproves of violence and specifically tells his followers to avoid it.'

'That's not a lot of consolation,' John glowered; any talk of the Australian angered him; he loathed the very mention of him. 'The man's a cult leader, and any cult gets extremists who'll act outside the guidelines of the leader to achieve the desired result.'

'There are no explosives,' Joe assured him.

'Keep on top of it,' John instructed as he looked at his watch. 'It's time for me to get dressed. I haven't seen Karen this afternoon. Make sure you put her through a security check, too.'

'She's your daughter, John.'

'She's a woman,' John stated flatly. 'We can go on about all the glass ceiling, equal rights, and political correctness bull when others are listening, but between you and me, women are too emotional when it comes to making the decisions for corporate America. It's why men have always run the world, apart from the rare exception who had the guidance of men, anyway. Check her.'

Joe's eyes were colder than usual as John walked away.

At eight that evening, the first cars were making a convoy from the security gates where the protesters gathered. They negotiated the first checkpoint where cars were inspected and then the second checkpoint where security checked invitations and personal identification. Then they moved to the front of the main hall where the guests alighted, and the cars went to an on-site parking lot four hundred meters away. A line of parking valets stepped up to move the vehicles, but the majority of guests had their own drivers, so the valets did not have a busy night ahead of them.

The arrivals were captured in photos and on video, and journalists were lined up reporting live to the world about the event. It was the glitz and glamour occasion that John had hoped for: the Oscars of the pharmaceutical world with all awards going to Pilatos and the new drug Stablex. The several thousand who gathered outside the center, waving their placards about kindness, the stallions, and evil pharmaceutical companies, were inconsequential. John smiled to himself and thought that once men learned what Stablex offered them, the vegan, new-age, tree-hugging animal lovers would be trampled underfoot as they stampeded to purchase the product.

John stood at the main entrance with the other heads of Pilatos, including Karen, welcoming the guests and handing them over to staff who would guide them to their tables. He was jovial and friendly, putting Karen in mind of a publican welcoming tourists to his country pub. This was not the distant and demanding man she was used to - he reminded her of some of the photos from her mother's house that showed him laughing and cheery in the earlier days of their marriage. It had all been an act, Isabella had once told her, he did whatever it took to succeed, and if success meant behaving like an affable man full of bonhomie, then that was the man he would be for the amount of time it took to achieve his end. Such as courting the heiress Isabella and winning her heart from the show jumping circuit.

'Lovely to see you, Karen,' a voice brought her back to her guests, and her eyes focussed on George, Marcus's brother, and his wife, Felicity.

'Hello, Senator. Felicity,' Karen nodded at them and smiled, her exterior as serene and calm as it always appeared.

'I adore your dress, Karen,' Felicity cooed, admiring the soft grey, flecked with silver, that poured down Karen's body like water, from the strapless top to a froth of white around her ankles.

'A new designer from Lexington that my mother found,' Karen informed her, 'and I'm guessing that fabulous dress is Ralph Lauren. Superb.'

'Thank you,' Felicity waved a hand down her dress. 'I do love the fabric. I must get the contact details of your designer, though. We must support the new blood, mustn't we?'

'Of course,' Karen nodded, wishing they'd move on so the next people could enter.

'So very sorry about you and Marcus,' George extended a hand to pat hers as though commiserating her on a great loss, his hand lingering a fraction too long, 'perhaps it will work out.'

'I doubt it,' Karen withdrew her hand from his and glanced at the table where Marcus sat with an arm slung around the shoulders of his date for the night, a Felicity-clone who looked as though she'd gone to the same school for producing perfect political wives. It would only be a matter of time before the doctor turned to politics, no doubt one of the reasons her father had encouraged their relationship and now blamed her for its demise. A Pilatos senator would be a wonderful asset; still, she was reasonably sure his brother's loyalties were for sale, and judging by her father's genial handshake and effusive greeting, he was already taking steps in that direction.

There were other senators, governors, and men who were the power behind the politicians, men who sat on boards of directors of many of the major companies in the country, men from Wall Street and Hollywood, Silicon Valley, and Washington. Present, also, were the medical and legal power brokers who could ensure Stablex had all green lights through the bureaucratic jungle that could be the stumbling block of any new drug in any country or legal system. There were international guests from more than twenty countries, as well as representatives from the press. The sector most represented was the medical fraternity, as it would be up to the doctors to write the Stablex prescriptions. John had many incentives set in place to encourage them to promote Stablex to their patients, starting with this night, and he was sure that by winning over the top of the medical tree, the demand for Stablex would filter down to all the men who could afford it.

Karen, with her remarkable memory, knew almost all their names after going over the guest list so many times; consequently, she had been placed ahead of her father so that he could hear her greet them before he had to receive them. Although knowing names was a tool he recognized as useful for these sorts of events, he didn't believe in wasting the mental energy learning and remembering them when he could rely on Karen's natural ability. The names she didn't recall were provided to her through a discreet earpiece from one of the techs who was using facial recognition technology to identify everyone as they approached her.

Although Karen had helped work on the guest list, it was only as she saw all the people gathering in this one place that she realized that they were almost all middle-aged and elderly, wealthy, and powerful men. There were women in attendance, but most were there to partner the men. It made sense in one way since these men were the individuals who had climbed the ladders of power in their various industries, but she found there was something distasteful about the gathering. It certainly highlighted the disproportionate power that men had in her world. In fact, it highlighted the imbalance of power in the entire world - the people in this one room controlled more wealth than a billion individuals at the other end of the income scale.

Such a concentration of wealth! She glanced around, seeing a necklace worth several million dollars. A watch worth almost as much. Dresses that cost the average annual wage, shoes embedded with gemstones, rings with massive diamonds. She thought that a Robin Hood-style thief could feed a thousand villages for a year with the wealth worn by the people in this one room. Her inner musings grew gloomier as she realized that every minute she stood there thinking about these two thousand, the same number starved to death elsewhere. And Stablex is for these men. And those stallions are locked up to produce Stablex for these men. And I'm at war with Lane over those stallions that are locked up to produce Stablex for these men.

'Ten minutes until we start the videos and holographic show,' the voice in her ear whispered.

Karen nodded and quietly relayed the message to her father, Phillip Reach, and Jeremy Murray, allowing them to move ahead of her to the tables at the front of the room. There were still some guests arriving, but the staff would show them to their places, and the Pilatos heads would take time to mingle later and speak to everyone.

As she made her way through the room, she was pleased to see the faces of those present showing signs of appreciation for everything around them, from the quality of the wine and abundance of delectable appetizers to the beautiful photos by Andy. Many of the guests were flicking through the small and expensive gift books of Andy's photos, each stamped with the Stablex logo. The atmosphere felt positive. It would only become more so when these men realized what Stablex could do for them.

Taking the stage, John Lawford waited for the murmuring to cease. He looked powerful, his tall, muscular frame clothed in tailored black evening attire that somehow gave him a presence as virile and commanding as the black stallions that appeared everywhere. He greeted everyone, thanked them for coming, and made some amusing comments delivered so flawlessly that they did not appear scripted at all, and laughter rippled across the room.

'Stablex,' he raised a hand to the logo that dominated the stage, the entire curtain covered with the black stallion on the green and blue background. 'You've heard the whispers and the rumors. You might not know that we've been working on it for close to twenty years, but rather than bore you with the details right now, just take a look at me. A good, long look. Three years ago, my body was aging as well as one might expect, given the stresses of my life, stresses that are echoed in each of your lives. Along with many others, I have been trialing Stablex for three years, and, last month, in preparation for tonight, I went through a series of tests to determine the relative age of my body. The whole gamut of tests: bloods, physicals, bone density, muscle mass, cortisone production, physical and mental responses, a brain and full-body MRI...if there was a test to determine age apart from what the calendar says, I did it. My age came back as thirty-five. The same age as my daughter. Chronologically, I am sixty-five. Look at me.'

He paused, and his words fell into a pit of silence as he stood, robust and vital, dominating the room. There was no muttering or whispering. Every person was mutely considering the implications of what John had told them, and it was beyond anything they had expected. The rumors about the drug being developed by Pilatos centered around sex drive, perhaps a drug that went beyond those currently available for erectile dysfunction, maybe something that gave men full sex drive and function similar to what they had in youth rather than a pill that was taken before sex. But this, this was the entire fountain of youth. He looked younger than forty, and he moved like a man in the prime of his life, he had the predatory litheness of the male lion who ruled his pride, and nothing even hinted at him being thirty years older than he looked.

Those who knew him recognized that, over the past few years, he had reversed his aging, but it had not been so apparent as now, with him standing before them, demanding they look at him.

'This is Stablex,' he strode across the stage to where a cord hung down under a single beam of light, 'and, tonight, you are going to learn about what this drug can do for you. For now, welcome, and enjoy the show.'

He gave the cord a tug, and the curtain at the back of the stage collapsed to the floor and disappeared. No one had noticed the fine haze that had drifted into the room, but it was just enough for the lasers to work on to create their magic. As the curtain dropped, black stallions burst from the back of the stage and cantered through the air over the heads of those sitting, staring up, their mouths open with amazement. They appeared real, with a three-dimensional shape that looked as though you could reach up and run your hand over their bodies as they passed, but if any hands did reach up, all there was to touch was the slight haze that worked as a canvas for the light. The sound of their hooves reverberated around the room, the deep notes being felt physically in the chests of all there each time the horses galloped past.

The stallions were doubled in size from their real-life counterparts, and it made them look like giants to be revered as they tossed their heads and cantered around the hall, calling to each other. Even Karen, who had seen the preview of this a few days earlier, was entranced by the stallions in the sky, marveling at the creative ability of the Pilatos computer techs who were artists as well as geniuses with technology. The herd of horses halted at the back of the room, and, on stage, another great black horse appeared. To the sound of dancing hooves, he rose on his back legs and reared high, striking out at the air with his front hooves. His call was almost deafening as he trumpeted his presence to the world, and Karen saw a few people cover their ears before he froze and morphed into the Stablex logo, his cry still echoing around the walls.

The irony of this symbol of Stablex calling so loudly struck Karen as so absurd that she shook her head and turned her attention to sampling some of the delicacies on the table. Picking up a seafood pastry so delicate and light that it almost fell apart in her fingers, she examined it carefully as the herd of laser-created stallions cantered across the stage and through the logo horse, neighing to each other as they ran. Listening to their voices, her appetite seemed to have left the room with the horses, and she placed the seafood pastry down on her plate without tasting it.

As dozens of large white screens dropped silently down all around the walls and the lighting dimmed, staff were quietly and efficiently delivering entrées to everyone in a choreographed dance of service that would be the envy of any catering firm. The diet preferences of all were taken into consideration, and allergies, vegetarian, vegan, gluten-free, kosher, halal, Hindu, and other restrictions were carefully noted in each dish served, allowing all to dine comfortably. It was another indication of the care and planning Pilatos took in everything they did.

On the screens, a movie about the black stallions of Pilatos began to play, starting with footage of thirty Friesians galloping along a beach towards the camera, their nostrils flaring as their heads nodded with every stride. They were magnificent. The camera zoomed up into the air above the stallions as they passed underneath and followed them in one unbroken scene to a lush green pasture above the sea. There, the horses slowed and halted, standing on the bright green grass, silhouetted against the brilliant blue sky, once more driving home the colors and logo of Stablex.

'Not all horses are created equal,' began the voice-over, an excellent Morgan Freeman imitation, 'the Friesian is perhaps the most majestic and recognizable of all horse breeds.'

The film flashed short scenes of Friesians carrying armored knights, pulling royal carriages, doing dressage, and running through their paces at assessment days, all showing the thick and long forelocks, manes, and tails flying like banners.

'Over twenty years ago, a Friesian came to the attention of Pilatos scientists – a stallion unique amongst his fellow horses. In some breeds, horses are considered old once they are in their twenties. In a few breeds, such as Shetlands and Arabians, some individuals live well into their thirties. Very occasionally, there is the rare exception of a horse that makes it to its forties.'

The images depicted old horses with sway backs and deep hollows above their eyes. They looked old.

'And then we have Sevvodarray the Third,' a kindly-faced black stallion filled the screens, trotting, cantering, bucking, and playing in green fields. 'Sevvodarray was fifty years old when these images were captured.'

Those in the audience who understood the normal aging of horses sat up straighter, surprised by a horse of that age looking so young.

'Sevv defied all known understanding of the aging process and was every bit as active, fit, and virile as a fifteen-year-old Friesian stallion. What was it that made Sevv so different from those around him that had grown old and died while he lived on with such great quality of life?'

The film moved to a laboratory with flashing images of centrifuges in work, genome mapping, scientists growing strands of DNA, long patterns made by the letters c, g, a, and t, and other scenes relating to genetic research.

'A gene was found on the Y chromosome, unique to Sevv and the male members of his family. A gene that is effectively their source of youth. The processes that allow cells to age in other horses were taking place at a much slower rate in Sevv. His cells could continue to make copies of themselves without the usual aging mutations and errors occurring. Sevv's body and mind were staying young long after he should have withered, faltered, and died of old age.'

'The gene, which we will call Sevv's gene, could not be harvested and put into other animals, but the unique chemical signals that Sevv's gene was producing - the chemicals, or hormones, that were telling the body and mind to stay young - could be harvested, processed, and injected into the bloodstreams of other species of animals with astonishing results.'

White mice, clearly geriatric and clumsy with age, were shown receiving the treatment, and, as the control group continued to age and grow feeble over the months that were marked across the screen, the treated group became more active and agile. The same result was seen with rats. Then the film moved to dogs, cats, and primates.

'It did not seem to matter which species of mammals were chosen - the hormones associated with Sevv's gene reversed the signs of aging. Not only did every treated animal in every group show every indication of age reversal, but also damaged cells were replaced by healthy cells, and diseased organs became healthy, cell by cell. Cancers disappeared. Failing kidneys recovered. Diseased livers returned to a fit operating state. And, most remarkably, mental disorders associated with aging withdrew and vanished.'

By now, the audience was palpably excited. Karen could feel it around her. No one dared talk as they didn't want to miss a single word of the revelation that was Stablex. What was being said in that introductory film was the holy grail of health for every person in that room. Correction, she told herself with a slight sniff of cynical amusement, it was the holy grail of health for half the people in the room: the men. As she looked around, it was clear that the more intelligent women present were noticing the sex bias in all the language used. It was all about males, with no female pronouns used or references made. When the video moved to the human subjects being used with numerous 'before' and 'after' cases flicking past, some women began to appear extremely concerned.

'When human trials commenced,' the narrator continued, 'they were surrounded with some of the highest security given to any new development in the pharmaceutical industry. It was clear within weeks that the same age reversal mechanisms being seen in other test subjects were also evident in humans. Quite literally, the old became young again. Not only did their bodies recover from the sickness we know as aging, their minds recovered from mental disorders, including dementia, Alzheimer's, and Parkinson's. No known adverse side effects. Just youth.'

At last, the faces of women appeared on the screens. 'The only negative so far associated with Stablex is that it is only effective on males of any species. The genes that create the receptors for the hormones produced by Sevv's Gene are located on the Y chromosome. The drug is completely ineffective on those lacking the Y chromosome – females. The final X chromosome associated with females has a gene that produces blockers for the chemical messengers that tell male cells to renew. Pilatos continues to search for the female equivalent of Sevv's Gene or a way to alter the switches in female cells, and after Stablex is released, we have no doubt that other pharmaceutical companies will join us in this search – it is coming.'

Karen noticed that a couple of women nearby met each other's glances and rolled their eyes slightly, their expressions clearly showing a sarcastic, 'Yeah, sure,' message of disbelief. She didn't blame them. For thousands of years, powerful men had tried to control women, and Stablex seemed like the ultimate control: women grow old and die; men stay young and continue to live. She chided herself for such nonsensical thoughts when she knew that profits lay at the heart of these pharmaceutical developments, and a female form of Stablex would be almost as profitable as Stablex promised to be, so if there were a way to extend this market to women, it would be found. Eventually.

The screens became filled with the black stallions of Pilatos Farm, standing in their stalls, their heads over their doors, looking with pricked ears at the camera. This was the bit that Karen had insisted was added to try and out-maneuver Lane, and it showed snippets of how the staff groomed and cared for the stallions.

'Twelve hundred mighty stallions, all related to Sevvodarray the Third, live in luxury at Pilatos Farm outside Lexington, their every need catered for by dedicated staff who love horses. Welfare organizations inspect them weekly, and equine veterinarians monitor their health several times a day. To minimize stress, humane surgery has been performed to help keep the stallions quiet and settled, and they live in cleanliness, care, and consideration, enjoying a level of comfort unknown by the majority of horses in the world. Each carries Sevv's Gene; each produces the hormones needed to manufacture Stablex. To date, no synthetic version of Stablex has been able to be developed, so these stallions are the only known source of Stablex on the planet.'

Once more, the black horses on the green pastures appeared, raised their heads, and began to canter across the tops of the hills that touched the sky.

'The spirit and vitality of these mighty stallions can be yours. Reverse aging. Rid your body of disease. Feel young again. Stablex – the source of youth for men.'

The final image was of a black stallion rearing, and like the laser horse earlier, it transformed into the Stablex symbol.

The screens lifted, the lights became brighter, and entrée plates were being replaced with main meals. A few men rose to their feet and began to applaud, soon followed by the rest of the men and many of the women. Applause washed in crashing waves over the room. There was no doubt, Stablex was the wonder drug that would make Pilatos one of the greatest pharmaceutical companies in the world, and although other companies and countries may try to copy it, without the Stablex stallions, it was impossible.

John Lawford was about to take to the stage again when the video screens once more lowered, surprising Karen. They weren't due to play the second film about Stablex until after her father spoke. Her annoyance increased when the lights dimmed. Didn't the techs read the timetable correctly? The evening was planned to the minute, and it was ten minutes before the screens should have come back into use.

The irritated look from her father raked across her nerves. It wasn't her fault. Everything had been checked and rechecked. Someone in the control room had lost concentration and wasn't following the schedule. She pressed the communication button on the underside of the ring of her right hand to activate the microphone in the jeweled Stablex brooch on her dress and spoke to the tech who'd been helping her earlier, but there was no response. Clearly, the man had better things to do than follow the allocated times or stay in communication with her.

The film that she had approved began to play, and with an infuriated glance at her father to show that she was every bit as angry as he, she sighed and sat back to watch the short documentary about the daily life of the Friesians on Pilatos Farm. It was the promotional film that would be released to the world to prove that life as a Stablex stallion was a wonderful existence for a horse.

Stills of Andy's images showed the beauty of the animals, and flowery quotes written in a flowing script about horses bloomed over the pictures. A female narrator began talking, her voice calm and wise, ageless and almost hypnotic. A voice Karen had not approved for this film. A chill ran up her spine as she listened.

'These horses are not happy. These horses are alive, but sometimes that is not enough.'

The images changed to closeups of sad eyes – photos Andy had taken and which Karen had been careful to delete from the Pilatos computers. Obviously, Karen grimaced, Andy had a backup hidden memory in her cameras.

Tragic music that pulled at heartstrings began to swell behind the voice, and Karen rose to her feet, meeting her father's fuming eyes and nodding with her own white fury as she indicated she would stop this. Where was Joe? She couldn't see him. What were the other Pilatos heads doing? She looked at their tables to see them sitting paralyzed with stunned expressions, doing what they did best in a crisis: nothing. Her father tapped at his microphone and shook his head at her to indicate that he wasn't able to talk over the video; someone in the control room had switched him off.

'These are the eyes of happy horses,' the voice rolled on as two-second grabs of horses playing, ponies with children, and horses working with kind riders, crossed the screens, and the camera zoomed into the eyes of each horse, one after the other. Once the viewer could see what emotions were in those eyes, the images changed to the sad eyes of the Stablex stallions. 'These are the eyes of horses whose souls are dying so that Pilatos can make the drug that wealthy old men will use to reverse their years of voluntary self-abuse.'

By this time, Karen had crossed to the side of the main hall and was trying to exit so that she could make her way to the control room. The first exit was locked. She tried to maintain a calm exterior over her rage as she attempted to open the door, but it would not budge. With a shrug and smile at the table nearest her, she moved along the wall to the next exit, only to find it also locked. Was this a security measure from Joe's men to stop unwanted entry by protesters, perhaps a way to prevent a waiter from opening the door to some of the Dimity people? Or was this an action to stop security within the room from reaching the control room that was broadcasting this anti-Stablex propaganda?

An image hung on all the screens as the voice continued, a photo of Lane holding the lowered head of one of the Friesians, his striking tanned face clearly showing his grief for the horse. Slowly, it zoomed in on the eyes of the animal, and tears were glistening in the corners. Tears, for god's sake, Karen cursed under her breath. Horses don't cry. They're not tears; it's the reflection of light in the eyes. Besides, these men, with the fountain of youth being waved in front of them, would not be concerned about a bit of light gleaming in the eye of a stabled horse.

'We steal their lives so that some men can cheat aging. Stablex is not a drug for humanity. It is not a drug to make the lives of children better. It is not a drug that can help men and women. This is a product for wealthy men who have made wrong choices regarding their health all their lives, and then, when the ill-effects of their choices are felt, they expect these horses to suffer so that they can overcome the consequences of their choices.'

Making her way up the steps at the side of the stage, Karen slipped behind the side curtains and saw several of Joe's security team at the two exits trying to get them open. One nodded to her, confident that the door would be open shortly, and before he returned his attention to the door, it swung away as men on the other side hoisted large bolt cutters out of the way and pulled off the blue Grade 120 chain that had tied the door handles shut.

'Sorry, Miss Lawford,' said the guard who pulled the last of the chain off the door handles. 'There was a distraction that took most of us to the car park, and these chains were put on doors everywhere to slow us down. Standard bolt cutters wouldn't work. We had to get these big boys from one of the work trucks.'

Karen waved away his explanation as she started to stride down the corridor, 'We need to get to the control room and stop that video.'

'On it,' he replied, snapping his fingers for his men to follow.

Back in the main hall, John Lawford was raising his voice to try and drown out the narrator's voice. He paced the stage and spoke to his guests, trying to maintain the air of someone amused by the efforts of annoying do-gooders, but he knew they'd gone beyond that.

'One of the obstacles on the path to great ideas and products,' he projected his voice over the audience, 'whether they are polio vaccines, space exploration, or the ultimate anti-aging drug, is that the ignorant flat-earthers fail to understand what progress means, and they fight tooth and nail to stop advancement. While we present science and facts and results to move humanity forward, they rely on religion and beliefs, emotions, pseudo-science, and outright lies and deception to hold us back. By all means, take notice of what they say, but be prepared to dismiss it when you see the real truth. The truth is, these horses are better cared for than ninety-nine-point-nine percent of horses on this planet. There is no welfare issue. Look at their emotional arguments, and then look at our factual proof.'

The narrator continued, her words competing with John's, easing into the minds of all present with a familiarity that they instinctively trusted. She sounded like someone who was revealing something important to them for their own good. On the screens, they could see horses in herds as well as in stables and gathered at events, and there were scores of sounds that they were making.

'A horse is a very vocal animal. The call to a friend across the distance, the nicker to the person who brings him his food, the challenge, the hello, the squeal of excitement, the soft sounds of meeting an old friend. They do not speak English, but they do speak, and their sounds have meaning and importance.'

A wave of gasps came from the tables as photos of horses having their throats cut open slashed across the screens, followed by close-ups of the scars on the throats of the stallions.

'The Stablex stallions have been robbed of their voices. Their vocal cords were surgically removed so that no one can hear their cries. They cannot call out to a friend or express fear in the night. The stallions are silenced. All one thousand, two hundred Friesian stallions at Pilatos Farm have been operated on to silence them.'

As Karen waited for the security team to cut the blue chain from the control room door handles, she listened to the seductive tones of the narrator telling the guests about the cordectomies, and she groaned. Of course, Lane was going to bring that information out, and she guessed correctly that there would be gruesome images to match the words. How much more could this video cover? Like her father, Joe, and everyone else, she had been distracted by the protesters and the fear of a violent demonstration disrupting the events and hadn't given enough thought to the possibility of their own employees turning against them.

The chain finally gave way after the men battled with the huge bolt cutters, and Karen followed them as they charged into the room. Banks of monitors and control boards filled the walls and benches with switches, wires, cables, and everything that a television studio would need, but there was no one there. It was running on an automated program.

Karen walked around, slamming every switch she could find to the off position, but she could still hear the woman's voice spouting the poison against Pilatos. There was an arrangement of large levers against one wall labeled *power, lights, main hall, air conditioning, heaters, kitchen,* and other main areas of the facility. Karen shoved them all to the off position, but nothing changed. The lights didn't flicker. The monitors still showed views of the Pilatos Centre. The voice continued.

'We started this protest because of twelve hundred stallions that are locked away, but as is often the case when you notice one unjust thing, it was merely an indication of all that is wrong with Stablex. The stallions aren't only kept in stalls until they die - they are surgically muted to prevent them from communicating with other horses. These are mutilated stallions locked up to produce a vanity drug to help wealthy men stop aging.'

Not even wanting to know what images were going with those words, Karen ordered the men to find the room where the controls for the center had been routed.

'They've diverted all this,' she pointed at the room of switches and controls, 'to somewhere else in the building. Find it, and shut it down. And someone better find the main power switches and throw them until we can stop this circus.'

She knew that every table had decorations that would provide light if the main power went down and the backup power was delayed in starting. So, even if they had to turn off the mains to stop the video, the guests would not be left in darkness, although they may well be in figurative darkness as they wondered what the hell was going on during this night of nights for Pilatos.

Kicking off her shoes that were beautiful to look at but difficult for any pace above a walk, she followed some of the men at a run along corridors searching for where the center's telecommunications had been transferred. Single doors were locked, and three more rooms with double doors and handles had the blue chains and padlocks on them, but Karen ordered the men to leave them as she was sure they were decoys to slow them down. These rooms had been open all day, and she imagined the renegade employees would have needed a room that guaranteed privacy as they set up the equipment necessary to support this operation. Somewhere like one of the rooms in the basement. Like the room for the backup generators.

'That's why the power wouldn't shut off,' she shook her head at the ingeniousness of the plan if it was as she guessed.

'Miss Lawford?' the man beside her cast a questioning look her way.

'The generator room in the basement,' she said as they jogged, 'I think they've had the center running on the backup generators all along, which is why we couldn't shut the power off. They transferred the control of everything there.'

Pilatos may not have employed the most loyal techs, as it turned out, but they did pay for the best, and she imagined it would have been a game to them to set this up so that time was lost as security tried to find them. She didn't know if they'd worked with Lane or if they'd operated as an independent group who believed in the views put forward by him, but it didn't matter. Lane was behind it one way or another, and she didn't even want to consider her emotions about him and this attack on her company; she simply wanted to get everything back under control. Pilatos control. Her control.

In the main hall, some of the security staff had found a few hooks on poles that were used for catching out-of-reach cords and cables, and they were going to each of the scores of drop-down screens to disconnect the cables from the back. As the screens went blank, one by one, the voice continued, coming from speakers hidden around the room, growing louder and more resolute. John Lawford continued his impromptu address to the crowd, but most of the attention was on the woman's voice and the scenes playing on the remaining screens.

'We began a campaign because of the suffering of horses, but this goes far beyond that. Stablex will change the balance of the sexes, and it will increase the gap between the rich and everyone else. Look at the couples around you: there will be no more growing old together. Men who can afford Stablex will watch their female partners age and die as they live. Men who can't afford Stablex will see wealthy men live decades beyond anything they can hope for. Stablex symbolizes so much of what is wrong with humanity: stop destroying in the name of your life, your ego, and your profits. Free the stallions.'

As the final demand resonated around the room, the music swelled to a crescendo, and the lasers created a storm cloud on the stage, with black stallions bursting out of it to race across the theatrical smoke that hung in the air. Some of the women looked as though they were about to applaud, while others stared at the men around them, realizing the truth of those words. These men would use Stablex to add twenty or thirty years to their lives, and how would that disadvantage the women around them? They would outlive their wives, even their second wives - they would outlive their daughters. It would give them extra decades to amass more wealth. It would provide wealthy men even more dominance over all other humans.

The air conditioning vents in the ceiling suddenly dropped open, and there were gasps as people looked up in surprise and confusion, not knowing what was going on but fearing violence. Timers attached to the grates had been synchronized with the film so that they opened when the film finished. Thousands of leaflets floated down from where they had been hidden in the vents, blown out by the increased airflow timed to coincide with the opening. Printed on paper, so thin and light that the sheets drifted down like snowflakes, were photos taken by Andy of the Friesians with slogans printed under them. Hands reached out to pluck the falling papers from the air.

A photo of a sad-eyed stallion with his head half-turned away so that the scar at his throat was clearly visible, and the words *SURGICALLY SILENCED* slashed across the bottom of the leaflet in blood red.

The beautiful eye of a horse with the reflection of man and a clock on the surface, and the words, *At what price?*

A line of stalls with the heads of the black horses out over the doors, and the statement, *Never to be released.*

The faces of four horses looking inquisitively at the camera, their long manes and forelocks falling in waves with the sentence, *We steal their lives so we can cheat aging.*

A moving image of Lane grieving as he hugs the lowered head of a stallion, with the claim, *Their souls are dying.*

As the last of the leaflets fell, Karen and the guards with her broke into the generator room. The four who had orchestrated the show had left a note taped to a laptop claiming full responsibility, along with their names and the brief message, *This is wrong. We quit.*

It seemed they had needed very little equipment to achieve all that they'd done, just a few laptops, cables, and connections, along with the chains, padlocks, and timing devices on the air conditioning vents. Once their program for the evening had been activated, they had been able to leave the building while the distraction was playing out in the car park, locking and chaining doors as they went to give their production the best chance of playing through to the end.

Leaving Joe's men to switch back to mains power and return the command of the facility's electronics and telecommunications to the control room, Karen jogged back up the stairs and along corridors to her temporary office, which, thankfully, was not locked. She grabbed her laptop and returned to the main hall, where the guests were being served their main meal. Her father was trying to minimize the damage from the propaganda film and leaflets by introducing the stars from one of Broadway's current hit musicals who were performing some of their songs. Originally, they were scheduled to take the stage after dessert, but it was a good move to bring their show forward so that the audience could move on from the debacle caused by the Pilatos traitors.

Although Karen was not proficient with everything in the control room of the Pilatos Centre, she had used the stage screens many times before and could hook her laptop direct to them. With all the movie clips and graphics they were using that night stored in her files, it meant that the audience could still see everything that was planned, just without all the drop-down screens and some of the fancier special effects, such as the three-dimensional laser images. The night would go on.

# CHAPTER ELEVEN

*'Kindness. That is something worthwhile to strive for. To be kind is to be a person who will help make the lives of other people and animals better and help to make this world a better place. Kindness shows in so many small ways – the smile for a stranger, a pat for a dog, a friendly face turned to a worried child. Acts of kindness are remembered by others, and sometimes they save lives, like hands reaching out to drowning souls. Words of kindness can heal and empower. Thoughts of kindness help cleanse our souls. Be kind to yourself and pass kindness on to others so that it grows and spreads and pushes back the darkness.'*

**Lane Dimity, when asked, 'What should people strive for?'**

**Arizona**

'Holy baloney bazookas!' Matt exclaimed, mindful of his language as he waved his phone at the crowd around the breakfast table at Tom's parent's house. He hadn't taken the time to count them, but he was reasonably sure there were six or seven youngsters under the age of ten running around. 'Look at these headlines!'

'Like, sure,' his twin grimaced at him, 'as though I'm able to read the tiny writing on a tiny screen when you wave it around madly at six in the morning.'

'Just another one of life's basic skills which you lack,' he grinned back at her, 'but let me swipe through a few of the headlines appearing on news sites this morning. Here's one, *Stablex Stabbed*, and there's a brief outline of the revolutionary anti-aging drug Stablex then a whole heap about the Pilatos workers who turned against the company because of the treatment of the stallions and the inequalities that will be associated with the drug.'

'Good one,' nodded Andy.

'And The Washington Post has the heading *Pilatos Pilloried,* followed by a rundown on the main points of our film, not that anyone seems to have realized it was our film. It looks as though they're laying the blame on the employees who turned against Pilatos.'

'Anything from Vicki Marshall?' asked Tom casually, hoping in vain that no one would think his interest in the journalist was anything apart from work-related. He should have known his friends better than that.

'Tom and Vicki, sitting in a tree,' teased Andy, doubly amused when Tom scowled darkly at her.

Lane's fingers spelled out the letters *k, i, s, s, i, n, g,* and Tom's scowl grew to include him while Andy's laughter tinkled infectiously.

'Hang on,' Matt said as he entered her name into the search bar and narrowed the search to the last twenty-four hours, 'here we go. She has a couple of articles out. One has used our leaflet heading *Surgically Silenced,* and it looks like she's written about what is happening to the stallions using the information we gave her, along with those photos the Pilatos vet sent us. This other one runs with the notion about what will happen with men able to live decades longer than women, and the headline is *Till Stablex Do Us Part.* I think I love this woman – she's really coming out to bat for us.'

Tom said nothing; he merely turned his attention back to the scrambled eggs on his plate, his dark hair falling over his eyes.

Taking pity on his friend, Matt added, 'And when I say *love,* I mean I love her like a sister. She's not my type.'

The crinkle at the edges of Tom's eyes when he glanced up from his breakfast told Matt that he was forgiven.

'This one,' Matt continued enthusiastically, 'says there should be a new award added at the Emmys for excellence in exposé because our film covered all bases in revealing the dark underbelly of Stablex. They're calling it inspiring. They've given the link to the video. Did we put it on YouTube?'

Lane shook his head and looked in askance at the others who replied in the negative.

'Those IT guys from Pilatos must have done it, then,' nodded Matt, knowing that, as of last night, no one else had copies of the video. 'I'm checking it now. Holy maloly - how does it get thirty million views in a few hours? And it's not the only video of it here. There's another one with nearly ten million views. The Lawfords are going to be royally peeved at this.'

'You must admit,' Andy smiled smugly, enjoying the fact that her work was being lauded, 'we did do a kick-butt job on that video. Three days and it looked slick. I sort of want people to know that we created it, but I also sort of don't want the Pilatos lawyers to know that we were responsible for it.'

'We expressed opinions,' pointed out Matt, 'they can't come after us for that.'

'Yeah, they could,' said Andy, 'it's pretty clear we made it with malicious intent to damage the company and the company's reputation, and even though we believe it to be true, all they have to do is push the point that one part is not completely factual, and we fall into the defamation pit of hell. I'm hoping that they'd rather ignore it and hope it goes away than bring it all into the public eye with a court case over it.'

'Forty million views,' Tom arched his brows at her, 'somehow, I don't think that is a good sign about it simply going away.'

'Cool, isn't it?' Matt chortled, ever the optimist.

'Is there any positive news about Stablex?' asked Andy.

Matt tilted his head back and forth as he searched, 'No. Not this. Not this. This one says your photos were art, sis, at first making us believe that life as a Stablex stallion was perfect, then showing us the tragedy that ripped at our hearts. I think this bloke has a thing for you.'

'I'm looking forward to when you reach your teenage years,' Andy answered him, giving him a flat stare.

'Keep waiting,' he replied, impervious to her looks and still searching through the news relating to Stablex. 'Oh, what do you know? This men's magazine has called Stablex a wonder drug and predicts it will make Pilatos billions of dollars. It also has naked ladies in the article under the Stablex one, so what would they know?'

'They're probably right,' said Tom, sitting back in his chair and looking around at his friends, brothers and sisters, parents, and some neighbors who surrounded the large table. 'People ignore the cruelty to foxes and wear fox fur coats, they turn their backs on caged chickens to buy cheap eggs, they cut down forests and consign the animals that lived there to die so they can use the wood. When it comes to money and things humans want, there's an awful lot who don't care about the collateral suffering. Ultimately, Stablex will be the same. They've paid off the welfare organizations. They have the lawmakers in their pockets. For all that we detest what they do, we can only stand around and point fingers at them, and the wealthy men will buy the drug anyway because our concerns mean nothing to them in the face of living longer.'

*Should we give up?* Lane signed. *Is it worth fighting?*

'Of course, it is,' Andy assured him, 'think of all those women stewing over the fact that their men will have access to decades more health and life than they…give them time to think about that, and it's not going to be pretty. Let the daughters see those photos from the Stablex vet haunt their dreams for a few weeks…they won't want their fathers and brothers and partners outliving them while those stallions pay the price. You'll see.'

'I wouldn't mind some of that Stablex,' Tom's father Atsa announced, leaning back in his chair and raising his eyes to the ceiling as if considering an important decision. 'Yup. I can see why a man would want it. So, if I started using it now, I'd be feeling as young as you, Tom, in a few months. Wouldn't you want a younger man, my dove?' he baited his wife, knowing she'd rise to the bait and get hooked.

'I'd be happy with a younger man,' Mai replied without missing a beat, her dark eyes gleaming wickedly. 'I'll start looking for one as soon as you take your first tablet of that cursed stuff because you'll die if you take it.'

'I don't think death is a side-effect,' Atsa shook his head slowly, his brow pinched as he thought of what Tom had told him about the drug.

'I will kill you,' Mai patted his hand affectionately, 'and I think other wives will feel like me. Death will be a possible side-effect of Stablex if I know anything about women.'

Her husband guffawed happily.

Lane grinned at the humor and love in this extended family where the door was always open to friends and neighbors, and where the local children could come and go safely. There was no great wealth, but there was always enough to be thankful for - food to eat, clean water to drink, clothes to wear, a safe place to sleep at night, and loved ones around. They were happier than most of the extremely wealthy people he knew, as it seemed that riches often gave them more to worry about and less to be thankful for. Plus, the wealthy seemed to live in fear that it would be taken away from them.

Tom's family was thankful for their food that day, while there were people in Karen Lawford's world who seemed to have no appreciation for the fact that they had money to buy food for three hundred and sixty-five thousand days – and it still wasn't enough. That massive desire for more than they needed, for more than others, for more than they could use in a thousand years, seemed to be the symptom of a human illness that caused so much suffering: greed.

He was greedy, too, he admitted, but greedy for love, friendship, peace, understanding, and knowledge. He was happy sleeping in a swag under the stars with a meal of wild berries and did not long to stay in expensive hotels or eat at five-star restaurants. He was happy spending a week alone on his station in outback Queensland, seeing no one from day to day except his horses, dogs, and other animals, and living small. Tom's family lived small – only using what they needed to stay alive and enjoy another day and not wasting more resources than they needed. Perhaps it was one of the reasons he felt so comfortable at their table. Humans could survive if they only used what they needed, but the greed to have so much more, to live big, and have every desire granted rather than every need met meant that humanity might not survive, and that worried him.

It was not within his power to change the world; he'd always known that, but if he could change the small parts he could touch, perhaps that would leave the world a better place for having him in it. Would Karen Lawford leave the world a better place for having been a part of it? He had faith that he could reach the hidden part of her that would make it so. Under the conservative, restrained, correct, and mature lawyer, the wild child who hurtled around on ponies still had to survive. If he could reach that child within, he believed he could help her become the person who would make her world a better place rather than make those around her wealthier at any cost.

'Stop dreaming about Karen Lawford,' Andy jabbed him in the ribs to bring his attention back to the conversation around him, 'I asked you three times if you'd heard from Karen, and you sat there with that faraway look on your face. You'll never save her, you know. She isn't a lost puppy who needs a home. She's Pilatos. Money is her god, and making profits for her company is her belief. You really need to stop thinking you can change her.'

*Maybe I was daydreaming about home*, he gave her a challenging look.

'Were you?' she smiled back at him, confident she was right with her guess.

*And maybe I was dreaming about a woman who can be changed,* he admitted, grinning back at her.

Andy shook her head and rolled her eyes, 'It's not going to happen, man, it's not going to happen. I know women. I am a woman...'

Matt made a questioning noise and was rewarded with a thump to the shoulder from his twin.

'...and she's a hard-nosed New York businesswoman who looks down that hard nose at this sort of stuff,' she waved a finger around the bustling kitchen. 'She doesn't think like you and me, Lane – she's not after friends, love, and happiness, contented horses, and rides into the sunset. She wants Stablex to be successful so that it makes Pilatos and her family a whole lot of money. You can't change that.'

He shrugged noncommittally, *You're probably right.*

'She's going to be hating you right about now, anyway, so that's going to be a big stumbling block in the way of trying to change her.'

He had no doubt that she was right about that. He had texted Karen after midnight, but there had been no response. She would not only be hating him; she would be furious at him, she would want to destroy him for how he had assailed her sacred stronghold of Pilatos. There would be a storm of emotions heaving around her internal oceans, but he knew that storms passed.

The person he had spoken to in the middle of those nights was an island within those oceans, and no person was meant to be an island. Even if she didn't realize it, he believed she was reaching out to him from the loneliness that makes itself felt during the nights when the oceans grow calm and the aloneness of an island in the vast sea becomes unbearable. She might tell herself that it was part of a plan to win him over to her side, but he felt the truth in her the same as when he stood in the yard with a wild horse that eyed him fearfully but stretched its nose out to him because it also desired connection.

'So, where do we go from here?' Matt asked his friends.

'Do we still agree that our ultimate aim is to free those stallions?' Tom looked around to see them nodding. 'Then, step one is to finish breakfast. Step two is to do the dishes for my mother. Step three is…'

'Can we skip all the steps about cleaning teeth, washing hands, putting our shoes on, and stuff?' Matt screwed up his face at Tom. 'Let's jump to an actual plan of action and not cover every incidental task that has to be done this morning.'

Tom shook his head, disappointedly, 'Always in a rush. That is your problem: always hurrying to reach the destination and not slowing to admire the scenery along the way.'

'Show me scenery,' Matt arched a brow at the sink, 'I'm not seeing doing the dishes as stopping to admire the scenery.'

'Then we focus on a plan to release the stallions,' Tom continued after flashing an amused smile at Matt. 'They're priming the market for Stablex. People know what it does. They're going to go into overdrive to try and negate the bad press from what happened last night. While they're doing that, we'll focus on winning over employees, and we'll get those stallions free.'

'We do have a few Pilatos people on our side now,' said Andy, thinking of the various workers who'd reached out to them. 'You can't have people who love horses, working with those horses, and then turning a blind eye to what is happening to those horses, so we should have at least ten or fifteen on our side before long. Maybe more.'

'We'll need more,' Tom tapped his fingers on the table, thinking. 'We need to see those stallions run free and feel the grass beneath their hooves. Lane, you need to keep working on Karen.'

'She's not a weak link,' Andy shook her head, thinking that it was a waste of effort to have anything to do with Karen.

'She doesn't have to be,' Tom replied, 'but having that communication open to the head sector of the company is going to come in handy for something.'

'Maybe she'll keep their thugs from bashing us senseless,' said Matt, 'or worse.'

'Probably not at this moment,' Andy laughed. 'I'd say that this morning, she'll be telling them to hunt us down.'

### The Pilatos Centre

The alarm buzzed Karen at eight, and she erupted out of a dream, her arms flailing. Staring around, dazed and upset at whatever had followed her from sleep, she slowly came back to reality. She was in one of the apartments in the Pilatos Centre in Lexington, and it was the morning after the Stablex launch, and it had been a disaster. No, she corrected, they had clawed the night back from disaster, and hundreds of millions of dollars of pre-sales were already being discussed.

Realizing how much demand there would be for Stablex, many wanted to tie up supply contracts early. It was clear that there would be a limited supply since it could not be manufactured artificially, so distributors knew they would have to move fast to be part of the supply line rather than part of the worldwide shortage.

Predictably, the representatives from China were promising to be the biggest buyers since they had an enormous cashed-up population of older men who would want a prolonged life of good health. There didn't seem to be a representative from any country present last night who didn't want to ensure a fast track of the drug through their country's regulations, followed by a guaranteed supply of Stablex.

It had taken more than two decades to develop, and a level of secrecy that she marveled. Prior to the preparation for the launch, she knew very little about Stablex, apart from the fact that it was one of a few drugs being developed, as she had very little to do with the pharmaceutical arm of Pilatos. Now, it appeared that Stablex was going to carry the company into the financial stratosphere.

This morning's headlines would be interesting, she thought. What would the news outlets say about the wonder drug that would change humanity for the better and grant decades to the lives of those who used it?

With a glance at the side table for her phone, she groaned as she remembered what she'd done with it. That Australian mime artist, she thought savagely, trying to denigrate the very thought of him, had texted her an hour or so after she'd gone to bed, and when she'd seen his number come up, her rage at him had exploded into action, and she'd hurled the phone at the door. As though she would want to have any conversation with that self-styled social media attention-seeking equine guru. The description of him that she'd used before rolled out of her thoughts, and she smiled. She wanted the chance to throw those words at him, not stew over them silently.

The bedroom door had a mark where the phone hit, and the broken remains lay on the carpet nearby. She rose out of bed and padded barefoot over to pick it up and examine the shattered screen and alarming dint in one corner. It wasn't working - another thing to lay at the door of that damned Australian. Removing the SIM card, she headed to the bathroom to shower and get dressed.

After putting on a minimum of makeup, she dressed in one of her favorite Dsquared2 suits in classic checked grey wool, with a double-breasted jacket, straight-leg pants, and a white collared shirt underneath. She slipped on a pair of Jimmy Choos, twisted her hair into a bun, and checked her reflection in the full-length mirror. She was the cool and calm epitome of the American businesswoman. Nothing was out of place. She wore her clothes like armor to protect anything behind them. She was in control, and, yes, she was out-manning the men in their world by being tougher, harder, and colder than they when it came to making difficult decisions. It was what she had to do to survive in this jungle, and she was a survivor.

As she headed to her on-site office with her briefcase, her fingers kept dancing around, missing the phone that she could have used to call ahead to order breakfast and coffee. Small things, she told herself, small things like a temporary loss of a phone and annoying animal lovers who had no concept of the importance of Stablex, were not going to get in her way of enjoying the wave of success that Stablex was about to ride on. She stopped at the lifts and tapped a foot on the carpet as she waited for one to arrive at her level.

Now that the world knew about the drug and what it would do, the demand would be insatiable. Her lips twitched in a small self-satisfied smile, and no one else in the world could provide the drug, so, even without the patents and licensing, they had a monopoly on it.

Her father had allowed her into the inner sanctum of Stablex in the days preceding the launch, revealing some of the secrets that he and his science team had been guarding for decades. Phillip, Jeremy, and other executives did not have access to what her father had revealed, and she understood why he had protected the knowledge so obsessively: the future of Pilatos depended on keeping the monopoly on Stablex for as long as possible.

All they had to do was protect the source, she hesitated as she entered the elevator and pressed a number on the panel, yes, protect the source of Stablex, and no one else could duplicate the drug. The source was the herd of stallions that were safe in the Pilatos stables, where security was being increased. The other pharmaceutical giants could search a million horses for Sevv's gene, but she doubted they'd find another horse with the mutation. Pilatos had assiduously researched Friesian stud books to find all living relatives of Sevvodarray the Third and test them, but the gene was not there. His sire may have had the gene, but he only had four daughters and Sevv before breaking a leg and being put down, so, at this stage, the only known source in the world for the genetic base of the chemicals in Stablex stood in the Pilatos stables.

Karen strode into her office, throwing a greeting to Sandy and requesting a new phone, coffee, breakfast, and a summary of the reactions to Stablex.

'Your coffee is on your desk, Karen,' replied Sandy, pushing her reading glasses back onto the top of her head. 'Breakfast will be here shortly - your usual. I've put a stick on your desk detailing most of the major articles. And here,' she pulled open a drawer at the desk she was using during their days at the Pilatos Centre and pulled out a box containing a new phone identical to the one Karen had smashed during the night. 'I always keep a spare version of your current model in case you need it.'

'You are officially amazing,' Karen laughed, reaching out for the box. 'I've never needed a spare one before.'

'But most people do,' Sandy told her. 'They get dropped in water or sat on, driven over or lost, and, generally, if you need a replacement, you need it immediately.'

'I threw mine at my door last night,' Karen admitted, grimacing at her behavior as she realized how churlish it sounded.

'Really?' Sandy looked at her, surprised. It was a revelation to learn that Karen had enough passion in her to indulge in an outburst like throwing her phone. 'The night wasn't that bad. You and your father dragged it back from ruin, and all in all, the segment that went off the rails was a small distraction from what was really going on. Stablex is going to be big. Mega big.'

'Let's hope so.'

'So, have you found out who the turncoats were who put on that show last night?'

'No need to find them,' Karen replied before she went into her office, 'they identified themselves in their notice about quitting their jobs. I don't think they've thought of the full consequences, though. Even if no action is taken against them, they'll find it hard to get work for any other company with a reputation for being a traitor to their employer.'

'Yes,' Sandy mused, absent-mindedly picking up some papers and stabling them together. 'You do have to wonder why they were willing to throw their careers away on a stunt like this. I mean, they're only horses, and horses are killed all the time for pet food, so how can they think the life of the Stablex stallions is worse than that? I don't get it.'

Nodding a silent yet meaningless response, Karen withdrew to her office, the smell of coffee beckoning irresistibly from her desk. As she sipped the potent brew, she switched on her laptop and scanned some of the headlines from the internet about Stablex. The name was everywhere, so perhaps the unscheduled events of last night would prove to be a blessing as it turned what may or may not have been a page one, two, or three news story into headline news. She could not click on an online news service without finding the words 'Pilatos' and 'Stablex' featured in large print.

Inserting the USB, she clicked on the collection of summaries from Sandy. There was the expected bad press because of concerns about the stallions and fears about the inequality that Stablex could encourage, but she didn't believe it would have an adverse effect on sales. Men who could afford Stablex to add a few decades to their life were not going to turn down that opportunity because of protests about the well-fed horses or because there were men who could not afford to use the drug. They wouldn't turn their backs on Stablex because women were not able to use it. No, they would walk over any objections to take their sip from the fountain of youth.

Interestingly, when she thought about the press releases from Pilatos, she realized that the term 'fountain of youth' had not been used anywhere in the information. Pilatos was leaving it to others to use those words. Legally sensible, she nodded approval. The drug slowed aging and reversed some health issues, but it wasn't really the source of youth.

Sandy quietly placed her breakfast of fresh fruit, yogurt, and muesli next to her as she continued through the news clippings. There were photos of the thousands who had gathered to protest outside the gates here and at Pilatos Farm last night and some complaints from prominent spokespeople, mainly women, about what it would mean to give some men the Stablex advantage. Whatever, she sniffed derisively - all their whinging wouldn't stop Stablex now. It was an easy guess that the men in charge of all the decision-making organizations, from the government to the FDA, would all be lining up for their Stablex script, so they weren't going to be swayed by the Lane Dimitys of this world.

Deep down, somewhere hidden in the bowels of her conscience, there was a twinge of something that she couldn't identify, a slight churning of emotions felt as she discounted all that Lane and his followers were saying. She put all that aside and mentally raised the flag of Pilatos over the battlefield to claim victory - Pilatos had beaten those who tried to stop Stablex.

She was sure Stablex would succeed beyond anyone's imaginings, a belief confirmed by the private memo from her father listing some of the expressions of interest in the drug from last night. Glancing over the figures, she felt the elation of the victor. Yes, they might have thought that they struck a blow against Pilatos last night, but these figures proved that when it came to staying alive, feeling younger, and being healthier, most wealthy men would not be deterred in the slightest by matters of conscience. Not that there was anything to feel bad about, she quickly adjusted her thoughts; nothing was weighing on her conscience or on anyone else's when it came to Stablex. Clear consciences all around.

'Your father asked for you to go to his office,' Sandy spoke from the door.

'Thanks,' Karen took a last mouthful of breakfast and carried her coffee to the office across the hall. It was not set up as luxuriously as his New York office, as it was often used by others when he wasn't in residence, but it was still the largest office in the building, with enough space for a dance floor. Not that anyone ever felt like dancing in her father's presence. John Lawford liked space. He liked his offices looking bigger than anyone else's. A man thing, she smirked to herself, her face registering none of her thoughts.

Not surprisingly, the usual crew was in attendance. Phillip and his lip-licking lizard tongue sat to the right of her father's desk, while Jeremy sat to the left, leaving an empty chair between, presumably for her to use. After terse greetings, she ignored the spare chair and stood near the window behind her father so that she could look out at the Kentucky sky. Joe's dour presence watched over them from the corner where he stood, arms folded and eyes narrowed, regarding everyone with all the expression of a sandstone carving.

'So, if this is a chess game,' her father's voice had a savage edge to it as he turned to speak to her, 'please tell me what move was that last night? It didn't look like we were several moves ahead in the game, or am I missing something?'

Karen's gaze clashed with his, flecks of ice glistening in the depths of her eyes as she replied in a calm, controlled voice. 'You're missing the fact that this was an inside job, and at least four Pilatos employees were so disgruntled with this company that they sabotaged the night. You're missing the fact that my specialty is contract law, not security, not personnel, and not public relations. You're also missing the fact that those moves last night bought us more publicity than we would have been prepared to pay for, and this morning, Stablex and Pilatos are being discussed all around the world. You're missing the fact that last night's debacle has proven that Lane Dimity and his followers, and even our disloyal employees, will not damage the demand for Stablex. The men who want to buy this drug will not be deterred by animal welfare or by women complaining about how unfair it is that men will have longer and healthier lives.'

Her father held her gaze for a few seconds before turning to Joe as though seeking confirmation of what she claimed. He inclined his head slightly to signify that he agreed with what Karen had said, but he remained silent. Jeremy and Phillip, on the other hand, let their mouths run away with them, believing that they could take advantage of the discord between Karen and her father.

'You can't guess at these things, Karen,' Jeremy drawled in patronizing tones, 'we have hundreds of millions of dollars riding on Stablex, and we can't afford to trust your women's intuition on this.'

Phillip barely hid his excited snicker at those words, and as usual, rushed to stick his boot in once he thought Jeremy had someone down, 'It would have been more helpful if you'd been able to make those points yesterday, before this all happened.'

Karen cocked an eyebrow at Phillip, 'Really? You want to go there?'

The steel in her gaze pinned him to his seat, and his tongue flicked nervously across his moist lips.

'For one,' Karen stepped closer and looked down at him from across her father's desk, feeling a primitive sense of enjoyment as he pressed back into his seat as though cringing, 'what you said made very little sense. In fact, it was quite idiotic. If anyone should have known about personnel, it should have been you, not me, the contract lawyer. The point on publicity could only be known after the event. The fact that the orders are flooding in could also only take place after the event. So, what exactly did you mean by telling me that I should have made those points before last night's fiasco?'

'You…I know…that Australian…' he blustered, trying to start a sentence that would make sense but finding it difficult under her gaze that withered his groin. 'I meant, well, you were supposed to keep that Dimity man neutralized and under control, and you didn't know what was going to happen.'

'Obviously, I didn't know,' she snapped back in a voice of lethal softness, 'I am not his keeper. I had no expectation of keeping him under control, only of staying ahead of him. Judging from the pre-orders coming in for Stablex, we have managed to neutralize his effect and stay ahead of him because he underestimated the selfish desire of men to live longer.'

'Selfish?' her father interjected, surprised she would use that word concerning people's desire for Stablex.

'Of course, they are selfish,' her eyes dropped to her father. 'They know this will make them outlive their partners and even their daughters, but they care more about their own lives than growing old with their partners, unless they are with another man who is also using Stablex. I think that makes them selfish.'

'Dangerous ground, there,' her father growled. 'We want to market this as the next smart move in healthcare, not the act of a selfish man.'

'Guess what, Dad?' she asked with an acerbic edge to her words, something she would never normally allow into her voice when she spoke to him. 'We can market it however we want, but the fact remains that men will buy it for selfish reasons. We don't have to say that publicly, but perhaps we'll be better off if we are realistic and acknowledge that detail privately.'

John's eyes grew frosty as he noted the tinge of insolence in her voice. 'Is it selfish to want a reprieve from cancer or Alzheimer's or any of the other diseases and illnesses that can be helped by Stablex?'

'Actually, yes,' she didn't feel like acquiescing and backing down from this disagreement like she usually did. She was glad she had been so busy working in other areas of Pilatos that she hadn't learned much about Stablex until this last week, and now she wanted to express some of the thoughts that had niggled at her over the past few days.

Her father waited for her to continue, a foreboding warning flashing in his eyes, but she ignored it.

'I gather from the figures you gave me that men will be paying around two thousand dollars for their weekly dose of Stablex, so we'll round that to a hundred thousand a year. If they live the projected extra thirty years, we're looking at three million dollars from each Stablex user. If even half of those men put the same money into medical research aimed at curing those diseases in all people, not just themselves, then that would be selfless. To spend that amount of money on themselves with no thought about all the others who will die because they can't afford the treatment, then that is selfish.'

Grunting a noise of disgust, John flicked a hand in the air as though batting away her words, 'With that argument, you could say that the polio vaccine was selfish or trying to avoid the flu each year is selfish, or any cancer treatment is selfish. Stablex is a revolutionary treatment that will improve lives – it isn't selfish to want to be healthy and alive.'

'Those treatments help everyone,' she shot back. 'Stablex is only going to the wealthy men who can afford it. Let's see - of the seven or eight billion people on the planet, there are about thirty-five million who can claim to be millionaires. Probably only ten million or so of them are men so wealthy that they can afford three million dollars over thirty years, but, likely, we'll only have enough for ten thousand customers annually, so the price will go up. Pilatos will make billions, and they will compete with each other – selfishly - to pay whatever we ask.'

'It seems like you've been listening to the Australian and his propaganda,' her father stared at her coldly. 'Perhaps those people last night aren't the only ones who lack loyalty to Pilatos.'

Karen faced him with a calm demeanor, but internally she was seething. How dare he doubt her loyalty to her company. Being accurate and realistic in the analysis and understanding of all aspects of the drug, from who would use it and why to the social ramifications of one select group of people having access to it, was not disloyal. It was a sensible approach to handling any arguments that might be used against them. Anyway, Pilatos was so much more than Stablex, even though the company's future might rise or fall on its success.

'I have always been loyal to Pilatos,' she vowed, 'and I don't need to listen to Lane Dimity to foresee problems in the future of Stablex when it is restricted to such a select group of people.'

'If you remain loyal to the company,' John steepled his fingers in front of his face as though considering his words carefully, 'you will change your way of thinking...'

'Stablex is one product,' she interrupted, speaking over him, annoyed that he couldn't see that looking at Stablex logically and impartially was not being traitorous to the company. 'Pilatos has thousands of products. Considering all the factors, possibilities, and consequences of Stablex is not an indication that I'm turning on my own company.'

'If you remain loyal,' her father repeated, louder this time, with an irritated look that made it clear he would not accept another interruption from her, 'then you will redouble your efforts to keep Dimity at bay. We will handle the other factors and consequences. You will minimize the Dimity effect. It seems more luck than anything else that last night didn't sound the death knell for Stablex, so I don't want him continuing his campaign against us, and I don't want to risk him eating into our profits. Luckily, demand will be so much greater than our supply that his influence hasn't yet balanced that out, but I don't want to give him the opportunity to do so. I don't like relying on luck.'

Phillip, growing bold as he watched father and daughter spar, advised, 'Hard work, Karen, not luck.'

As soon as he uttered the words, he regretted them. Her testicle-shriveling look swung to him and drifted down his face to rest somewhere in the region of his tie.

'Hard work?' she inquired, arching an eyebrow, her voice deceptively smooth. 'Would that be like how my father and I worked last night to minimize the damage and return control of the evening to us, or is it like how you sat in your seat staring about like an overfed prairie dog looking for a hole to dive into?'

'Don't be emotional, Karen,' her father warned, his distaste showing in the tightness of his mouth, 'you know I have no time for it.'

'I am not emotional,' Karen stated flatly, wishing that, for once, she *could* be emotional and yell and throw things, and, maybe, land a blow right in Phillip's thin-lipped moist mouth, but her father had trained her since childhood to hide her emotions behind this damned mask. Her eyes narrowed imperceptibly as she thought of how she had changed her life because of all the things her father had no time for, molding herself into his notion of the perfect daughter. How dare he accuse her of being emotional when she was merely demonstrating the coolness that he so admired.

'Good,' John nodded at her, not entirely convinced. 'We need you to bring that Australian to heel. Perhaps, in your late-night chats with him, you can ensure he comes around to our point of view.'

As soon as he admitted to knowing about the communications between her and Lane, Karen felt anger surge in her chest, and she fought it to maintain her calm exterior. Her father could only know about that aspect of her contact with Lane if he'd been spying on her or accessing her phone records. To be accused of being disloyal and emotional was more than enough for her to handle in one day, but to learn that he didn't trust her enough to grant her full privacy was beyond her limits of tolerance.

'I can guarantee that he will not come around to our viewpoint as surely as I know we're not going to see his,' she spoke levelly, battling to keep the churning anger from finding a vent and erupting forth. 'So, don't rely on me changing his mind. And I advise you to stop monitoring my phone use – I have an expectation of privacy in my own time. As have these men,' she indicated Joe, Phillip, and Jeremy, 'and it can be assumed that if you are spying on my phone use, you are also examining theirs beyond what is acceptable or legal, and I'm fairly sure they wouldn't appreciate that. Am I right?'

With her final words, she looked at each of the three men and noted their reactions. Joe remained impassive, and she doubted that he would have anything that he wouldn't gladly share with John, from his phone records to his innermost thoughts. Jeremy looked slightly alarmed at the thought of John investigating his phone use, while Phillip looked positively sick at the idea of John examining anything in his private life.

'So, please desist from checking up on me. I'm not a twelve-year-old using your phone while you are in the bathroom. I own ten percent of this company, I have a clear expectation of privacy, and I will take action if you breach that. Do you understand?'

Father and daughter stared at each other with their mirrored eyes, true combatants for the first time in their lives, with neither giving quarter. It was a revelation to John to see Karen square up to him rather than facilitate his wishes and bend to his will. They had navigated minor clashes many times, but this was more, this was her refusing to accept his authority, and she was issuing a challenge. As his galloping thoughts raced around the slow passing of seconds, he realized that his daughter was dangerous. He had worked to create a suitable heir to his Pilatos kingdom, and here she was, capable and intelligent and hostile...but was she traitorous?

He thought not. At least, not at the moment.

He raised his hands and gave ground, smiling at her with a pale imitation of warmth, his voice conciliatory, 'Don't bite my head off. You have your privacy. I had been tracking the calls people were making and receiving during this critical time for Stablex, but no one has been taping calls, just seeing who is speaking to whom. And it can stop.'

'Good,' Karen inclined her head without going to the effort of faking a smile.

'And do whatever it takes to keep that Australian out of the way between now and when people are buying Stablex. I don't need any more of his stunts. We got away with this one, but that's no reason to invite more.'

'I do have other things to do,' she replied, annoyed that he seemed to think that by saying the words, it would happen, 'including trying to get the Maine land deal worked out, and I don't know how I'm expected to keep him *out of the way*, but I'll try to come up with something.'

'Do that,' he nodded and dismissed the topic. 'Now, to the Maine deal. Fill us in.'

Karen spent ten minutes explaining the latest developments with the tract of forest before they went over some other issues that had emerged in various sectors of Pilatos. After an intense hour, they had covered dozens of points that John had listed for the unscheduled meeting and then circled back to the subject of Stablex when one of the assistants brought in the latest expressions of interest in the drug. The publicity from the night before was growing exponentially as time zones came awake around the world, and people read the headlines and became fascinated by the wonder drug that seemed too good to be true.

The pre-orders meant that the future of Stablex was assured. The stallions would continue to live lives of luxury in their stalls. Protesters could jump up and down and demand change, but the only change coming was Stablex.

Karen almost felt sorry for Lane: his campaign could not possibly succeed against this rising demand for the drug, and there was nothing left that he could reveal that would damage sales. If his images and words about the muted horses did not impede interest, then he was left with nothing to use against them.

Or so she hoped. It occurred to her that her father hadn't informed her of the surgery performed to silence the stallions, so there was a chance that there was something else hidden away. The fact that he scoffed at her suggestion that there could be other secrets that might become weapons in the hands of the protesters did little to reassure her.

# CHAPTER TWELVE

*When you notice a wrong, keep in mind that they rarely travel alone. It often grew from something that should never have been and leads to many more problems that need to be addressed. You might not be able to mend them all, but if we all try to improve the problems that we do encounter, we leave the world better than when we arrived.*

**Lane Dimity, in an interview for the documentary Our Quiet Leaders.**

### Bisente Farm

After the meeting with her father, Karen felt mentally exhausted. Corporate battles usually energized her, leaving her walking on a high of adrenaline and other fighting hormones, but this was different. Perhaps it was because she had never faced her father across the battlefield before. Maybe she was tired after the big night of introducing the world to Stablex and having it go so wrong. Or she could be coming down with something.

At lunchtime, she sat at the desk in her temporary office at the Pilatos Centre, staring out at the clouds that floated by in the blue Kentucky sky. She decided that, instead of going straight back to New York that afternoon, she'd visit her mother. The urge to go home to Bisente crept up on her and became an overwhelming desire as soon as she rang the farm and heard her mother's voice.

Two hours later, she was stepping out of a company car and into Isabella's arms. As she felt the comforting embrace enfold her, she found herself melting into the warmth that was her mother instead of stiffly withdrawing as was her habit. The seconds stretched out as she gave herself over to her mother's hug and absorbed the love that flowed to her.

'I am so glad you came,' Isabella patted her on the back softly and soothingly before stepping back to smile at her, 'and I have your room ready, so please tell me that you will stay tonight instead of rushing off.'

'I think I will, Mum, thanks.' Karen found some of the stress eased from her spine as she agreed to stay the night. The thought of sleeping in her childhood room seemed strangely appealing at the moment. Seeing her mother in blazing color was reassuring. Her bright green jodhpurs covered in brilliant yellow sunflowers, plus the sky-blue polo, showed a life that her own subdued greys lacked. Her mother was a field of flowers under a blue sky, while she felt as though all the color had been drained from her wardrobe. Metaphorical clothes, she smiled to herself.

'Now, come and try my latest concoction,' Isabella spun away and stepped lightly like a dancer towards the house, 'carrot, apple, hemp seed – the legal sort – cucumber and berries. You will love it.'

'It sounds…interesting,' Karen grinned behind Isabella's back.

'No need for that look,' Isabella tossed the words over her shoulder. 'Just because I'm not looking at you doesn't mean I don't know the expression on your face.'

'You always were a bit spooky,' Karen joked, humming the theme song to *The Twilight Zone*, 'Isabella Lawford: she knows what you're thinking.'

'That is true,' Isabella paused at the open front door and indicated for Karen to go inside, 'and do you want me to tell you what you're thinking?'

Karen gave a dramatic shudder, 'Absolutely not. Well, not until I have a glass of your cucumber-hemp-hippy-juice in me, anyway.'

'Then we shall take our juices out to the balcony and watch the horses working as we drink, and we shall talk. I do know you need to talk.'

'Do I?'

'Darling, you are making and selling Stablex,' Isabella shrugged and raised her brows as though that statement made it clear that Karen would need to talk. 'Such a tacky name, too, by the way: stallion blood extract. I have no doubt your father thinks it is a brilliant name.'

There was a jug of thick, dull orange liquid on the kitchen counter, and Isabella added ice to it plus a sprig of mint, collected a couple of glasses, and led the way to the balcony overlooking the arenas. Motioning to one of the armchairs at a small round table, Isabella poured the drinks as Karen sank into the soft leather of the old chair and gazed out at the six horses working in the dressage arena.

'There are the young horses,' Isabella nodded at the arena. 'Those ones are all five-year-olds and ready to start some serious work. They have their first competitions next month. Which one do you like?'

'All of them,' Karen sipped her drink tentatively, wrinkled her nose at the unusual flavor, then decided she liked it and had more.

'Don't be diplomatic,' Isabella said, 'it doesn't suit you. I want you to judge those horses, not pander to my feelings.'

Karen snorted, 'I can be diplomatic.'

'It still doesn't suit you, dear.'

'OK, then,' Karen's eyes swept over the horses as they cantered down the long side of the arena, then turned at the large letter 'A' halfway along the short side and trotted over the poles that were placed one stride apart. 'The big brown horse will go all the way; he's the obvious pick. Great athlete and born to jump. The grey is stepping short and won't go above low level. The bay with the two hind socks is sweet-natured and will make a good junior horse but not a top-level open horse. The bay with no white has potential but lacks the attitude of a star. And the little chestnut that's a hand and a half smaller than all the others looks completely out of place.'

'Does he?'

'And he's my pick,' Karen turned to look at her mother. 'He has more heart than all the others put together, and he is out-thinking them, too. He wants to jump, doesn't he? He reminds me of the incredible pony, Teddy O'Connor. He has that same indefinable air about him - smaller than the others but more ability than all of them. He's your star, isn't he?'

Isabella laughed incredulously, 'The little chestnut? So you think that little fifteen hand horse is going to jump better than the huge brown horse?'

'Yes.'

'I don't know why you gave up horses,' Isabella shook her head and tut-tutted, dropping her act of disbelief, 'your eye is ridiculously good. Yes, that little chestnut gelding is a superstar in the making. I would back him against all those others in any jumping competition, but most people think I'm joking when I say that.'

'He has heart.'

'And if you can see that,' Isabella looked sideways at her daughter, 'why can't you see what Lane sees in the Stablex stallions.'

'Not you, too, Mother,' Karen groaned, not wanting to argue this point now.

'I am curious, that is all,' Isabella pointed down at the chestnut, now trotting calmly over two small jumps along the other long side of the arena, 'it took all of a few seconds for you to spot the spirit in that little horse and recognize the greatness in him, yet you've spent more

189

time with those black stallions and can't see that their spirits are dying.'

'Their spirits are *not* dying, Mother,' Karen rolled her eyes. 'They're well looked after, and all the major welfare groups will testify to that.'

'Because your father pays them,' Isabella dismissed her claim. 'Charities like those are mostly about making big incomes for the people running them. I imagine that the well-paid heads of those welfare groups will be lining up to buy Stablex as soon as it is available.'

'You're such a cynic,' Karen sniffed and took another sip of the orange-colored blend.

'And you're not?'

Karen snorted into her drink and glanced up at her mother from under her lashes, 'Apples and trees, eh?'

Isabella reached over to pat her hand, 'Two trees, and one apple has fallen somewhere between the two of us. Your father has tried to claim all of you for most of your life, but you fell from this tree, too, remember, and look at you here at Bisente watching our horses. No, you haven't fallen all that far from this tree.'

There were a few minutes of comfortable silence as Karen breathed in the air of Bisente and thought of how different her mother's rural lifestyle was from her own New York existence. Could she settle for something like this after working so hard to achieve what she had in her corporate world? She doubted it; even her own thoughts made that clear as she had considered this as something she would have to settle for rather than choose. This was her mother's world and the home of her childhood, while she belonged in boardrooms and high-rise offices. Still, it was pleasant to sit overlooking the horses as they worked, and she did like the look of that little chestnut.

'Has Lane been in contact with you?' Isabella asked casually. Too casually.

Karen looked at her sharply, 'Why do you ask?'

'I'll take that as a yes,' her mother arched her carefully shaped eyebrows at her. 'I could tell he liked you.'

'We're not high school kids, Mother. He's an animal activist, and I represent a company he'd like to destroy.'

'Minor details,' Isabella waved her hand as though shooing away mosquitoes, 'and you are being overly dramatic. He doesn't want to destroy Pilatos; he wants to see those stallions released so they can run on pastures and feel the sun on their backs.'

'That's not going to happen,' replied Karen. She lowered her glass and leaned back in her chair, closing her eyes as she enjoyed the warmth of the sun on her face. 'If you've had time to read the updates that Dad sent us about the origin of Stablex, you'd know that those stallions are the only source of the hormone in the world. It can't be made synthetically – yet – and the gene hasn't been found in any other horse or any other animal for that matter. It's produced by what appears to be a random mutation in their sire, and Pilatos is not going to risk anything happening to those horses.'

'I did read that this morning. How sad for the horses that such a gene was discovered. They truly are like the goose that laid the golden egg,' nodded Isabella, her eyes troubled as she looked from her daughter to the horses in her paddocks. 'I can't help but agree with Lane on this…those stallions represent an evil at the heart of Stablex, and in turn, Pilatos, and one wrongdoing is usually an indication of others.'

At the mention of Lane, Karen opened her eyes and looked at her mother. 'So, when did Lane say that? Which is a total load of nonsense, by the way. Or have you become an avid reader of his works?'

'We text each other most days,' Isabella spoke with half-closed eyes, as though she was drifting off to sleep, but she was watching Karen intently.

The astonishment on her daughter's face didn't go unnoticed, and there was something else in her eyes. Was she dismayed that a friendship had formed between them? Or jealous? Lane had mentioned that he had communicated with Karen several times late at night. He said he found her intelligent and funny, and he regretted that his actions would turn her against him. Isabella wondered if her daughter was feeling possessive of the Australian and didn't like sharing his attention.

That guess felt right, and Isabella hid the twitch at the corner of her mouth as she speculated on the alien emotions that must be invading her daughter's mind and heart in regards to that handsome young Australian. It was about time Karen experienced something that she couldn't control or switch off with logic. No, she closed her eyes for a moment, picturing Lane's face when he'd looked at Karen that day here; there was no way she'd be able to switch him off. He was an unstoppable force.

Rather than think up a response to the unexpected information that her mother and Lane were text buddies, Karen narrowed her lips and studied the horses as they moved to one of the show jumping arenas and started working over a small course of obstacles. She didn't want to examine why the thought of Lane and her mother being friends made her feel uncomfortable.

'He mentioned that he had talked to you, too,' said Isabella softly, trying to ease into a conversation with her daughter that covered feelings, not just facts.

'Then why did you ask if he had been in contact with me?' Karen looked at her mother challengingly, her guard up.

'Because I wanted to see if you were prepared to tell me about it or if you'd slam the door shut on talking about him, which you did.'

'There's nothing to talk about,' Karen said stiffly, 'we've been in touch a few times at night after I've finished work. I doubt it will happen again. We don't have anything in common, and I know he was behind the sabotage last night, so, right now, I'd rather kick him than talk to him.'

'Emotions are hard things to understand, aren't they?' Isabella sighed. 'I remember falling in love with your father – it was like holding my arms up to a tornado and letting the winds take me. He was an unstoppable force, too, back then. He filled my thoughts and my heart, and I didn't notice that there was a fundamental difference between us, or I didn't care. I loved horses. He had little empathy for any animal.'

'He's not much of an animal lover,' Karen agreed.

Isabella exhaled slowly at the thought of John's attitude towards animals. It was something that she had struggled with all of her marriage. 'That is one thing you and Lane have in common. You really do love horses. You know them. You understand them. I know you've turned away from them to pursue your career, but look at how you knew those horses down there with just a few minutes of observation. Which, again, makes me wonder how you can accept what is being done to those Friesian stallions.'

'There's nothing *being done to them*, apart from making sure they are the best cared for horses in the world.'

'Oh, Karen, in your heart, you know that's not right. How did you feel when you learned about those vocal cordectomies?'

The moment lurched back into Karen's mind, accompanied by the sick feeling that had wrung her insides when she realized that all the stallions had been surgically silenced. For a few seconds, her mouth moved as though she was trying to find words to hide behind, but they didn't appear. She rubbed a hand over her eyes, seeing the scars on all the throats.

'I admit, it was awful,' she confessed honestly. 'I wish Dad or the head vet had told me about it so I could have kept Lane and his friends away from the horses. I wish I'd had time to learn that the procedure is painless and makes the stallions' lives more peaceful without the constant noise and alarms from the other stallions.'

192

'Part of you has to realize that there is no justification for silencing them like that. It doesn't matter if the procedure is painless; it's wrong. You know it's wrong. And if that was kept from you, what else is hidden?'

The question rattled Karen, though there was no sign of her unease as she examined the table surface. Only a few hours ago, she had been wondering the same thing, and it was unsettling to hear her mother give voice to Karen's thoughts.

'Sometimes, Mother,' she spoke softly, not meeting her mother's eyes, 'we have to trust that the vets and the welfare groups, the FDA, and all the other checks and balances along the way to keep the chain of production ethical and honest, are doing their job and there's nothing hidden.'

With an eye roll and a harrumph of skepticism, Isabella shook her head, 'No evil is an island – there will be more. I know you are a lawyer, and you've had almost nothing to do with this branch of Pilatos, but, darling, it's time to step up and find out what is going on.'

'There's nothing *going on,* Mother – they are using the blood of those stallions to produce a revolutionary drug. That is quite straightforward and not worthy of conspiracy theories.'

'No, I know there's more,' Isabella tapped her fingers on the table, looking perplexed. 'I know your father too well. He has been keeping you away from Stablex for a reason.'

'Honestly, Mum, he hasn't been keeping me away from Stablex; I've been busy in lots of other sectors of Pilatos that needed my attention.'

Cocking an eyebrow at her daughter, Isabella gave her a *what did I just say?* look. Keeping Karen busy with other sectors amounted to the same as keeping her away from Stablex.

Karen shrugged, 'He was probably worried that I'd go all *horse lover* on him and want the stallions to have a better life.'

Isabella pounced on her words, 'So, you agree they deserve a better life?'

Karen laughed, 'This is becoming like a Sixty Minutes interview. That's not what I meant. And you know it.'

'I don't mean to grill you,' Isabella apologized ruefully. It was a rare event to have her daughter visit more than a few times a year, so a few times in a month was a treat she shouldn't waste arguing over Pilatos business. There was so much to talk about, but, as usual, there was so much that couldn't be said. If she led this particular horse to water, she was guaranteed not to drink, so she needed to make her realize that she was thirsty.

'Come and look at my latest paintings,' Isabella rose gracefully from the table and held out a hand to her daughter.

'More from Alicia? I purchased a wonderful one from her a few days ago.'

'No, these are ones I'm painting myself.'

'Really? I'm so glad you are painting again. You were so talented.'

Isabella gave her a dry look over her shoulder as she led the way into the house, 'I never stopped painting, dear.'

'Didn't you?' Karen looked surprised. She had thought her mother stopped painting years ago, back when she went off to college. An uncomfortable awareness washed over her: it wasn't that her mother had stopped painting, it was that she had stopped showing an interest in her mother's life.

'There,' Isabella waved a hand at a large canvas on an easel as they entered the art studio, a huge room at the far end of the house with beautiful views of the farm through glass walls on two sides.

The painting currently being worked on showed a black stallion, a Friesian by the looks of him, rearing against a sky of violent reds. The blood-red sky was reflected in his mane and on his glistening black coat. Karen felt moved by the raw spirit in the horse's eyes as it gazed at her from the canvas.

'It's beautiful,' Karen murmured. She turned to look around at the other paintings in the studio and saw several of a child on horseback, and the child looked startlingly like her when she was young. There was a life-like painting of one of the Bisente stallions going over a jump with Julian on board. There were also some botanical watercolors of the flora found on Bisente, and Karen was impressed by her mother's ability.

'I had no idea you were this talented,' she looked at her mother, her brows creased as she puzzled over the fact that she had not known how well her mother painted.

'Of course, you didn't,' her mother smiled at her fondly, 'I exist outside Pilatos, so how would you know what I was up to?'

'Ouch,' Karen said with contrition. 'Am I that obsessed with work?'

'Yes, but it's who you are at this time, so I love you anyway.'

'Is that the little chestnut horse?' Karen pointed to a half-finished painting leaning against a wall.

'He's not that small,' Isabella protested, 'he's over fifteen hands. He's small compared to the seventeen hand horses. And, yes, that's him. Would you like that one when it's finished?'

'I'd love it,' Karen smiled, sincerely pleased to be getting one of these paintings. 'Why have you been giving me store-bought presents all these years when you could have been giving me these paintings?'

'I didn't think you'd want any,' Isabella replied as she moved the painting of the chestnut to an easel so that she could complete the artwork.

'How could I want any when I didn't even know you were doing them?'

'Exactly,' Isabella smiled as though pleased at Karen for coming up with the answer to a question by merely asking the question.

'If I'd known you were painting these,' Karen said with patience, 'I'd have wanted them.'

'If you'd been at all interested in my life, you'd have known I was doing them.'

'You are impossible,' Karen laughed, shaking her head.

'So your father says,' Isabella chuckled with her.

Karen spent twenty minutes admiring the paintings and making small talk about artists, colors, and subjects before Stablex was mentioned again.

'Why don't you bring your things in and have a shower before dinner?' Isabella asked. 'I imagine it was a rather difficult night last night, and you can have a well-earned break from Pilatos and Stablex for this night, at least.'

'I don't *need* a break,' said Karen, making her way back to the kitchen, 'but I will be happy to take one for the night.'

'Good,' Isabella stopped in the kitchen and began to brew up some coffee as Karen leaned against the breakfast counter, watching her. 'I would like to know what you think – really think – about Stablex. I can't believe that you think it is such a great product.'

'All the tests show it is reversing many illnesses and adding decades to the users' lives.'

'Male users,' Isabella pointed out. 'Don't you find that at all unfair?'

'Oh, absolutely,' Karen nodded, 'but it's going to make huge profits for Pilatos. It is a business, Mum – we're meant to make a profit. Pilatos supports a lot of lives who depend on us to pay them so they can eat.'

'I'm sure they'd find a way of being able to eat if we didn't pay them,' countered her mother, 'we are not the world to the employees; we are merely an employer who can be replaced.'

'And we won't have to be replaced if we make such a profit with Stablex that we can grow and provide more jobs for more people.'

'Is it worth it?' Isabella paused and looked at Karen, her head tilted to one side.

'Stablex?'

'Yes. It just seems such a discriminating drug that will cause more division in our world.'

Karen shrugged, 'I'm sure the men who will be taking it will argue that it is certainly worth it.'

'And I'm sure their wives would say otherwise as they trudge into old age and death. I'm sure most wives would prefer their husbands to age gracefully alongside them rather than rely on pharmaceuticals to keep them virile and hunting for younger women.'

'It doesn't change their morality,' scoffed Karen, 'if they are the sort who go looking for other women outside of their permanent relationship, they are going to be that person, whether or not they take Stablex.'

'At least without it,' Isabella's lips quirked, 'there is always the hope that they might drop dead of natural causes.'

'What every wife hopes for, I'm sure,' said Karen sarcastically.

'Not *every* wife, dear, but you might be surprised.'

'I would be surprised,' Karen tweaked an eyebrow at her mother, 'especially after you said that most wives would want their husbands to age alongside them. Such a contradiction, mother – they want to grow old with them, and now they want them to drop dead.'

'We are contrary creatures,' Isabella smiled, enjoying the verbal sparring with her daughter, 'and you are an expert at not answering direct questions when you can deflect.'

'When did I do that?'

'Is it worth it?' Isabella repeated the earlier question, pinning her daughter with her gaze and making it clear she wanted an answer this time.

'I think… no, I am sure it is worth it,' Karen's voice seemed to hold a tremor of doubt, but the meaning of her words was clear, 'it will aid health and help people, granted, only those wealthy men who can afford it at this stage, but I'm sure all stops are being pulled out to try and develop a similar drug for women, as well as a cheaper version that can be made available for more people.'

'Do you believe that?' Isabella held two empty coffee mugs in one hand and stared at her daughter.

'Yes, I do.'

'Then you'd be a fool, dear. Sorry, but if this drug can make the company billions, I don't see the men in charge of the company working hard to develop a similar one for women. Have they been searching for older female mammals to try and find an equivalent gene?'

'No idea,' Karen shrugged, 'and it's not my department, so it's not something I'm likely to know.'

'Then let me tell you what I know,' Isabella placed the mugs down on the counter and held up a hand to list off points. 'One, this drug is patently unfair: it gives a huge advantage to wealthy men over all other men, and over all women. Two, it's going to make Pilatos so much money that they won't bother trying to develop a female equivalent; they'll be too busy trying to expand this one, the ultimate bird in the hand. Three, your father has been keeping you away from Stablex and will continue to do so, as there is more you don't know. I don't know either, but I know there has to be something there because I know how John works. Four, you need to make it your job to protect those horses, Karen, as it's the right thing to do, and until you do it, it's left to outsiders like Lane to do something about it. And, five, talk to Lane tonight – he's the Yang to your Yin or vice versa, and you need to work with him to help those stallions, which, in turn, may prevent those megalomaniacs outliving everyone else and feeling like gods.'

When she stopped, she expected Karen to erupt into counter-arguments and was relieved to see her daughter stand silent for several minutes, digesting the words, a frown creasing her brow. A couple of times, Karen's chest rose as though she was about to launch into her rebuttal, but she remained silent.

'Actually, Mother,' Karen finally said with some determination, 'there is way too much there for me to worry about now. I'll work on it later. I'm going to get my things from the car, have a shower, and then enjoy a cup of that coffee with you. Promise me, though, no more talk of Stablex, those stallions, or Lane, or I will get in the car and drive away.'

'I promise.'

'And I don't believe you,' Karen grinned, 'but that's OK. We'll deal with it later.'

They did manage to make it through coffee, a tour of the stables, and dinner, without mentioning the forbidden topics, much to Karen's incredulity, and when she lay in her childhood bed that night, she turned her mother's words over and over in her mind, looking at them from all angles.

There were valid points, she conceded, but when she honed all non-essential options down to what she needed to do, it came back to the fact that Pilatos needed Stablex. It was going to be the savior of the company, so she had to do whatever she could to ensure the production and release of Stablex proceeded, unimpeded by Lane or anyone else.

At midnight, she had nearly managed to find the elusive sleep when her phone vibrated under her pillow. For several minutes she lay on her back, staring at the ceiling with its glow-in-the-dark stars, ignoring her phone. She knew it was going to be Lane. No doubt, he'd been chatting to her mother and knew she was here at Bisente. I don't have to respond, she told herself, counting the stars she had stuck to her ceiling when she was eleven.

Reaching for the phone, she unlocked the screen and flicked to messages. There were two: the unread one from the night before that had resulted in her pelting her phone at the door, and the one that had just come through. She shut the phone and put it back under her pillow and lay still, wondering where sleep had gone. She took the phone back out, turned it on, and went to the controls to turn the vibrate function off. She put the phone back under her pillow. Now she wouldn't know if he messaged.

Ten minutes later, she decided to read his messages. It's not like they could hurt, she told herself, I'll just read them and put the phone away again.

*I'm sorry about what happened. I'm trying to save the stallions, not hurt you*, was the message from the previous night.

Yeah, sure, she glared at the words and flicked to the next message. *I can be at Bisente before dawn if you want to talk.*

Karen's hand tightened on the phone, and the muscles in her arm tensed as though she was about to throw it, but she took a deep breath and relaxed. There was no point in feeling upset. There wasn't anything he could do to harm Stablex. He'd tried his best at the launch, and though plenty may have felt outraged, the pre-orders by the close of the business day had been overwhelming.

Placing the phone on the floor, she gave it a push so that it was out of reach. No need to answer, she smiled at her stars above.

A few minutes passed before she rolled out of bed and reached for the phone. She couldn't be one hundred percent sure that there wasn't *something* he could do to harm her company. He did have all those followers – his cult, she said with vicious tones inside her mind. He did find those employees who pulled last night's stunt. Perhaps it would be best to follow her father's orders and stay in contact with the man and try to keep him busy.

### Arizona

Lane didn't expect a reply. Isabella had made it quite clear that Karen was not likely to separate herself from Pilatos and see his actions as anything but an attack on her. He wanted her to understand. He wanted to find the right words to help her recognize what was wrong with the treatment of the Stablex stallions, but nothing had worked so far. The campaign against the drug was about to be ramped up, and he wanted to contact her so he could make it clear that it wasn't personal: what was coming was not about Karen and him, but about a drug that should never have been developed. The more he learned of it, the surer he became that it had to be stopped.

He lay back on the sand, feeling it crunch under him as he wriggled to even out some of the bumps under his flannelette shirt and jeans, and gazed up at the vast star-laden sky. It wasn't as brilliantly clear as his outback skies where the stars blazed down on him like old friends, and he couldn't see his beloved Southern Cross or either of the Magellanic Clouds, the two dwarf galaxies orbiting the Milky Way, but he could still make out various constellations and features.

Words were so important, he mused, and it was ironic that so many millions of people seemed to be addicted to his words while he couldn't find the right ones when he needed them. His words failed to stop his father on that day so long ago. Now, with this strange and distant woman whose life was so different from his, he could not find the words to reach her, to help her see what he could see. He could not find the words to help her rediscover the child within who would see the suffering of those stallions.

He couldn't speak to her about what lay at the heart of Pilatos Farm as he only knew fragments of the truth, and he needed more before there was any chance of changing her views. He knew that the fate of a single horse would seem inconsequential compared to the billions of dollars that Stablex would make the company, so he needed to learn more in order to outweigh those profits with the weight of his knowledge and words.

The theme song to *Spirit, Stallion of the Cimarron* interrupted his thoughts, and he smiled at his piece of the sky. That was the tune he'd attached to any incoming calls or texts from Karen. It was a text. He didn't want to look at it immediately. He wanted to enjoy the feeling of knowing she had replied before letting her anger into his night.

There was always the chance that she wasn't angry, but he imagined her level of frustration as she tried to deal with the disruption at the Pilatos Centre, and knew that it was a very small chance. The computer techs had detailed all that they'd done to ensure the longest possible time for their little documentary to run, and it didn't take a genius to realize how irritated Karen would have been as she tried to shut it down.

Some horses snorted in the distance, and one of the dogs back at the Claw house a few hundred meters away growled, the sound traveling easily on the cool night air. Next to home, he thought, this is my favorite place in the world. Good people. Horses. Dogs. Clear skies. Far from town. Here it is peaceful…and it makes me want to go home.

A deep yearning for Ellamanga raised its head within his chest, and he squeezed his eyes shut, imagining, just for a moment, that he was home in Australia under southern skies. He wanted a quiet life and an end to running and hiding. He wanted to stop trying to fix the problems of the world.

Let someone else do it, he spoke in his mind to the stars, I want to go home.

He shoved those thoughts away and picked up the phone

*How far away from Bisente are you? Not that I want you to get here before dawn, I want to know so I can send my suicide squad out to get you.*

Laughter bubbled out of him as he read her words, not believing for a second that she was serious. She might have wanted him dead when the Stablex launch was going down the toilet, but he knew she wasn't a natural-born killer.

*Sorry, I'm half a continent away. I was going to have a pilot friend fly me there if you wanted to talk before dawn.*

*Damn,* her message came back almost instantly, *I was kinda hoping you were in Lexington so my hitmen wouldn't have far to drive.*

*Does the desire to kill me mean that you are angry at me?*

*No. Not at all. I loved your documentary. I thought it was great to be running barefoot around the center trying to get chains off doors and shut your movie down while 2,000 guests were wondering what the hell was going on. Why would I be angry?*

*You're angry.* He added a little angry devil face to his message.

*Genius.* She added an image of Einstein.

*If you missed the other message, I did say I was sorry for what happened. I'm not trying to hurt you, just save the stallions.*

*I didn't look at it when you sent it. I hurled my phone into the bedroom door and broke it. If I'd read your message, I'd have broken the phone anyway. Maybe with a gun.*

*Do you have a gun in your bedroom?*

*Since meeting you, yes. Just in case you ever turn up before dawn.*

Once more, Lane laughed out loud. He liked her sense of humor. Unless she wasn't joking, of course…he pursed his lips and reread her messages. No, she was joking. She didn't have a gun waiting for him. He hoped.

*Note to self: do not visit Karen's bedroom before dawn.*

*Unless invited.*

He stared at the two words. It was ridiculously hard to guess at the tone she was using. Was that only joking around, or was there an element of flirting, suggesting that maybe, one day, she would invite him to her bedroom. Lane scratched his head and had an internal argument over his next words. He didn't want to reject a possible flirtatious overture, but he didn't want to think it was one if she was being totally jokey.

He wrote, *I'm hoping for an invitation,* and then deleted it as it made him sound like a smooth operator, and he was anything but that when it came to women. *Sounds interesting,* was his next try, but after looking at it, he deleted it, too. *I'll check the mail for my invitation.* Stupid. Delete.

He'd use a question. There was no harm in that, was there? He gritted his teeth as he tapped in *What are the chances I'll ever be invited?* He sent it before thinking too deeply about it.

*About a million to one.*

Thank the stars I deleted that other rubbish, he nodded to his bright friends overhead, that could have been awkward. And yet the odds aren't that bad, he snorted, I've been known to buy lotto tickets with a forty million to one chance of winning, so I'm still in with a chance.

*Good to know. What are the chances you are going to free the stallions?*

*Zero. Mind you, it's not my call, anyway, so you're wasting your time trying to get me to free them.*

He started a reply to that, but she sent another text before he could finish his.

*Can we talk about something other than Stablex? Please.*

*How's the weather where you are?* Lane shot back, grimacing at the dreary nature of his question as soon as he'd sent it, but at least it was a change of subject.

*You really aren't here in Lexington?*

*Nup. Arizona. I'm staying with Tom's family.*

*Thanks for letting me know. Squad on their way.*

*I'll put the kettle on.*

Karen sent a gif of a woman laughing hysterically and falling on the floor.

*I sure hope that gif is because I'm being funny and not because you're amused that I'm about to die.*

*I may have wanted that to happen last night,* she wrote, *but I'm not feeling homicidal at the moment.*

*It's always a relief when the person you're talking to says they're not homicidal.*

*Back to the weather. It's fine here. I can see stars.*

That's a coincidence, he thought, both of us looking at the stars. *Me, too. I'm sitting outside doing some star gazing.*

*Then you're looking at real stars. I'm looking at glow stars I put on my ceiling when I was eleven.*

He smiled at the image of Karen as a child sticking stars on her ceiling. When she was eleven, he'd have been…his smile vanished. He didn't want to remember. It was the source of all that followed in his life, and though ultimately, it had led to him helping so many, it remained a well of pain and hurt at his core. His way of coping was to not go there, just cover it up and move forward. Or up. He looked up at the stars and relaxed back into the comforting hold of the earth as he looked at those millions of suns shining at him from across the galaxy.

*The real stars are bright tonight. You should go outside and look at them.*

*Great idea. I will. Sure. Maybe. Nah. Bad idea. Bed is really comfortable right now. I'm not moving. The stars will still be there tomorrow and tomorrow…*

*…and tomorrow,* he began, wondering if she was intentionally quoting Shakespeare because it could just be a repetition without reference to Macbeth's speech, or maybe she was testing him to see if he had any education in literature, or…He stopped himself. He was overthinking it. His first reaction was to complete the quote, so he would run with that. *Creeps in this petty pace from day to day, To the last syllable of recorded time; And all our yesterdays have lighted fools the way to dusty death. Out, out, brief candle!*

There was a sense of relief when she quickly sent back the next four lines, confirming that she had been thinking of the Scottish play. A part of him was hoping that she appreciated his knowledge, he wanted her to be looking at his words with eyebrows raised, thinking how intelligent he was. My ego, he sniffed in amusement at his thoughts, is trying to make me the hero in my own mind, but I suspect it will get a nasty touch up from this woman.

*Signifying nothing,* he provided the last line, sent it, and then read and reread the two words. Signifying nothing. Signifying nothing. There was something depressing about those two words.

The refrain from Spirit interrupted his thoughts, and he read her next words that echoed the ones that had run through his mind. *There is something depressing about those two words.*

He wrote without thinking, he put down the words that came at that moment, *I was thinking that. Does it really signify nothing? All that we do, all that we believe and love and achieve…does it really signify nothing?*

*I hope not. They're just words in a play written long ago, about a Scottish king who lived even longer ago. I want to think that what I do has some significance. Of course, if you want to look at my work in the context of a million years or as one of seven billion humans, it probably doesn't signify much. Maybe it only has to signify something to ourselves.*

*Perhaps,* he let his words flow out again without filtering them through the mesh of questions about what he should and shouldn't say and what the other person would think, *but whatever I do seems insignificant as I look up at these stars that have burned for billions of years. I'm here and gone, and does anything change?*

*Who are you kidding? I've looked at your social media following. You make their lives better. You do change things. Don't judge yourself by what you have failed to do, look at what you have achieved.*

*That is deep.* He was heartened by the fact that Karen seemed to want to help him feel better about himself in this time of introspection.

*You wrote it,* she replied.

Laughter flew from him like a flock of escaping sparrows. He sent her a gif of Steve Carell bursting into laughter.

*You write lots of good things,* her next message read, *they're not likely to change me, mind you, but I'm sure they improve the lives of many others.*

*What would it take to change you?* he asked.

*Do I need changing?*

*No, you are perfection herself. You have reached Nirvana and cannot change, develop, or evolve any more than where you are right now.*

*Thank you. I'm glad you realize it.* She added a laughing emoji to make it clear that she wasn't serious.

*I would like you to rediscover the child within, though. That's not a change. That's a reintroduction to someone you've lost.*

*Urg.*

*Eh?*

*Urg. As in a low, guttural sound made to indicate my disapproval of that psychobabble claptrap.*

*When did you last ride a horse bareback and race the wind?*

*Like, never.*

*Liar.* Lane had seen some of the photos of her on horses when she was young. He knew she was the sort of rider who vaulted bareback onto a horse on a moonlit night and went charging around the countryside.

*When did you last do that?* Karen asked him.

*About six hours ago.* He attached some photos that Andy had taken with his phone of him, Tom, and Matt galloping bareback on three palominos in the late afternoon, with the intense reds, oranges, and yellows of the desert popping vividly from the images. They'd taken the horses for a ride down to the waterhole when Andy had pictured a scene in her head for a future ad campaign, so she had them race towards her as she snapped photos on each of their phones, then sent the images to herself so she could digitally enhance them, and she intended to pitch the photos to clients. She was sure someone would pick up on the pictures to develop them into an advertisement. Color, action, handsome young men, horses, the desert, laughter: excellent concepts to associate with any product.

*It looks fun, but I have actually grown up and left childhood behind.*

*Growing up shouldn't mean the child in us is left behind or dead to us...so much of our happiness can come from our inner child.*

*Psychobabble claptrap.* She added a gif of a small girl rolling her eyes in disdain.

*OK. It's childish, but it's fun.*

*I don't need to charge around bareback on a horse to have fun.*

*What fun do you have? Think of one thing in the past month that you can describe using the word 'fun'.* If he'd guessed correctly, Karen simply didn't do 'fun'. She worked. She was responsible and an overachiever. Everything she did, she did well. But she no longer had fun, and there was something about the notion of her always working that seemed a little sad. In some way, she had chosen a life where she was every bit as locked up as those stallions.

*I thought chatting to you late at night was fun, but not now. It's not fun now.*

Her words hit him hard. He didn't think she was joking or being manipulative or even being light-hearted. He felt that it was a cry from her heart, and he felt bad for putting pressure on her. Right now, she wasn't the high-powered executive from a large company, she was a friend, alone at night, reaching out. His musings were interrupted by a flash in the sky as a fragment of space dust streaked across the heavens, leaving a blue trail behind.

*I saw a shooting star,* he wrote, moving on from the examination-of-self that had bogged down the mood, *it was so bright it lit everything up and left a blue trail.*

*You do know that it's not a star. It would be the end of the world if an actual star shot across our atmosphere.*

*It's the end of the world as we know it.* He wondered if she knew the R.E.M. lyrics.

*And I feel fine.* Obviously, she did.

*It's like we're playing Game of Quotes and we're one for one so far.*

*That you know of,* she replied with a laughing emoji, *what if I've been doing others and you didn't find them?*

*I'm going to have to go over everything we've written now and look for them.*

*Jkn*

There was something that tickled his sense of humor about her replying with the old-fashioned shortened text for 'joking' after they'd both been writing grammatically correct sentences for so long. He could imagine her dark blue eyes with their hint of grey twinkling as she held a serious countenance, the slight raising of one eyebrow the only other indication that she was deeply amused by the small trick.

*I don't know why that seems so funny, but I'm lying on the sand laughing like a loon. And scrolling back in case I did miss quotes.*

*I'm laughing, too, for the first time in days. It feels good.*

*I imagine executive stress and contract law at your level don't lend themselves to hilarity.*

There was no reply for the space of a minute, and he wondered if there was something in his words that had offended her. It was difficult relying on text without the backup information coming from facial expressions and voice to give the words refined meaning, not that he ever had the voice to rely on, but he'd speak to her one day. Was she lying in her bed with the phone in pieces across the room? Had she just fallen asleep? Was she writing a longer than usual answer? Was she considering an answer?

Her message arrived at last. *This is strange, odd, peculiar, this texting each other in the middle of the night.*

*In what way?* He was genuinely curious about where she was going with that line of thinking and didn't want to deter her by adding his opinions. There were several minutes before a message came through, and he guessed, correctly, that she was busy writing.

*It's like I'm knowingly getting catfished, but I can't help myself. I know that you and I can't get on in real life because we are continents apart in more ways than our homelands. Yet, I chat with this version of Lane Dimity, and it's like you're my best friend, this person I can laugh with and share with, but I know it's not real. People get catfished because they think the person they're talking to is handsome, wonderful, and perfect, when they're actually nothing at all like the person they're pretending to be, but I know what you look like and what you believe, and I know there is no way we could be friends in our real lives, but here…oh, I don't know, here it's like we're friends, but we can't be. Sorry, that sounds convoluted.*

Lane read her words carefully. He understood what she meant and tried to find an explanation that would help. It was something he'd thought about often since their first session, and he believed he had a concept of what was happening in their relationship, and as intermittent and hostile as it could be, it was a relationship.

*Perhaps, alone at night, texting each other, we're talking to the essence of each other, that which lies under all the layers of our daily lives. My layers are the activist, the author, the social media guru ('urg,' to quote someone I admire), and yours are the lawyer, the Pilatos executive, and so on. Our layers are what face off across the Stablex battlefield, but our essence, our inner selves, get on perfectly well. Does that psychobabble claptrap make any sense?*

Her immediate reply was an image of someone lying on a psychoanalyst's couch with Freud looking over them, followed quickly by a sagely nodding head.

Then she wrote, *It sounds plausible enough tonight, but wait until tomorrow.*

The sentence rang a bell in his mind, so before answering, he did a quick search, then wrote the next line from the H.G. Wells novel, *Wait for the common sense of the morning.*

*You are GOOD*

*I Googled.*

*Ha ha ha.*

They continued as the earth slowly rotated under the stars, avoiding the subjects of the stallions and Stablex, and managing to spend thousands of words discussing nothing of great importance, and yet it seemed significant. As the messages flew back and forth between them, Lane began to work on a plan that would help Karen as well as the stallions because he believed that both human and horses needed to be freed. He did not know if it would change the course of Stablex, but he hadn't set out to change it all, he had seen the unjust treatment of the stallions and had known he had to do something about that.

In life, he had noticed that it was often the case that one wrongdoing grew from an earlier one and led to more, and it was easy to get lost in the enormity of all that was wrong by trying to consider the entire maze of transgressions. The fact that he was learning more about aberrant situations and events that led to the existence of the Stablex stallions, along with problems that would result from their existence, firmed his resolve to do all that he could to help them. He knew Karen wasn't ready to see the sickness that he believed lay at the heart of Pilatos Farm, but he wanted to lead her in that direction. The campaign against Stablex was about to intensify, and he knew that their friendship was likely to be blown away by the coming storm.

# CHAPTER THIRTEEN

*Free the stallions! These magnificent Friesian stallions are locked away from the sky and the fields, living in the sort of luxury as prescribed by the scientists and business people who had them surgically silenced so that their cries can never be heard. Their blood is taken to provide a drug for wealthy men so that they can outlive their female counterparts and less wealthy men. It is time to stand up and demand the stallions be freed, so all that is sick and wrong about this drug can be stopped by our morality, compassion, and empathy. Do not use violence, do not resort to hatred – just step up and be counted on the side of what is right. The spirits of these stallions are dying, and it is up to us to help them. Free the stallions.*

**Lane Dimity, in a Facebook post that was shared over fifty million times on the first day and crossed to other social media. It was reproduced in part on memes and in full on news sites and discussion pages.**

### The Pilatos Building - New York

The days following the introduction of Stablex to the world were hectic as media representatives jostled to score interviews with Pilatos executives. John employed the services of a leading public relations firm to script every meeting with the media. In addition, they advised using Karen as the company spokesperson because it was important to see a woman speaking on behalf of the drug. She did not enjoy the public attention and was busy with her other duties, but she stepped up to become the face of Stablex.

Following the instructions of their advisors, Karen downplayed the stunt on the night in Lexington, calling it the act of extremists who didn't understand the level of care granted the stallions. Representatives of various welfare groups spoke to assure the public that they were more than satisfied with the wellbeing of the horses. The media themselves appeared to accept the Pilatos version of the truth, but the general public seemed less convinced.

Demonstrators continued to build in numbers at the gates of Pilatos Farm and other Pilatos buildings and factories. At that time, there was no direct proof that Lane Dimity was mobilizing his followers, but it seemed there were growing numbers of people who believed what he said and who had no faith in either Pilatos or the welfare organizations. Their protests remained peaceful as they waved signs and placards proclaiming *Free the Stallions* and other maxims.

When Lane's 'free the stallions' message hit social media four days after the events at the Pilatos Centre in Lexington, there was a dramatic increase in the number of protesters. The four or five thousand that lined the road into Pilatos Farm were eerily silent as vehicles drove past or media filmed them. They had drawn scars on their throats, referring to the vocal cordectomies inflicted on the stallions, and even when journalists tried to interview them, they did not speak - they would only write answers to questions.

It was inevitable that the media also made the connection between the silence of the protesters and Lane's mutism. In various ways, the media reported that lacking a voice did not make the message any less loud as it reverberated around the world.

Karen found that she was being kept busy with many tasks from various sectors of Pilatos other than the pharmaceutical division that handled Stablex. She had to speak publicly about the stallions and the drug, but she didn't have the opportunity to visit the stallions or learn more about the development of the drug. She suspected her father kept her out of the way and would have challenged him over it if she had found the time or inclination to do so. As it was, she focused on the work at hand and went up to her apartment late every night, more often with a headache than without one.

Isabella made an uncharacteristic visit to New York, five days after Karen had stayed at Bisente, and watched her daughter disapprovingly as she worked through digital files, as well as folders of contracts and paperwork pertaining to the activities of Pilatos.

'You own ten percent of the company, dear,' Isabella said to her that evening as they relaxed in Karen's apartment at the end of the day. 'You need to delegate more and not take it upon yourself to check every one of those contracts.'

'It keeps me away from Stablex,' Karen shrugged, 'and I think that's what Dad is trying to do. He controls ninety percent of the company, and I don't think he trusts me to have anything to do with Stablex at present, so his ninety trumps my ten, and I do my work while he focuses on Stablex. There seems to be more talk of disloyal workers at the stables, and he's concerned my past attachment to horses will cause me to act irrationally.'

Isabella groaned in disgust at the notion that John could worry about Karen being either disloyal or irrational. 'And that is exactly why men should not live thirty years longer than women. They are quite insufferable as it is without giving them an extra few decades.'

'The way I feel at the moment,' Karen leaned back and rested her head on the back of the armchair and closed her eyes, 'I don't know why anyone would want to add thirty years to their life. I'm thirty-five, and I feel seventy.'

'Your father has never had reason to consider that he should not go on living. He'd be happy if Stablex made him immortal, and you can be confident in assuming that he is spending more money on that male immortality research than on trying to find the equivalent that works for women. As though the world isn't misogynistic enough without the kings and emperors of misogyny having thirty percent longer to live. It makes me rather ill as I think of the inequalities that this drug will cause. Quite honestly, I understand what Lane is saying, or writing, or whatever. How much have you researched the development of it?'

'Not much,' Karen shrugged. 'They found an old stallion who seemed young. They discovered he carried a gene that produced a hormone that works on XY individuals, but not us XX ones. They bred an army of stallions from that horse to get access to large quantities of the hormone produced by that gene. Therein lies the story of the Stablex stallions.'

'There's always more to any story,' Isabella narrowed her eyes and pursed her lips as she thought through what she knew. 'If there were nothing more, your father wouldn't want to keep you away from it.'

'Oh, I don't know that he's actively keeping me away from the production of Stablex; he's just keeping me busy elsewhere.'

'Hmm,' Isabella frowned at Karen's acceptance of that. 'Normally, you would object to being manipulated in such a way.'

'Normally, I'd care. But, as I've said countless times before, the horses are fine, the drug has been through all the checks, it's been safely used on trial subjects like Dad for years now.'

'And pharmaceutical companies never lie, fabricate, conceal, or alter facts in any way,' said Isabella, her voice dripping with cynicism.

'Sometimes, you have to assume they are telling the truth,' Karen pointed out. 'And it's going to make Pilatos a ridiculous amount of money as men are clamoring to get hold of the drug before its release date.'

'What does Lane have planned?'

'How would I know?' Karen snorted at the idea of knowing Lane's plans.

Isabella sighed, 'I am in contact with him, too, you know. I know he has a thing for you. He would tell you if you asked.'

Opening one eye, Karen looked at her mother with a wry expression on her face, 'I don't think he has *a thing* for me, Mother, we are simply facing off across the battlefield and enjoy a truce at times. That's all. And I'm sure he wouldn't tell me what he plans.'

'He told me he's meeting with your father tomorrow.'

That caused Karen to sit up and open both eyes. She stared silently at her mother and blinked as she digested that information.

'You didn't know?' Isabella asked her.

'No. I didn't. I was supposed to go out to Maine tomorrow to deal with more issues about the land we're buying there, but Dad told me to stay here, that's all.'

'Then he's expecting you to be available if the need arises.'

Karen tilted her head from side to side as she weighed up ideas about what was going on. 'He did want me to keep Lane neutralized and out of the way until Stablex was rolling out to the customers, but I think I failed at that job, judging by this *free the stallions* speech that's gone viral.'

Laughter tinkled from Isabella. 'How typical of John! Imagine trying to neutralize a man like Lane Dimity. No offense, darling, but even someone as beautiful and intelligent as you isn't going to deter Lane from his mission if his mission is to destroy Stablex.'

'I doubt he'll succeed at that,' Karen rubbed her temples wishing the throbbing would subside, 'the demand has already outstripped all expectations. It seems more men are willing to spend millions on adding years to their lives than we ever imagined.'

'It doesn't surprise me. I wonder if women would act the same if the drug only worked on females.'

'Interesting thought,' Karen turned her head and looked out the window at the cityscape of lights beneath a black sky. There were stars there, but she could never see them. They were hidden from view by the brightness of a billion little lights. The thought seemed to refer metaphorically to something else, but she couldn't identify what that was at this moment. Damn this headache; it made it hard to think. She rubbed her temples again.

'As a mother,' said Isabella, her eyes soft as she regarded her daughter, 'I know that if I could take a drug that would mean I'd watch my child die of old age before me, I would not take it. I would think any woman who had a son would be reluctant to take a drug that could not also add the years to his life. Sadly, it doesn't surprise me that John is taking Stablex. He will watch you, his daughter, age, weaken, and die while he takes his strength from those stallions, injecting their spirit into his life.'

'Dramatic, much?' Karen asked dryly, raising a brow at her mother. *'Injecting their spirit into his life* – is that a Lane quote? You do realize it's merely a hormone harvested from their blood. It's not their spirit. Anyway, you know I don't believe in that spirit and soul stuff.'

'You used to.'

'I used to believe in the Tooth Fairy, too, Mother.' Karen leaned back again and closed her eyes.

'Headache?'

'All the time of late.'

'You should take a month off and come home to Bisente. Relax, enjoy the country, maybe ride a horse. Pick out any horse. You liked that little chestnut, Shandy – ride him. If you like him, I promise not to sell him out from under you. He'll be yours for life.'

'God, I used to hate it when Dad sold my horses.'

'I know, I'm sorry,' Isabella apologized, remembering back to those times when Karen's ponies and horses were sent away, and hearing the sobs coming from her room night after night. 'I was young, I didn't realize that I could stand up to your father. He would say that it would toughen you up and help you survive in this world. Maybe it did. I don't know. If I could, I would go back in time and make sure you didn't have to give up any one of those horses.'

'It was so long ago, it doesn't matter anymore,' Karen murmured, her thoughts drifting to the horses that belonged to a child called Karen who loved them more than her human friends, a child who rode bareback on moonlit nights and believed that the world could be conquered from the back of a good horse. That child seemed to live in a world of bright colors and hopes and dreams, and, yes, she believed that her horses had souls that would wait for her in heaven.

Silly child, she spoke to that innocent of long ago who remained as a ghost in her mind, your father was right. You had to toughen up to survive in this world. You have ambition, not hope. You have plans, not dreams. Horses die, and their souls are not waiting for you in heaven.

'It does matter,' Isabella said, moving to stand behind Karen's chair and placing her cool fingertips on her daughter's temples. She massaged gently, pushing the ache back into her hair, trying to take the pain into her fingers. 'Loving your horses and believing that they had souls was not a weakness, my sweet, it was your strength. Believing in the love you had for those horses was the beauty of your heart, and your father couldn't understand it, so he removed it.'

'My heart?' Karen smiled, her eyes still closed, trying to make light of the conversation. The headache was easing under her mother's touch.

'No, silly,' Isabella snorted and tapped a finger on Karen's temple to gently admonish her for her levity, 'he removed the things you loved.'

'How different do you think I'd be if he hadn't done that?' Karen asked in a small voice, wondering for a brief moment about possible lives that had been taken from her by those actions of her father.

'You would still be you,' Isabella assured her, 'but you wouldn't have to hide under all this grey and all the serious masks and the hard shell that you need in this world. You would have laughed more and worn color and been every bit as successful, as it's always been in your nature to be so, but your father wanted a clone of him, not a feminine, outspoken, funny, warm, colorful woman who rode horses and loved life. He couldn't destroy that woman, but he was able to bury her under all this...' she waved her hand around the apartment, taking in the grey clothes, the neutral decor, the very building itself that represented Pilatos.

For a few minutes, Karen remained silent, enjoying the mothering that had been absent for most of her life. Right now, she thought, I feel like Isabella's daughter, not someone who touches the edges of her life, but someone who grew inside her body and was given life from her: we are mother and daughter, entwined in life together. A warmth grew in her chest, and she was aware that she was feeling love. It hadn't gone from her life, it was still there; it had lain dormant, hiding away at her core, so that this brutal corporate life could not obliterate it.

'That's helped my headache. Thanks.'

'I should have been removing your headaches long before this,' Isabella withdrew her hands and returned to her chair. 'Perhaps I can start to make up for it. Will you come and stay for more than a night and perhaps take that chestnut out for a ride?'

'Maybe,' Karen nodded sleepily, her lips quirking, 'but I still don't think he has a soul.'

'Of course not,' Isabella smiled, 'this world you've chosen is a soulless place.'

With a maternal gentleness that had been lacking when Karen was young, Isabella put her to bed and retired to her apartment next door. It was always kept ready for her, but she rarely visited New York these days.

The next morning, Karen chose an Emporio Armani outfit of cream pants and shirt with a thigh-length grey jacket, twisted her hair up onto the top of her head, grabbed a tub of yogurt and went down to her office early. There was a pile of papers on the left side of her desk to work through before lunch and more files on her laptop. As she signed off on the paper versions, they went to the right of her desk, a simple routine, but it helped her move through it as swiftly as possible. Sandy would take the pile from that side of the desk and file or send them to where they belonged.

She paused halfway through a page detailing contract details on a new shopping mall and thought that there was no reason why Sandy couldn't do most of this work. It had already gone through the Pilatos legal department and only came through her as a final check, something her father had instituted as he believed in family keeping control in a family company and knowing everything that was taking place. Sandy had worked here for longer than she had and was every bit as smart as the majority of people with a law degree, and she had lived and breathed this work for many years.

Putting her pen down, she buzzed for Sandy, and within seconds, the door opened.

'Sandy, are you ready for a pay rise?'

Sandy's dark brown eyebrows shot up towards her dark brown hair that was neatly arranged. She nodded, 'I'm always ready for that.'

'Good,' Karen motioned towards the left side of her desk, 'find an assistant to take over most of your work and then sit here at my desk and go through these. There are a few more files on the laptop, too – you made up the USB, so you'll know which ones. I'm only checking up on work that is already done. There are occasional changes I make or suggest. I tend to cross-reference different deals and contracts and people in case there's a pattern emerging of which I should be aware, and I look at the financials when something niggles at me. Do you know what I mean?'

Sandy nodded confidently, 'I've been working with you for a lot of years now, Karen, I know what you do and what you look for. I've seen the things you've highlighted, and I've chased up the information that you've felt prompted to find. I know what to do.'

Karen stood, stretched her shoulders back, and smiled, feeling her muscles release some of their tension. 'Good. You're now earning an extra fifty thousand a year, and until I find you a better office, you'll be sharing my desk. Go through these and think like me. If you find anything worth bringing to my notice, just make a third pile somewhere.'

Unruffled, as always, Sandy calmly stepped forward and slipped into Karen's chair as she vacated it.

'You might want to go to your father's office,' Sandy looked up at her employer, her brown eyes astute. 'I heard that Lane Dimity and his friends were due to arrive about now. I notice that we haven't received a memo about it, but I imagine you will be interested in how that goes.'

'How right you are,' Karen nodded. 'I wonder why they're coming to the lion's den... it seems a little foolhardy given the recent actions and posts against Pilatos.'

'Lane knows what he's doing,' said Sandy with a show of faith that surprised Karen.

'Are you a fan, Sandy?'

Sandy blushed slightly and looked down at the paper in front of her, 'He's a fascinating man, Karen. I like some of the things he writes. I don't like his attacks on Pilatos, of course, but, you know, I wouldn't like to be married to a man who was using Stablex, if you don't mind me saying.'

'Between you and me,' Karen tapped the side of her nose to indicate a secret, 'I wouldn't want to be married to one, either.'

Leaving Sandy at her desk going through the work felt like the right thing to do, as though life's problems were one large combination lock and the first pin had clicked into place. She would clear it with her father, of course, and the work would still be completed to the high standard he expected. He would still be apprised of anything that hinted at problems, and she would know what was going on in the company, so there would be no change for the worse. She trusted Sandy. Distrust was one of the traits that her father believed paved the way to success, but she realized now, at this moment, that perhaps trust had more of a place than her father was willing to assign.

For a long minute, Karen stood outside her father's office. No voices could be heard, but the soundproofing was excellent, so there was little chance of hearing anyone beyond that door. Her hand went to the right hip pocket of the jacket, and she felt the silk scarf Lane had given her. It was far too bright to be worn, but she felt an element of comfort in having it on her person where she could touch it if she wished. For a second, she envisioned taking it out and wearing it jauntily around her neck, but this was not a place of frivolity and brightness, so she gave it one last pat, took her hand out, and opened the door.

She did not knock. If her father wanted privacy, he locked the door.

The tableau inside the office consisted of seven people in two groups, blue jeans versus suits, facing each other across her father's enormous desk, and there was an entire story to be told from her first glance. Lane, Matt, Andy, and Tom were seated on four straight-backed chairs, side by side, in front of the desk. Opposite them, standing, stood her father, his body language declaring that he was the emperor of this room, the king, the principal, the head honcho. His shoulders were back, and his chin raised. Every inch of his body demanded that homage be paid to him as the dominant being in this group.

Behind her father, leaning against the window was Joe; his eyes narrowed as he regarded Lane and his friends. His body appeared relaxed as he stood, arms crossed and legs apart, but Karen knew that, like a cat, he was always poised for action. At her father's shoulder stood BJ, one of his favorite dog-loyal assistants whose specialties were accounting and brown-nosing. He was another she had little time for, though she appreciated his ability to find errors accidentally or deliberately hidden in a thousand figures.

Although there were chairs available, BJ, like John and Joe, remained standing as though to remind those sitting down that everyone at Pilatos was higher than they were. The intent failed miserably as the three Australians and Tom managed to sprawl in their chairs as though they were at home in front of the television, comfortable and relaxed. There was something almost insolent in the way the younger men sat. Matt with his right ankle crossed over his left knee, Lane with both his legs splayed out in front of him, and Tom leaning back with his left arm on the back of Lane's chair, his right on Andy's chair. Andy had her legs and arms crossed, looking up at the three suits with a slightly amused expression on her face as she regarded their intimidating stances like she might look at toddlers trying to be threatening.

All faces turned towards her as she entered, but only Lane's face showed any sign of being pleased to see her. She did not allow her gaze to linger on him any longer than it stopped on the others, only coming to rest when she met those deep blue eyes so similar to hers. An infinitesimal tuck at the edge of her father's mouth indicated that he was irritated that she had turned up unannounced and uninvited, and a hardening of her eyes told him that she didn't care.

'I heard there was an interesting meeting taking place this morning,' she nodded at her father, 'and as one of the owners of Pilatos, I thought I'd like to sit in.'

'Me, too,' a soft voice spoke from behind Karen.

She turned to see Isabella standing there, hands on her hips, smiling broadly at John Lawford. A quick glance at her father saw him battling to maintain his neutral façade and not glower at the small and feisty Isabella, dressed in a flaming red dress that would have looked more at home in a Parisian fashion show than in a business meeting.

'Isabella,' John growled her name, then nodded at his daughter. 'Karen. I believe you both know everyone.'

'Wonderful to see you all again,' Isabella said effusively, smiling at the four who were sitting. Seriousness dropped like a shade over her face as she turned to those standing, 'John, BJ, Joe.'

'Take a seat,' John motioned to a couple of chairs on his side of the desk.

'I believe I'll stand if that's alright with you,' Isabella tilted her head coquettishly at John and laughed provokingly. 'Of course, it is alright with you. You're standing. Mind you, I don't really understand why you're standing, looking like some predator waiting for the deer to come to your waterhole.'

John's eyes narrowed in warning, but Isabella waved a hand airily at him as though shooing him away. 'You are altogether too serious, John. What's the point in living thirty years longer if you spend it being angry?'

Andrea snorted a laugh, and Karen cleared her throat and gave her mother a look that pleaded with her to not antagonize her father too much. She wasn't sure at what point in life Isabella had gone from being the quiet wife who acquiesced to all her husband's wishes to this jaunty creature who delighted in tormenting the man, but it was a change that did not win favor with John Lawford. Clearly, Isabella did not care.

'Karen,' John motioned to the chair next to him, expecting her to take it.

Her habitual reaction was to follow his instruction and sit, but as she took a step towards the chair, Isabella placed a restraining hand on her arm.

'You know,' Isabella said reflectively, 'I think I might sit. Would you be a dear, BJ, and pull that chair around here to the end of this desk.' She patted the wood and batted her eyelids at her husband. 'Such a big desk, John! It must be bigger than anyone else's.'

Another odd sound came from Andrea. John's response was to stare at his wife without speaking, his expression stony.

'We could both sit here,' Isabella continued merrily, looking around as though noticing how much room there was at the end of the desk. 'What do you think, dear? We two Pilatos girls can sit here at the side, sort of like umpires at a tennis match.'

Karen looked to her father to see his reaction, but he merely shook his head as though despairing at finding any sense in his wife.

'BJ,' John nodded at two of the spare chairs, and BJ quickly moved them to the end of the desk for Karen and her mother.

'Do go on,' Isabella told John airily, then laughed playfully. 'Oh, listen to me, telling you to continue! You go on all the time without me urging you to do so.'

The four visitors to Pilatos seemed fascinated by the exchange, with Isabella chatting lightly and John glowering darkly. John Lawford was a daunting figure, standing behind his desk like a warrior king defending his kingdom, but Isabella seemed to have no concerns about teasing him. The man almost looked slightly perplexed by it, as though he was used to his scowling countenance frightening others into silence, and this chatty, laughing creature offered up something he was not equipped to handle.

They didn't realize that Isabella was quaking on the inside. She had never dared to speak to John in this fashion or challenge him in any way. It wasn't that he had ever been violent or threatening with her. It was more that she felt violence was never far beneath his surface. He had such an ingrained expectation of the females around him being subservient that he didn't know how much fear he could engender in them with a disapproving look or raised brow of inquiry. It was apparent now, in this moment of mischievous mocking from Isabella, that he lacked the tools to deal with a woman behaving insubordinately and without the respect that he took as his due.

In a moment of clarity, Isabella realized that this is what Karen should have seen growing up: a female role model who did not have to become like the men in order to work with the men or to challenge her father. Strong women came in all packages, in dresses as well as suits, with giggles as well as frowns, with compassion as well as callousness. The choice of how to behave in this man's world of business was never offered to Karen: to succeed, she believed she had to act like them. It wasn't even a *belief* as much as *acceptance*. If it had merely been a belief, she would have known that there were choices to that belief, that she could have remained true to herself and allowed her world to adapt to her rather than automatically adapting everything about herself to fit into that male world.

Looking at the Pilatos men standing so aggressively, Isabella knew this really was a male world. They would have scoffed if she had called them chauvinistic, but where were the women in Pilatos? Karen, the highest-ranking woman, wore colorless suits and blended into the background. The other women tended to be assistants. It was an equal opportunity workplace, but thinking and behaving like men was expected. If a woman turned up with flouncy dresses and laughter, she was not considered suitable. If a woman turned up with a baby, the workplace would not adapt to her. There was no creche in this building. This was not a workplace for mothers. There was no allowance for a woman being wonderfully, uniquely female. There was no mindfulness of compassion and generosity or of working together as groups of women had worked together throughout history. It was all about a male leader who dominated all the way down the chain. It was about greed, success, testosterone, and control.

The thoughts tumbled over each other in Isabella's mind as the epiphany rolled through her. The successful women had to submerge their estrogen beneath a layer of testosterone to succeed in this world, but it was still called 'equal opportunity.' Yes, if those women were prepared to forget they had ovaries and grew a set of balls, she grimaced internally at the offensive words but knew them to be true. And by withdrawing to Bisente and being obsequious to John, she had let her daughter lose her female identity, she hadn't provided the role model that could have shown Karen that there was a choice between adapting herself to this male world of business that had not changed in essence for two thousand years, and forcing this world to adjust to her as a woman.

It became clear in those moments as she sat observing the people around her what Lane had meant when he told her that her daughter was every bit as imprisoned as the stallions. How could Karen know if this was the life she wanted if she had no concept of alternatives? John had shaped her, bit by bit, with disapproval for this and approval for that so that she fitted into his world. She should have been able to see that the world could also change for her if that is what she wished. If she wanted to be a mother and have mothers working alongside her, then Pilatos should adapt to the needs of mothers...but it didn't change, it just claimed to be 'equal opportunity,' as long as all those who wanted to succeed changed themselves to fit the expectations that had always been there.

Never underestimate the fight in a mother, she said to herself as she looked at John with an innocent expression covering her deep thoughts. I may be decades late in realizing what I have to fight for, but I will be fighting.

'We were discussing our impact on Pilatos,' explained Andy, looking at Karen and Isabella. 'Understandably, Mr. Lawford wants us to desist with our campaign, but he insists that we are not having an effect on Stablex. Equally understandably, we believe that Lane's *free the stallions* post yesterday is going to have an effect.'

Isabella clapped her hands together like a delighted child, 'What exciting times! The Goliath of Pilatos versus four people with social media power. It's like you four are David, and your sling and stone is social media.'

'It's nothing like that,' growled John, his intense disapproval of his wife's bubbling presence oozing out of him but having no effect on her.

'Nonsense, John,' Isabella shooed him with her hand again, 'it is exactly like that. Pilatos is a giant on this battlefield, and look at these four beautiful people. They aren't our competition; they aren't a corporation or a government department – they are simply four people who don't like what is being done with those stallions. Twenty years ago, their voices would have counted for nothing, now their voices get multiplied fifty million times, a hundred million times, and we are forced to listen.'

'Isabella,' John seemed to loom over her even though he hadn't moved, 'I would prefer it if you left this meeting.'

Everyone held their breath as the unspoken threat seemed to swim around beneath the surface of his words. Karen looked back and forth between her parents with no small measure of astonishment. She had no idea of what was going on, but she could not believe that her mother had chosen this time, in front of these people, to stand up to her father. It wouldn't end well; she knew it. Her father always won.

'John,' Isabella said sweetly, shoving her quivering anxiety down to her womb, the one her daughter had grown in, 'remind me again. You have control of ninety percent of Pilatos, is that correct?'

There was a surprising hesitation as John seemed to mentally masticate those words carefully, chewing ten times before swallowing.

'Correct.'

'As of this moment, consider that control of sixty percent,' Isabella leveled a stare at him, the lioness within revealing herself. 'I believe, if you check the documentation my lawyer drew up giving you control of my thirty percent of Pilatos, you will find on page sixteen a small paragraph that states, in effect, that I can overturn that and resume control of my share of the company any time I desire, without notice. Naturally, you assumed that the time would never come as long as I was playing around on Bisente with my horses, but guess what, John? This is the time. I believe I want to stay at this meeting and be a part of the decision making.'

For several silent seconds, they stared at each other before John's gaze dropped to Karen. 'Did you know about this?'

She raised her hands defensively, 'Don't look at me. It's news to me, too.'

With a slow intake of breath, John kept control of his emotions. Isabella's announcement had no impact on this meeting, apart from those present witnessing an unsavory disagreement that should never have taken place. He was still in control.

'Your campaign is an annoyance,' he spoke down to Lane and his friends. 'We offered to pay you to assist us in providing those stallions with the level of care you believe they need, but you refused to work with us. You need to realize that no matter what you say publicly, it will not impact the sales of Stablex, but, I admit, it is an irritation. My concern is that you may move beyond using words against us and damage our facilities or contaminate our product. Clearly, you have people within our corporation prepared to work for you, as demonstrated last week, and without being able to determine how many more you may have corrupted, we have agreed to meet here to try and work something out.'

*We want the stallions set free,* Lane's hands spoke, *no more throats cut, and remove the permanent cannulas.*

Karen discreetly watched what he signed and checked that against Matt's words.

'We want to see the stallions set free, and there are to be no more vocal cordectomies and no more permanent cannulas. The cannulas cause a high risk of bleeding out if the stallions damage them.'

'Impossible,' John said firmly. 'Those stallions are far too valuable to be running around in paddocks, where they increase their risk of injury and death. Also, we are facing a massive threat from pharmaceutical espionage, and we are unable to provide the required level of security for them outdoors. The gene that is unique to these horses will be the most sought-after property in pharmaceuticals, so we must keep the stallions stabled where we can provide the highest level of security.'

*Total bull,* signed Lane, his fingers moving savagely, though there was no hint of anger in his eyes, *that entire farm has security that is more than adequate to protect those stallions while they are out in paddocks.*

'Lane wonders why they can't be adequately protected in the Pilatos fields,' said Matt, 'the perimeter of security fences, surveillance, guards, and dogs seems to provide enough security for them.'

'That's not enough,' John shook his head as though explaining basics to children, 'you need to have a concept of the billions of dollars at stake here and the desire of other companies to get a share.'

'Aren't they likely to get that,' queried Isabella, 'whether the stallions are stabled or in fields? Surely the weak point lies in our staff releasing material, not someone stealing a field full of stallions.'

'You don't understand,' John looked at her witheringly, before his eyes swept the others, 'none of you understand. We have done all we can to make those stallions comfortable without compromising the security of this firm. Your claim that their spirits are dying might make exciting headlines for horse lovers, but there is no more substance to that than someone claiming angels, ghosts, aliens, and leprechauns are real. It sounds like a wonderful idea, but there's no proof.'

For the next ten minutes, the discussion went around and around the same ground, with neither side relenting. John claimed they would not harm the sales of Stablex or change the conditions of the stallions. Lane asserted that their campaign had only begun and would damage Pilatos. Finally, John hit the desk with his hand and stopped the pointless back and forth discussion that achieved nothing.

'Tell me what it will take,' he demanded, 'to get you to back off and leave our company alone. Tell me something achievable.'

After some quiet conferring, Matt raised his eyes to John and cleared his throat, 'Lane would like you to spend five or six days with him seeing how other stallions are housed, and seeing how conditions for yours could be improved.'

'No,' John shook his head, 'I don't have a day to spare, and it would serve no point.'

'The point would be,' Matt spoke after watching Lane sign, 'that you could show the world that you care about your stallions, and you tried to learn more about them to improve their lives.'

'That would be a total waste of time,' John scoffed, looking at BJ to see the ridicule reflected there, as he knew it would be, 'I don't need to go and see other people's horses.'

'You asked for something achievable,' continued Matt, 'and this seemed like something that was possible. Give us five days, and during that time, we will stop all social media attacks on Pilatos and ask our protesters to back away.'

That caught John's attention. He turned his steely gaze to Joe, who gave the slightest of nods. Anything to slow the growing tsunami of public enmity would be worth taking if it could be bought cheaply enough.

'Take Karen instead of me,' he countered, ignoring the flash of surprise on his daughter's face. It would suit him to keep her away from Stablex for the better part of a week, as his gut told him that when it came to those horses, she might claim to be logical and concerned with facts, but she was likely to let emotions interfere with judgment.

Having her go on the fool's journey with Dimity would be a small price to pay for a break from his campaign.

'No,' said Karen, adamantly.

Lane looked to be considering the substitution, then shook his head and made it clear that he wanted John to accompany him.

'Lane thinks,' said Matt, 'that it's important for you, Mr. Lawford, as the face of Stablex, to show the public that you are attempting to learn more about the welfare of the stallions.'

Lane was not about to let on that Karen was the one he wanted. He understood men like John well enough to realize that the key to having him agree to something was to make him feel that he had won the negotiations. As he sat, blandly regarding the man across the table, he could almost see his thoughts. Calling him the *face of Stablex* and making reference to the public was a way to put those images together in his mind so that he would make the connection to Karen, who had been the face of Stablex in the media since the night in Lexington. John wanted Lane's followers to back off for five days, and he didn't want his daughter around those stallions, so the result was predictable.

'Impossible!' John declared, 'I can't afford the time away. None of us do. But, Karen,' he turned to his daughter, 'you can move your schedule around and go. You're the one the public sees on the news when Stablex is being discussed, so you can be the one they see trying to learn more about horse welfare.'

'Absolutely not!' she exclaimed, astonished her father would suggest such a thing. 'I don't have enough time to do the work I'm already doing. I can't take five days or six days off just to learn about how other people's stallions are being cared for.'

'If these people,' John waved an imperious hand at the four opposite him, 'can guarantee to call their protesters away and stop their campaign against us for the time that one of us is with them, then you can find a way to delegate or postpone your work. You will be the Pilatos representative to go.'

Lane appeared to be unhappy about the suggestion, which made John more determined that his idea would be the one adopted.

'It's that or nothing,' John glowered at everyone. 'You get a Pilatos executive to go with you. We get relief from the protesters and your opinions. If you don't agree, that's fine – the future of Stablex is already assured, and you and your groupies are merely an annoyance that we can work around.'

With a frown, Lane nodded reluctantly, agreeing to John's terms.

John began moving towards the door, talking as he walked. 'This meeting is over. Karen, you can go with them as you will be buying time for Stablex. You agree,' he glanced at Lane and his friends, 'to cease making any reference to Stablex or Pilatos or those stallions for the next week and call those protesters away from our gates.'

Offering a shrug as though backed into a corner but accepting the conditions, Lane held out his hand to shake on the deal.

Ignoring the outstretched hand, John said, 'I'll have that agreement drawn up for you to sign before you leave. And, Karen,' he showed her the palm of his hand to silence her objections, 'you're the obvious choice for this as you've been the face on the media. Also, you know more about horses than I do, so go with them and find the flaws in their arguments. If by chance, you do end up with any suggestions to alter the conditions of the stallions within the parameters of what we expect for security, then we'll work on that.'

With a final nod to the others in the office, he called BJ to heel and said he had other matters to attend to, but they could stay in his office until someone brought the papers for Lane to sign.

'Isabella,' he nodded at his wife, a slight look of disappointment on his face.

'Lovely to see you, as always,' Isabella smiled cheerily at him, glad to be free of the cold dread that used to clutch at her whenever he showed disappointment.

After John and BJ left, Joe remained in the same position, quietly watching over everyone. Karen stood and moved to the window to look out as she wanted time to cover her seething emotions at being traded off to these people by her father. It had been humiliating, and she tried to conceal any evidence of that feeling before engaging in conversation with anyone.

'You needed a break,' Isabella's positive voice reached out to Karen, 'five days away from here will be good for you.'

'You think?' Karen turned, the neutral mask firmly in place. 'I had hoped to get my work done, not waste my time - no offense, Lane - looking at horses.'

*Tell her that it will be more than looking at horses*, Lane signed, *explain that I want to give her the chance to rediscover that horses do have souls.*

'Lane says that it isn't about looking at horses,' Matt put his spin on Lane's message, 'it's about reconnecting with them and learning to understand their needs.'

'They need food, water, shelter, exercise, vet treatment when required, a farrier and regular worming,' Karen replied dryly, not buying into their spiritual beliefs, 'all of which are provided at Pilatos Farm. So, I hope that while you are trying to convince me of your ethereal notions, you will be open to my ideas based on facts and science.'

Tom stood, stretched, and looked down at Lane, raising his brows, 'And you want to spend five days with her? Better you than me, man.'

'Charming,' Karen sniffed, not missing the implication that Lane wanted to spend this time with her. She focused on him, 'Is this what you intended all along? To have me go with you on a horse tour?'

Lane lifted one shoulder in a *maybe* movement.

'And who else is coming if Tom's not going to be there?'

'Not me,' said Matt quickly.

'And I'm going to be busy getting the demonstrators to stand down,' put in Andy.

'Wonderful,' Karen looked at her mother, and another suspicion formed. 'Did you know, Mother? Did you know that this was the intended outcome of this meeting? That I was going to be sent off on this wild goose chase?'

'It's not a wild goose chase, dear,' Isabella sidestepped the questions. 'I doubt you'll be seeing any geese, much less chasing them. I've thought for ages that you are working too hard, so a few days traveling the world looking at stallions will be a good thing.'

'The world?'

'Not all of it,' Isabella smiled, 'what did you tell me, Lane...Vienna and the stallion drive at Rauris Valley in Austria?'

Lane nodded.

'So, you see,' Isabella continued with maddening jollity, 'not all the world, just here and there.'

'Several moves ahead,' Karen muttered to herself as she turned back to the window, too infuriated by the manipulations around her to continue talking to any of them.

Joe leaned towards her and said softly, 'I thought we were the ones who were meant to be several moves ahead in this game.'

'Don't start,' she warned him, glancing sideways to see an unexpected gleam in his eyes.

'Don't be too upset by it,' he advised gently, 'they are outside the realm of what we are used to. It's like playing chess with pigeons – it doesn't matter what moves you make, you're going to end up with pigeon poop.'

Karen sniffed in wry amusement at his comment, 'So, I guess that is what I've ended up with.'

'Seems like it,' he nodded and gave the briefest narrowing of one eye as though he'd almost winked at her. It surprised her.

**Pilatos Farm**

### Jacinta and Nia

'I don't know how much more I can take of this,' Jacinta whispered to Nia as they waited for the commuter bus to pick them up after their shift at the stables.

Nia looked around nervously to see who might be listening in on their conversation. Most seemed to be further than an overheard whisper away, but she had become paranoid about listening devices, so motioned to Jacinta to follow her away from the bus shelter. With its artistic design and busy swirls and patterns, it would be easy to hide a microphone to catch out unwary employees plotting against Pilatos.

'Another one?' Nia asked, trying to smile as though she was asking about a recipe or family matter.

'The one I call Hugo,' Jacinta nodded. 'There wasn't much warning. He was fine yesterday, then this morning, he looked exhausted and tired. Shortly after lunch, he lay down and died.'

Nia cursed, then asked, 'What the hell is happening?'

'I don't know, but I can't take it anymore. I'm going to resign.

'No. No, don't do that. You'll hate yourself for leaving the other horses.'

'But it's killing me,' Jacinta wiped away a tear, pretending for anyone else watching that she had something in her eye. 'I love these horses. I can't handle standing there and watching them die.'

'L.D. will do something,' Nia nodded with conviction, 'I know he will. We need to wait for him to act.'

'He called off the protesters this morning,' Jacinta shrugged, not understanding what was going on. 'Do you think he got bought off by the Lawfords?'

For a few seconds, Nia considered this possibility before shaking her head, 'No, absolutely not. He's going to save these stallions; I know he will. If he's called the protesters off, it must be because he's up to something else. We need to stay put until we know what he's doing. Have you tried contacting him?'

'I will this evening. Not from home, though. I'll go to town and use a computer in the library.'

'Let him know there are two of us,' Nia told her, 'actually, there's probably more. I know some of the fellows in the workshop are tired of seeing their forklifts carting the bodies of the stallions over for autopsies.'

'I don't know if my message will get through,' Jacinta finished quickly as the bus pulled up, 'but the others in my stable block would come on board. It's breaking them, too, seeing what is happening.'

**Pilatos Farm**
**Noah and Abhirka**

Noah walked into the staff kitchenette like someone drunk, one hand on the doorframe as he entered, then the other reaching for the counter to steady himself as he took a step towards the sink. He began salivating uncontrollably, so knew he was close to vomiting. He grabbed at the door under the sink, opened it, and reached for one of the empty ice-cream containers stored there. Falling to his knees, he held the container in front of him and began retching.

'Noah!' exclaimed Abhirka, running into the room behind him. She had been waiting to assist him with another autopsy and had expected him ten minutes ago, so she had come looking for him. 'What is wrong? Have you been poisoned?'

He managed to wave one hand to indicate that he had not.

'Are you ill?' she asked, taking a hand towel and running it under cold water so she could give it to him to wipe his face when he was ready.

'No,' he mumbled as he gained control of his heaving.

'Here,' she offered him the towel.

Wiping his face, he took a deep breath and noticed that his hands were shaking.

'So, what is wrong?' Abhirka insisted, adding in an attempt to lighten the mood. 'Was it that dish the canteen called *curry* that you ate at lunch? I can tell you that is not curry.'

'Let me get rid of this,' he motioned at the bowl.

'No, no, no,' she shook her head, 'you will tell me now. If you wander off to the bathroom to clean that, you will think of what not to say when you get back. Tell me now.'

'You're probably right; it was most likely lunch. I'll go clean up.'

With a deft movement, Abhirka removed the sick bowl from his hands and smiled at him when he gave her an alarmed look, clearly concerned that she was handling his vomit.

She waved away his objections, 'I have cleaned up enough stomach contents in my time as the older sister to several brothers. This does not worry me. But you do. Your hands are shaking, Noah – something has happened. Tell me.'

'Nothing happened,' he denied, 'my stomach is just a bit weaker than it used to be. Autopsies make me ill.'

'Well, of course, the number we've been doing of them of late makes me ill, too, but, Noah, you are not telling me the truth. Perhaps, if you were sick *after* this autopsy, that might be a bit more believable.'

Noah sat on the floor with a resigned slump of the shoulders, his back against the cupboards, his head bent down. Abhirka placed the bowl on the sink and filled a glass from the water cooler, and handed it to him. Then, she sat next to him, waiting silently. She knew that, sometimes, a person needed a minute or two to collect their thoughts and begin to talk. It was clear Noah needed to talk.

'I can't tell you what I saw,' he murmured in a dull voice. 'because of security clearances. Uh, who am I kidding? That's not the reason I can't tell you, I'd ignore that, it's just that I *saw* something today, and I want to forget that I ever saw it. The chief vet in the research area - in the white cube - has been away this week, and they called me in to help with a problem. A horse. I...I...' His voice dwindled away, and his hands began to shake again.

'There was a horse?' she enquired.

'I think I need to leave. Leave here. Leave Pilatos,' he looked up at the walls of the kitchenette. 'I always think there are microphones and hidden cameras. I'm always performing autopsies. Wondering why the horses are dying. And today.' His voice caught, and he wiped a hand across his eyes. 'I can't work for them anymore.'

'You need to stay,' Abhirka whispered, mindful that there could be microphones in the kitchenette. 'I spoke to Lane's friend, Tom Claw, yesterday. They are going to free the stallions. They are. We need to be here for that. We can help.'

Noah shook his head, 'I want to believe that, but it's hard. It's all too hard. You know, I became a vet because I loved horses. Now, I want to stop having anything to do with being a vet because I love horses.'

Seeing how deeply upset he was over whatever he had witnessed, Abhirka patted his hand gently. 'I have faith in Lane, Noah. Let us stay here and see what he does. Perhaps everything will work out.'

'No,' he sighed, despair in his voice, 'it won't all work out. Not for the horses.'

'Yes, it will. Sometimes we have to have faith.'

He raised his eyes to hers like a drowning man reaching for the rope that had been thrown to him. 'This place needs to be shut down.'

'Yes. And we will help do that. For now, we have work to do.'

# CHAPTER FOURTEEN

*You learn a lot about a horse by taking the time to sit down and watch him.*
*Your horse is communicating all the time – he's speaking his language, not*
*yours, and you need to take the time to learn what he is saying.*
**'Ride With Heart' by Lane Dimity, p.41**

### New York to Vienna

Within hours of the meeting at the Pilatos Building, Karen was
heading to the airport to board a direct flight to Vienna. She had
expected to have another night to prepare, but working with Lane was
like being swept along by a flood, and it was easier to go with the flow
than fight the current. It seemed he had organized the flights in
advance of the meeting, so was arrogant enough to believe his plans
would work.

The flight left New York in the late afternoon, and with time zones
adjusted, would have them in Vienna by eight, local time, the next
morning. It was organized for her without any input from her and paid
for by Lane. She tended to forget how wealthy his books had made
him, she thought, as Sandy handed her the Business Class tickets on
their way to the airport. Not surprising, she told herself wryly, since he
liked to behave like a broke-arse cowboy most of the time.

Sandy accompanied Karen as far as the airport, taking notes as
Karen ran through all the things to be done in her absence. With such
a quickly organized trip, there were sure to be things that she forgot,
but she and Sandy would remain in contact, and much of the work
could be done on her laptop anywhere in the world.

As Pearce drove away with Sandy, leaving Karen standing at the
airport with her carry-on luggage, she was hit by the realization that
this was madness: she'd woken that day with an expectation of another

day at work, not a flight to Europe with a man she barely knew. With a great exhale of breath, she resigned herself to getting on with the journey, and, forcing her shoulders back and chin up, she walked smartly to the departure area. She was glad that the Business Class tickets gave her a speedy trip to the members' lounge, where she drank a glass of wine to settle her nerves. She wasn't worried about flying, but there was a certain trepidation about traveling with a man who infuriated and intrigued her in equal parts.

She did not see Lane until after she'd been seated on the plane for ten minutes, and, finally, he boarded with the last of the passengers. It occurred to her that he might not turn up, and she wasn't sure if that made her glad, sad, or downright furious, but he turned up, almost a head taller than the passengers around him, all of whom seemed to know him and competed for his attention. His blue jeans and checked shirt looked so country next to the urbane outfits of the rich and famous who surrounded him, but he wore them with such confidence that it somehow made the designer clothes look pretentious.

When he reached the seat next to her, she nodded to him silently, her eyes hard, wanting him to know that she was not happy about this. No, not in any way. At least the flight attendants seemed pleased about his presence as they helped him into his seat.

Eight and a half hours of this, Karen fought the impulse to roll her eyes and, instead, turned her head to look out the window as two flight attendants fussed over him. In the seats in front of them, she could see a movie star and two sporting stars who weren't receiving the attention that was being lavished on Lane. Of course, they hadn't shown that dazzling smile and clear appreciation that Lane had offered. He was just so darned friendly, she mused, like a Golden Retriever, pleased to see everyone, and they responded in kind.

'Let us know if there's anything you need, Mr. Dimity,' the willowy blonde smiled down at him, her eyes shining.

*Lane*, he signed with another stunning smile.

'Lane,' she uttered softly, her cheeks dimpling.

Oh, of course, they understand sign language, Karen forced her eyes to remain facing forward and not roll back in her head.

'I'm reading *Ride With Heart* for the third time,' breathed the brunette. Poppy, according to her name tag. 'I swear it's the best book I've ever read.'

If not the only one, Karen thought with sourness as she gazed at the tarmac, since it was more interesting than watching two women simpering over the Australian horseman.

His hands moved again, and Karen had to tilt her head slightly to see what he was saying. The reflection in the window was too confusing with its reversal of everything.

*Thank you. How's that bay horse going?*

'You remembered!' Poppy exclaimed, clearly delighted that Lane had remembered her from a previous encounter. 'He's a different horse since you helped me, isn't he, Liana?'

'Absolutely,' she enthused, 'Poppy is taking him to their first competition next month, all thanks to you.'

*Let me know how you go.*

'Really? Oh, I will. I'm so glad to catch up with you again. The other girls will be so jealous. Now, let us know if you want anything. Anything at all.'

I think he gets the message, thought Karen, as she raised an eyebrow at the effusive Poppy, silencing her.

'Are you comfortable, Ma'am?' inquired Liana as Poppy moved away to tend to the other passengers in their section.

'Perfectly. Thank you.' Her voice was as cool as her attitude.

When they were left alone, Lane turned to look at her, a speculative expression on his face.

'What do you expect?' she snapped defensively, her voice pitched low. 'I get trapped into this…' she waggled a finger around at the plane, trying to indicate the journey with him, '…whatever this is…'

*A plane*, he mouthed silently, his eyes gleaming.

'You know what I mean,' she narrowed her eyes at him, hating the feel of not being in control and not knowing what was going to happen and detesting her inability to intimidate him in any way. 'I was tricked into this trip or vacation or excursion or whatever you want to call it. I thought the last thing I wanted to be doing was flying to Europe with you, but it turns out I'm mistaken. In fact, the last thing I want to do is listen to horsewomen vomit up their love and gratefulness to you as we fly to Europe.'

Lane's response was to laugh, his eyes warm with mirth as he regarded her. When her lips tightened in anger at his amusement, he quickly reached out to lightly touch her hand, shaking his head, wanting to let her know that he wasn't laughing at her. Raising a finger to ask for a moment, he removed his digital notebook from the back of the seat in front of him and switched it on, throwing her a grateful look as she waited for him to get ready to talk to her through written words.

*I was laughing at that expression you used about vomiting up love and gratefulness*, he wrote, looking up a few times to make sure she was reading the words that were appearing on the screen faster than talking speed. *And I'm sorry you feel tricked and trapped into this. I believe we can achieve an understanding of the Stablex stallions with this trip.*

'I can't see how,' she spoke firmly but softly, aware of the other passengers sharing Business Class with them, 'you have one idea, I have another, and neither of us is likely to change.'

*We'll see,* he wrote.

'Are you always so annoyingly positive?'

Lane seemed to think about that for a moment before nodding with enough hesitation to indicate he was almost always this positive.

'I prefer realism to optimism,' she replied, trying to withdraw emotionally to hide behind a frosty façade. It was one thing to text a man she barely knew and chat like friends. After all, tens of thousands were getting catfished because of how easy it was to open up to a fictional character. And that's all he was when she was texting him: someone who was only partly real, and she invented the missing pieces to suit her imagination. This was too real. Sitting next to him left little for her imagination to modify or invent. She needed to hide from this all-too-real person.

He nodded agreeably at her as though he'd heard her thoughts and was fully understanding of their rambling.

'So where exactly are we going?' she continued crisply, refusing to allow her lips to smile at the man. 'I didn't read the itinerary that someone gave to Sandy because I was too busy trying to organize everything for my unexpected absence.'

*Vienna,* he wrote, then looked at her and waggled his eyebrows as though sharing a joke with her.

'Really?' her voice dripped with sarcasm, 'I hadn't noticed the word Vienna written everywhere, from my ticket to the screens in the departure lounge. What I'd like to know is, where in Vienna or Austria are we going?'

He grinned at her, and instead of typing a response, he used a finger to draw directly on the screen. A stick figure of a person sitting by a river appeared, a fishing line in his hand, with bait on his line and a fish about to grab the bait. He pointed to the fish, then at her to show that she was the fish rising to his bait.

Being teased was not new to her. When she was a child at school, everyone seemed to tease everyone else, but for the last fifteen years or so, she had not suffered teasing. It was as though this man had no notion that she was an important corporate lawyer worth many millions of dollars. It was as though he didn't see all her trappings of success, her office, her law degree, her reputation, her impeccable wardrobe. It was as though he looked through all that and saw the person at the center of it all. She wasn't sure she could stand up to that sort of scrutiny. It was easier dealing with men like Marcus, who had only seen the outside layers and been impressed by them. She could have been a hollow person, and Marcus wouldn't have cared, but this man, this annoying Australian who teased her, looked past everything to the person beneath.

'Very funny,' she snorted softly and blinked back a smile that almost broke through. 'So, you keep baiting the hook, and I keep biting.'

He winked at her, an infectious smile spreading across his face.

For several seconds, she looked at him. He was absurdly handsome, there was a deep intellect behind that teasing, and he had a way of looking at her as though she was the only person in the world at that time. And they were sitting together for the rest of the night, and then goodness knows what he had organized for accommodation during their stay. This was a dangerous place to be, she told herself as she realized, with surprise, that she was not immune to his charm.

Her thoughts were broken by the Captain introducing himself and giving a brief rundown of flying conditions ahead of them; then the cabin staff went through the safety talk as they taxied out to the runway.

*The Spanish Riding School tomorrow*, he wrote as the plane waited for take-off, looking up at her to see if she looked at all excited about visiting there, *and then the release of the stallions in the Rauris Valley, about a five-hour drive from Vienna.*

'We won't get in to see the dancing stallions,' she said, shaking her head. 'I was in Vienna last year, and all performances were booked out months in advance, and you can't tell me you've planned this visit that far ahead. I suppose there might be tickets for the morning exercise session available. And I have no idea what the release of the stallions refers to.'

Lane shrugged, *I hope you enjoy it.*

The engines whined as their power was increased, and the plane turned on to the runway, accelerating quickly. Karen looked out the window and decided that, no matter how often she flew, she never tired of the sensation of speed and then that raising of the nose of the aircraft as it pushed up into the sky. Watching the ground rapidly distance itself from them, she smiled for the first time since boarding. There was a sense of freedom in escaping from work so unexpectedly and setting out on what amounted to an adventure. It was almost as though her life at Pilatos was a gilded cage, and the door was open, and she was flying…she closed her eyes briefly and scolded herself for such fanciful nonsense.

The passing smile wasn't lost on Lane, who was watching her as she gazed out the window. It had been his practice to observe horses before working with them, seeing what alarmed them and what interested them, what made them comfortable and what they enjoyed. It was something his father had taught him as soon as he'd been old enough to toddle around the horse yards. He closed his eyes for a moment, and his father's voice came back to him from across the years.

'Watch them, son,' he'd spoken gently to Lane as they leaned on a rail watching a yard of two-year-old Australian Stock Horses that had been trucked in from a station up in the Territory. Lane may have been three or four, he wasn't sure, but he remembered he was small enough to be looking between the bottom two rails. 'See who's the boss, which one is the gentle one, which one is spooked. That chestnut with her head up in the air, she's ready to bolt, she's scared, nervous. Look at her ears twitching back and forth as she's trying to catch every sound that is upsetting her. She's going to take some careful and gentle handling, or she'll be ruined. She'll prefer your mother to me. That bay gelding, though, look at him. He's resting a leg, his head is held out straight and relaxed, he's moving this side ear only, listening to my voice. He's a laid-back dude of a horse that one, he'll be your buddy, that bloke. Now, look at the big black horse that's standing well back watching us. He's facing us because he's not scared. He doesn't feel the need to be half-turned away ready to run – he's measuring us up, and there's neither fear nor respect in his eyes. A horse like that can kill a man if you give him reason. You have to win his respect – use brute force on that one, and he'll use it back at you; out-think him, and he'll respect you. He'll be a champion if handled properly, and pet-food if a fool gets to him.'

A few years later, the bay was the favorite riding horse for the neighbors next door while Lane's mother rode the nervous chestnut, and she was beginning to place in campdrafts. His father won two campdrafts on the black horse, then sold him for one of the top prices at the Landmark Sale at Tamworth. Six months after the sale, he found his father crying at the kitchen table. The black horse had attacked his owner in the stable, and the man had shot him.

'I should never have sold him,' he shook his head, his eyes tragic. 'I knew what he could be like if he didn't respect a person. I heard his owner spurred and reefed him till his sides were bloody, and his mouth was cut a half-inch each side. The horse only did what was in his nature; it wasn't his fault. It was up to us humans to know him - we're meant to be the smart ones. It shouldn't have to be up to the horse to work us out. He could have been the best; instead, he's dead because a man wasn't smart enough to do the right thing. I did the wrong thing by selling him, and now it's too late. You make sure you always do the right thing by horses, son. Always do the right thing by them.'

The image of his father crying at the table over the black horse melted into the memory of him that final day as Lane begged him to stop.

'Lane. Lane.'

A voice that didn't belong in the horse yards called him.

'Lane,' Karen spoke his name, her hand on his arm gently shaking him.

His eyes opened, and he saw Karen Lawford staring at him, her beautiful eyes wide with some emotion.

'I think you were asleep,' she said, looking at him strangely.

He nodded, his thoughts still emerging from the memories of his father. He hadn't realized he'd been that tired. He'd looked at Karen during take-off, then shut his eyes for an instant to think of something his father had said. There was no recollection of drifting down into sleep, but as the memories receded into his mind like dreams, he recognized them for what they were. He'd been dreaming.

No wonder she looked alarmed, he thought wryly: to dream, perchance to speak, he misquoted to himself.

'You were talking,' she leaned in close so that her voice only to carried him, 'I mean, talking. With words. I could hear you.'

Sighing, he nodded. Taking up his notebook, he wrote, *Sometimes I talk in my sleep. Sorry, I hadn't realized I'd gone to sleep. I'm not usually such bad company.*

'No, no, that's fine,' she assured him, her deep blue eyes troubled, 'and if you went to sleep like that, wouldn't it be me that's the bad company? Less than twenty minutes sitting next to me, and I've bored you to sleep.'

He grinned and was glad to see her smile back.

*Believe me, it's not you. I haven't had much sleep this past week, and it caught up with me.*

'It sounded like a nightmare,' she said, suddenly realizing she still had a hand on his arm. She looked at her hand resting on him and removed it before continuing. 'You were asking someone not to do something. To stop. It sounded...it sounded...' she struggled to describe how his voice had begged, '...desperate. I thought I should wake you.'

*Thanks. If I fall asleep again, feel free to elbow me - hard.*

'Really?' she grinned at him, a wicked glint in her eyes. 'I might have to practice that a few times. I apologize in advance for any broken ribs.'

*Forgiven in advance.*

'So, the talking?' she tilted her head as she looked at him, her eyes narrowed as she tried to understand why he didn't talk when awake if he could talk when asleep.

*There's no physical reason why I can't talk*, he wrote, not meeting her gaze as it embarrassed him to talk about it. It made him feel vulnerable when he tried to explain. Maybe it even made him feel less of a man. While he was signing and writing to others and listening to them, he didn't think about being mute; it was simply how life went on around him. If he had to explain the details of it, well, he tried to avoid that. It wasn't possible to fully explain it without going into the events of that day. It was something he avoided. *I'll explain in a few days.*

'Would you care for a drink?' Poppy leaned over Lane, smiling at him as she addressed both of them and held a hand towards a drink cart with champagne, spirits, and other beverages.

'Mineral water, thank you,' said Karen, realizing that it wouldn't be a good idea to drink alcohol in the company of this man. She didn't need anything to lower her guard any more than it was in the moments when she heard his voice for the first time, and she realized that he was haunted by something in his dreams that made him beg with fear.

The plane leveled out and sliced through the night sky towards Europe. The hostility she felt at the start of the flight had evaporated as New York was left behind and Austria beckoned. They enjoyed a meal of filet of trout with forest mushrooms followed by a light and fluffy Salzburger Nockerl, shaped like snow-capped mountains. Karen then spent an hour going over documents on her laptop, though she was careful to select ones that weren't a security risk if Lane happened to see any part of them. While she perused her Pilatos files, Lane typed another chapter to his latest book, and they worked in comfortable silence. When the passengers around them had converted their seats into beds, they followed suit, stretching out in a way that would make every economy class passenger envious.

The intimacy of trying to sleep so close together was enough to keep them both awake, lost in their thoughts, and wondering if the other was asleep. Karen was worried she would snore. Lane was worried he would talk in his sleep. Neither knew when sleep crept up and claimed them.

# CHAPTER FIFTEEN

*You learn the alphabet before you learn words. You learn words before you learn sentences. You learn sentences before you write paragraphs. You write paragraphs before you write a novel. That is how it is with training a horse. Take your time with the basics, and know that alphabet of communication between you and your horse before moving slowly up the ladder of learning. Do not expect to start with competition riding if you have not laid the foundation first.*

**'Training The Young Horse With Heart,' by Lane Dimity. P.6**

### The Spanish Riding School

'Should I be worried about how we're going to get around Austria?' Karen asked as they moved through customs.

She knew that, after today, there was an overnight stay in Vienna, then they were visiting towns elsewhere in Austria, but Lane seemed to scorn the need for in-depth itineraries and careful organization with a shrug, a grin, and a laid-back Australian attitude of *she'll be right*. With her preference for a meticulous organization that verged on obsessive, she found his devil-may-care approach to be quite irksome.

With one of his careless shrugs, Lane gave her a perplexed look as though he had no idea but believed it would all work out. She found her mouth beginning to contract into a disapproving line when, a few seconds later, he was waving to someone waiting in the crowd. A tall, slim man with brown hair and an outdoors flush to his cheeks waved happily to Lane and pushed forward to greet him. He looked about the same height as Lane but perhaps ten years or so older. As Lane stepped forward, he cast a quick look at Karen, winked, and motioned with his hands as though he was fishing. She wanted to hit him.

'Lane! So good to see you!' The man opened his arms to wrap Lane in an affectionate hug. 'It's been too long since we boiled the billy on a barbie and talked the bulldust.'

He spoke English with a slight Australian drawl overlaid with a classic Austrian accent, and, apart from his first greeting, she had no clue what he was talking about.

Releasing Lane, his attention went to Karen. She was perfectly attired in a deep grey Tagliatore trouser suit and cream silk shirt with a favorite pair of E. Vogel custom-made riding boots peeping out from the hem of the trousers. It wasn't that she was expecting to be riding a horse, but she believed in sensible foot protection when around horses, plus the boots were comfortable and, in some strange way, comforting.

'You must be Karen!' he exclaimed as though meeting his new best friend. 'So wonderful to meet you!'

He almost stretched his arms out to hug her but took note of her impassive expression and held out a hand to shake, instead, which she accepted.

'I am Lukas Waldberg, your guide for the next few days. We will have the ripper time with no drama and no worries. It will be bonza.'

Karen arched a brow and stared at him. She knew he was speaking English words, but it made little sense.

Seeing her restrained confusion, Lane grinned, smacked Lukas's arm, and signed, *She might not understand the Australian slang.*

'Ah, my Aussie words confuse all but Australians,' Lukas told her with a sympathetic nod. 'I spent several vacations in Australia with Lane and his friends, and they teach me to speak like a true-blue Aussie. By my words, I mean that we will have a good time.'

'Excellent,' Karen murmured without conviction.

'But let us go. You only have the carry luggage? Good. Where to first? Breakfast?'

'We did eat on the plane,' began Karen, only to be interrupted by the rapid-fire words from Lukas.

'Ah, plane food. Even the best is still plane food. You need to start today with a good Viennese breakfast, so the buffet at the Imperial it is. And so close to the horses - we're on a winner there!'

Lukas seemed possessed of boundless linguistic energy, with words tumbling busily out of him, often sprinkled with Australian colloquialisms that made no sense to Karen, but she found his enthusiastic delight in everything to be rather endearing. He led them to his vehicle, and she hid her surprise at seeing the Mercedes-AMG S63. There had been something so casual about the man that she was expecting an economy car or van of some sort, perhaps with roof racks and camping gear on top.

'My driver is Simon,' Lukas introduced them. Simon was a muscular grey-haired man who looked as though he might have retired from Special Ops, with a serious eye and the movements of a fighter. He appraised them, then nodded a silent hello as he stowed their two travel cases in the trunk. 'He is the best of drivers, so you can relax. You two take the back seat to be together, I will sit with Simon.'

The car slid along the A4 on the half-hour trip to the heart of Vienna, where they were to have breakfast. Lukas and Lane did most of the communicating, with Lukas explaining the signing to Karen so that she had both sides of what was being said, though she found her understanding of Lane was almost perfect now. They talked of friends and horses and events, and by the time they were being dropped off for breakfast, Karen still had little idea about Lukas apart from the fact that he was wealthy, liked horses, and loved Lane and his friends.

'Leave your bags in the car,' Lukas instructed them with one of his ready smiles, 'after breakfast and visiting the horses, Simon can take you back to my apartment while I finish work. You did not give me much notice, my friend,' he lightly punched Lane's arm, 'otherwise, I could have had today off as well, but, no matter, we hit the road tomorrow.'

'I can stay at the Hyatt,' Karen offered, not because she didn't want to impose on a man she had just met, but because she knew she would much prefer the solitude of suite in a hotel.

'Nonsense! We are friends now,' Lukas turned in his seat to give her a warm smile, his blue eyes shining with bonhomie. 'Any friend of Lane is a friend of mine. Perhaps you are worried that my apartment is small?' He held a thumb and forefinger close together, 'Smaller than a possum's pouch? No, no, no. It is plenty big for all of us, plus room for a kangaroo to hop.'

Both he and Lane laughed at his description of the size of his apartment, and against her better judgment, Karen found herself thawing to the humor and gave a small chuckle, shaking her head at the ridiculousness of the moment. What was she thinking? Agreeing to stay in Vienna with a man she'd just met, accompanied by an Australian who couldn't talk and didn't know she could understand his sign language, while he tried to convince her to destroy her own company because of the welfare of stallions that had no welfare issues…it was crazy. She looked at the two attractive men laughing together, and an errant voice in her mind said, *and it's fun*. Somewhere, in growing up, she seemed to have become alienated from the notion of fun, and there was a sense of discomfort trying to fit it back into her life but also a sense of longing.

As soon as they arrived at the café, a few people came up to Lane to ask if they could have photos taken with him. Karen was proud of herself that she managed to refrain from grimacing at the deity-like status offered to him by his fans.

Lukas was well known at the café. The staff treated him with genial respect as they were shown to a table, and several customers greeted him, while a few others whispered to their friends as though explaining who Lukas was, and she noticed a few phones discreetly taking photos of the two men.

As soon as she could politely do so, Karen excused herself and went to the bathroom so she could use her phone to Google him. Lukas von Waldberg. His mother was a von Croÿ. He was a member of the ancient noble families of Austria, and he could use the title Count if not for the 1919 Law on the Abolition of Nobility that officially abolished Austrian titles. He was one of twelve Riders at the Spanish Riding School, which meant he had been working with the Lipizzaner stallions for at least eight years to qualify for that position. The dedication and hard work over so many years that was required to become a Rider seemed at odds with this carefree, quick-to-laugh man.

And he lived in his grandfather's palace in the middle of Vienna. An eight-hundred-year-old palace, the Palais Rosen, famed for its sculpted roses in the stonework of the palace and, also, for its rose gardens.

As sophisticated and cultured as she was in New York, she still felt a silly urge to jump up and down with excitement at the thought of staying in a palace at the invitation of a member of the nobility. She had met members of the royalty and nobility before, but there had always seemed to be a circle to which she wasn't invited in, and a vague feeling that they didn't have a great deal of respect for her position as one of the heads of a large family-owned American company. They had always been gracious, even friendly, yet there remained the niggling feeling that they saw her as new-money while they were old-money, even if they didn't have much of it left, and invitations to stay as a guest in their homes – or castles – had never eventuated. It had taken an audacious Australian horseman who didn't seem particularly concerned about correct protocol and etiquette around Count von Waldberg to get her invited to stay in a palace.

Returning to the table, she pretended to know nothing about Lukas that hadn't been told to her by the two of them, but it was difficult. When she had thought he was a mere horse-riding friend of Lane's, perhaps a farmer or a worker with a show jumper, she had barely taken note of him. Once she had seen his car, she had reassessed her view of him and found new respect. Discovering that not only was he one of the famed riders of the Spanish Riding School but also an aristocrat with a pedigree that went back many hundreds of years, connecting him to most of the royal families of Europe, Britain, and Russia, had quite unnerved her. Now, she felt that she should show him the correct level of deference while also trying to impress him with her own importance.

As he joked with Lane about some event in Australia that sounded like he had tried to start a campfire by emptying the fuel from Lane's brand-new chainsaw over it, only to have the fire whoosh up the fuel and set fire to the chainsaw, Karen realized that Lukas was at ease with Lane. It wouldn't have mattered to Lane whether Lukas had been a farmer, a retail worker with a horse, or a titled aristocrat; he responded to the character within, not his station in life. Karen had prided herself on being like that - hadn't she been upset with Marcus for treating Pearce disrespectfully? But her changing attitude towards Lukas over the hour she had known him was a sad indication of how she was swayed by external factors rather than the character within.

She recalled one of her mother's oft-repeated stories about one of her school friends whose parents had been a duke and duchess. Isabella had stayed with them a few times during her high school years, and she reported how the duchess treated everyone with equal respect, speaking to the man who came to repair their toilets, or the gardener, with the same respect and interest that she granted the Bishop or a fellow aristocrat. The duchess could also be scathingly cutting to any person, regardless of wealth, family, or position, if they were cruel to animals or rude. True class, Isabella would say, lies in seeing the person in front of you, not their job or their bank account or who their parents are. The duchess had taught Isabella that, but Karen had failed to learn that lesson, and although neither man at the table in Vienna was aware of her introspection, she was ashamed of what she learned about herself.

'Are we boring you with our outback stories?' Lukas asked her as he returned to the table with his second helping from the breakfast buffet. 'You must tell me a bit about your life in America. Not that city, business, money stuff, but life at Bisente. I met your mother once, years ago. Charming and beautiful. And I know Julian, of course. Who in the horse world doesn't? Your Bisente horses are quite remarkable.'

'Sadly, they are not my horses,' Karen smiled, trying to find the horse-girl within who responded to other horse people on equal footing, rather than the veneer of Harvard-Law-School-Graduate-Corporate-Executive who wanted to rank people according to their social, political, and financial importance. 'Julian is doing great things with Mum's horses, and we're hoping to see a few with the Bisente prefix at WEGs and the next Olympics.'

'Cracker horses,' nodded Lukas wisely, using what she assumed was another of his Australian terms that didn't mean much to her. 'Lane sent me photos of you riding. Do you compete now?'

Throwing a dry look at Lane for making free with images of her, she replied, 'I haven't ridden for years. Life is too busy. Though I did spot a chestnut gelding at Bisente the other day that interested me.'

'Then you must ride that horse,' Lukas announced, 'you must listen to your heart when it comes to horses. Think with your mind. Act with your heart. Be true to your soul.'

Lane stifled a snort of laughter and signed, *Haven't I heard that before?*

With a broad smile at his friend, Lukas said, 'Lane thinks he has heard those words before. Of course, I may have quoted something out of some book I've read sometime by an Aussie horse whisperer, but they sound like words I might say.'

'I think I read the same lines in the same book,' Karen nodded, amused by the play of words and looks between the two men.

'Lane did not tell me you were a fan of his works,' Lukas waggled his eyebrows at her. 'He seemed to think that you might not have a lot of respect for his ideals and ideas.'

'Is that so?' She glanced at Lane with speculation as to what else he'd told Lukas about her. He shrugged with a show of embarrassment that she didn't believe for a moment. 'We do have differing views on some things, but I don't mind the notion of thinking with the mind, acting with the heart, and being true to one's soul. Not a lot of places to practice that in my corporate world, of course, but when I move to fairyland, I'm hoping to take them up.'

With a guffaw, Lukas slapped Lane on the back and nodded at her, 'You are a funny one. Spirit and humor, what all humans and horses should have more of. When you move to fairyland.' He laughed again.

'I gather you have horses,' she said as she selected another Viennese delicacy from her plate, 'is that how you met Lane?'

'I competed on my own horses when I was a teen,' he told her, 'but have been working with horses down the road from here for nearly twenty years, and we met there many years ago.'

'You're at the Riding School?' she asked, trying to sound as though she didn't already know. She was a lawyer, she told herself wryly, she knew how to obscure the truth.

'I thought Lane would have told you,' said Lukas with a dramatic sigh, 'sometimes getting the full story out of him is harder than catching bunyips.'

'Bunyips?' Karen queried the odd word.

'Mythical Australian creatures of the billabong.'

'Billabong?'

'That is a pond or waterhole.'

Karen snorted, 'Just how long did you spend in Australia? All these words I've never heard of before.'

'They may have made a bit of sport,' confided Lukas, 'out of teaching me extreme Australian, and we laugh a lot about it.'

*You loved it*, signed Lane, *and you took to it like a rat up a rafter.*

'Lane is saying,' Lukas explained to her, 'that I was a natural at the Australian words. I was like a rat up a rafter.'

Karen grimaced at what that expression could mean and said, 'I don't even want that one explained.'

When they had finished breakfast, Lukas called for Simon to pick them up, and they continued to the Spanish Riding School, which was just over a kilometer away. Karen would have been happy to walk through the historic streets of Vienna as it was one of her favorite cities in the world, but Lukas had to be working horses within the hour, so that didn't allow enough time for walking.

'I have organized one of the students to accompany you,' Lukas explained after signing them in as his guests. He had become efficient and businesslike as soon as they entered the prestigious building in the Hofburg. 'I must change into my riding uniform for the morning practice. The Director has been told you are here, Lane, and gives you his regards. He is away at present but has cleared you both to join us for the performance tonight. Of course, all seats are booked out, so you will be with the grooms and students behind the scenes, but you will have an excellent view of everything.'

*I appreciate this*, Lane signed.

'I owe you more than I can ever repay, my friend,' said Lukas, hinting at more in their history than a casual friendship, 'so this is nothing. Tonight, when we go home, I might convince Grandfather to open up the cellars and bring out a bottle of our favorite Australian wine, now that would be something towards repaying you.'

Karen missed what Lane signed since he was half-turned away from her. She wasn't concerned with their conversation, though, as she was enjoying staring around at the building and soaking up the history. Her head swiveled left and right, up and down, and about as she followed the men further into the building. She could hear horses. There was snorting and whickering and a couple of squeals, and she felt a rising excitement about meeting the famous white horses.

'There are my boys,' Lukas waved a hand down a corridor with wooden doored stalls so close that stallions could reach out to touch the nose of the horse in the stall opposite if he also extended his nose.

Noble heads in every shade of grey lined the corridor as the stallions watched the riders, students, and grooms moving about with gear, getting horses ready for the training session. The darkest heads of the youngest horses had the most cheek in their eyes, stretching noses out and nodding audaciously as people passed, while the older horses watched the action with wise calmness. The older stallions grew progressively whiter as the grey gene instructed their hair follicles to flood forty years of hair pigment through their hair in the first ten or more years, so the young horses were dark from the high levels of melanin, but as they aged, there was less and less color, eventually greying out to white in the older stallions. It was surprising how colorful the many shades of grey could appear.

Lane glanced down at Karen's face and smiled when he saw the magic shining there. He imagined that seeing them for the first time like this brought back a flood of childhood thoughts on the dancing stallions of the Spanish Riding School, from the Disney movie covering their rescue during World War II to all the images of the incredible stallions doing their haute école movements. Perhaps she had some porcelain figures of the stallions with their riders doing the courbette, the capriole, and levade like his mother had kept in her china cabinet. He knew that if she had been anything like him as a horse-mad youngster, she would have dreamt of these beautiful white stallions, so to see them here was to be immersed in the enchanted memories of childhood imaginings.

'They're beautiful,' Karen murmured, entranced by the scene before her.

'I will be working that second horse on the left, first,' Lukas told them, sounding brusque compared to his earlier casual self. 'I will leave you with Jenna here,' he held out a hand towards a blonde, blue-eyed girl who barely looked old enough to be out of school, 'and she can show you around and answer any questions. Jenna, this is Miss Lawford and Lane Dimity.'

'Karen, please,' Karen held out a hand to the girl and was impressed by her sure grip. Horse girls, she thought, there's no doubt that handling horses gives them confidence.

'I understand sign language, Lane,' Jenna smiled winningly at him, her Austrian accent adding charm to her voice, 'I have always hoped to meet you and talk, so please feel free to converse.'

*That's great,* he signed, *would you mind introducing us to some of the horses?*

'Yes, of course. Come this way.'

Oh sure, Karen grumbled to herself, everyone learns sign language so they can chat with Lane. Then she caught herself with a snort of amusement as she realized she also learned sign language so that she could understand him, it was just that she was being deceitful and hadn't let him know that she could understand it. She realized that it would make the trip far easier if he knew that he could sign to her, but it was a bit late to admit to knowing it.

'See you when I am dressed to ride,' Lukas nodded to them and strode off.

Jenna led the two of them down the line of stalls, explaining the details about each horse, including where he was up to in his training. Karen fell behind Lane and Jenna, listening to her explanations and enjoying the atmosphere of the stables.

'The young horses are worked in snaffle bits,' Jenna explained as one of the dark grey horses was led past them, all tacked up and ready to commence work, 'and spend many years on foundation work, developing fitness and strength before starting on the airs above the ground.'

'Will we see any of those this morning?' asked Karen, hopeful of seeing one of these magnificent animals launching itself into the air.

Jenna shook her head, 'Unlikely in the training session. As you can imagine, the movements require a great effort, so they are infrequently done in training sessions once the horses have learned them. They are mainly for the performances.'

They left the stables and made their way to the gallery shortly before the public was admitted. Jenna continued her work as a guide, explaining the history of the building and pointing out the features.

Two dark grey horses entered the arena, their hooves silent on the sand, their riders dressed in brown tailcoats, white breeches, black boots, white gloves, and bicorne hats. Jenna quietly explained the tradition behind the outfits and noted that the young horses were wearing the black bridles and dressage saddles for the practice session, adding that the older stallions in the performances would have different gear from what they would wear this morning.

'There is lots of trotting,' she smiled as the horses transitioned upwards into working trots, 'many who come to the practice sessions do not realize how much of the walk and trot goes into training the horses.'

As the riders passed, Karen saw that the lead rider was Lukas, and he was so absorbed in his riding that he didn't even glance up to see them. The young stallion was quite exuberant and threw in a couple of playful bucks down the long side of the arena, and Lukas barely moved in the saddle, his hands holding the reins lightly so that the horse didn't receive even the lightest of jerks in the mouth as he played up.

'The young horses,' explained Jenna, 'they have much energy and can test our riders, but Lukas, he does not fall off. He has the glue seat.'

They remained there for almost two hours, watching various horses come out, work around at the trot, do some lateral work, and some canter. Spectators came and went, some understanding the training, some wondering why the horses weren't leaping into the air every five seconds to entertain them. Towards the end of the second hour, four of the white stallions came out, and Karen found her eyes drawn to their power and grace as they trotted several laps then seamlessly flowed into passage, an extremely powerful and elevated trot.

Without realizing it, she put a hand to her heart as she watched. Lane glanced sideways at her, pleased to see her emotionally moved by the stallions. He wanted her to understand that the essence of a stallion was so much more than an object that was to stand in a stall all day, every day, providing blood for an anti-aging drug that wealthy men wanted. These stallions showed one aspect of the nature of stallions that he was sure she once knew but had forgotten: the incredible ability of man and horse to work together to create art. Passage was art.

Looking up and seeing his intense gaze, Karen immediately shut down her emotions and sealed them away from view. She knew he was gloating over her reaction, and she wanted to prove to him that seeing these stallions in no way altered her view of the Stablex stallions.

'Stop looking so smug,' she whispered, folding her arms across her chest. 'You think that I'll see these stallions and think they are so much better off than our Friesians, but you know what? I am not going to think that. These horses don't ask to work, they are made to work. I'm sure, given a choice, any horse would rather stand around doing nothing except eat, drink, and sleep, have safe exercise, and be kept away from danger – like our stallions.'

He shook his head sadly, trying to let her know that she wasn't seeing the point of what was happening with these Lipizzaners.

'You think this,' she threw an arm wide to encompass the six horses working in the arena at that time, 'is so much better than what our stallions have? Do you think a horse is born wanting a human to get on its back and make it work day after day in heavy sand, with a bit in its mouth and spurs on its side? Look at that horse.'

Karen pointed to one of the older stallions in a double bridle being asked to perform piaffe, a strenuous trot on the spot. The off-hind was not lifting very high, so it was receiving a soft tap from the rider's whip to remind him to lift, lift, lift.

'Look at the ear set on that horse – he's not happy. He doesn't want to be forced to do piaffe by a rider who is insisting on perfection. He doesn't want two bits in his mouth, a rider on his back, spurs on his sides, and a whip tapping at him and telling him to work harder. So, don't start on me about how our stallions don't want the lives they have. This life may be different, but I don't see that it is better. Our stallions exist to provide a drug that will save lives...'

That claim caused Lane to shake his head. Stablex wasn't about saving lives, it was a vanity drug.

'...no, don't pull that disapproving face,' Karen said, frowning at him and trying to keep her voice low, 'you can focus on the wealthy men who will buy it to live longer, but it *will* save lives. Just because they are wealthy doesn't mean that their life isn't of value and that they should be forced to die of cancer or some other disease that Stablex will help with. So, our stallions exist to save human lives – at first, yes, they will be the lives of wealthy men, but a life is a life. These stallions exist to entertain people. Our stallions have a life of luxury. These have a life of servitude. Granted, they are beautiful to watch, but I don't want to rush home and insist all our Friesians start working under saddle so that they can be entertainment for people.'

Jenna stared at Karen, completely lost and alarmed that she was using words like 'servitude' and 'entertainment' to describe the Lipizzaner stallions.

Turning to Jenna, Lane signed, *Could you please tell Karen this: I don't expect you to change your mind today. I just want you to watch and experience these days without judgment.*

He waited until she spoke the words, and when Karen was about to reply, he gave her an apologetic look and asked her to wait a bit longer with a 'just a moment' shake of his forefinger.

*We are on a journey that will take five days. We won't arrive at our destination on the morning of the first day.*

When Jenna had spoken those words, Karen replied, 'If the destination is a metaphor for me thinking our Stablex stallions are suffering a ghastly life, then we're not going to arrive at all.'

Lane gave a noncommittal shrug. He didn't want to fight about what they saw each day on the journey he'd planned, but he realized that Karen was going to be confrontational whenever she thought that he was trying to manipulate her to change her mind on what constituted a good life for a stallion.

Not wanting to continue using Jenna as a go-between for his messages, as he felt it was unfair on her, he took out the digital notepad that he could use to speak for him, turned the volume off, and typed in, *Do you want to go back to Lukas's place now? We're not due back here for the performance until 5.*

Karen read it, chewed her bottom lip as she looked around the palace for Lipizzaners, and thought about what she wanted to do that afternoon. There was plenty of work on her laptop that she intended to get through while away. 'I'd rather stay at a hotel. I'm sure the Hyatt would have a room available. I can do some work this afternoon and meet you back here.'

He shook his head and wrote, *Lukas's place is like a hotel. You'll have your own suite and can work this afternoon if you wish. I won't bother you.*

After texting Simon, they said their farewells to Jenna and asked her to let Lukas know that they would be back for the performance, and went out to meet Simon for the short drive to Palais Rosen. Located in a street containing several other palaces, the Palais Rosen stood out with the display of roses unequaled in any of the gardens around, and the rose motif was repeated in stone and glass across the front of the building. The imposing three-story stone front of the palace seemed to extend a great distance down the street, and there were plenty of tourists walking along, taking photos of the gardens and the building itself.

After parking, Simon escorted them to their rooms and explained that Lukas's grandfather was out for the rest of the day, so they should make themselves at home, and feel free to call on one of the staff if they needed anything. He added that Lane knew his way around, and if he wanted anything to eat, or if he wished to show Karen about, feel free to show themselves around the palace. There were paying guests at the far end of the building in the section that had been turned into accommodation, but Karen and Lane were staying in the family's private quarters.

Karen's rooms on the second level comprised a spacious sitting room with an antique lounge suite that would be the envy of any serious collector, an equally large bedroom with a four-post bed, and a modern bathroom that had been installed in what had once been a dressing room. There was a desk placed under a window looking down on the magnificent rose gardens in the courtyard at the center of the palace. The window was slightly open so that the fragrance drifted in with the summer warmth.

*Would you like to see the gardens?* Lane held up the notepad, his face hopeful.

'I can see them from here,' she replied, indicating the window, 'and I really want to get some work done.'

*Ten minutes,* he wrote, *just to show you where the kitchen is, how to find the front door, and see the gardens.*

Arching a skeptical brow at him as she knew that would take more than ten minutes, she nodded and followed him into the corridor that was wide enough to drive a truck along. He pointed to the door opposite hers to show that he was staying there and then walked quickly along the stone floor to a stairway that went down to a reception room. He wound his way confidently through the rooms and hallways, and she was glad they were only staying the one night as there was no way she'd remember how to find her way around this maze of grand rooms and corridors.

Lane showed her a small kitchen not much larger than the one at Bisente, but before she could remark on it being small for a palace, he opened a door through to another kitchen as large as a community hall. Obviously, that was the main kitchen. In the small kitchen, they made some salad sandwiches to take into the garden, then followed another twisting route to the rose gardens in the courtyard. Motioning with a hand to ask her to follow, he led her to a wide seat enclosed by a horseshoe-shaped hedge of pink roses.

He sat, took out his sandwich, and began eating. It would have been rude to have done anything except sit and eat the early lunch with him, so Karen joined him. They ate in companionable silence, and she thought of how many perfectly good silences people filled with words when the calm of not talking was so very restful. It allowed her to appreciate the sounds, sights, and scents of the rose garden without muddying the moment with small talk or arguments.

For a few seconds, she closed her eyes and drew in a deep breath of the rose perfumed air. This was a good memory to keep, she told herself, sitting in a palace garden with Lane Dimity and not fighting. She smiled. She had to admit, she didn't hate arguing with him; he was challenging but always good-natured no matter what she said. If they didn't come from such different worlds, perhaps…perhaps… she couldn't finish the thought as there was nothing productive to come of it.

Karen spent the afternoon in her room doing Pilatos work on her laptop, lost to the passing of time as she read various documents, made some alterations, and emailed them back to Sandy. At four, when Lane knocked on her door, she realized she hadn't changed out of the clothes she'd been wearing all day.

'Give me a few minutes!' she called to him, shutting the laptop and pulling another grey pants suit from the wardrobe where she'd hung her clothes on arrival. She'd intended to shower, but there wasn't enough time, so she dressed, spent less than a minute touching up her makeup, and shoved her boots back on, brushing her hair as she headed towards the door.

Lane gave her an appreciative look and a small bow as a compliment.

'Thanks,' she smiled, 'you don't look too bad yourself.'

He wore an open-necked shirt of indigo blue and his usual Wrangler jeans and boots. There was an indefinable movie star *je ne sais quoi* about him that caught at the heart. When he smiled at her, he looked so delighted to see her, as though she was the only person in the world he wanted to be with at that time, and she was not immune to the effect. She met his gaze for several seconds before looking away, feeling disconcerted, and she rushed to fill the silence with words.

'Let's go, then. Sorry, I was busy working and hadn't noticed the time. Do you think it will be very cool? I haven't brought a coat, only the jacket that's part of this outfit.'

Lane took a step to the side and picked up a stylish brown leather jacket from a chair in the hallway, offering it to her if she was cold.

'I'm not cold yet, but thanks,' she tried to stop the free-fall of words from her mouth. She didn't know how this silent man could unnerve her so much. Marcus hadn't made her feel this tumbling of emotions, and they'd been lovers.

They walked together down to where Simon waited with the car and traveled in silence on the short trip back to the Spanish Riding School. Simon must have told Lukas that they were coming as Jenna was waiting for them when the car stopped as close as it could get to the Hofburg.

'I hope you had a pleasant day,' she greeted them, 'Vienna is beautiful in the summer.'

Karen didn't tell her that she had spent the afternoon indoors doing office work.

'Please, come this way,' she entered the building and led them back to the stalls where there was a rush of activity preparing the stallions. 'This is the only performance this month and the last before the stallions leave Vienna for their summer holiday.'

'Holiday?' Karen asked.

'Yes, the stallions spend six to eight weeks in July and August at Heldenberg relaxing and just being horses. They need it after the long hours of training here.'

Karen glanced at Lane to see his lips twitching as she heard another difference between the lives of these stallions and the Friesians at Pilatos Farm.

'Don't start,' she muttered to him, 'I really don't think horses have a concept of what a vacation is.'

He shrugged and put a finger to his lips to indicate that he didn't want to argue with her over anything. Lightly tapping Jenna on the shoulder, he asked her to pass a message on to Karen.

'Lane says that he hopes you two can enjoy the night watching the stallions without arguing. I hope so, too. It is too magical, too beautiful to watch with anger in your heart – they are my words, not Lane's. One should just experience the performance and feel the beauty of it.'

'I shall try to do so,' Karen assured her and Lane, 'as long as Lane doesn't give me any more of the smug looks that I find so annoying.'

He shrugged and mouthed, *I'll try,* to her.

They made their way to where the riders and horses were making final preparations for the performance. Lukas waved to them but was clearly too busy to come and talk, though he sent a groom walking briskly to see them. He spoke to Jenna in German, which Karen understood perfectly, but she waited for Jenna to translate.

'It is good luck for you,' Jenna grinned at them, 'Lukas has been told that there are two cancellations in the front row Royal Boxes, and they are now yours.'

She led them to their seats and departed after telling them that Lukas would join them after the performance.

Before long, eight white stallions and their riders entered in single file, walking between the pillars in the center of the arena before dividing off left and right at the end. The next seventy minutes swept them both along in a celebration of what horses and humans could achieve together as the riders and their horses demonstrated the movements of classical dressage, including the airs above ground that had the audience applauding after every move.

While she was watching, Karen was able to forget all about her life at Pilatos and just be the girl who loved horses. Her face glowed with emotion as she watched the stallions perform, her applause coming automatically as she experienced the excitement of watching the horses bound on their hind legs in the courbette and leap into the air and kick out with the capriole. When she shared a look with Lane, there was no animosity; they were merely two horse lovers relishing the chance to see the legendary stallions perform.

'How did I do?' Lukas asked them after the audience had departed, and he had changed back into his street clothes and joined them.

'It was remarkable,' Karen spoke with genuine respect, 'and I was impressed with how light you have the curb rein.'

'Lightness is what we are aiming for,' he nodded, 'harmony between the horse and the rider. So,' he clapped his hands together, 'are we ready to go home and enjoy the company of another fine Australian?'

'I'm not very familiar with Australian wines,' confessed Karen

'Grange Hermitage,' sighed Lukas, as though mentioning the name of a loved one. 'My grandfather has quite the collection. I would like to try the '58 Bin 46, but he might disinherit me if we did. He did say we could have a bottle of the '58 Bin 95, though, so let us go home and become acquainted with that excellent Australian.'

With the light-hearted banter of Lukas, along with some of his grandfather's wines fuelling the evening, they talked into the night, entertained by Lukas's stories of his outback encounters with snakes, eccentric people, and kangaroos. Lane urged him to recount more stories that had them laughing until Karen was dabbing at tears and gasping for breath. There was something intrinsically hilarious about Lukas's soft-spoken Austrian accent, sprinkled with Aussie colloquialisms, telling them about being accidentally locked in a car with an angry kangaroo or being chased half-naked across a claypan by a love-struck emu, that had Karen laughing like she hadn't laughed since she was a teenager.

As the night had worn on, she had even been cajoled into telling tales of some amusing incidents in her life, and she had felt strangely exhilarated that the two men laughed so much at her take on being a woman in the U.S. where, in some places, the attitudes of men were distinctly Biblical towards women's rights.

Perhaps it was the wine, she thought as she slid between the crisp sheets sometime after midnight, but she could not remember enjoying a night like that, ever. She'd been able to curl up in a two-hundred-year-old armchair and listen to the comical stories of Lukas's outback adventures with Lane and his friends and let her guard down. She'd told stories from her life and felt like a comedian on stage with an appreciative audience. There was no talk of Pilatos or the welfare of stallions or what Lane wanted to achieve with this trip, it was as though they were three friends who had known each other forever and were catching up on the things that made them laugh.

She checked her phone before nodding off and found a text from her father. Her mood plummeted back to her normal cool level, and she debated for a moment whether to leave it until the morning. Too late, she thought, I've already lost the feeling. She tapped the message open. *Good job. No protesters here. The media is settling. Orders are huge, and we are ready to get Stablex on the shelves as scheduled. Keep him busy and away from here for as long as possible. Whatever it takes.*

Whatever it takes? She snorted and dropped the phone to the floor. Just what did her father include in that 'whatever'? Lies? Violence? Sex? Would he prostitute his daughter to give Stablex a clear run to consumers? She shook her head and rolled over onto her side, tucking her arms and legs in to become small in the large bed. Why was she even asking herself that question? Of course, he would. He'd prostitute himself if it helped Pilatos. Mind you, an errant smile touched her thoughts as the image of Lane laughing at one of her stories popped into her head, it wouldn't be that much of a chore if he were willing.

Across the corridor, Lane lay awake in his bed, staring out the window at the black sky, wishing that the stars were visible from cities. Seeing Karen relax and laugh at Lukas's stories had given him hope that he could save her from the shackles she'd placed on her own life in Pilatos. He knew she wouldn't recognize it as that, but the restrained, constrained, and inhibited woman who always dressed in grey and found nothing to laugh about in her day-to-day life was imprisoned every bit as much as those stallions. This was her taste of freedom, of laughing, relaxing, and seeing a life that existed outside the stable she'd locked herself in.

Would it be successful? He wasn't sure, but he knew he had to try. Not trying was far more of a failure for him than trying and not succeeding. He had always felt compelled to make an effort to change what he felt was wrong, and seeing this extraordinary woman locked into a belief system of greed and commerce-above-life felt so wrong to him. She was so much more than the lawyer who went through contracts or the executive who made decisions that put profits above all else. Tonight, as she'd laughed until she cried at Lukas's anecdotes, he'd seen her inner light shine through the small crack in the armor that she wore. The sound of her laughter lifted his spirits, and he drifted to sleep thinking of it, and her flashing blue eyes, and the way she'd looked at him and understood his thoughts without him needing to say the words.

# CHAPTER SIXTEEN

*I think every horse person should take the time to go out to their horse at midnight and just stand with them in the silence of the night. Not expecting anything. Not asking anything. Not wanting anything. Just stand with your horse, and for that brief moment, simply 'be.' If happiness comes in moments, then grab that moment of happiness: just you and your horse, alone together in the night, there for each other. In that moment, you will find happiness.*

**Interview with Lane Dimity, when asked to describe happiness.**

### Heldenberg and Alpengasthof Bodenhaus

The knock at her door woke Karen from a deep pit of sleep, and she took a few seconds to get her bearings as she looked around her room in the palace.

'Yes?' she called, trying to sound less sleepy than she felt.

'Wakey, wakey,' the distinct tones of Lukas's voice called back to her from the other side of the door, 'time for breakfast and then adventures.'

Karen groaned and touched her temple, there seemed to be adventures going on inside her skull at present. Just how much of that wine had she consumed last night? At least ten thousand dollars' worth, if she knew anything about the value of wine.

'Are you decent?' Lukas asked, 'Can I come in?'

'Come in,' she replied, after quickly checking that she had put her dove-grey silk pajamas on, 'I don't think I locked the door last night.'

Lukas opened the door and grinned at her without stepping in, 'No need to lock doors in a palace – if you can't trust the aristocracy, who can you trust?' He waggled his brows at her to show that he wasn't serious. 'The nobility never did anything wrong – all the kings, emperors, and princes were lovely people who respected the rights of others, I'm sure.'

'I should have locked the door, obviously.'

'Well,' he rocked a hand back and forth, 'you can trust me, but I wouldn't trust that Australian hombre if I were you.'

His body jerked as if hit from behind, and he stepped into the room, followed by Lane, who had delivered the thump. Lane held out a glass of water and a range of packaged tablets. She was about to refuse them but realized the pounding in her head could use some help to move it on its way.

'Did I drink that much last night?' she frowned at his offering.

Lane nodded.

'We may have all been as full as the cows,' Lukas dipped his head sadly at their state the previous night.

*As full as bulls*, Lane corrected Lukas on his misquote of the Australian expression for drinking too much.

'As full as bulls or cows – they are all bovine to me,' Lukas shrugged.

'And that means nothing to me,' Karen snorted, 'but there did seem to be a few empty bottles.' Meeting Lane's eyes, she asked, 'Can I assume they are legal, over-the-counter headache pills?'

Lane gave the German brand packets a *maybe* look, then looked at her, his eyes shining with good humor to show he was joking about not knowing what they were, and held them out to her.

She took a couple of ibuprofen tablets and the water.

'Thanks, I don't know when I last woke with a headache like this.'

'It was a good night, wasn't it?' Lukas sat on the end of the bed as though they had been friends for years rather than a day, but she didn't find it to be an imposition, she rather liked it that he was comfortable around her. 'We will be heading off to Heldenberg as soon as you are ready. Do you want breakfast here or along the way? I recommend breakfast in our rose garden, but I also recommend a very nice bakery on the way.'

'I'm happy with either. I'm not particularly hungry. Coffee wouldn't go astray, though.'

'Coffee it is, then we shall drive!' he announced cheerfully, tapping her foot through the bedcovers and standing up. 'You do whatever it is women do to get ready in the morning, and we will be waiting downstairs in the rose garden with your coffee. If you get lost, phone Lane, and we will come and find you.'

The men left, shutting the door behind them, and Karen rose, showered, donned a pair of grey jeans, a white cotton shirt, and her riding boots, then packed the rest of her items in her bag and headed downstairs to join them. She only took a couple of wrong turns before making it to the rose garden, and, true to his word, Lukas had a tray with coffee waiting for her, along with some Austrian pastries.

'Just in case you found your appetite in the last fifteen minutes,' he said as he held out the plate to her.

While they enjoyed coffee together, Lukas gave a rundown on the history of his family's palace and the rose gardens, then Simon arrived and carried their bags out to the Mercedes. With Lukas in the front and Karen and Lane in the back, they made their way out of Vienna and headed towards Heldenberg, a rural area an hour north-west of the city. They stopped briefly at the bakery Lukas had mentioned for baked goods that were as good as he promised.

When they turned off the main road, Lukas gave her more information about the farm they were visiting.

'Our stallions spend their holiday here every July and August. They have not arrived yet, but you will see many of the young stallions working, and the best of those will train here for some years before graduating to Vienna. Riders can also receive instruction. It is quite the center for those who work with horses.'

Feeling that the friendly and casual ambiance was about to evaporate in the face of another lesson to try and teach her that these stallions lived wonderful lives while hers suffered, Karen withdrew into herself, erecting the cool façade that chilled the memories of last night.

*There are also the retired stallions,* Lane signed the reminder to Lukas.

'Lane has pointed out that we also have the retired stallions living here. They spend the rest of their lives in the pastures and stables of Heldenberg.'

'Which is obviously better than living out their lives in the stables of Pilatos,' Karen muttered dryly.

'That is not what I meant,' Lukas looked hurt that she had become so defensive. 'I can only tell you about the horses I know, not about the horses I do not know.'

They left Simon and the vehicle in a car park and went to explore the stables and one of the riding arenas where young horses were being worked. Some of the young stallions were being long-reined, while others carried riders, and although Karen could admire their work, she did not see any evidence that these horses were happier than the Friesian stallions.

A couple of young women in riding clothes were watching the horses when they noticed Lane. They whispered to each other and nodded in his direction, then came over with nervous giggles to ask if they could have a photo with him. He cast Karen an embarrassed look, but she was getting used to the adoration he received from horse people, particularly the female ones.

After Lukas had caught up with some of his fellow riders and admired the up-and-coming stallions, he asked Karen and Lane if they would care to ride the older schoolmaster Lipizzaners that were used for teaching classical dressage to riders. He pointed towards three white stallions being led out of the stalls, all tacked-up with English saddles and double bridles.

'I asked to have these three ready for us in case I could convince you to have a ride,' he said as he led them to the horses, 'and you both have riding boots on and jeans that are not as good as long boots and breeches, but we will make an exception on outfits today.'

'I haven't ridden in years,' Karen began making an excuse, but she found her heart beating a little faster at the thought of riding one of these magnificent horses, and she realized that she *wanted* to ride one. Hadn't she dreamed of the white stallions of the Spanish Riding School when she was a child? It would be unforgivable to pass up the chance of riding one just because she had been so preoccupied with work for so many years that she had given away riding.

'They are the bicycle you will get on,' Lukas winked at her, 'and you will not have forgotten how to ride.'

'I rode showjumpers,' she snorted, 'not bikes, and not horses that can perform capriole and courbette.'

'You talk nonsense,' he scoffed genially, waving away her concerns, 'you ride over big jumps, these horses do big jumps – it is the same.'

'Of course, it's not the same,' she laughed, 'but, yes, I would love to have a ride on one of the stallions.'

'And you, Lane?' Lukas asked.

*As if I'd say no*, he signed, shaking his head.

'I shall be your instructor,' Lukas told them, 'so first, introduce yourself to your horse and lead him to the center of the arena. He should stand as you mount, but do not become the cowboy once in the saddle, be the soldier who sits tall and still, with your height up through your head and your weight down into your heels.'

After adjusting the stirrup leathers to her length and checking the girth, Karen placed the reins over her stallion's head and ran her fingers up through the pair of reins so that they were straight, then, ensuring the snaffle rein had contact while the curb was light, she put her foot in the stirrup and lifted agilely and softly into the saddle. A sense of being home ran through her as soon as she settled in the saddle, and she closed her eyes for a moment to savor the feeling. It had been too long since she'd sat on the back of a horse.

'You will find that if you ride correctly,' Lukas told them, 'when you think of doing something, like walk forward or turn right or trot on, your body will make almost imperceptible movements from that thought, and these horses will feel those actions and respond. To you, it might feel as though you are merely thinking turn right, but you will have looked to where you want to go, your seat will have shifted, your legs will have shifted, and the horse will go to where you are looking. Remember, we do not pull the right rein to go right as we don't want to pull his head right, we want all of him to go forward into the right turn, so we ride all of him to the right.'

The three of them walked together, and Lukas ran them through some basic exercises of halt, collected walk, extended walk, and some turns, so they adjusted to the lightness required to work with the horses before they began trotting. The power in the horses was astounding, and Karen had a sense of being on a loaded spring that could leap upwards at any moment. Just thinking about the collection required to signal the horse that he should sit back on his haunches and leap skywards had her horse cantering on the spot with an action that felt like the precursor to an air-above-ground.

'Did you think capriole?' Lukas asked her with a gleam in his eye.

'I may have,' she laughed, 'I have no idea of the aids for that, but I was wondering...'

'Beware the thought,' he warned with a grin, 'many the new rider has been unseated by a stray thought and a stallion who was looking for the excuse to leap.'

When they came back to a working trot after cantering circles, Karen noted, 'It's quite a different action from our Bisente show jumpers and eventers. They have those big, scopey strides always reaching forward like there's a jump coming up, but the energy in this boy feels so contained and controlled as though passage or piaffe are only a breath away.'

'They are forward movements,' objected Lukas as his horse transitioned smoothly into the slow-moving, high stepping passage, 'you will be penalized if they are not seen as forward movements,'

'Yes, I know they are forward,' she gave him a dry look, 'I'm saying that it feels very different from a Warmblood that is trained for jumping. I wouldn't think of pointing this horse at a five-foot cross-bar, just as I wouldn't expect a Bisente horse to do the elevated collection that results in a levade or capriole.'

Lukas laughed and nodded, 'I do know what you mean. I will not ask this old boy to do them, but I feel he is ready at any moment to respond to those signals. They do teach the riders how to ride them, but it takes more energy than I want to ask for during a short ride for fun.'

They brought their horses back to a loose reined walk, and Lukas asked Karen to stay in the center while he ran Lane through some of the more advanced movements. It gave her the chance to observe Lane, and she was ready to admit that he was a better rider than she was, with his horse responding more willingly while hers had been flicking his ears back and forth with some confusion about what she wanted. Lane's horse *looked* confident with his rider, and as Lukas asked for some lateral movements, then passage and piaffe, which were performed faultlessly, horse and rider in total communion, she realized the horse had reason to feel confident.

'Please tell me that isn't his first time riding that horse,' she said to Lukas when he halted his horse next to hers to watch Lane ride a trot half-pass which flowed into a canter and a faultless canter pirouette, the hind legs describing a small circle as the horse maintained his three-beat canter stride while spinning. 'It's like they've worked together for years.'

'What can I say?' Lukas gave her an apologetic shrug. 'It is his first time on that horse, but that is Lane. He doesn't ride a horse so much as become one with a horse. If I did not like him so well, I could stab him in the eye for being that good. I have spent twenty years to ride like that. He plays around on some brumby mustang horses like a wild west cowboy, and he can get on any horse and ride better than I can. I don't think it is natural - I think he is magic.'

Karen snorted at his joke, 'Magic. I haven't noticed him waving a magic wand over any of the horses.'

'But I am not jesting,' he shook his head at her, 'it is like he can speak to them, and they understand him. He does speak to them. Did you know that?'

'I think someone mentioned it at some stage, but I've never heard him speak, so I wouldn't know. Though, he did say something while sleeping on the plane the other night.'

'Ah, the nightmares,' Lukas said knowingly, 'they are always worse at this time of year.'

'In Summer?'

'The Solstice. Summer Solstice tomorrow. Winter Solstice where he comes from. That is his birthday.'

'I didn't realize,' Karen's gaze rested on the Australian as he asked the stallion to do one-time canter changes across the diagonal of the arena, giving the impression that the horse was skipping as he changed lead every stride. It was impossible to see what aids he was giving as he rode so perfectly still that it looked as though he was sitting doing nothing, and the horse was coming out with the movements all by himself.

'He doesn't like to celebrate his birthday, so I am not surprised he didn't tell you.'

'What an awful way to spend it, though, dragging me around to look at horses and trying in vain to have me change my mind about the Pilatos horses. It won't work, you do realize that, don't you?'

'Sometimes, we have to take the journey even if the destination isn't guaranteed,' Lukas said as he began to walk his horse. 'I believe that is a quote from one of Lane's books, and it may be fitting for this situation. Come. It is your turn to try some of what Lane is doing.'

With a grin that lit up his face, Lane rode back to them. He touched the fingers of his right hand to his chest then placed it on the wither of the horse, and even if Karen hadn't learned sign language, it was clearly a way of saying he loved the horse.

'You love all horses,' Lukas sniffed, 'and that one is better than most, so of course you love him. And, as always, the horse seems to think you are some sort of horse god, as do your spectators,' he tilted his head in the direction of the twenty or so people who had gathered to watch and film Lane riding. He added, to Karen, 'I am sure his adoring fans would not worship him quite so much if he had the beer belly and the unpleasant face, but he looks like the movie star, so he is easy to adore. Good riding, by the way.'

Lane lifted a shoulder as though to say it was nothing.

While Lane dismounted and loosened his girth, Lukas gave Karen a brief lesson in advanced dressage. She had been riding most of the movements through her teen years on the Bisente horses, but she'd never felt anything quite like the sheer muscular power of these Lipizzaner stallions. Lane observed her closely as she quickly adapted to the signals the horse understood, her face intent as she listened to Lukas's instructions and lifted a shoulder or felt the reins. Within five minutes, she had progressed to some of the more difficult actions, her face drawn with concentration as she listened to both her horse and Lukas.

She rode as he thought she would – with heart. She did not fight the horse or try and force her knowledge on him, she listened to him and let him lead her to what he needed in a rider. On the back of a horse, Karen Lawford was everything she could not be in her corporate world: she was kind, strong yet empathetic, working in harmony with another to reach a goal together rather than flattening all before her to achieve her own ambition. He could see that in the way she moved with the horse, her hips and spine moving supplely as she adapted to him, moving with him, being as one with him...

His cheeks warmed as he realized that focusing on the supple movements of her hips had an effect on him that was, luckily, hidden by the tautness of his jeans. Still, he drew in his breath and looked away, turning his body in to the shoulder of the horse. This was not the time to have those sorts of reactions to this particular woman. With them in opposing corners over the issue of Stablex, it was difficult enough to make any overtures of friendship without introducing the notion of a romance to the relationship.

He knew full well that she was only accompanying him on this trip because he had agreed to call off the protesters during this time. What she didn't realize was that while he was here with her, Andrea, Matt, and Tom were working tirelessly on orchestrating another demonstration to irrevocably damage Stablex. Karen and her father were so focused on keeping his influence at bay that they forgot he was not the only one outraged by what was happening in those stables. His friends were as important as he was in trying to bring about change.

So, while Karen thought she was neutralizing him, he was distracting her from realizing that this was about much more than one man versus the pharmaceutical company. This was about an entire way of thinking in conflict with her company. His friends were gathering information and reaching out to people within Pilatos, quietly gaining strength and leverage as growing numbers of individuals realized that it was time for a change.

'That was brilliant,' Karen's voice broke into his thoughts as she and Lukas rode stirrup-to-stirrup back to where he was leaning against his horse.

'You ride very well,' Lukas complimented her, 'for an American.'

Karen playfully swatted at his arm for his comment. 'We Americans do alright on the world stage with our horses.'

Lukas laughed and continued to tease her, 'Yes, you do. Your Bisente horses are almost good enough to be European.'

It was heartening to see her laugh, thought Lane as he watched them banter like old friends. He felt her life in Pilatos was probably a lonely one, living in a castle made remote by money and power, unable to relax like this because she had a role to play, and she always had to be that person without ever letting her guard down. He didn't know how to convince her that she deserved more than what she had without it sounding as though he was dictating to her, like so many other men dictated to women about what they should be. He hoped that by spending these hours with horses, people, and places outside her Pilatos life, that she might want it to continue.

After the horses had been led back to their stalls, some of the spectators came over to speak to Lane, have photos taken with him, and get his autograph. Lukas and Karen watched on with some amusement, passing droll comments to each other as Lane managed to satisfy their wishes before extricating himself from further demands. Lukas left briefly to thank his friends for allowing them to ride the horses, then returned to Karen just as Lane was re-joining them.

Lukas slapped him on the back, 'It is like traveling with a celebrity.'

*Only around horse people,* signed Lane with a grin, *away from them, I'm a nobody.*

'You could never be a nobody,' assured Lukas, heading back to their car, 'and it's not just horse people who love you. Last month, I visited my uncle in Berlin, and my little cousin Julia, who can't stand horses, asked me to get your autograph. She has two posters of you on her bedroom wall, alongside boy bands with names that all seem to be initials, capital letters, or questions. Really, what happened to good band names that were simple nouns and adjectives?'

'Those flight attendants,' put in Karen, able to catch the gist of the conversation without giving away that she could understand Lane's part, 'seemed fairly well enamored of you, too.'

*They had horses,* Lane gave her an amused look.

'Lane is arguing that it is because they had horses,' provided Lukas.

'Only one of them, the other drooled over you without needing a horse to stimulate the drooling.'

'Drooling?' Lukas wrinkled up his nose in distaste. 'That sounds quite disgusting.'

'Oh, it was,' Karen nodded sagely, 'I was sitting next to him and was suffering from second-degree drooling as they focused their attentions on him. I had to ask for a towel.'

Lukas laughed. Lane narrowed his eyes at her and mouthed, *ha ha,* pretending that he didn't think it was funny.

'Drooling,' she repeated, teasingly.

'Enough, children,' Lukas waved an imperious finger in the air, 'we have a long trip to the Alps, and I will not have you fighting in the back all the way.'

'How far is it to where we're going?' Karen asked.

'Alpengasthof Bodenhaus,' said Lukas, 'up the end of the Rauris Valley. Beautiful place. Very beautiful. And it is about four hours if we drive like the clapping. It is only three hundred kilometers as flies the straight crow from here, but the road winds around.'

Lane snorted at Lukas's muddled expressions and signed, *Like the clappers. And as the crow flies. You don't have to add straight. It means straight.*

'Whatever,' Lukas shrugged, his eyes gleaming.

Karen suspected that he knew the expressions correctly but enjoyed teasing his friend by mixing them up.

'And we go through Salzburg?'

'Yes,' Lukas opened the car door for her, 'we can stop there if you like, and anywhere else. I always find that visitors enjoy seeing Seewalchen am Attersee. We are staying tonight near Alpengasthof Bodenhaus and watching the stallions tomorrow in the Hengstauftrieb, which is when they are let loose.'

'Correct me if I'm wrong,' began Karen as Simon steered the car onto the road, 'I gather this is a once a year release of stallions who all run together over summer.'

'Yes,' Lukas confirmed, turning in his seat to speak to her and Lane, 'it has become quite the tourist attraction there, with thousands turning up to watch the stallions led out by their handlers and released together.'

'And they fight?' she asked, looking from Lane to Lukas and back again. 'I mean, stallions do fight when put together.'

Lane rocked a hand back and forth and crinkled one side of his face in thought as though to say that they did fight, but it was more than that.

'It is not the movie version of stallions fighting,' explained Lukas, 'it is difficult to explain until you see with your own eyes.'

'I'm imaging that a whole lot of stallions let loose with each other will result in a whole lot of biting and kicking. I've seen photos of people who've been savaged by stallions, so I can't begin to imagine what they'd do to each other.'

'We are told so much about stallions that is not correct,' said Lukas, looking to Lane to see that he agreed, 'and there are too many idiot moron fools handling them so that you often see or hear the bad side of stallions that has been manufactured by bad handling. These are working stallions handled by people who have a good understanding of, and respect for, the stallions.'

'And, just so I'm clear,' she met Lane's open gaze, 'you somehow think that me seeing these stallions fight each other will make me think differently about our Stablex stallions? Because I'm not seeing it. Stallions injuring each other, potentially causing death, seems a good reason to keep our stallions safe in their stalls.'

*I don't know if it will change your opinion,* signed Lane, waiting a moment for Lukas to explain the meaning to Karen, *but perhaps it will help you see stallions as a complicated life form deserving of so much more than a life in a stable.*

As Lukas spoke his words, Lane looked weary, as though the futile task of trying to give Karen a greater appreciation of the importance of the lives of the stallions was wearing him down. It should have made her feel a sense of victory as, in essence, this was a competition to see whose ideas would win, and she always liked to win, but there was a hollowness in seeing him look almost defeated.

'We should have taken a helicopter,' Lukas said, looking out his window at the passing scenery, 'We would be there so much quicker.'

'But sometimes it is the journey that is important,' Karen paraphrased his earlier words, 'and how many times in my life am I likely to have the opportunity to spend four hours in a car with a world-famous celebrity horse whisperer,' she gave Lane's leg a nudge with her boot and offered him a cheeky smile, 'and an Austrian nobleman from the Spanish Riding School, along with whatever interesting special forces past there is to Simon.'

'Jagdkommando,' said Simon over his shoulder, his eyes remaining on the road.

'Pardon?' Karen asked.

'Jagdkommando,' he repeated in his clipped, accented English, 'our Austrian special forces. Hunting command.'

'I am officially impressed,' declared Karen, pleased that her guess has been correct, 'although I also feel that we could be part of a joke on a stage somewhere. An American lawyer, an Australian horseman, an Austrian aristocrat, and a retired special forces operative get in a car to drive to the Alps...'

'If you can come up with a punch line for that,' laughed Lukas when her words ran out, 'I will give you one of my grandfather's prized wines.'

'That's as far as I've gone with it,' Karen smiled at him. 'I know it should be funny, but I only know the start.'

'We will work on it,' nodded Lukas, 'but perhaps we only ever need to know the start.'

*Very philosophical,* signed Lane, raising one eyebrow at Lukas.

'He says I am the philosopher,' grinned Lukas, 'I think we were all philosophers last night after several bottles of wine to bring out the truth.'

The trip from the low country to the Alps went surprisingly quickly. If someone had told Karen a few weeks earlier that she was to travel over four hundred kilometers in a car with two Austrians and Lane Dimity, talking all the way from Vienna to the high end of the Rauris Valley, she'd have called them mad. She did not do road trips. Time was short in her world so, if she had to travel any distance by car, she turned the back seat into an office while someone else drove, usually Pearce. But this was a road trip. They talked and laughed. They stopped to admire views. They took photos with their phones. They sampled foods from several different places.

The four-hour trip stretched to six, and it was late afternoon as they approached Alpengasthof Bodenhaus, the restaurant next to the field where the stallions would be released the following day. There were already crowds gathering for the spectacle of the stallion release, after which they would be driven up into the mountains to spend the summer grazing together at the Grieswiesalm. It did not surprise Karen in the slightest that the hosts at the restaurant knew Lukas and Lane and had a table reserved for the three of them. Simon left them and took their bags to a lodge some kilometers back down the valley. It was owned by a cousin of Lukas, and they had it to themselves for the night.

Once more, Karen witnessed Lane's popularity as scores of people vied to have their photos taken with him. She wished they could visit a place without horse people so that they would not be interrupted by this level of hero-worship. He was just a man, admittedly, a charming man, she told herself, but this adulation was almost religious in nature, and so many wanted to touch him or be noticed by him.

After dinner, Simon drove them back down the valley to the charming alpine lodge that was used in vacations by some of Lukas's family. As they sat on the balcony overlooking the valley and the mountains, Karen made some light-hearted remarks about feeling as though they were in *The Sound Of Music*, which prompted Lukas to break into *Edelweiss*, and Lane held up the curtains against himself as though measuring them for clothes. For the rest of her life, whenever she remembered that night in the Austrian Alps, Karen remembered the sense of lightness and laughter and friendship. It was a good night.

Not long after Karen put on her silk pajamas and slipped into bed, her phone vibrated on the nightstand next to the bed.

*It's good to see you laughing,* Lane texted.

Their rooms were only a wall apart, so she imagined him lying in his bed an arm's length away on the other side of the wall. She wasn't sure if the thought was disturbing or comforting.

*It was a good night. Lukas can really sing.*

*Lukas is great at many things. I am proud to call him my friend.*

*You have many friends,* she pointed out.

*Don't you?*

Karen looked at the simple question and thought about it for several minutes before replying.

*I don't think I do. Family and acquaintances, yes, but there's not a lot of room in my life for friendship. I'd always be letting them down, not making it to this or that because of work, being too busy to meet for coffee, putting work first.*

*I think we're becoming friends.*

*It almost seems that way,* she wrote, *but what we have here can't exist at home. We aren't on the same side. I will let you down because I will put my work ahead of my relationships. That's how I am.*

*When you do,* he wrote prophetically, *it will be important for you to know that I understand why you are doing it. If you think you've let me down, you haven't – and I will want you to forgive yourself because, as far as I'm concerned, there won't be anything to forgive. We merely act in a way that is true to ourselves at that time, and what is true now may not be then, and what is true then may not be later.*

Karen started her reply with a smiling emoticon, *I'd like to say that I understand that, but I think you've lost me.*

*I'll never lose you.* His words struck an arrow into her heart, but she read on to see that he was making a joke. *I can track a black ant across the bitumen.*

*Sounds like a useful skill,* she replied, finding a dozen little ant symbols to add to the message, *If I'm ever lost on the bitumen, I'll know who to call.*

*Try not to get lost.*

*I'll try. Oh, look, it's midnight. Happy birthday to you.* She reached over her head and lightly tapped the first line of *Happy Birthday* on the wall.

*Thank you. And good tapping, by the way.*

*I don't have a present for you, sorry. I only found out back at Heldenberg that it's your birthday today.*

*This is as good a birthday present as any,* he wrote to her, *chatting to you and not feeling alone on my birthday.*

*How can you ever feel alone?* Karen asked, thinking of all the people he had in his life, including his three close friends in his inner circle, friends all over the world like Lukas who loved him, and all the admirers who longed to spend time with him wherever he went. *You're the least alone person I know.*

*What about you? You are surrounded by people at Pilatos every day, but does that stop you from feeling alone or even lonely? At night, alone in your bed, don't you ever wish that there was someone to talk to like we're talking now?*

*I haven't thought about it,* she lied and changed the subject. *Lukas said you don't like to celebrate your birthday. Why is that?*

*It's part of that long story that I was going to tell you one day.*

*That has to do with your parents dying and you not talking?*

*That's the one. It's all tied in together.*

Karen tapped her fingers on the bedcovers thinking about the clues she had to this particular story: someone told him not to speak, his parents died, his birthday. *Please tell me your parents didn't die on your birthday.*

There was no reply for several minutes. She turned her face to the wall, tapped on it, and spoke, not knowing if he would hear her through the wall. 'Did your parents die on your birthday, Lane? When you were a child?'

There was a drawn-out silence before her phone vibrated. *On my eighth birthday.*

Tears suddenly burned Karen's eyes, and she wiped at them, looking at the moisture on the back of her hand, surprised that those four words seemed to hold an infinite sadness that touched her. She imagined a little eight-year-old Lane, with tousled hair and a grin that could light up the world, trying to make sense of a birthday that saw him lose both his parents.

'I'm sorry,' she spoke to the wall, 'I'm so very sorry.'

She sat for several minutes, grieving for a little boy she hadn't known, and then he sent the story of that day.

*There was a drought. We'd lost almost all the stock. Dad meant to shoot the last of them before I woke that morning, and then he and Mum and I would drive away from Ellamanga, our property, and start a new life. I got up early. I heard the shots from the cattle yards. Mum tried to stop me, but my horses were in those yards. They were my best friends back then. Punkin was my pony, and we went everywhere together. And Jess, and Dusty.*

Karen read the words, a feeling of dread creeping into her chest as she imagined how much that little boy loved his pony. She thought of how her heart had broken when her father had sold her horses, but this…this, she thought, seems like it is going to be so much worse than anything I ever knew.

*When I reached the yards,* his next message read, *Dad had already shot most of our horses. I begged him not to shoot Punkin. He told me to shut up, that there wasn't any choice, and words were useless. He shot Punkin, and then he shot himself.*

The scene played out in Karen's mind as though she was witnessing it. That little boy, watching his friends die. Watching his father die. A soft sob burst from within, and she covered her face, overcome with grief for something that happened so long ago to a child so far away. She didn't want Lane to hear her crying, so she muffled her crying with a pillow and read his next message as soon as it arrived, trying to control her breaths that were breaking in her chest.

*My mother came to the yards and thought I was dead as well as Dad. Our neighbors found her dead at the house a few hours later. I was in shock but alive. My neighbors raised me. The people in the district put up the money, so the bank didn't take Ellamanga. It rained eventually. I never talked again, except to horses sometimes, or in my sleep. I don't like my birthday. I'm sorry if it made you sad, too.*

The fact that he was worried about making her sad when he'd confided the saddest story she had ever heard was her undoing. The distress over what that child had gone through on his birthday ruptured the barrier that she had erected between her emotions and her day-to-day life, and the flood that ensued had her sobbing uncontrollably. She grieved for the eight-year-old Lane. She felt the anguish of losing all the horses she had loved because her father wanted her to toughen up. The torment of struggling to gain her father's approval all of her life caused more tears. And the loneliness. He was right. The feeling of being alone at night, even when Marcus had been there, was a malignancy that ate away at her. There was just too much sorrow in the world, and she felt so alone.

Her breath came uncontrollably in dots and dashes as she cried for Lane, and she cried for herself, and she cried for all the heartache that had ever been.

A soft knock at her door had her grabbing tissues from next to her bed and wiping frantically at her face to try and remove the excess of fluids that seemed to flow from her eyes and nose. Lane opened the door, and in the faint light, she could see his white t-shirt and bright flowery board shorts that he chose as sleeping gear. She could also see his worried look, and once more, his concern for her opened the floodgates to her emotions, and she turned her head away in a vain attempt to hide the crying.

He shut the door quietly behind him and went to her, upset that he was the cause of this pain. Reaching for her face, he placed a finger under her chin and gently turned her head so that she was looking at him.

*I'm sorry*, he signed, *I didn't mean to upset you like this.*

She gazed up at his face, her tear-filled eyes locked on his, and at that moment, she knew he could stop her from feeling lonely.

*I know you can understand me*, he continued, lowering himself to sit on the edge of the bed, *I figured that out at the beginning, so we're as crafty as each other on that one.*

'How did you know?' she sniffed.

*Someone let on that you speak a lot of languages, and that you can learn a new language faster than most people. It seemed logical that you would learn my language so that you would have an edge in any conversations.*

'That sounds like Isabella,' she said, knowing that few others knew about her ability with languages.

*Yes,* he nodded, *I don't think she intended to be disloyal to you. Perhaps she wanted to help me understand you. She is very proud of your language skills.*

Karen nodded up at him, her tears still rolling down her cheeks. 'I am so sorry for all that happened to you when you were eight. I can't even begin to…' She stopped as her words choked in her throat.

Patting her hand like he was consoling a child, he took a deep breath and exhaled. *It was long ago. It comes back on my birthday, but mostly I don't think about it.*

'I wish life could wash away the bad memories and experiences,' she muttered, sniffing at the end of her words.

*Then we would not be living. Life is meant to have the good and the bad, the grief and the joy, the loneliness, and the friendship. If we do away with the negative, how can we know the value of the positive?*

'I think I'd still know the value without all the sorrow,' she sighed and wiped her eyes with more tissues. 'If ever there was a good reason not to cry, this has to be it – weepy, red, swollen eyes and a sniffly nose are just not a good look.'

*You are beautiful.*

'Thank you,' she smiled up at him and sniffed.

He rose from the bed and took a step towards the door, still facing her. *Get some sleep. I'll see you in the morning.*

For a second that cradled a small lifetime in its passing, they held each other's gaze.

Karen stretched a hand out to him, tentatively. 'Will you stay? Not for sex or for any reason that would make sense when we get back to New York. Stay to keep the loneliness away for just one night. I might regret it in the morning, but right now…'

Lane held a finger to his lips to stop her flood of words, *Sometimes, words just get in the way. No need for explanations or the regrets of tomorrow or over-thinking.*

He stepped back to the bed, and she moved over, holding up the covers so he could slip quietly in beside her. He lay on his back, the arm next to her outstretched to welcome her to his side, and she curled up against him, closing her eyes and breathing him in as she used to bury her face into the neck of her horse and breathe in the essence of horse.

'Thank you,' she said softly, feeling safe in the crook of his arm, held against him, hearing his heart thud under her ear. She knew she would regret this later, but for now, it seemed so right.

The sense of loneliness and aloneness that plagued them both went elsewhere that night.

When Karen woke after sunrise, she was alone in her bed. Her immediate reaction to the memory of asking Lane to stay with her was a feeling of sweet contentment that was quickly replaced with anger at herself for being weak and needy, then worry about how it would change things between them.

'I'm so stupid,' she cursed herself softly, 'he's going to think I want a relationship.' She sat up and dropped her head into her hand, shaking her head with regret. 'He'll think this changes everything. I can't believe I asked him to stay. What was I thinking? I wasn't thinking.'

A piece of paper on her bedside table caught her eye, and she picked it up. A note from Lane. His hand-written script was as neat as the penmanship of a nineteenth-century calligrapher. Her stomach plummeted another few stories as she wondered what he'd written about their night together. It meant nothing, she knew that, but what if he thought it meant something? What if...?

*Stop over-thinking*, she read, with a snort of amusement at his perceptiveness, *if it worries you, pretend it never happened. It's alright for something to just be – we don't have to label it or fear what it will lead to or autopsy it with words. Come down to breakfast when you're ready. I hope you'll enjoy today. Lane.*

For several minutes, Karen sat up in bed, re-reading the note. She thought that it was probably exactly what she wanted to read, but on the other hand, there was a niggling sense of disappointment that he didn't want her to remember last night as something special. With a sigh, she committed to the day and rose from the bed, showered and dressed in another outfit of grey and cream, though, today, in a small act of defiance against herself, she took out the scarf Lane had given her and knotted it loosely around her neck for a splash of color.

'Good morning, good morning!' exclaimed Lukas when she came down the stairs to the kitchen where he, Lane, and Simon were sitting having breakfast. 'Coffee?' He raised an old-fashioned percolator with one hand, tilting his head questioningly.

'That would be fabulous, thanks. And good morning to you all,' she nodded at the three men.

Lane pointed to his throat and gave her a thumbs up to indicate that he recognized the scarf around her neck.

'Glad you like it,' she smiled at him, trying to block out the image of lying her head on his shoulder and watching the rise and fall of chest as his heartbeat against her ear. 'I thought it was time for a bit of color.'

*It looks good on you,* he signed, *color suits you.*

'Thanks, but I can't promise I'm about to overhaul my entire wardrobe. A scarf today, perhaps a jaunty hairband next week.' She even managed a mischievous wink as though she was entirely at ease joking around with him, and not at all concerned about falling asleep in his arms some hours ago.

'And what is this?' Lukas looked from her to Lane and raised his arms in a dramatic shrug of perplexity. 'You understand the sign language now?'

*She always did,* Lane told him with a grin, *we just pretended that neither of us knew. Karen hoped to catch me giving away any secrets, and I may have wanted to lead her on a wild goose chase.*

'Such tricky people,' Lukas clicked his tongue in mock disapproval and shook his head as he handed Karen her coffee, 'so were there any secrets and goose chases?'

Karen tilted her head to one side, considering the question. 'How would we know?'

*Good point,* Lane laughed.

Noticing some birthday wrapping paper on the kitchen counter behind Lukas, she looked around for a gift and saw a small framed pencil drawing of a Lipizzaner head near Lane's elbow, between cups, plates, and pastries.

'I'm sorry, I don't have a birthday gift,' she apologized, 'but happy birthday, all the same.'

*I don't need gifts, but I'm happy to have been given this by Lukas,* Lane picked up the tiny drawing and passed it to her to inspect. It was quite simple and striking but did not look like the work of a professional artist.

'It is by Colonel Podhajsky,' explained Lukas. 'He was the Director of the Spanish Riding School for many years and is responsible for saving the Lipizzan horses in World War II, evacuating the stallions to the mountains. They still may have perished, but he met a great American horseman, your General Patton, who placed the horses under the protection of your American forces.'

'I remember the Disney movie about the events,' said Karen, admiring the drawing with more appreciation now that she knew who the artist was. 'This really is a treasure, then.'

*Yes, it is,* Lane nodded.

'Pastry?' Lukas offered a plate with several types of Austrian pastries piled on top of each other. 'They are fresh from the bakery this morning. Simon knows where to find all the best bakeries across the length of Austria.'

'An admirable skill,' Karen took one and thanked him. 'Lukas, this valley is one of the most stunning places I have ever seen. Even the air seems better than anywhere else.'

'What can I say?' he spread his arms wide, 'Austria – where God perfected the art of making mountains and valleys. Of course, Lane misses his vast outback of rolling plains, it calls to him, but a day or two here won't hurt him.'

*The outback called you back to it a few times, too,* Lane pointed out.

'I admit, there is something enchanting about your ancient land, but then I see the Alps, and I know I could not live anywhere else. I visit, but my heart will always be in Austria.'

*Where does your heart belong?* Lane asked Karen.

She narrowed her eyes at his loaded query, but his guileless expression didn't look to be offering up a trick question, merely a geographical one. 'Nowhere. I like the area around Bisente in Kentucky, and I'm used to the city life of New York. But I don't think any one place calls me home, like you two are describing.'

'Everyone should have a special place to go home to,' Lukas smiled at her kindly, 'a place that is where you want to be when you need to escape the rest of the world.'

'My office?' she offered tentatively. 'That's about the only place I go when I need to escape the world.'

'Pah!' Lukas looked disgusted by that revelation. 'We will work on finding you a home. It could be anywhere,' his gaze slid to Simon and then to Lane, 'or anyone. Sometimes, a person can feel like home.'

Karen snorted at that and bit into her pastry.

After breakfast, they walked around the extensive gardens, and Lukas named various plants and birds and pointed out some of the landmarks that could be seen from the elevated levels. The alpine peaks surrounded them, and she gazed up at the jagged tops as Lukas named some of the highest mountains. She breathed in the crisp, high-altitude air, agreeing with him that this was closer to heaven than anywhere else on the planet.

Lane seemed relaxed, and she was glad that there didn't seem to be any awkwardness lingering between them after she asked him to stay with her in the night. It was almost as though it hadn't even happened. As though the man and woman who talked during the night were people from a dream, and this was reality. There was a faint sense of regret that what they shared in the night could evaporate so entirely in the daylight hours.

After packing their bags, Simon drove them back to the Alpengasthof Bodenhaus, where thousands of people had gathered to watch the release of the stallions. Karen wasn't sure how they would find a good viewing position around the small field where spectators stood ten deep, but both Lane and Lukas were recognized by many, and the crowd parted to allow them to have a rail side position to view the action. A few asked to have photos taken with either Lane or both men, and Karen grimaced at Lane to express her irritation about his movie-star status. He laughed at her, his eyes crinkled in amusement at her look of exasperation. She found it impossible not to laugh with him.

*Here come the stallions,* he told her as they stood together, her body in front of his and tucked against him so that she had to twist against him to watch his hands.

Handlers led the strong-bodied Noriker stallions into the small field shaped like a long triangle with a small bulge along the short side. Around them, people began betting on which stallion would be the lead stallion that year, pointing to different animals that looked particularly large or bold or keen to get loose and dominate the others.

'Oh, God, they're not going to let them all loose, are they?' Karen turned her head to look up at Lane, her eyes dark with worry about what would happen when the horses were released. 'I know I read about it, but so many stallions, and such big horses. I thought they were just young colts, not mature breeding stallions. They'll kill each other. Look at the size of them!'

*They do this every year, it is the way of the studs around here.*

'They are boys meeting each other again on summer camp,' Lukas bent over to speak to her above the noise of the crowd, 'they don't want to kill each other, they just want to have a bit of a yell and tussle to remind each other who is the boss. They love it. Feel the energy of them.'

He waved a hand towards the stallions that were now being stood up by their handlers around the field. Some stood like statues, staring at the other horses with a 'bring it on' glint in their eyes. Some moved restlessly, keen to be free. Long manes tossed, and tails swished as they measured each other up, and the stallion noises coming from them ranged from deep grunting noises to squeals of excitement.

*They talk to each other,* Lane's hands spoke in front of her, *they boast, and they threaten, and they speak of their excitement and their joy. You can feel their messages.*

He tapped his heart and looked searchingly into her eyes to see if she understood him. It wasn't just noise, there was conversation and emotion, and he was right; it was something she felt in her heart. The power of these stallions was reaching into her soul and plucking at strings that she had forgotten existed.

'I like the big silver boy,' Lukas pointed to a taffy-colored dark brown horse with a silvery-cream mane and tail that towered over his handler. The stallion was staring at a black horse, a few horses away. 'Those two know they are the two leaders when there can only be one leader. Look at them staring each other down! Magnificent.'

'Aren't their owners worried about them being injured?' Karen asked Lane, standing on tip-toe to speak closer to his ear. 'They're obviously valuable animals and this… this…' she waved a finger at the field of stallions challenging each other before being released, 'it could be total carnage.'

*Watch them closely when they are free,* he explained, *most of it is bluff, noise, and shoving. They will mostly kick at the air and stand nose to tail, like boys giving each other shoulder shoves.*

'It is very interesting to view,' added Lukas, 'there will be a few kicks that connect and, if they hit you or me, we'd be dead, but they seem to kick on fleshy parts where noise is made, and strength is felt, but no damage is done. Most of it is posturing, like boxers facing up to each other before the match, eyeballing, and talking the trash.'

Karen remained unconvinced but was swept along with the emotions of the crowd as the release of the stallions came closer, and the tension and excitement became tangible. Finally, the handlers unclipped the halters, and stallions surged towards each other. Combatants who had been eyeing each other rushed in with squeals and roars, their front legs slashing the air in violent strikes. Three massive black stallions met in front of where they were standing, and one shoved his chest against the side of a taller horse while the third wheeled around and began double barrelling at them, his hooves punching rapidly through the air with the power to break legs. No kick connected, though, he seemed to pull the kicks just before they touched the other horses. Then he swung around, roared, and struck at the other two who were now standing nose to tail, shoving at each other as they sniffed flanks.

The silver stallion that had caught Lukas's eye rushed straight to the big black as soon as his lead dropped. Without hesitation, his head snaked out, and he grabbed the black's shoulder in his teeth, roaring in his throat at him. The black screamed, shook himself free, and reared up, striking his forelegs at the silver. But there was no skull smashing blow delivered, he was showing his height and dominance before dropping to the ground, spinning, and kicking out at the silver. Tossing his magnificent creamy mane and forelock, the silver bounded on the spot and snapped at the black a few more times before shoving him and nearly knocking him off his feet. The black stumbled, then stood firm and stretched his head out to the silver, his nostrils quivering as he snorted loudly. They squealed a few more times; then the silver bucked his hindquarters up in excitement as it seemed he had secured his position as the lead stallion over the big black.

Other pairs and small groups of stallions showed very little interest in actual fighting; they just seemed excited to be able to sniff each other and squeal, strike and kick at the air. The big silver-maned horse trotted around the other horses, shoving some, kicking at others without connecting, squealing, snorting, and roaring as he asserted his dominance over all in the field.

Karen heard a couple of loud cracks as kicks connected, but she didn't see any horses limping, and a couple of men with whips intervened when two horses looked like they wanted to get serious about fighting. There was some blood from bites, but, mostly, they were settling their disputes with the noise and posturing that Lane and Lukas had described. It was exhilarating to watch the raw power and mastery of these stallions as they sorted their pecking order and friendships out, and, within minutes, some stallions were already grazing muzzle to muzzle.

'They are glad to have this time without the worry of girls,' Lukas told her, his cheeks dimpling as he smiled. 'Their breeding is over for the year, and they will hang out with the other boys through summer, gaining energy for the next breeding season. Look at how happy those ones are!'

He pointed to three stallions, a brown, a black, and a leopard spot who stood with their nostrils touching, their ears pricked forward, and their necks arched proudly. Every few moments, one would let out a small squeal and strike the ground with a front hoof, but there didn't seem to be any aggression in the action, just exhilaration about being able to touch the other stallions. The big silver-maned horse raced at them to break up their boys' club, and the leopard spot horse reared up at him playfully but did not offer a fight. The black and the brown bounded away together, shoulder to shoulder, soon joined by their spotted friend, keen to leave the antagonistic stallion to his plans of dominance.

*They want to be friends and not fight*, observed Lane.

'They might have been friends last year,' said Lukas, 'I've been told that they have lifelong friendships and can be seen with their besties every year.'

Eventually, it was clear that the stallion that Lukas had picked was the herd leader for this year, with the big black he had initially challenged a close second. The fight gradually left the herd, and they began to start the business of grazing with just the occasional squeal or strike when two stallions discovered that they hadn't passed words with each other yet.

'Such astounding energy,' marveled Lukas, admiring a pair of black stallions who trotted past with massive strides. 'It is raw power to see them move,' he tilted his head to look quizzically down at Karen, 'and it makes me wonder how you keep all this energy, this great force of life that is inside a stallion, locked inside a small stable, year after year.'

'They're happy,' she replied flatly, 'and, in case you haven't noticed, most of the stallions in the world *don't* get released like this together. If they did, there wouldn't be these crowds here today.'

'Most still get to release this energy outside of a stall at some time,' he countered, then smiled winningly at her, 'but we shall not spoil the day with a dispute. This is for you to see, not for me to lecture.'

They turned their attention back to the horses, and Karen pushed the comparison between these stallions and the Friesians in Kentucky out of her mind.

The crowds were still intent on the horses when Lukas tapped Karen's and Lane's arm and motioned to follow him back to the car.

'We need to get you to Munich to catch your plane home,' he told them as they walked with him. 'If you have seen enough and don't need to see more of the same, we can be smacking the road.'

*Hitting the road,* Lane grinned at him.

'Same, same,' Lukas winked back at him.

'I could watch them for at least another week,' remarked Karen, feeling quite emotionally moved by what she had seen. She touched Lane's arm so he would look at her and know she meant her words, 'Thank you for showing me this. It was quite amazing. I would never have known about it if you hadn't organized this trip.'

He arched an inquisitive brow at her, *But it hasn't changed your mind about your horses.*

'Of course not, but I haven't processed it all yet. There was a lot to take in.'

He nodded, *There was a lot of language going on. You are talented with languages. You will work it out.*

With a start, she realized he was right. She was thinking about the use of language she had observed with the stallions, not just the sounds they made, though they were varied and many, and rich with meaning, with all the posturing and body language, ear movements, tail swishing, staring, and sniffing. It was a language she had been fluent in when she was a child, but she had not immersed herself in the richness of their communications for so long that she had almost forgotten the nuances and intricacies of the equine language.

'We have a three-hour drive to Munich,' said Lukas as they settled into his car once more, taking on the voice of tour guide, 'many mountains to cross, many places to see. Sit back, relax, and enjoy another Austrian road trip.'

'Three hours?' Karen raised her eyebrows, 'As an American, I find it astounding that you can drive three hours and be in another country. We drive for three hours and can still be in the same state.'

'Don't drive in circles, then,' Lukas advised with a grin before holding a hand out towards Lane. 'And now, of course, I must hand us over to our Australian who, no doubt, will have some remarkable and astounding fact about how far you can drive in his vast country.'

*You can drive for twenty-four hours in a straight line and full speed on a highway and still be in Queensland*, he grinned triumphantly.

'Nonsense,' Karen shook her head in disbelief, 'that can't be possible.'

'I know that one,' put in Simon who rarely added anything to their conversations apart from the occasional eyebrow twitch or frown, 'Coolangatta to Cooktown on Highway One, and if you leave the highway and continue north, you can drive another twenty-four hours and still be in Queensland. I've driven it. The going is much slower, of course, and there are crocodiles.'

'Crocodiles, of course,' nodded Lukas knowingly, 'a road hazard in north Queensland.'

Karen narrowed her eyes and looked suspiciously at Lukas, 'A road hazard? Really?'

'They eat cows,' said Lukas, as though that explained the road hazard comment, 'whole cows. They catch them and eat them.'

'And that makes them dangerous on roads because...?'

'Because the roads have to cross the rivers, and there are no bridges, so you are driving through the water in a four-meter-long car where there are six-meter-long crocodiles that can catch and eat cows...and you are much easier to eat than a one-tonne cow.'

'Remind me to avoid a road trip in that region of Australia,' Karen shuddered, 'it sounds very Jurassic Park to me.'

The rest of their trip to Munich passed with the companionable small talk that had no place in Karen's working life, and she found it enjoyable to discuss and banter about all manner of topics, apart from those that could lead to serious disagreements. They stopped in several places for food and to admire views. Karen managed to do some work using her phone between stops and conversations while Lukas kept up his tour guide explanations for the places they were passing.

'Lukas, I am officially in love with Austria,' Karen announced as they arrived at the airport, 'I feel like I've been here for weeks, not three days.'

'Then you must come back as soon as you are able,' he smiled at her, his face showing genuine warmth, 'you will always be welcome at our Palais Rosen, Karen.'

She was surprised at how emotional she felt at his invitation. They weren't words tossed off without thought – he truly meant that she was welcome in his home.

All four climbed out of the car, and as Simon removed their bags from the trunk, Lukas and Lane hugged each other.

'It has been so good to spend time with you, my friend,' Lukas patted him on the back affectionately.

*Thank you for everything,* Lane smiled, his eyes conveying the love he felt for his friend, *I owe you.*

Lukas waved away that notion, 'You owe no one. We all owe you, Lane, and we always will. You have made the lives of millions of horses and millions of horse lovers better with your thoughts and your words, and your kindness. Call any time, and I will be there. We will be there,' he extended a hand to Simon, who nodded his agreement.

With an embarrassed shrug, Lane accepted the words and thanked them again.

While Lane was picking up their bags, some fans recognized him, and a small crowd began to gather, asking for the usual photographs and autographs. While he was busy with his flock, Lukas stepped in close to Karen and opened his arms, offering an embrace if she felt comfortable accepting one. She did. In these few days, she had come to admire him as a rider and a person, his sense of humor never far from the surface, and his serious dedication to his riding something to respect.

'Take care of Lane,' he spoke softly so only she would hear.

'He's not mine to take care of,' she replied with a smile.

Lukas almost rested his forehead against hers, leaning over to talk for her ears alone, 'He looks at you like I had always dreamed he might one day look at me, but it was never to be. I have never seen him look at anyone like that. And I worry about him. He sees the good in you, of which there is much, but there's also much hardness, and I worry that you might break him.'

There were several points to his talk that had her doing a double-take. She hadn't realized he was gay, not that it mattered, but she had been almost piqued that he hadn't once shown any interest in her, so the admission about his sexuality bolstered her faith in her own. It was also astonishing to realize that the easy friendship he had with Lane was underscored by the fact that, while Lane loved him as a friend, he was in love with Lane, and yet he had no expectation of that love going anywhere, it just was.

She hadn't noticed Lane looking at her in any way different than how he looked at others, but there were moments when she sensed his eyes on her, so maybe it was in those instants that Lukas had seen something that she hadn't recognized. And as far as the hardness that he saw in her, she knew he was right. This break from the reality of her normal life brought out the softer workings of her character, but once back at Pilatos, there was little room for them. She had to be hard and make hard decisions for the company to survive and grow and for all the employees who depended on it to keep their jobs. It was also quite possible that she would have to make decisions that would upset Lane, but she was not responsible for how he felt.

'I'll try not to break him,' she smiled weakly, knowing it was far from a promise, 'and I'm sure he doesn't look at me how you think.'

'Like something more precious than breath itself?' he arched his brows at her. 'Believe me, I know that look, and he has that look when you don't know he's watching you. But you are not accountable for his heart, so be true to yourself and hope that someone is there to pick up *your* pieces when they break. If you call me, I will be there. Remember that. You have my number. I can help you pick up all the little pieces when all that is hard and brittle finally shatters.'

'I...well, thank you. I hope I don't need to call. You make it sound as though nothing will end well.'

'It rarely does,' he shrugged, 'most marriages end in divorce, most love ends in hatred or apathy or heartbreak – and which of those is worse than the others? The animals we love die before we do, and eventually, death comes for us all. But the ending isn't always what is significant. Just as the journey can be more important than the destination, the love story does not need to have the happy-ever-after ending to be remarkable. Sometimes, just the fact that there is love at all is what is so extraordinary. And when all else has withered and died, the memory of that love shall be the beacon of our life, even if nothing came of it. Lane will never love me as I love him, but the fact that such love exists at all is what is beautiful.'

There was something so deep and meaningful in the gently spoken words that Karen felt as though pieces of her life within her mind were shifting slightly, like fragments of a puzzle that had been forced together to form a shape and were now drifting apart to create another picture. This language of emotions was new to her, but she realized that Lukas spoke it knowledgeably, and she should hold on to his words to examine at a later time.

'Lukas?' Simon interrupted them, holding the front door of the car open for him and nodding to the sign that indicated the time limit for this drop-off zone.

As Karen observed Simon, she suddenly became aware of the look that Lukas had mentioned in the eyes of the taciturn, retired special forces soldier who drove the car for the blue-blooded Austrian. Life, she thought, is far more complicated than the binary way in which I have chosen to live: so many stories, and yes, so much love, and not always a love that is returned, and yet it exists.

'Simon says I have to go,' he smiled at her, and as Lane disentangled himself from his followers and joined them, extended his smile to him. 'My life is richer for having had you these few days, and I hope you both feel the same.'

For a crazy few seconds, Karen wanted to ask him to wait. She wouldn't go back to America, she would stay for another day, another week, in Austria. She had felt happy, and she had laughed in these few days, and there was a camaraderie that she had never experienced before as they drove and chatted or sat over a glass or two or three of wine and talked. An overwhelming urge to stay clawed at her: she wanted more of what she had experienced in these Austrian days and nights. Then common sense reasserted itself, and she shoved those feelings down into a dark place and said her final goodbyes to Simon and Lukas. She doubted she would ever see them again.

# CHAPTER SEVENTEEN

*If you live to be ninety, and in the final hour of your life, you are given a chance to recall all the treasures of your life – what is it that you will remember as your life's treasures? It won't be the money or the things that money bought. It will be the achievements, the love, the memories of the best dog you ever owned, the nights you sat around with friends and laughed all night until the sunrise surprised you. You'll remember those who looked at you with love, you'll remember those who held out hands to help you, and those who you, in turn, reached out to help. You'll remember the moments, the love, the goodness, and the kindness. Those are the treasures of your life. Don't spend so much time and effort and money trying to buy the things you are told are valuable, as, in the end, they will be forgotten, and it will be the moments and the emotions and the memories that are your treasures.*
**Lane Dimity, Facebook post.**

### A Sad Horse

Once more, side by side on a plane in Business Class, Karen and Lane soared across the planet, only this time they were a little more comfortable with each other. When he had something to say, he signed; when she spoke, he listened. They had an understanding, not that she was sure what that was, but she knew it was there.

The mood was relaxed, Karen thought as she settled back into her seat and enjoyed the privileges of not flying economy. No mention had been made of her asking him to spend the previous night with her – was it only last night? She frowned at the question because it seemed as though time was stretching and warping like a Dali clock, so that a day seemed to pass faster than an hour, and three days seemed as though they might have been a year. She was glad they had managed to push her momentary weakness and the subsequent hours out of their minds as she knew it should never have happened.

For too long, the only thing on Lane's mind had been how Karen's body had felt tucked up against his. He understood she had locked the memories down in the basement of her mind, but the way she felt in his arms was too perfect ever to lock away, and it would remain as one of the treasures of his life even if he were never to hold her again. He glanced over at her, working on her laptop and going through the correspondence she had downloaded at the airport so she could put in a few hours' work on the plane. That dedication to work was admirable, and, obviously, her mind wasn't caught in a spin of remembering last night like his.

That was alright, though, he sighed softly with an equanimous acceptance of how things were, we move forward slowly, but we move forward.

When he was sure that Karen was absorbed in her work, he opened an email that Tom had sent him with the subject, 'FYEO FYEO FYEO,' to make it clear that it was for his eyes only and not for anyone else to see. He knew Tom was rarely dramatic, so this had to be important, and he had the screen angled away from Karen so that she couldn't accidentally read anything.

It began with some brief greetings, followed by a mention of Sean, Lane's 'double' who worked in the stables at Pilatos and was happy to trade places with Lane whenever he wanted access to the facility. Then he discussed the meeting he'd had with one of the Stablex vets, Noah, and he outlined what Noah had told him about what lay at the heart of the laboratories at the center of the stables. A heavy, sick feeling settled in Lane's abdomen as he read.

He stopped before he had reached the end and closed his eyes, trying to focus on breathing slowly as he attempted to remove the image from his mind that Tom's words had painted. Stealing a glance at Karen, he felt the sick sensation turning over like an oily growth on his insides. She couldn't know. She couldn't. She couldn't be defending that. But she was Pilatos. She was an owner of the company. How could she not know?

Feeling tired beyond life itself, he continued to read as tears formed in his eyes and ran down his soul. He didn't care what it would take; he would close them down. What Noah had brought to Tom would nauseate any person who cared for horses, or who respected life, but if it were made public, Noah would lose his job, and the Pilatos money would pay for welfare experts to state that it was acceptable and that there was no suffering, and nothing would be gained. It would go on.

If she didn't know, he looked at her from under the lashes of his half-closed eyes, if she didn't know, he would think of a way that would ensure she would shut it down herself. If she did know…pain ached in his chest at the thought. If she did know, then the world had gone to hell already, and he doubted there was a place left in it for him.

He would find the pattern in all the chaos, and he would fix this. On this day, all those years ago, he had been unable to save his horses from his father's bullets. No words helped on that day, but he would find the right ones to save these horses. He thought of the people who were coming to their side, the people inside Pilatos who could help him, and the scenario needed to bring about change that could not be stopped. He believed he would find the right way to heal this suffering. A phrase danced on the edge of his mind, and he brought it into the center of his slowly forming plans: *great change requires great sacrifice.*

'Are you alright?' Karen turned to look at him, her deep blue eyes seeming as endless as the oceans. 'You look pale.'

He stared at her, struggling to stay afloat in the oceans of thought that heaved within his mind but which grew calm when he looked into her eyes.

'Lane? Everything OK?' she asked again, her voice worried.

He had to ask, but he wanted the question to be exact and not open to any misreading, so instead of signing, he opened a new page on his notebook and wrote, *What do you know about The Source?*

'The source of Stablex?' she asked, then shrugged. It had been told to all on the night at The Pilatos Centre, so there was no risk of revealing classified information to him. 'Only what was made public and not much more.'

He stabbed a finger at the question so that she knew he was asking it again and looked at her searchingly to see if she was telling the truth or hiding it from him.

'I think we both know the same history to Stablex,' she gave him a curious look, wondering why he was asking about something that he already knew. Unless, of course, there was more to the source of Stablex that she hadn't yet learned. She repeated what she knew in case he hadn't seen all the information film. 'There was the Friesian stallion, Sevvodarray the Third, who was found to have a rare mutation, or a unique mutation, perhaps, as no other horse was found to have Sevv's gene, and it caused him to produce a hormone that kept his body younger than others of the same age, right down to a cellular level. The Stablex stallions were bred using him so that the gene and its effects could be studied. All the stallions there now are his sons and grandsons, perhaps even further generations. And their blood is the source of Stablex.'

The seconds stretched as he examined her face, not knowing if he would be able to detect a lie by omission if she chose to hide what she knew from him. So much depended on whether or not she knew about The Source and the other information that Noah had passed to Tom.

'What have you learned that I don't know?' she asked, then tilted her head to one side as she considered what was going on. 'It's something that you think I know, isn't it? Just tell me, and I will tell you if I'm aware of it or not. If it's something you already know, it's not like I'd be giving away classified information by admitting I know or don't know, because you already have the information.'

Hesitating, Karen ran the words she'd just uttered through her head a second time and grimaced at them. 'If you understood what I said then, you're better than I am. What is it about?'

Using his hands to sign, he replied, *I'll talk about it later. There are people who might lose their jobs if I explain now.*

Like I'm going to let that go, thought Karen, narrowing her eyes and feeling her Pilatos loyalties stir. 'Someone in Pilatos has told you something that I don't know about the source of Stablex?' Her mouth twisted thoughtfully to one side before straightening. 'They probably will lose their job, anyway, not because you've told me about them, but because security is higher than most would think, and I imagine Joe Kaiphas's men already know they've spoken to you.'

*Do you want to finish our trip early and go back to New York?* Lane asked, unsure of her answer. If she wanted to cut it short, he could use the extra time to form and modify a plan that would deal with this new information about Stablex, but he also wanted to give as much time as possible to help Karen rediscover her affinity with horses, as that would be an integral part in any plan that he was currently creating from the bedlam of thoughts.

'No. Do *you* want to finish early?' She looked at him suspiciously. He had agreed to keep the protesters silenced for the duration of this trip, so if he wanted her to go back to New York, did that mean he had some new disruption planned for Pilatos? The closer they could get to the release of Stablex without any more Dimity problems, the better it would be for the company.

After a pronounced hesitation, he shook his head.

'I'm curious to see what you have planned next,' she smiled guardedly, 'flying into Chicago instead of New York is interesting. I've been able to do some of my work as we've traveled, a bit here and a bit more there, so I don't need to rush back to that. I think we should play this out to the end.'

He nodded, *I wonder where it will end.*

'It will end with you realizing that our stallions are fine, and perhaps you'll make some suggestions to improve their lot in life so that you feel happier about them. It will end with Stablex helping the people who use it, and, hopefully, a female equivalent is found, and the production becomes cheaper and more people benefit from it.'

*Where will it end for us? You and me?*

'Hopefully, with some sort of friendship,' she suggested, deliberately ignoring the previous night and whatever it meant. 'I still have hopes that you might become an advisor for us so that the stallions are kept more in line with how you want them to be kept, within reason, of course. There may be a compromise.'

Lane shook his head, *I will not compromise. I want freedom for every stallion. I want it shut down. Stablex should never have been and should never be.*

'Maybe you should tell me what you've learned, or think you've learned,' she sighed, trying to avoid the escalating conflict, 'maybe it's false information. There are lots of interested parties who'd like to see Stablex disrupted and who wouldn't be above planting information to increase attacks on the company.'

There had been a moment when he'd considered the same possibility, but he knew Tom well: the information would be verified. There was nothing he could do about it now, ten kilometers above the earth, far from the stalls where the stallions were living. He had to assume that Karen did not know the full story of The Source, and now was not the time to discuss it. The sensible approach, at this point, was to nurture their friendship, show her the final acts on his magical mystery tour, and then complete the shutdown of Stablex.

*Ask me again tomorrow night under the stars,* he signed, adopting a nonchalant, lop-sided smile to hide the pain he felt when he thought of The Source.

'The stars?' her eyebrows nearly met her hairline. 'Please tell me we're not camping out. I don't go camping. Palaces. I do palaces and Alpine lodges, but camping is not my thing.'

*You'll be fine,* he assured her, *I've been told the scorpions and rattlesnakes aren't too active at present.*

'Oh, I don't mind them,' she snorted, 'I deal with them every day at the office, only a lot bigger and on two legs. It's the camp beds – I like a comfortable bed.'

With the mood somewhat restored, Lane strove to avoid any more mention of The Source. He would attempt to bury those thoughts and feelings, just as Karen had entombed her memories of asking him to stay with her last night. Karen continued with her Pilatos work, this time adding some emails asking her father, mother, and some of the other executives to give her full information relating to the source of Stablex so that she would be able to answer any questions the media might ask. She omitted to mention that her curiosity was because of something that Lane had asked.

Although the flight back to the U.S. took ten hours, because of the seven-hour time zone difference, it was just before midnight when they landed in Chicago. Karen had organized a Pilatos courier to deliver a package to her at the airport, and shortly after walking through customs, she spotted the courier holding a card with her name written on it. Excusing herself from Lane, she went to fetch the object and brought it back to him.

'I know your birthday began over 30 hours ago,' she began, taking a present wrapped in birthday paper from the bag the courier had given her, 'and I know you don't like to celebrate it, and I think we only have a few minutes left before it's over, so I'd be pleased if you'd accept this from me.'

He gave her a *you shouldn't have* sigh and motioned towards some seats where they could sit down. Once seated, he unwrapped the gift to reveal a small porcelain scene with some snow-capped mountains at the rear. In front of the peaks, there was an Alpine lodge, along with a rider from the Spanish Riding School on a Lipizzan horse doing levade, the classical low rear made famous by the dancing white stallions. There were some white flowers, presumably edelweiss blooms, and across the green grass at the front of the figurine was written *We'll always have Austria.* He regarded it in silence, realizing that she had selected it carefully, and it had meaning.

Exhaling after realizing she'd been holding her breath while he looked at it, Karen rushed in with words, 'It's hideous, I know. It's a tourist trade, mass-produced figure, so you don't have to think I spent lots of money on your present, I just liked it.'

He placed it on his knee so he could sign, *So do I.* Smiling at her, he extended his hand to lightly brush her cheek with his fingers. *It's the perfect present. Thank you.*

'When all this is over,' she twirled a hand in the air to indicate all that they were doing on this strange journey of his, 'if we arrive back at where we started, we will still have Austria. I enjoyed those days…and nights.'

It was the closest she came to acknowledging their night together, and he knew horses and people well enough to release pressure when they gave something, so he changed the subject.

*I will treasure this,* he patted the porcelain ornament. *We have an hour of driving to reach our beds. Shall we go?*

'Sure, but where are we going?'

*Near Tonica.*

'Is someone picking us up?' she asked as she stood and followed him to an airline information counter.

*I'm driving. A friend has loaned us a car.*

'Mr. Dimity, welcome,' a uniformed man behind the counter smiled in recognition and held an envelope out to him. 'It's a pleasure to see you again, sir. Ms. Parkinson's vehicle is ready for you. I've informed the valet to have it in the usual spot.'

Taking the envelope, Lane gave him a grin, a wink, and a thumbs-up sign to thank him. So very Australian, thought Karen, watching him, everyone is his best friend.

'Let me guess,' she said dryly as they walked out to the car, 'your friend who's loaned you a car is Laura Parkinson, the head of this airline.'

Lane nodded and signed, *She has horses,* as though that explained everything.

He opened the envelope to read the card inside and chuckled, handing it to Karen to read.

*I think you'll find the car fitting. I don't trust you with my Viper, but I know you're good with wild horses. Give my regards to Karen and have fun. LP XX*

Arching an eyebrow at her, he asked, *Do you know her?*

'We went to school together,' she explained, 'Laura's a few years older, but our parents mixed in the same circles, so we saw each other at social events, too.'

It was no surprise to see a parking valet emerge from a red Mustang and hand the keys to Lane.

'You borrow her cars often?' she quizzed, her mouth twitching at how the employees seemed to know him and accepted that he had free access to the CEO's cars.

*Only if I need to. She has cars at a few airports.*

Stowing their bags on the back seat, he held the keys up to Karen and asked if she'd prefer to drive.

'I'd get speeding tickets all the way from here to Tonica, so I'm sure Laura would prefer you to drive.'

The Mustang rumbled richly as they pulled out of the airport, and Lane handled it as proficiently as she imagined he would, leaving her feeling safe as he focused on the job of driving through the night. In an hour and a half, they turned through white gates with *Bellagrai Farm* written on them, and up a tree-lined driveway with white railed fences on either side. The car pulled to a stop in a car park next to a block of stables, and horses looked out at them, curious about the disturbance to their sleep.

'I know this place,' she informed him, 'they've bought a few of Mum's horses over the years. They have some great eventers here.'

*They do. We have rooms there,* he pointed to one of the four identical stone cottages next to the stables.

'Do we need to meet anyone, or can we go straight to bed?'

*Bed. It's been a long day.*

'Yes, it has.' She wanted to say more, but she didn't want to start a conversation that could keep them up any longer. Sleep was calling her name.

They exited the car and walked to the cottage where a note pinned to the door said in jaunty writing, *Hi Lane! Make yourself at home. See you in the morning – sleep in. Molls.*

He took the note down, folded it, and placed it in his pocket, then showed Karen into the cottage where she had a large bedroom and bathroom on one side of the spacious living area while he had a mirror image of it on the other side.

*Coffee?* He held a hand towards the kitchen.

It was tempting. Nighttime seemed to weave a spell that made her want to talk to him, but she fought it. This wasn't far from home, this was in her own country where she had to remember her responsibilities to Pilatos.

'I think I'll turn in,' she replied, trying to keep the regret from her voice.

*Thanks again for the gift.*

'I hope your birthday wasn't too tough for you. I can understand why you don't want to celebrate them.'

*This year, it was a good birthday.*

'Sleep well,' she turned to go into her bedroom suite but hesitated in the doorway, her shoulders slumped as she tried to find something else to say. There were words entangled inside her, but she didn't know how to bring them out in any order that made sense. Looking back at him, she realized he was waiting in case she had something else to say.

Lit from behind by his bedroom light, he looked so damned sexy in his open-necked shirt and jeans, his eyes shadowed. Karen felt a tingle run through her as she looked at him. This is madness, she scolded herself, this can never be.

His hands moved, and she looked at them closely. *So much to say. So much that we can't say. Words don't always do the job we want them to do.*

She nodded sadly. He understood. Taking another step, she closed the door behind her and leaned back against it, closing her eyes, aware of a longing but refusing to give in to it. She turned her phone off, showered, and went to bed.

It was after eight when she woke, and, after dressing in another pair of grey jeans and a white cotton shirt that had been rolled up alongside the similar sets and crammed into her travel bag, she added Lane's scarf around her neck, pulled on her boots, and went out to find him. He'd already had breakfast and left the cottage, so she grabbed a bottle of water and an apple from the fridge and headed to the stables as she was reasonably sure he'd be with the horses.

Several young men and women were busy carrying buckets and saddles and pushing wheelbarrows of manure around the extensive stable complex. The sounds and smells of the stables were welcoming, and she couldn't help but compare them to the New York streets outside the Pilatos building where she lived. Did she ever feel at home in the city like she did standing amongst the bustle of horse stables? She doubted it, but she had turned her back on this life and accepted the city.

Horses extended noses to her in greeting as she passed, and she rubbed a few on the forehead when they seemed to beg for acknowledgment from her. Behind the stables were some dressage and jumping arenas, so she headed there, imagining that Lane would be where the horses were working.

Turning a corner, she saw the diminutive Molly Vitale in her trademark bright purple jodhpurs and sunflower yellow polo shirt standing in the center of one of the jumping arenas, watching Lane work a big bay gelding around her on a loose-rein canter. When Karen had been competing as a child, Molly had started wearing purple and yellow and was recognizable by the color combination from across a crowded competition arena. Now, in her sixties, the woman was still a little dynamo, riding horses at national competitions and producing top-level event horses from her Bellagrai stables.

Bringing the horse back to a walk, Lane signed to Molly that he was a super horse. He dismounted, and one of Molly's riders led the horse back to its stall. It was only then that Lane looked up and noticed Karen standing in the shadow of the stables. A grin lit his face, and he waved, clearly happy to see her.

'Hello there, Karen,' Molly strode up and held out her hand to give a brisk shake, 'haven't seen you since you were this high.' She held her hand out from her shoulder, which wasn't much higher than Lane's waist.

'Good morning, Mrs. Vitale,' Karen nodded, 'thanks for letting us stay last night.'

'Molly, dear. Or Molls. Whatever,' her staccato way of speaking fired words at her. 'You're not ten now. And always glad to have any chance to get Lane to look over the horses. Off to see some mustangs, eh?'

'Are we?' Karen blinked at Lane, 'I'm just along for the ride, Lane's picking the trail.'

'Yep. Best place to see Lane's work,' Molly strode into the stable corridor, 'wild horses love him. But, before you go, check Jokester, Lane. He'll be glad to see you. He's not doing too well since...since...' her fast words stopped, and she sniffed, shrugged, and waved her emotions away. 'Well, you know.'

They followed her through the stable block to a large, roomy stall with Jokester written on the door. Karen looked in to see a massive black horse standing against the back wall, his head lowered, his ribs clearly outlined under his coat. He looked sick. There were several feed bins with different tantalizing feeds in them, all untouched.

Opening the door, Lane walked slowly towards the big horse. Stopping at his shoulder, he lay a hand on the black's neck and stood still. The horse, as though just realizing someone was there, raised his head slightly, looked at Lane, and let out a heart-rending sound, somewhere between a groan of pain and a nicker of recognition. Moving to his head, Lane put both his hands on the horse's forehead and rubbed. The horse leaned into him and seemed to draw strength from his presence.

'He was Ben's horse,' Molly spoke quietly next to Karen, who recognized the name of Molly's son. Her voice slowed from her usual machine-gun pace as she dabbed at tears between words. 'When he came here six years ago, he was a right mongrel of a horse. He'd kick down stalls, attack grooms, and buck like a bronco. But so much natural talent. Lane came and worked with him for a week, and to this day, I don't know what he did, but he turned that horse around. In a week. He still had some quirks. Still does. But Ben took him on, and they were magic together. Magic. Pure magic. Badminton. Burghley. The Rolex. They were unstoppable. God damn, but that horse loved Ben. Loved him.'

Molly took a wad of tissues from her pocket, wiped her eyes, and blew her nose, taking some seconds to control her crying. Her sadness was contagious, and Karen felt moisture burning in the corners of her own eyes. As far as she knew, Ben Vitale hadn't died, but Molly was speaking as though he had. He was shortlisted for the Olympics with this horse, she remembered that from somewhere, probably her mother.

'It was Jokester who found it, you know. The cancer.' Molly dabbed at her eyes again and sighed. 'He kept pushing at Ben's back whenever he could, and Benny-boy told me it was as though Jokey knew he had a painful lump there and wanted to make it ache more than it did. I had a look. I took him to the hospital immediately. Riddled with it. Full of tumors like the one that came out on his back. He doesn't have much time left, our Ben. Came home for the first time in three weeks last night but hasn't been to see Jokester yet. He'll be down when he wakes. Never used to sleep in, but, you know...' her voice trailed off again.

'I'm so sorry,' Karen whispered, 'we shouldn't have imposed on you.'

'Nonsense,' Molly patted her hand, 'Lane makes everyone feel better. He has a gift. We're always more than pleased to see him.'

Looking at him, Karen was prepared to admit that he did have a gift with horses. Jokester had raised his head slightly, and it seemed as though Lane was whispering to him as his ears were moving back and forth. He took a handful of feed from the nearest feed bin and offered it to the horse. Jokester took it and began to chew.

'I think Jokester knows Ben is dying,' said Molly, 'he's barely eaten a thing since Ben went into hospital. I'm frightened he'll die of grief.'

Karen thought it was unlikely the horse was grieving. He was ill, obviously, but with grief? In her childhood, she had believed horses had emotions, but her father had made it perfectly clear that anthropomorphizing animals didn't do them any favors, and, in fact, it could lead to major issues because they didn't have human emotions. She had learned that they didn't understand the world as humans did and needed to be appreciated for their uniqueness rather than how humans wanted them to be.

Whatever the cause of Jokester's illness, Lane did seem to be providing some relief, and the horse was now nibbling at his food.

'Mum?' a male voice called from the entrance to the stables.

A gaunt man in a black tracksuit leaned on a walking stick, a beanie on his head. Karen had competed against Ben when they were on the junior circuit, but she would never have recognized this shadow of a man as the dynamic youngster she'd once known.

'Here, Ben,' Molly replied, 'with Lane and Jokester. And Karen Lawford – you remember Karen?'

'Karen,' he forced a smile that seemed too much of an effort as it soon faded. He walked slowly towards them. 'Great to see you. It must be close to twenty years.'

'Getting close,' she agreed.

Her attention was drawn back to the stall as Jokester started to whicker softly. His head had come up, and he was staring at the door, his eyes intent, his ears pricked.

Ben said something else, but Karen missed it because she was fascinated by the transformation of the horse when he heard Ben's voice. He released an ear-blasting whinny and rushed to the door, staring into the laneway at Ben, his nostrils quivering as he repeatedly made soft noises, not unlike a mare gives her newborn foal.

'Hello, Jokesy,' Ben got close enough to pat his outstretched face, 'I hear you haven't been eating, you old devil. Neither have I.'

Stepping away from the stable, Karen watched the horse rest his head gently against Ben's frail chest. The sigh the horse uttered spoke of relief at being reunited with his human.

'He loves Ben,' Molly whispered to Karen. 'Don't you ever let anyone tell you that horses don't feel love. He might not write love letters or speak English, but I know love when I see it.'

When Ben stood back from his horse to let Lane out of the stable, the two men held each other in an embrace that told of sincere friendship.

'I was just speaking to Tom,' Ben told him, 'he says you're headed out to Betsy's ranch.'

*She has some new horses and wants me to look at them.*

'Give her my love, won't you? I probably won't get the chance to see her again. You know how it is.'

Lane nodded, his eyes so filled with kindness that it brought a lump to Karen's throat. He was a good man. Gentle and strong and good. He would be destroyed by companies like Pilatos. Men like her father would have nothing but disdain for the traits they saw as weaknesses. She was still coming to terms with it herself.

They talked for a few more minutes before Ben said his farewells and started to make his way back to the house, leaning heavily on his cane. Jokester watched him until he was out of sight before turning his attention to his breakfast, happy to eat now that he had seen his person.

It was interesting to witness, thought Karen, but it was entirely plausible that the horse merely associated Ben with eating and wasn't pining for a friend as much as missing the Pavlov's trigger in his life that stimulated the eating response. Perhaps Ben always fed him, so he had become trained to the routine of only eating the food Ben brought him, and when Ben was in hospital, the horse wasn't smart enough to eat because he was hungry, he required the presence of Ben to initiate eating. That was far more plausible, she thought as they said their goodbyes to Molly, than believing the horse felt love, grief, and a loss of appetite because of his heartache. She would not accept that horses had human emotions. As far as she was concerned, humans credited them with human emotions to explain what they saw, even when a more believable scientific explanation was available.

# CHAPTER EIGHTEEN

*This is a war between those who believe that having more money than they need is the most important thing in life and those who believe that life is more important than all the money that can tempt them. This is the fight to save our souls by saving the lives of the animals and the trees and the vast myriad of life that our greed threatens. This is about understanding the importance of all life and realizing where our insane greed is taking that life… we have to change.*

**Lane Dimity, in response to a question on 'Sixty Minutes' about greed.**

### The Mustangs

There were almost five hours of driving to reach Betsy's ranch, the last stop on their tour. It was located on the edge of Mark Twain National Forest in Missouri. This time, Karen shared the driving, and Lane used his text-to-speech device to talk to her as they traversed Illinois and crossed into Missouri. He explained that Betsy took in truckloads of mustangs from out west and gentled them until they were safe to handle, then adopted them out to responsible homes. When he had the time, he'd drop in and do some work with her horses, and they'd become friends. As far as Karen could work out, everyone who met him became his friend.

He said that he wanted Karen to see one of the mustang stallions that had recently arrived at Betsy's because it would be interesting to compare his behavior to the Lipizzaner and Noriker stallions that she had seen in Austria and contrast all that she had observed with the Stablex stallions.

'Different, but not necessarily better or worse,' she gave him an exasperated look as she pulled into the driveway he'd indicated and slowed to a crawl as the potholes in the dirt were tire traps.

The track wound between fields and patches of forest, and, ahead,

297

mountains cloaked in trees stood guard over the lower slopes. She stopped the car in front of a run-down, wooden building that may have once had paint on its surface but was now the bleak grey of weather-worn timber. A couple of the rails along the front porch were broken, and four hound dogs raced from under the house to bay at the intruders. Karen looked at the house with unease. Unlike the other accommodation Lane had organized for the trip, Betsy's ranch offered little in the way of elegant design or luxury, though it may have made an excellent setting for a horror movie.

'Suddenly, camping doesn't seem such a bad idea,' she muttered, trying not to wrinkle her nose at the untidy, overrun, and neglected house and surrounds nestled into a clearing in a forest at the base of a hill.

*Don't judge a book by its cover,* Lane signed to her as he strode up the pathway to the house.

'I'm not,' she retorted, 'I'm judging a building by the fact that it should be condemned.'

He stopped to face her, *You're a very fussy person.*

'Having standards isn't fussy. Is that a dead raccoon?'

She pointed at the body of a raccoon on the end of the porch. Lane snapped his fingers a couple of times, and the body stirred, stood, and tottered towards him.

'A drunk raccoon?' she asked suspiciously, watching the uneven pace of the little animal.

*He's special,* Lane signed. *Hit by a car, saved by Betsy. She saves things.*

'She's certainly saved money on her renovations,' she looked dubiously at the steps that looked in imminent danger of collapsing.

*You don't mix much outside of your income bracket, do you?* Lane asked when he reached the top of the steps without them caving in on him.

'And just what does that mean?'

*It was a question. It had no meaning.*

'It had meaning.'

*You didn't answer the question. Your answer would have meaning.*

She shook her head at him and sighed, 'You really are a most infuriating man.'

'Yoo-hoo!' A cheery voice called from the trees at the edge of the clearing around the house. 'Lane! Over here!'

A stout, dark-skinned woman with wiry grey hair that stuck out at all angles waved to them. She wore a red checked flannel shirt and patched blue jeans and had five or six dogs dancing around her legs.

'More dogs?' Karen looked incredulously from the pack around Betsy to the hounds that now flopped on the porch.

*These are the old ones, they mostly sleep. She likes dogs. They're her family.*
'And, no doubt, she saves them, too,' she remarked in dry tones.

Lane winked an affirmative, made his way back down the rickety steps, and strode over to the older woman to envelop her in a hug.

'Ah, my favorite man in the world,' the gruff-voiced woman slapped him on the back as he released her, 'it does my heart good to see you, son, it surely does.'

*You are looking beautiful, as always, Betsy.*

She laughed like a schoolgirl and stepped back from him, taking hold of his arms so she could look him up and down. 'And if you ain't the sexiest beast our dear Lord ever put breath into! I bet this city girl can barely keep her hands off you.'

Betsy released Lane and turned her attention to Karen, who was trying to ignore the comment about handling Lane. 'What a long, cool drink of neutral tones you are, child. Karen, I assume?'

Karen stepped forward to shake the offered hand, 'Yes, ma'am, and I gather you're Betsy.'

'That I am, that I am. And these dogs are Collie, Yeppie, Red, Killer, Buster, and Pocket, but you don't have to remember their names, I reckon they'll be forgetting yours.'

She laughed again in the pealing scale of teen laughter that seemed so at odds with her weather-beaten skin and wiry grey hair.

'But we're not going to spend the rest of the day chit-chatting here, come and see the horses, and then we can have ourselves some supper.'

'Lane mentioned that you have some mustangs here, Betsy,' said Karen, trying to engage this eccentric woman in conversation so that she didn't appear the sort of person who only mixed in her own income bracket.

'Sure as heck do!' she exclaimed and laughed. 'They carry the blood of the great warhorses and cavalry horses and conquistador horses, and the government wants to round them up and shoot them! Not on my watch, they won't, not if I can help it.'

*Betsy organized a group of landowners, and they take the ones the government wants to shoot,* Lane explained with his hands. *The stallions are gelded, all the horses are handled, some are broken in, and they have homes for the rest of their lives.*

'Here's my latest lot,' announced Betsy as they walked out from under the shady branches and into another clearing.

Karen's eyes swept over the complex system of horse yards as well as neat log-cabin-style stables and several small fields with high fences. Alert, nervous horses of all colors swung their heads to stare at the three humans. Their heads were high in alarm, and many snorted loudly as a signal to the others that there was danger.

'It's one whole herd,' Betsy stopped well back from the fence so as not to disturb the horses too much. 'There's the big old buck over there.'

She nodded towards a yard where a chestnut and white pinto with a long, knotted mane and tail pounded at the ground with his front hooves, frustrated at being separated from his mares and locked in his own yard. He swung his head to glare at them, anger in his eyes as he regarded the humans.

'And there's fourteen mares, eight foals at foot, and a couple of yearlings, all wild as skit - 'scuse me, Karen, I'm trying not to cuss – and getting used to eating hay and oats and being locked in yards. I haven't laid a hand on any yet, but they'll quiet given time. They deserve a chance. Their families have been here on the land a sight longer than those Washington men who want them dead.'

Karen wasn't sure how this herd of horses that had been taken from their free life on the range and locked in the yards owned by a rather peculiar woman was likely to alter her perception of the Stablex stallions. As far as she could see, these scared and flighty animals were far more imprisoned than the calm and content stallions: these longed for the life they had lost, the stallions couldn't miss something they had never known.

Stepping forward to the rails of the stallion's yard, Lane watched him in silence for a full minute. The stallion raised his head defiantly and stared at him, only breaking his gaze momentarily to check on his mares.

*He's hurting,* Lane turned to look at Karen and Betsy, his dark eyes mirroring the pain he saw in the stallion, *he knows his purpose in life is to protect them from harm, and he feels he's failed them. He doesn't know what to do to help, and it's confusing him.*

'Poor boy,' Betsy cooed, sympathizing with the stallion, one hand going to her heart. 'I thought that might be the case, but he has to stay separate from them. We don't want any more in foal.'

*Perhaps put a couple of the mares that are heavy in foal with him,* Lane scanned the herd of mares and saw a few that were clearly well along with pregnancies, *he's never been alone like this before.*

'Good thinking,' Betsy nodded enthusiastically, clapping her hands lightly together as though this was something to celebrate, 'we'll do that before nightfall.'

Noticing the look of doubt on Karen's face, Lane caught her eye and asked, *You have something to say?*

'Probably not something you want to hear,' she said, a wry twist to her lips.

He dipped his head and opened his hand, asking her to share it anyway.

'You want me to learn about stallions so that I feel sorry for our Friesians, but this,' she waved her hand about airily, 'this attributing human emotions to them, it's not helping. It simply makes me wonder that if you are inventing those emotions on their behalf, what else is believable and what is made up?'

*Why do you think I'm inventing emotions for them?*

'Let's see,' she raised her hands to begin listing off the points on her fingers, 'he's hurting; he knows his purpose in life; he feels he's failed them; he's confused; he's feeling alone. Really? They sound an awful like the human feelings and thoughts you want him to have.'

As they squared up to each other verbally, Betsy leaned against a fence and watched them thoughtfully, chewing on a piece of grass she'd plucked from the base of a post. She knew you could tell a lot about a critter by observing them interacting with others, and she was learning about this city gal and how she and Lane worked together. There was a lot of emotion going on between them, not that she understood it all, but she could feel the air fairly buzzing with all sorts of feelings from both of them.

*Are you sure he doesn't have them?*

'I don't have to be to see that these horses are irrelevant to the situation of my stallions. You want my stallions to be set free, but you want these horses to go from freedom to captivity.'

*I would prefer they be shot than live like the Stablex horses*, his eyes glinted with a touch of steel that she rarely saw in them.

Never one to back away from a steely adversary, she narrowed her eyes and argued, 'So, *your* idea of how a horse should live is the only right way. You think these horses should be tamed and live in captivity because, in your opinion, that is best for them. And you think my stallions should be freed and live out in fields because, in your opinion, that is best for them.'

*There is a lot more to it than that.*

'It seems to me that the crux of the problem is that you are so sure your view is the only correct one.'

*No, the core of this problem is that you don't even know what is going on at Pilatos Farm,* he glared at her challengingly.

'I do know, and what is going on is the top-quality care of stallions who are being used to produce a drug that will save lives.'

*A vanity drug to make wealthy men live longer so they can continue to increase their wealth at the expense of everyone and everything else on this planet*, his fingers were snapping rapidly in an uncharacteristic release of anger. Anger at her and at Pilatos and at everyone who thought that all that mattered in the world was their own desires, their own lives, and their own wealth. Anger at being unable to change what he wanted to change. Anger at what he was learning, bit by bit, about the inner workings of the laboratories at those stables in Kentucky. Anger at feeling locked into a role of being a hero to all the people who wanted a piece of him when he just wanted peace. Anger at himself for not using his voice when there was no physical reason to stop him.

'Again, your opinion,' she cracked back at him, feeling a slight loss of control over her usual cool demeanor.

*The opinion of many who work for you at those stables and who are sickened by what is going on there. Have you learned about The Source? Do you know how many stallions are dying there? Do you know what happens to the horses that don't make it to the stables? If you do know about that, then you are a part of the sickness, the disease, at the heart of Pilatos.*

After focussing on his hands so that she didn't miss a word, she threw up her own hands in frustration and exclaimed, 'What melodramatic drivel! There's no sickness at the heart of Pilatos. It's just another company doing what companies do. *You* have a problem with animals being used to make money, but there's no problem with those animals.'

Lane turned away from her, fastened his hands onto a timber rail in the fence, and shook it rather than direct any more anger at Karen. She infuriated him with her inability to see what was happening, but this was not how he hoped to enlighten her. This fighting head-to-head would only polarise them more, not lead her to an understanding of his views.

'Seems like it's time for some coffee and cake,' Betsy broke in cheerfully, realizing that the two of them had a whole lot more going on than a disagreement over horses. She'd never seen Lane rattled over anything, and this fine-looking woman was flushed in the cheeks and fiery-eyed. Yep, she thought to herself, there was a whole lot of emotion going on here that neither of them understood.

'Thank you,' Karen said with a brittle voice, 'I'm not feeling hungry. I think it would be better if I organized to leave now.'

'Leave?' Betsy smiled curiously at her. 'Because you and Lane had a bit of a spat? Pfft, that's nothing. My husband and I used to scream and yell at each other, we'd throw things and break things and storm around like bears in traps. That bit of a tiff you two had was a mite entertaining for me, but it's nothing that can't be fixed up with my chocolate mud cake. Come on, let's get back to the house.'

Imagining the mess inside the dilapidated house did nothing to tempt Karen, and the thought of eating cake baked by this odd woman and her hands that must smell of dogs was enough to convince her that she needed to contact her office and organize an immediate evacuation. This was no place for her. She didn't belong with these people.

*I'm sorry,* Lane sighed, his anger dissolving into the pit of sadness that sat somewhere near his heart, *I don't want to fight. We only have tonight, and then you can go home tomorrow.*

'And then you'll get your protesters back at our gates?' she asked, anger coloring her words.

'Honey,' Betsy intervened, patting her on the arm, 'take this from an old woman: when a man as good as this one says he's sorry, don't go on the attack. If a dog hasn't been coming up to you when you wanted him to, then he does, you don't go hittin' the dog for coming up to you when that's what you wanted. He said he's sorry. Go forward together from that, don't go driving him away with meanness.'

It was on the tip of Karen's tongue to tell the woman to mind her own business when a handful of realizations pierced her consciousness. Betsy thought she was mean. Lane's eyes had a desperate sadness to them that shouldn't be there. She was offered hospitality, and she was about to throw it in their faces. There was only one night left with Lane. If she left now, the protesters would return to Pilatos a day early because of her - Lane's agreement only covered the time she spent with him. She didn't like seeing him look sad. He shouldn't have to apologize to her. The points listed themselves off in her mind.

Meeting Lane's eyes, she nodded, acknowledging Betsy's words.

'Cake then?' Betsy asked.

'Sounds like a good idea, Betsy, thank you,' she said, trying to put sincerity into the words.

Anyway, she told herself unconvincingly, exposure to germs could help boost the immune system, so eating a slice of cake in the decrepit house might help her fight off next season's influenza. Or give her food poisoning tonight, she snorted, as she followed Betsy and her swarm of dogs back up the path to the trees that divided the horse yards from the house clearing.

'And after we've had coffee,' Betsy chattered away to Karen, 'we'll get Lane to do a bit of his work with that stallion back there. Chances are, you've never seen him work with a wild horse, have you?'

Karen shook her head, glancing at Lane, who walked an arm's length away from her, his expression reflective.

'Hoo-ee,' Betsy slapped her thigh, 'then you have a treat in store for you.'

Glancing at Lane, Karen saw that he looked faintly embarrassed by Betsy's enthusiasm, but the woman's chatter jumped on to another subject, then another, and they were soon through the wooded section and back in the house clearing. The old hound dogs once more raced out, baying loudly, and the rickety raccoon wobbled along the porch rail to be picked up by Betsy and cuddled like a baby. They negotiated the shaky stairs and followed Betsy into the dark interior of the house.

Much to Karen's surprise, the house didn't smell like dogs and cat urine; it smelled of roses. As her sight adjusted to the interior, she could see polished timber floors and pale green walls with high white ceilings. Paintings of country scenes and horses and other animals covered most of the walls, not prints in cheap frames, but genuine works of art in carved wooden frames. The antique furniture was polished and clean, the house was neat, and there were vases of fragrant pink roses on several tables. The inside of the house was nothing like she had expected.

Betsy flicked on a couple of lights. 'I find keeping the curtains drawn during the day helps keep it cool in summer, but it does get a little dark when you come in out of the sunshine. Bathroom's down the corridor there, second on the left, Karen, you go wash your hands and freshen up. Lane, you use the bathroom out the back. I'll put the kettle on and wash up in the kitchen.'

As Karen hesitated, looking around the well-appointed rooms that wouldn't look out of place in any older style mansion, she caught Lane looking at her with a smug look. She glared at him, disliking the intense emotions he provoked within her, and he waved a hand around at the house and listed three words, *book, cover, judge,* before grinning at her and heading to where Betsy had sent him. She wanted to snarl at him but adopted her serene expression and went to the bathroom to wash up. It was a large, clean bathroom with a 1950s décor but modern fittings. Nothing like she'd expected.

When Karen brought up how different the inside of the house was from the outside, Betsy had a chuckle.

'I get told to do up the outside, but I figure it works fine for me. Some no-good thieves pull up at my door, a good look at the hounds and broken timber and unpainted surfaces should be enough to convince them that there's nothing here worth stealing. It also keeps the salesmen moving right along to the next place – this doesn't look like a house belonging to someone who can afford to buy anything they're selling.'

'As I always say, it certainly pays to not judge a book by its cover,' Karen smiled at Betsy, then threw Lane a self-satisfied look.

*Ha ha with sarcasm*, he signed back when Betsy wasn't looking, but there was genuine humor in his eyes that softened Karen's resolve to be at odds with him.

'I also think the house is a bit like me,' continued Betsy, 'you look at the run-down old exterior, and there's no hint of what's inside. You know, I still burn on the inside.'

Her voice wavered and stopped, her eyes focusing on something beyond their sight as she tried to find the words to express her feelings about aging. 'I still have passion and dreams and hopes. I'm still the seventeen-year-old who went to college to study science. I'm still the twenty-five-year-old who fell in love with the most handsome man who ever lived, I'm still the fifty-year-old who grieves his passing. I'm all those things on the inside, but the outside grows shabby. But that's alright. It's the inside that counts.'

'My mother often says the same thing, that it's the inside that counts,' nodded Karen, 'of course, that is easy to say when she's so beautiful on the outside.'

'Still, sounds like a wise woman,' Betsy winked at her. 'Another piece of cake?' she asked, holding out the plate to Karen.

As they talked of Betsy's rescued animals and her plans for this lot of mustangs, Karen felt herself slipping off her high-horse, where she'd been when she'd wanted to call home to organize transport away from this farm and these people. This was far out of her comfort zone, yet she found herself warming to Betsy. Certainly, her cake was genuinely the best cake she had ever eaten, and inside her house felt like a grand old southern manor rather than the ramshackle ruin it had seemed from the outside. And, once more, she felt herself lulled into calmness by the mesmerizing movements of Lane's hands as he talked.

'Do we have time for an hour or two with the stallion?' Betsy asked Lane, who tilted his head in agreement.

'Wonderful! You two head on down, and I'll join you in a few minutes once I tidy this.'

'I'll help,' said Karen, rising and taking the three empty cups to the sink.

Lane carried the plates and cutlery. With Betsy's happy chatter as background noise, they quickly did the dishes, then gathered up the swarm of dogs and left the house.

When they entered the clearing around the horse yards, Betsy placed a restraining hand on Karen's arm and pointed to a log nearby, 'We'll stay back here, well away from his corral. We can sit and watch.

He'll go into his own world, and we'll only be a distraction. I know what he's doing, so I can explain it to you.'

*Thanks,* Lane gave Betsy a thumbs-up sign, and raised his eyebrows questioningly at Karen.

'Suits me,' Karen replied, thinking that she knew enough about horses and horse handling to understand what he was doing.

She was wrong.

The first thing Lane did before entering the horse yard was to remove his boots, socks, and shirt so that he stood bare-chested with bare feet, wearing only his jeans and belt. His upper body was muscular and lean, and he flexed left and right, forward and back, to stretch before working with the horse. Karen found her eyes riveted on the smooth, tanned skin of his back as he reached for the sky, and, without realizing it, she licked her lips as she drank in the sight of him moving in the late afternoon Missouri sun.

'He sure is something, isn't he?' Betsy spoke softly, almost reverently, as she regarded Lane's back.

'Pardon?' Karen looked sideways at her. Was the woman feeling hot under the collar for Lane? That's a distasteful notion, she thought.

'Lane. He's something. Look at those muscles. What I wouldn't do to be thirty years younger and looking like you.'

'I want to know why he's half-naked and bootless when he's about to handle a horse,' said Karen, deliberately ignoring Betsy's comments. 'It is hot, but not hot enough to strip down, and any reasonable horse person knows to wear protective footwear around horses.'

'It's about connecting,' explained Betsy. 'Lane believes that we are all connected: you, me, the animals, the ground, the sun, the air. Everything is connected on an atomic level, and he is anchoring himself to those connections. The power of the earth can flow through his bare feet. The power of the sun can flow through his skin. Just as the horse is connected to the earth and the sun and the air, so now is Lane connected to them, and it will allow him to connect with the horse.'

Arching one eyebrow skeptically, Karen regarded Betsy. Surely, she didn't believe that new-age drivel. She also noticed that Betsy's speech had changed slightly from the folksy farmgirl drawl to a more grammatically correct and clipped voice as she used expressions like 'atomic level.' Was all this an act staged to deceive the woman from Pilatos?

'And you believe that?' Karen questioned her.

Betsy smiled at her and nudged her with her elbow, 'Twenty years ago, I'd have been like you, a cynic and disbeliever in anything like this. You see an eccentric old lady surrounded by too many animals now, but I was a molecular biologist.'

Karen's eyes widened in surprise, though she remembered that Betsy had mentioned being at college studying science.

'My husband and I both worked for a multinational chemical company that produced pesticides and herbicides. He died because of the so-called safe chemicals we were working with, and I walked away from all of that. I could have sued, but money was never going to replace what I'd lost, and without him, I had no fight left. I couldn't live in the city without him. But here…here, with the trees and the animals and the old house, I can live without him physically being here, but he's here in every breath I take. Billions of atoms in every breath were also in his body. It's something Lane wrote about, and it helped me with my grief. Every breath connects us. So, once I wouldn't have believed this drivel, as you call it, but science doesn't know everything, and now I believe in the possibility.'

Lane slid between the rails and stood perfectly still as the mustang eyed him nervously from the opposite side of the yard. From where she sat, Karen couldn't see his face, but from the angle of his head, she assumed he was looking at the ground and not at the stallion.

'He's giving the stallion time to see that he means no harm,' said Betsy softly. 'He's not staring at him aggressively, like a predator about to attack, he's not chasing him or moving. They're together in the yard, and he'll start connecting with the horse. Soon, he'll start the horse moving – not with fear or panic, though; he will want him to move in response to where he puts his body, how he leans or looks. It's a language of the body, and the horse will understand and connect.'

As Betsy had predicted, Lane started the horse moving. He took a step sideways so that he was closer to the hindquarters of the horse, moved his hand, and clicked his tongue to encourage the horse to move forward. He seemed to control the horse by positioning his body in relation to the animal in ways that made the horse move or stop or turn. It looked choreographed. A step behind the eye of the horse and he went forward, a step back away from the horse, and he moved towards him.

'He's getting the horse tired without being scared,' Betsy whispered. 'A scared horse doesn't learn anything, it just remembers being scared. A relaxed and tired horse can learn. Watch how the horse's ears keep flicking towards Lane, showing that he's attentive. When he looks at his mares, Lane will move a hand or take a step to get the horse's attention back on him – he is becoming the center of the horse's world for now and showing that they understand each other.'

After half an hour, the stallion was sweaty and puffing but not showing any sign of fear, just respect for this two-legged creature that was having him move, turn, and stop. Lane relaxed his stance and turned his head away from the stallion, and the horse stopped to catch his breath. As the horse stood watching him, Lane took two steps towards him, stopped, then three steps back, and stopped. He repeated it several times, stepping towards the stallion and then moving away, and the horse kept his eyes on him.

'He's showing the stallion that approaching him isn't a trap,' said Betsy, 'if he tried to walk right up to the horse, he'd feel trapped and attacked and would run. This way, he steps in then steps away – the stepping in puts pressure on the horse, and because the horse stood still, he was rewarded by taking the pressure away and stepping back. If the horse moves, Lane will make him do another twenty or thirty circles of the yard. The idea being that standing is rewarded with more resting, but moving means he keeps on moving, even when he doesn't want to. As he gets tired, he'll learn to make the choice that avoids the work.'

A few seconds after she'd finished, Karen saw what she'd described. When Lane stepped in closer to the horse than before, the stallion snorted and whirled away from him, so Lane kept him moving, around and around, left and right, moving, moving, moving. The stallion wanted to stop, and when Lane took the pressure off and he halted, they started the step-close and step-away routine again.

'You can see the stallion is beginning to understand what is going on,' Betsy pointed at how the stallion almost wanted to run when Lane came within an arm's length of him but stood his ground. 'He doesn't want to do another mile of trotting, and he's realized if he stands still, it doesn't happen. I don't really know what else Lane is doing. I've seen lots of other handlers do a similar quietening technique, but no one else has the ability or the connection or whatever it is, to get to what Lane will do in the next half hour. Maybe he hypnotizes them, I don't know, but watch closely. You're about to see the real magic of Lane Dimity.'

'I thought this was the magic,' said Karen, meaning all that had happened so far.

'Sure, it looks impressive,' agreed Betsy, 'he's entered the yard with a completely unhandled mustang, and look, he has his hand on his shoulder and is touching him for the first time... here it comes...look at the horse.'

Karen would have expected the stallion to become extremely tense at the first touch of a human hand, but instead of snorting, backing away, or striking out at Lane, the stallion immediately became relaxed, his head lowering, his eyes growing calm, and his expression tranquil. Lane kept his hand on the horse's shoulder, standing motionless and...and what? Karen wondered, what was he actually doing? It looked as though the stillness that was at the core of Lane flowed through his hand to the horse, and they stood together, connected by the flow of calming energy through his hand.

When Lane stepped away from the horse, it followed him. He stopped, and the stallion moved close to him and looked as though he was asking to be touched. When Lane reached out his hand and placed it on the back of the stallion, the horse immediately looked comfortable and at peace with what was happening.

Over the next ten minutes, Lane moved around the yard with the horse following, leaning into him whenever he stopped and appearing to enjoy his touch. Then, Lane began to run his hand all over the horse, and it stood still as he moved around it, running his hand over the chestnut and white patterned coat. It did look as though he was hypnotizing the horse as it no longer looked like a wild mustang; instead, it seemed quiet, like a well-handled horse that was used to human contact.

When Lane began resting his body over the horse's back, Karen leaned forward, biting at her lower lip. Surely, he wasn't going to try and get on the horse. This groundwork would have to go on for several days before anyone would consider getting on the stallion. She knew that the serene surface of the animal covered a wild mustang that could explode at any moment. This was the time to stop and leave the horse, not push it beyond what it could possibly handle.

With a lithe and easy action, Lane slipped onto the back of the mustang and sat quietly, patting him gently. Remarkably, it didn't show any sign of being upset. With a quick and sure movement, he slid a thin rope around the horse's neck and tied it off so that it formed a loop. He made a clicking noise, and the horse moved forward, hesitant at first as it adjusted to the weight on its back but not in any way upset about having the man on his back.

'I don't believe it,' Karen looked at Betsy and frowned, 'this must be a set-up. That's not a wild horse. It has to have been ridden before.'

'I know, it's crazy, isn't it?' Betsy grinned back at her, seemingly delighted that she didn't believe her own eyes. 'I've seen him do it a heap of times now, and I don't know what is going on. Everything I know about horses tells me the horse should object to this, it should buck and rear and even throw itself down. It should be scared and angry and determined to get him off its back, but – look – the horse is happy. I swear, it's like the horse loves having him there.'

'No wild horse is going to accept being ridden like that,' Karen said with conviction.

'Not by anyone else, it wouldn't, but, I'm telling you, there's something about Lane that defies logic and science and belief, and yet it happens. It's like he and the horse have started to share thoughts, and he knows what the horse is thinking, and the horse knows what he is thinking, and they work together. You don't have to believe it; it's just a small piece of the puzzle that is Lane. And what an astonishing, amazing, wonderful puzzle he is. He makes the world a better place.'

As they talked, Lane began to trot and canter the horse around the yard, using the neck rope to tell it to slow, stop, or turn and clicking to make it go forward. Betsy reminded her that, in the groundwork over the past hour, every time he asked the horse to go forward, he clicked his tongue so that the horse knew what the sound meant.

'Do you want to take him out?' Betsy called to Lane.

Nodding, Lane pointed to the gate.

'If he takes that horse into the field,' Karen said to Betsy as she stood to go to the yard, 'then I'll know that this is a setup. There is no way he could ride a wild horse for the first time with just that little neck rope and take it into the open.'

'Honey,' Betsy looked at her almost sadly, 'it doesn't matter what you believe, it's not going to change what is. You want to believe that we went to the trouble of having a well-broke horse posing as a mustang just so you can witness some scripted performance, then you go ahead and believe that. It won't change the facts, just your perception of them. I know I'm seeing something amazing, and it makes my heart soar, so it's a bit sad that you're looking at the same thing and seeing what's not there and feeling sour about it. I guess it's how you and Lane look at those stallions and see something completely different.'

She didn't wait for Karen's answer. Instead, she walked to the gate in one of the panels of the mustang's yard and swung it open. With a smile at her, Lane used the neck rope to guide the stallion out of the yard, then he pointed the horse across the clearing at the woods beyond, and they began to canter. By the time they reached the trees, Lane was bent low over the horse's neck, and they were galloping like wild things together, escaping into the wilderness.

Karen heard the hoofbeats for some seconds, then silence as the trees caught and held the sound. Betsy climbed up on the rails of the yard and pointed to a clearing on the hill above the woods. There, still galloping, was Lane on the mustang, moving in total harmony together, as though they ran from a common enemy and sought sanctuary in the mountains beyond. Once more, they disappeared into the trees, and Karen was left with the image of man and horse linked in a way she couldn't understand as they raced together across the land.

Even if they had fabricated the wild mustang scenario and the horse was well-trained, it was still remarkable to see the man and horse working together without force or fear. If the horse was, indeed, a wild stallion, then Karen had witnessed something extraordinary, even mystical, only she didn't believe in fairy-tales, so it couldn't have been that.

Surely not. And yet…

Twenty minutes later, Lane returned, riding the stallion at an easy walk out of the trees, across the grass, and through the gate into his yard. Betsy and Karen remained well back so that they wouldn't spook the horse, even though Karen was having doubts about his wildness. The horse had dried off after their gallop, indicating they'd been walking for long enough for him to cool down and seemed very comfortable with being ridden. Once in the yard, Lane slid off his back, removed the neck rope, and shut the gate, looking back at the horse with an expression of regret, as though he'd rather spend more time with the horse than return to the people.

'What happens with the horse now?' Karen asked Betsy as they watched Lane pat the horse between the rails, his full attention still on the horse.

'He's still wild,' Betsy said, 'you and I wouldn't be able to touch him like that, believe me, I've tried. The horses are drawn to him like moths to lamps. So, I'll spend another few weeks trying to get him calmer for people who aren't Lane, and then he'll be gelded, then we'll spend another few months giving him some basic handling so he can go to a new home. It may not be as good as being free on the range, but it's a helluva lot better than being shot dead and left to rot on that range.'

Karen could concede that point, but she was still puzzled as to how this was relevant to the Stablex horses, and, for a moment, her guard dropped, and she felt she could trust the judgment of this woman next to her. She so rarely felt that she could trust anyone in her world, but Betsy, who rescued dogs, horses, and raccoons, seemed to radiate a warmth of care and protection, and some instinct told her that she could be trusted.

'Betsy,' she began tentatively, unsure how much Betsy knew of the situation with the Friesian stallions and what Lane was trying to accomplish, 'can you see how any of this relates to what Lane wants with our Pilatos horses? Your horses are losing their freedom, while he wants ours to gain their freedom, so I don't see the point.'

Slowly, Betsy's gaze left Lane and turned to rest on Karen, looking her up and down and seeing, perhaps for the first time, what Lane had meant when he had described Ms. Lawford as someone who had lost herself and needed to find her way back. Her dark blue eyes, so Arctic cool at first, now seemed genuinely puzzled, almost guileless, as she tried to work out the reason for being here in Missouri. Once, she had been a horse person, Lane had said, but she had forgotten what that meant, and he hoped that if she found that little girl who still lived somewhere inside, the child who had loved horses, then she might open her eyes and see what was wrong within the Pilatos stables. He believed she was the key to saving the stallions, though, until that moment when Karen looked at her with an earnest expression and genuine bewilderment, Betsy had believed that massive protests and even sabotage would be the only ways to stop what was happening.

'Maybe, it's not just about comparing these horses to your horses, child,' Betsy replied softly so that her voice would not carry to Lane, who was still communing with the stallion. 'Maybe, it's about you reconnecting with the magic of horses. And there is magic. Not the abracadabra-wave-the-magic-wand type, but the sort that catches at your heart and makes you realize that the world is a better place because of horses. The sort of magic we knew in childhood when we were little girls who dreamed of unicorns and pegasuses while we rode ordinary ponies that we loved as much as life itself.'

She took a deep breath, her eyes shining as her mind flooded with her memories of horses from her past, then she continued. 'Do you remember riding bareback on a horse you loved, racing the wind, and leaving the world behind, as you and the horse were one? Do you remember teaching a horse something new, and he understood, as though he could read your mind and knew what you wanted? That's the type of magic that horse people know, the sort of magic that connects us back through the millennia with all those who loved horses and explored the world on their backs, and plowed the fields, and conquered the nations, and ran the races, and sat on their backs as kings and queens of the world even if they owned nothing apart from their horse. I think Lane wants you to see these horses and spend a night sleeping under the stars because he hopes you will remember those things and then look at your Pilatos horses through the eyes of the child who loved horses, the child who still lives within you.'

The words resonated in Karen's mind, and she looked down at her feet as she considered the message behind them. She was reluctant to admit that there was something in them that appealed to her, even called to her, so she remained silent as she thought about the child she had once been, before hiding behind an observation.

'You sound quite different from when we first arrived, Betsy,' she looked sideways at the older woman and smiled. 'I could have almost imagined you cooking up possum stew and wrestling mountain lions barehanded, but now you sound like you could be lecturing at Harvard, well, a spiritual, new-age, mystic version of the Harvard I knew, but your voice has definitely changed.'

'Has it now?' Betsy snorted and winked at her. 'Maybe, I'd just spent too long alone with my hound dogs and raccoons, but speaking to a fancy city lawyer like you has tightened up my talk. And, maybe, I can rustle up some possum stew *and* lecture at Harvard...you shouldn't be too quick to judge the whole of a person from a bit here and there.'

'I think Lane has said something similar.'

Betsy laughed, 'A lot of my words come from him. He says the things, so many of us think and feel but can't find the words to express. I guess it's ironic that a man who doesn't speak ends up writing the words that so many of us want to say.'

The rattling of the gate drew their attention back to Lane.

*Can we put some mares in with him?* Lane signed to them once they were looking.

'Sure thing,' Betsy replied, 'we'll sort them up so those in-foal ones can be with him.'

*Good.* Lane nodded and smiled at the horse as though he'd agreed to do this for the stallion and was honoring his side of the bargain.

Betsy worked one of the gates in the mares' yard as Karen and Lane quietly moved the mares around until the three they wanted were near the gate, which then opened to let them through to a smaller enclosure. From there, Betsy was able to move them along a connecting laneway of high fence panels to reach the stallion yard.

The stallion was whickering, snorting, and snuffling as his mares approached one of the gates into his yard, and when Betsy swung it open so that they could enter, he welcomed them with enthusiastic tail swishing and stomps of excitement. He went up to each mare and stretched his neck out to greet them, muzzle to muzzle, sharing breath through quivering nostrils and making what appeared to be happy sounds about being reunited.

*He'll be happier now,* Lane signed, a smile touching his lips as he regarded the stallion and his mares, *he's never had to spend a night without touching another horse, and it was killing him being separated from them.*

'It won't be so bad once he's gelded,' added Betsy, 'but, as usual, you're right, Lane. This is what he needs for now.'

Watching how the stallion rested his head over the back of one of the mares and closed his eyes, breathing a great sigh of contentment, Karen could understand how easy it was to overlay human emotions on the instinctive actions of the animals. He did look happy to have the company of his mares, but how could she know what he really felt?

A few hours later, after they'd fed the horses and had dinner, Betsy took some lanterns and helped them set up inflatable mattresses and bedding near the horse yards, explaining to Karen that camping out next to the mustangs was a good way to get them used to the presence of humans. Karen had been going to wear jeans and a shirt for the night as she wasn't prepared to wear her silk pajamas in the wilderness, but Betsy had found some navy-blue sweat pants and a matching t-shirt in her size, assuring her that they would be much more comfortable for sleeping than jeans and a buttoned shirt. The clothes were clean and smelled faintly of lavender and roses rather than dogs and raccoons, so Karen was happy to accept the offer.

When Lane saw her in the casual clothes that hugged her figure, giving her a more outdoorsy look than office executive, he raised his brows and pointed at them, signing, *Not grey.*

She gave him one of her dry, *Really?* looks, and made a V of two fingers on her right hand to point at his eyes, and replied, 'Not color-blind,' before glancing down at his garish colored board shirts and orange t-shirt, adding, 'although, the jury might be out on that because I'm fairly sure anyone who could see in color wouldn't put those together.'

He merely grinned at her, amused by her remarks about his clothes. On the front of his t-shirt was an image of a cowboy riding a bucking bull and a clock hitting the eight-second mark with the words, *Time Is Up.*

*Time is up.* They were merely words on a garment referring to the eight seconds of a bull-ride, but Karen found herself frowning at them, thinking they were telling her more. The background of Betsy's chatter had faded out as she tumbled through her thoughts, and when they pierced the bubble of her awareness, she realized she'd missed most of what she'd been saying.

'And it's something completely different from your life in New York, I bet,' she chuckled as she plumped up Karen's pillow, 'out under the moon and stars in a field surrounded by ancient trees, hugging the edge of the mountains.'

'I'm not one for camping,' said Karen stiffly, standing slightly apart from Lane and Betsy, who were preparing the beds. She was not at all comfortable with the notion of sleeping outside and was once more wishing she had ended the trip early and called someone to come and get her.

'You'll like this camping,' Betsy assured her, 'these beds are more comfortable than any motel bed I've ever slept in.'

'Hm,' Karen eyed the two double airbeds dubiously.

'And you'll be back at your desk tomorrow afternoon,' Betsy assured her, 'so don't be scared of doing something out of the ordinary, like going to sleep under the Missouri stars tonight. And don't you be worrying about dangers out here – with all these mustangs on two sides of you and my dogs standing guard on the other sides, nothing is going to get you. Enjoy the clean air, clear skies, and the sounds of horses. Could life get any better?'

'I could be thirty stories up in a five-star hotel with a bathroom ten steps from my bed. That could be better.'

'Nonsense,' scoffed Betsy, 'you're higher above sea level here than thirty stories in New York, and there's a bathroom and flushing toilet only forty yards away in that first stable.'

'Perfect,' Karen said dryly.

'Here's a basket of goodies in case you get peckish during the night,' Betsy placed a wicker basket between their two camp-beds, 'and you'll find water and some of my apple cider in there as well.'

*Thanks for everything,* Lane gave Betsy one of his heart-stopping smiles.

'No need for that,' she leaned in and gave him a hug, then rested a hand on his cheek in a gesture of affection as she looked up into his eyes. 'If any of my babies had lived, I could have only hoped that they'd be like you. You give me hope that the world can be cured.'

He snorted softly and gave a small shake of his head to show that her expectations were a little high.

'No,' she insisted, 'you make people better versions of themselves. Don't underestimate your ability to bring change. Your words are powerful. And wherever there is a great power of good, it will be balanced with the strength of evil trying to destroy it. So, you be careful in coming days,' she glanced sideways at Karen and narrowed her eyes thoughtfully. 'If Lane is the light and what Pilatos is doing is the dark, then you are the point where they meet, Karen. You are the tipping point, balanced between the two.'

One voice within Karen's mind wanted to shout belligerently that her words were melodramatic garbage, while another voice hid in a shadowed corner and bowed her head, sensing the truth in what she said. Her lips remained sealed: silence was sometimes the best option.

Betsy sighed when Karen didn't speak into the silence. 'Ah well, you two enjoy your night out here. No fighting, now – it's your last night together, and you should count your blessings, not be all prickly about what one wants that the other doesn't want when it comes to those black horses.'

Slapping at an insect that landed on her arm, Karen twitched an eyebrow and asked, 'Blessings?'

'Not used to counting them, are you?' Betsy looked at her, the soft yellow light of the lantern, that rested on the ground near the beds, casting hauntingly unusual shadows across her face.

Karen slapped at another insect. 'I'm just not sure what the blessings are when I'm being eaten alive by insects and sleeping on the ground.'

'There's insect repellent in the basket,' Betsy told her, 'so that's a blessing. And you're going to be an arm's distance away all night from a man who millions of others dream of knowing. That's a blessing. And in the seconds it's taken for me to say this, probably a hundred people, even two or three hundred, have starved to death or been tortured or raped or murdered, and you're standing there, well-fed and safe and free, with a home to go back to and the power to do what you want in life…if that isn't a whole ship-full of blessings right there, I don't know what is. So, count them, honey. Count them.'

With that, Betsy and her cloud of dogs walked away into the gloom, finding the path back to the house easily in the moonlight.

# CHAPTER NINETEEN

*Let your young horse learn to be a horse first. He needs to understand the other horses before he can understand you. Don't put too much pressure on his mind or his body while he's young. Take him slow. Don't be in so much of a hurry that you lose twenty good years for the sake of one hard year under saddle early on.*

**Lane Dimity, Hints For Horses, p. 68**

### Under the Missouri Stars

Karen and Lane stood rather awkwardly between the two beds, with the lantern placed down past the foot of the beds. There was enough light from the moon to see, even without the lamp, but Karen guessed they would talk before sleeping, and the extra light would come in handy for what Lane's hands were saying.

'Our last night,' Karen began, not knowing where her words were going but feeling compelled to drop some sound into the heavy silence. 'It's been quite the trip. One of those experiences that seem to have been going on for weeks, but it has passed in a blink.'

*I hope you enjoyed it,* he signed before lowering himself to his bed and lying on top of the covers, as the night was still warm.

'Yes, I have,' she replied, almost surprised that it was the truth. Following his lead, she stretched out on the bed and found it to be remarkably comfortable. Lying on her left side, she propped her head on her left arm and looked over at him lying on his right side with both hands free so he could sign. 'It's probably the strangest thing I've ever done for Pilatos: go on a whirlwind tour around the world looking at horses with Lane Dimity so that he'll call off his protesters.'

*Is that the only reason you came?*

'I don't know. Maybe. Perhaps I was curious to see what you'd show me.'

*Was it worth giving up these days? Or was the only worthwhile thing the fact that the protesters have been quiet?*

'It's been good. No, more than good,' she rolled onto her back and gazed up at the stars, suddenly struck by their brightness and number. 'Meeting Lukas, going to the Spanish Riding School, seeing the Noriker stallions released that day, these mustangs, Betsy... there's so much to take in. It was all worthwhile, though.'

When she finished talking, she turned her head so that she could see his hands speak to her.

*I have loved these days,* he smiled at her, causing odd palpitations of her heart, *I'm sorry I don't speak. This signing or texting instead of speaking must be very tiresome for you. I want to speak, but the sound doesn't come. I'm sorry.*

'Don't be sorry,' she said earnestly, 'words from you have meaning, rather than the endless chatter that becomes arduous as people shovel never-ending words into empty spaces. You give the empty spaces significance. I haven't once thought it was tiresome or that it was anything you should apologize for, and I'm tickled by the fact that I hear your signing and your texts with an Australian accent. Who'd have thought?'

*Thank you*, the soft expression in his eyes added depth to the simple hand movements.

'No, thank you,' she said, bringing up one of the thoughts she that had bubbled to the surface in her dreams the previous night. 'I think I've spoken more openly to you than I've ever done before to anyone. I'm not sure that's a good thing, mind you, but I've never had the inclination to talk like we have talked these past few days, so thank you for that.'

*I hope it's a good thing,* he inclined his head.

'If we've done enough thankyous,' she rolled back on her left side to face him, crooking the pillow in her left arm and leaning her head on it, 'what happens after this? Do we just part ways and go back to you trying to free the stallions and me trying to prove that they have happy lives?'

*I hope you will visit the stallions and look at them closely, comparing them to all the horses over the past few days. I hope you'll remember how you loved horses when you were a child. I hope you'll find out more about The Source. I hope you'll find out why your stallions are dying. I hope you'll consider that what is happening to them is more than happy horses kept in stables. I hope you see that Stablex is a drug of unfairness and inequality. I hope you'll see that earning more money than you would ever need is not the way to being happy. I hope so many things, and I hope you forgive yourself if it's too late when you see all those things.*

'That's an awful lot to hope for,' she smiled at him, admiring his high hopes but knowing he was setting the bar too high. 'I hate to see your hopes dashed, but I can't see all that happening.'

*At least I tried*, he signed and shrugged.

'A quick change of subject,' Karen remembered something she wanted to ask about, 'before when Betsy said *if any of her babies had lived*, what did she mean by that? What happened to her children?'

Lane held up a finger to ask her to wait, then he reached into his bag on the other side of his bed and took out an electronic device with two detached screens and a keyboard. Sitting up on the edge of his bed, his feet crossed in the grass, he handed Karen one screen and set an identical one next to his feet where he could see it, and placed a keyboard on his knees.

Nodding at her, he signed, *I can type faster than I can sign.*

His fingers began flying over the keyboard as his attention was divided between looking at his screen to check for errors and looking at Karen.

*This will make it easier,* he typed, *and I can be more accurate with my words. You can still talk while I write, and I hope you read my words with an educated and intelligent-sounding Australian accent, not a bogan one.*

'Bogan?' she cocked an eyebrow at him, having no idea what that meant.

He grinned, *Houso, bogan, westie. A bit like the Aussie equivalent of redneck white-trash.*

'I understand. I'm imagining a good accent, not a *bogan* one. So, Betsy?'

*Betsy had three babies,* he looked at her as he typed, *two were stillborn, the other lived for a week. She thinks it was the chemicals she and her husband were working with, but the company had studies proving it was safe. Other women working there had miscarriages and stillbirths, as well. She felt their profits were more important than the babies. She doesn't like corporate America.*

There was not a lot Karen could say to that since she was a part of corporate America. She knew that denying responsibility for any ill-effects of drugs and chemicals in the hope that litigation would go away was always the first line of defense. Producing research that was biased in favor of the company's chemicals was standard practice. Being desperate to disprove any link between deaths of babies and their chemicals would have been the path any company would have taken, it was just what they did. But thinking of Betsy having three dead babies and losing her husband to cancer somehow made the standard defensive actions of a company seem sickening. It was what Pilatos would do, though.

'That is tragic. If the company was responsible, they should have compensated her. '

Lane looked at her sadly because she still didn't seem to understand that money was not compensation for losing the people you love. *There was no compensation for what she lost. If she had tried for it, they would have fought her, and she didn't want to fight, she wanted her husband and children. She quit. She receives an anonymous donation every year that is more than her salary, so I think someone at the company feels responsible.*

'She looks like she'd have been a good mother.'

*She mothers all these animals who need someone to love them. I try and save the horses that I couldn't save when I was a child. You try and be the person your father wants you to be. We're all locked into our own lives, doing what we feel we should do.*

'I think I'm more than a woman seeking her father's approval,' Karen frowned at him, irked that he was right.

*Much more, but that is part of you. The part that stops you from seeing what is happening in those stables.*

'We're heading back down that road where we end up fighting,' she told him, 'so tell me about that mustang stallion, instead. Is he really wild, or was that all scripted?'

Lane laughed, *Scripted? You think we took a quiet horse and pretended he was wild?*

'I think it's highly possible.'

Lane shook his head, *He was wild. He still is. I haven't tamed him. We just worked together, but I would have to start all over again if I worked with him tomorrow.*

'When you put your hand on him, he seemed to change. It was as though you were speaking to him through touch. Betsy said it was magic,' she snorted, 'I know it's not. I don't believe in magic.'

*It's not magic.* He held up a hand and examined it as though looking for something that wasn't there, then he stretched it out towards her and hovered it above her arm, his eyes asking permission to touch her skin as he'd touched the stallion.

She nodded, holding her breath as his hand softly, gently, tenderly lowered to rest on the bare skin of her arm. His eyes were on hers as he thought of laughing with her, smiling with her, sharing happy moments, feeling content together. Karen didn't know *what* she was feeling, but it felt good. There was a warmth that flowed from his hand to her body, and she felt heated within from the touch and strangely content. Yes. She felt a sense of contentment, as though all was well with the world now that he was connected to her by the soft touch of his hand. She realized that she was reacting much the same way as the horse.

'That is unusual, to say the least,' she said when he withdrew his hand, 'it was as though energy was flowing through you to me.'

*Energy flows everywhere,* he wrote, *that was why I had bare feet, so the energy could flow from the earth to me and then to the horse.*

She gave him a doubtful look, 'I can buy the notion that energy flows from you to me, or to the horse, but you're losing me when you say it flows from the earth. That's a little too new-age and cosmic-monkey for me.'

With a shrug, he pointed out, *Not so much new-age as ancient. Something many old cultures believe.*

'Believing something doesn't make it true, as I've pointed out before with the tooth fairy and Santa. Some of them believed sacrificing virgins made their gods happy, so I hope you don't practice that simply because it's an ancient belief.'

The wry look she gave him caused him to laugh. *I'm very selective.*

'Selective about which virgins you sacrifice?'

He laughed again and met her eyes as he wrote, *Selective about which beliefs I follow. What beliefs do you have?*

'I struggle with the whole notion of belief when it relates to that which can't be proven. As I just said, believing something doesn't make it true, no matter how many others you brainwash or kill for your beliefs – not your beliefs, as in Lane Dimity's beliefs, just a generic use of the word *your*. I might not be able to prove that this or that belief system is flawed or false, but then, I can't prove that we're not sentient beings living within a virtual universe.'

She expected him to be bewildered by her reference to the virtual universe theory and was surprised when his eyes lit up with enthusiastic interest. The words raced across her screen as his fingers flew over the keyboard, their gaze often meeting as she looked up from the words, and he watched her without looking at his keyboard.

*I wonder the same thing. When I think how far we've come with computers in fifty years, then I try to imagine what we will be doing with them in a hundred years or a thousand years, I can see humanity inventing computer-based universes with sentient life forms in them, all following the laws of physics as we understand them. And then I have to wonder - if we could do that in the future, how would we know that we aren't the sentient beings in a computer-generated universe created by another intelligent race?*

'Exactly!' Karen sat up on her camp bed, excited about her

galloping thoughts being met by a similar mind. 'And the more I look for evidence to prove that we're not within that computer-generated universe, the more I'm unable to find any proof. Even the way we think and make decisions seems to be binary. If we have ten things to choose between, we tend to think this-or-that through them, choosing between two, and then choosing between the next two.'

*I thought that, too,* he nodded as he wrote, *and I thought that perhaps death could be used as proof that we're not in a simulated universe, but it supports the simulation. Assuming the computer doesn't have infinite storage, then the program space taken up for an individual's experiences, thoughts, and actions is going to be needed for another individual, so one life program is ended, and the space is used to write another life program.*

'I hadn't thought of that aspect,' she enthused, her eyes bright as she leaned forward to speak to him, 'but I had wondered about how our DNA is composed of just four proteins, Cytosine, Guanine, Thymine, and Adenine, and it's the almost infinite shuffling of those four that gives us all the variations of life on this earth, which isn't that far removed from how using a one and a zero gives us the infinite range of digital information we can have on computers.'

*And if you were using a computer program to design your simulated life forms, then having four bases to form all life forms, from plants to whales to the dominant intelligent life, would be a logical move.*

'Of course,' she grinned at him, 'if we *were* in a simulated universe, it would mean that all your work trying to prove to me that horses have souls is just a waste of time as they would be bits of computer program, like us, and none of us would have souls.'

*Ouch, you have me there. I might opt out of the simulated universe theory.*

Suddenly, Karen was struck by how bizarre their conversation in its context had become, and she burst out laughing. An Australian and an American camping next to corrals full of mustangs, communicating with speech and writing to discuss the possibility of being simulated life forms.

'How ridiculous are we?' she asked, her shoulders shaking with mirth. 'We're real, talking about not being real.'

*It's like a gym workout for the brain,* his words popped up before her, *and considering all possibilities helps free us from being tied to one belief.*

'But there's so much we could be talking about that is important, and we're dabbling in theoretical nonsense that is meaningless.'

*Not meaningless,* he shook his head, *we've shared ideas, we've seen that we both have abstract thoughts and that we consider unusual possibilities.*

Karen exhaled, seeing sense in his words. 'I guess if I had to be stranded on a desert island for a decade with one other person, I'd much rather someone whose mind danced with possibilities than a person who trudged in ruts of thinking.'

*Are you saying you'd like to be stranded on a desert island with me?* He waggled his eyebrows at her, making her laugh again.

'You should be so lucky,' she snorted, 'but I'll concede that it's not unenjoyable talking to you.'

*Is 'not unenjoyable' an expression?*

'It is now. Think of it as unenthusiastic praise.'

This time, he laughed, *I'm feeling ever so faintly complimented.*

'Good. You have far too many people fawning all over you, so weak approval should be a necessary change. I hope those close friends of yours don't deify you – with your army of followers, you might need to be reminded of your mortality.'

*They remind me of it*, he grinned, thinking of how they teased him about his fans. *They'll be here in the morning if you want to see them give me a hard time. They're flying in on the plane that will be taking you home.*

'Home,' she mused, looking around at the moonlit field, the horses, and the stars, 'it seems to be in another universe from here. Where will the plane land?'

*Betsy's neighbor to the east has an airstrip. There'll be a car there for them. They'll come over, and you can leave, and then this will be over.*

'Do we even know what *this* is?' she asked, looking directly at him, deeply aware of the short distance that separated them. He could reach forward and touch her like he had earlier when he gently laid his hand on her arm.

Meeting her gaze, he shook his head. Words were unnecessary to explain the confusion he felt about what drew them together when every logical part of life dictated that they should be adversaries. They searched each other's eyes, both feeling the tightness in their chests that made it difficult to breathe.

If Marcus had ever made her feel like this, she would never have let him leave. If she had been at a dinner somewhere in New York and had met a man who made her feel like this, she would have gone back to his place and given herself to him or dragged him back to her apartment. If this had been any other man apart from the indefinable, enigmatic, complicated, and unfathomable Lane Dimity, she would have known where these feelings would take them, but he was so unpredictable, and so unattainable, that she had no inkling where any of this was going. He looked at her as though he hungered for her, and yet he would not reach out and take what she offered.

She began to lean forward, taking the initiative since some code of honor, shyness, or old-fashioned values were holding him back. The naked desire in his gaze as he glanced down at her lips and back to her eyes was clear, and she wanted him to give in to it, as she was doing by slowly, ever so slowly, moving towards him.

A massive clash of steel against steel caused them both to swing around to look at the horses. One of the metal gates between yards had come undone, and a horse had crashed against it, slamming the gate back onto a metal fence panel. The horses could move into another yard, and though they couldn't escape, the distraction allowed Lane to escape. He stood and went to check on the horses, absconding from the kiss that had only been moments away.

Karen slumped back onto her bed and stared at the tall, lean Australian as he walked away, her cheeks warm with humiliation. She had been going to throw herself at him, and he knew it, and he walked away. Perhaps she had mistaken the expression in his eyes, and he hadn't felt desire for her at all. Maybe he just felt confusion that she had been staring so intently at him like a predator about to pounce on her prey. But there had been the night in Austria. What did that night mean if he rejected her now? He had come to her bed, and he had held her…and now he walked away.

'I don't understand,' she called to him as he leaned against the fence, watching the horses ten meters away.

He turned his head to look at her.

'I don't understand what this is,' she continued, an unexpected vulnerability in her voice.

She felt emotional and hurt and could have curled up in her bed and blocked this out of her mind, but she wanted to understand. She thought that whatever this was between them could have been unique and amazing, sexual and sensual, addictive, inspiring, erotic, remarkable, and life-changing. It could have been all that, or maybe she imagined it, and there was nothing there at all. She couldn't let it go, she had to know.

'I haven't felt like this before,' she confessed, her voice soft as she knew he would hear her easily on the still night air. 'Maybe I just didn't feel. Marcus left me, and I felt nothing. I went home and packed up his things as though I was moving a stranger out of my life. But this,' she moved her hand back and forth between them to indicate a connection, 'I don't know what this is. I know it hurts because I was going to kiss you then, and I thought you wanted that, too, but you rejected me. Was I wrong?'

In the pale light of the moon, she could see his eyes on her and sensed a sadness in them. He moved closer so that she could see his hands.

*You weren't wrong,* he signed, *I wanted you.*

'But not now? You wanted me a few minutes ago, but not now?'

*I always want you. I always have and always will.*

The words brought tears to her eyes because of the enormity of the admission in those words. They implied that he would not give in to his desires, that this was destined never to be.

'Is there any reason why we can't have what we both want tonight?'

*Too many reasons.*

'Don't be abstruse or obtuse,' she shook her head, 'we're here, together. It seems we both want the same thing. It's not 1950. Why not?'

*I don't want to complicate what's coming with more emotions, more guilt, more issues than are already there. I didn't want to make it about us.*

'I think it's too late for that,' she smiled pensively.

*I want us to have the chance of a relationship next month, and the month after, and next year, and the year after. If we start now, then whatever might happen in the coming weeks with Stablex will most likely kill what we have tonight.*

'If you're planning to do something that will destroy any relationship we might establish tonight,' she argued logically, 'then it's going to kill whatever chance we have of a relationship in the future, anyway. So, we may as well have tonight.'

He shook his head sadly at her sensible words, uttered without longing, and lacking any hint of the emotions that tore at his heart when he looked at her. Part of him was sure that she had deep rivers of passion coursing through her body and soul, but her calm words sounded more like she was offering to have a game of tennis with him rather than make love under the stars next to the wild horses.

*May as well?* He questioned her choice of words. *You make it sound as though us being together is distasteful, but we may as well do it because we're here.*

'That's not how I meant it,' she sighed, wishing she was able to put emotions into words as easily as she could argue law, facts, and business. There was a tangle of feelings moving within, trying to break free from all the years of being shackled and hidden in the locked rooms of her mind. They scared her with their intensity. It was as though they threatened to break her entire life apart if she let them loose, but looking into his eyes made her want to release them and disregard the consequences.

*Tell me what you're thinking,* he looked at her as though he could see into those locked rooms, and his gaze coaxed the words from her.

'I don't know how to describe what I'm thinking and feeling,' she admitted. 'Believe me, I want this so much more than I've wanted anyone - or anything - in a long time, perhaps forever. I don't know. But I can't put it into words. It's bigger than words.'

*I know what it's like to discover that words aren't always adequate.*

'Then, can we both forget words?' she whispered, realizing that her desperate craving for him in this moment was something far beyond the power of words to describe. 'Please? Can we have this one night?'

*One night will never be enough for me.*

His eyes dropped to her mouth, and the image of him kissing those lips filled his thoughts, driving all reservations away. He wanted her. She wanted him. He could see that in her eyes and in the parted lips that beckoned him closer.

He gave in to desire and went to her. He knelt on the grass next to her bed and placed his hands on either side of her face, knowing what would happen once he touched her. He saw her eyes open wide in surprise as the tingle of energy flowed from his hands, and then she leaned into them, hungry for more. She closed her eyes and inhaled, breathing in the cooling night air and feeling the magic of Lane's touch unlocking all the hidden rooms in her mind and soul.

There were no words to describe the euphoria that enveloped her as the power from his touch flooded her senses. She desperately wanted more; she wanted everything. She wanted him.

When his hands left her, the current of energy that had been filling her was cut off, and she opened her eyes to look at him. He regarded her wistfully as he waited for her to see the words from his hands.

*Will you try to forgive me for what may happen over the next few weeks?*

She nodded blindly, agreeing to anything if it would make him touch her again.

*And will you forgive yourself for whatever you do? I need you to know that I will not blame you, even if you think you have betrayed me. We do what we have to do.*

'I won't betray you,' she whispered, believing her words at that moment when her body was desperate for his.

You will, he thought to himself, as I will you, and I don't think I want to live in the world where we do that to each other.

Leaning over to the side, Lane turned out the lantern, leaving them awash in the reflected light of the moon. He reverently brushed his hand through her hair, moving it away from her face so that he could burn the image of her perfection into his memory.

Her eyes, heavy with desire, gazed up at him as he placed a finger on her lips and traced their outline. He felt a shudder in her body as his other hand moved to the skin of her back under her shirt and traced its way up her spine. Her eyes closed as she was lost in the sensations of his hands exploring her skin.

'You are so beautiful,' he whispered softly as he lowered his mouth to hers, and the tsunami of desire carried them away.

# CHAPTER TWENTY

*In any moment, always remember that all you will ever be will grow from that moment. Make your moments count.*
**Lane Dimity on Twitter. Twenty million likes.**

### Back to the Pilatos Building - New York

The Embraer Phenom 100E jet taking Karen back to New York passed over Evansville in Indiana before it hit her like an unexpected medicine ball to the chest. Lane had uttered the only words she had ever heard him say directly to her, calling her beautiful as they lay together under the Missouri skies. The instant the memory pushed her other rampaging thoughts aside, she clasped her hands together in front of her chest and bowed her head over them, gasping for breath. Tears burned her eyes and rolled down her face.

Oh, it hurt, a voice in her mind cried as her body folded around her clasped hands, collapsing in on itself. It was like the pain she'd suffered when she found the empty stall after her father had sold her pony. It was like the feeling of holding her dog when he died in her arms, and she felt pain like the shattering of a glass heart in her chest. He had spoken to her, and she knew she would never hear his voice again because she was going back to Pilatos to betray him. She couldn't do it, but she had to do it. It would destroy her, but it had to be done. It was the wrong thing to do, but it was the right thing to do. He had spoken to her, and he never would again.

She rocked back and forth in the cream leather seat of the small jet, the only passenger in the four seats, overcome with emotion. Guilt and grief and pain and a desperate longing for last night to have never ended broke every brittle piece of her insides. She was broken, and she sobbed for the loss of the most remarkable person she had ever known.

The night had been like an erotic dream that was so perfect that some part of her knew it could only ever be the one night. When he'd finally fallen to sleep, their bodies entangled, she rested her head on his shoulder, watching his chest rise and fall. She wished that the moment would become stuck in a vortex of time so that she could spend eternity in those minutes, forever having just finished making love and about to drift into sleep, feeling connected to perfection.

But as that had passed, so may this, and her memories of their night fragmented into pieces that were being swept away by her return to her real life. In all the days away from the office, she had remained tethered to her work by the documents on her laptop that came in each day to be perused and checked and sent back. Now, that tether was pulling her back to the colorless and structured world of Pilatos, where she had responsibilities. And she knew that her job was to serve the company and all the employees who depended on her and do what was right for them.

It was time to let go of that bubble of freedom, where she traveled with Lane, met his friends, and fell under his spell. That was the dream, and it was over. Flying back to her waking life in a luxury jet loaned to Lane by Laura Parkinson was that period of waking, where the dreams were left behind, and the duties of work imposed themselves over all that she did. She could not choose the dream over wakefulness, no matter how much she wanted to cling to those moments with him. She would wake, and she would betray the man from her dreams. His words, 'You are so beautiful,' would be locked away in her mind, along with the empty stall and the dog she'd loved.

*You do not let emotions get in the way of business,* her father's voice boomed in her mind, blowing away more fragments of her broken memories. That was the reality she was returning to, and the memory of Lane's fingers caressing her flesh with worship in their touch had to be pushed away. But it hurt. Oh, how it hurt.

When she'd woken not long after sunrise that morning, alone in her bed, the Missouri air was chilled, and she pulled the covers closer around her and looked for Lane. He had already thrown hay to the horses and was leaning against the fence, watching the stallion and his heavily pregnant mares eating. Her heart skipped crazily at the sight of him, and she melted a little on the inside at the memory of their night.

'Looks like a bloody beautiful day to be alive!' A distinctly Australian voice shouted from the trees towards Betsy's house. Matt.

Karen immediately felt for the t-shirt and sweat pants and quickly pulled them on, then reached over to ruffle Lane's bed a little more so it looked slept in. Looking up, she saw Lane gazing at her regretfully, knowing that their time together had passed. She wanted to mortgage the rest of her life to pay for a different ending to their night, but it was ending with his friends and their loud voices, and judgemental looks, arriving to take him away from her.

*I wish...* he signed to her, the expression in his eyes telling her a dozen different wishes, none of them involving disruptions by friends.

She nodded, signing to him for the first time, *I wish, too.*

'Hey, bro!' Matt called as soon as he entered the clearing and saw Lane. 'Long time no see.'

With a wide grin, Matt strode towards Lane, pausing briefly at their campsite to give Karen a cheeky wink and a, 'G'day' as he cast a look at the two inflatable mattresses to ensure that both showed signs of use. Continuing, he wrapped his friend in a bear hug and lifted him off the ground.

'God, it's good to see you again!'

*It's only been five nights*, Lane signed, once released from the enthusiastic greeting.

'Yeah, but do you realize how few times we've been apart for that amount of time these past few years? We're joined at the hip, the four of us, and it hurts when one isn't there. So, how'd things go?'

*I can't speak for Karen, but I had a great time.*

'A great time?' Matt chortled, 'I thought you were trying to prove to our corporate friend here that stallions deserve better treatment than what her horses get, not have a great time. How did you find it, Karen?'

She had risen to her feet and was heading to the bathroom in the small stable complex with her towel and clothes but stopped to look at Matt, a strained smile on her face. 'It was interesting and educational and very different from anything I've done before.'

'Huh,' he grunted and nodded his head, 'so, not that great for you, eh?'

'That's not what I meant.'

*Where are the others?* Lane asked him, giving Karen the chance to remove herself from the conversation, which she did.

'Having a chat with Betsy about her raccoons. I said I'd come and get you two for breakfast and help feed the horses, but it looks like you've beaten me to it.'

Once in the small, clean, and utterly white bathroom, Karen had a quick shower, put on the grey jeans and cream shirt she had worn before, and spent two minutes putting on some light makeup. She wasn't looking forward to seeing Lane's three friends as they would remind her that she and Lane weren't on the same side. Would Lane tell them about the developments in their relationship? She hoped not, but what if that had been his intention all along, and she had been played? A cold lump formed in her stomach as she considered that last night had merely been part of a calculated plan in their overall scheme to attack Pilatos.

Her face was paler than usual when she re-joined the men, and Lane looked at her with concern in his eyes. Real concern, she told herself, this was not feigned.

*Everything OK?* He signed to her as Matt began walking back towards Betsy's house.

'Yes and no,' she said quietly, 'but they're my problems, not yours.'

His hand reached for hers, and, for a few seconds, he held it in his grasp and looked at her with warmth in his eyes. He raised her hand and pressed his lips to the back of it, and a shiver ran through Karen.

Matt stopped before entering the corridor of forest between the mustang's clearing and Betsy's house and looked back to see Lane and Karen standing in their own world. He watched Lane raise her hand and kiss it, and he could see the expressions on both their faces. This is not going to end well, he thought as he watched them, two powerful, strong-minded people looking like love-struck teens when they are about to retire to their corners and come out fighting.

'Come on, you two,' he called as he entered the trees, not wanting them to know he'd seen that tender moment between them, 'the jet is waiting next door to take Karen home. Betsy said to leave the beds there; we'll come back later and tidy up.'

'Jet?' Karen arched a brow at Lane as he released her hand, and they picked up their belongings from next to the beds.

*The fastest way to get you home,* he smiled at her, trying to keep the sadness of goodbye from his face.

They followed Matt back to the house without any further conversation. Karen was running through all the things she would have to do as soon as she reached the office, including trying to solve the headache of the Maine acquisition for once and for all, while Lane was planning the messages he would send out, once Karen was gone, to initiate the action against Pilatos. Neither wanted to think about saying goodbye.

Once they came in sight of the house, Andy ran to Lane to hug and kiss him, and Tom gave one of the smiles that Karen rarely saw. Clearly, they were overjoyed to see him again. They gave Karen a quick hello before dragging Lane ahead to talk to him about the past few days.

A stranger stood at Betsy's steps, a middle-aged man of military bearing with silver hair, dressed in black pants and a white shirt.

'Morning, honey,' Betsy greeted Karen, then held a hand towards the stranger, 'this is Ammar. Ammar, Karen Lawford.'

They shook hands as Betsy continued.

'Laura Parkinson has kindly loaned Lane her jet for the day, and Ammar is your pilot.'

'Nice to meet you, Ammar.'

'Pleasure's mine, Miss Lawford,' he spoke with a British accent.

'Karen, please,' she insisted.

'Did you have a good night camping out with the mustangs?' Betsy asked.

'It was interesting,' Karen replied, 'and you were right, those inflatable beds were very comfortable.'

'I hope you'll consider more camping, then – it's good for the soul. Now, will you have breakfast before leaving, or are you in a hurry to get back to the big smoke?'

Hearing the excited chatter of Lane's friends on the porch as they asked about his trip and told him about things they'd been doing, she realized that she didn't belong here. It was time to go. The sooner, the better.

'I should get back. I imagine there's food on the jet.' She looked questioningly at Ammar.

'Absolutely,' he inclined his head, 'Ms. Parkinson always has a range of food on board, and she gave instructions that you are to make yourself at home.'

'I have a few things in the house,' Karen told him, 'I'll get them, say my goodbyes, and be with you shortly.'

Betsy and Karen went into the house together, the older woman chatting away about the mustangs, the dogs, and the weather. The Dimity gang were seated at a polished antique table in a front room, with Matt and Andy doing most of the talking in their loud Australian voices. Karen gathered her travel bag, made sure she had everything, and went to say goodbye to Lane and his friends.

As soon as she entered the room, he looked up at her, his eyes flooding her with memories and messages of all the words that hadn't been said. She tried to guard her expression, but she feared that he could see everything she thought and felt, and she tightened her lips and looked down at the polished floorboards to try and prevent him from having access to her thoughts.

'Time to go?' Andy asked, looking at the travel case at Karen's feet. 'Sure you won't stay for breakfast with us?'

Karen shook her head, 'You all look as though you have a lot to catch up on, and I'll have something to eat on Laura's jet.'

'She has the best food,' Andy told her with enthusiasm. 'We've flown in it a few times now, and there's always something scrumptious there.'

'You'll be home by lunch,' said Matt, 'it's only twenty minutes from here to the airstrip, and the jet will make short work of the trip back to New York.'

'Excellent,' she nodded, trying not to look at Lane, but his hands caught her attention.

*Do you want me to go to the airstrip to see you off?*

'No, no, it's fine. You stay here with your friends.'

'What?' Matt guffawed, looking back and forth between them. 'Did you learn sign language while you were away?'

'I learned it in the week or so before we first met,' she shrugged, 'sorry for the deception, but, you know how it is.'

'You're not at all sorry,' Matt laughed with good humor, 'but that's OK. All's fair in love and war. And how can you learn it in a few weeks, anyway?'

*Karen has a knack for languages,* Lane explained.

They spent another few minutes with meaningless chatter before Karen left. Lane half-rose to follow her out and speak to her, but she motioned for him to stay with his friends. There was nothing more to say to each other. She was the outsider here, and it was easier to leave without him attempting to make her feel as though she had a place with them, or with him, when it was clear that she did not.

Ammar had borrowed a car from the farm where the airstrip was located, and it was parked behind Laura's Mustang. He held the back door open so she could put her bag in, then opened the front door for her. For a few seconds, she looked at the car seat as though contemplating not getting in, then sighed and climbed in. He shut the door gently but firmly, and she felt it was closing on more than just the car.

Betsy and Lane stood on the porch, and she raised a hand to them, trying to look competent, calm, and in control to mask the chaos that fought within.

'Come back anytime!' Betsy called.

*I will miss you,* Lane signed.

*Thank you. For everything*, she signed back.

He touched his right hand to his heart and pointed to her.

And like that, it was over, and she was driving away from the most unusual five days of her life. The best five days, she thought.

They traveled slowly down the rough driveway, making small talk about the landscape around them and the current flying conditions.

When Ammar reached the main road, he stopped the car and felt his pockets.

'My keys,' he said, 'I must have left them on that shelf at the front door of the house.'

He turned the car around and made the slow journey back over the potholes. His phone rang as he pulled up behind the Mustang, forty meters from the house, and Karen offered to get the keys so that he could take the call.

The dogs were silent as she approached the steps, watching her with wagging tails as they relaxed in their favorite spots on and under the porch. Not trusting the sturdiness of the steps, she climbed carefully and made her way across the worn and faded floorboards to a set of distressed white shelves placed against the wall between the front door and the room where Lane and his friends were talking. She was going to call out to let them know she was there. She didn't intend to eavesdrop, but when she heard Matt's loud voice say *Pilatos* twice, she stood next to the shelves and listened.

Taking a quick look at Ammar, she could see him using his hands animatedly as he talked on the phone, so he wasn't going to notice if she stopped here for a moment and listened. She couldn't see anyone through the open window, so that meant they couldn't see her, either.

'Like Matt was saying,' said Andrea, her voice clear through the open window, 'it's all organized for next Wednesday at Pilatos Farm.'

'Your doppelganger, Sean,' Tom chimed in, his voice softer than the others but still easy to understand, 'is on the Pilatos security team. He has access to all the laboratories.'

There were a few seconds of silence in which, she assumed, Lane was signing something.

'That's right,' Matt agreed with whatever Lane had communicated, 'he can get into the main Pilatos laboratory, and you can see The Source for yourself.'

'It's worse than we ever guessed,' Tom spoke, his voice heavy with emotion, 'Sean told me something this morning, and, well, man, I wanted to puke. We're working on getting it verified by one of the vets who has been feeding us information. It's the first I've heard of it, and I don't want to believe it.'

Another silence indicated Lane was signing.

'He's going to meet us that afternoon before his shift starts,' Andy explained, 'he has a set of fingerprints for you which he says will work on the pads; he's tested them, as well as contact lenses that he's had made up. He's worn them this past week, and the eye scan hiccupped the first few times over them but has adapted and accepted them. He doesn't think you'll need them, anyway, as the security card he has grants access to wherever you want to go; it's just backup.'

'You'll be in for eight hours,' Matt told him, 'from nine at night through to five the next morning. Sean is going to coach you about what to do in that time, so you hold your cover. You can do what you need to do during those eight hours, as he spends most of it alone on patrol.'

Lane must have asked about being mute as, after another pause, Andy said, 'He's been telling people he has a sore throat. Today he's going to have laryngitis and not speak at all, then get it back but still be croaky, and lose it again at the end of the last shift before you take his place. No one will be expecting you to talk.'

'If you need more time,' said Tom, 'you can do another shift in his place the next night, but you should be able to get it all done in the one shift.'

'Now, the protesters,' Andy changed the subject, 'do you want me to send the tweet to get them back at the gates? OK, done. You can do your call to arms today or tomorrow, and hell will arrive at their door.'

'More bacon?' Betsy's voice trilled over the talk.

Karen carefully closed her hand over Ammar's keys, so they remained silent and quietly departed. After three minutes of eavesdropping, the chess game had changed dramatically because she knew their next moves. Her loyalty to Pilatos and her analytical mind kicked in, and she began plotting possible moves to checkmate them.

Ammar was still lost in his phone call when she arrived back at the car, so she slipped into her seat and waited. In another minute, he finished and apologized for the phone call, explaining that his wife was purchasing an investment house, but he knew it was a bad investment. Karen wasn't interested, though she managed to make the sounds and facial expressions of someone who thought the story was fascinating.

On the ride to the airfield, during take-off, and until they left Missouri, she remained lost in a tangle of possibilities regarding Lane's planned visit to Pilatos Farm. There wasn't much they could do to stop him before he got there, but once he was on Pilatos land, something could be done to prevent him from bringing any harm to the facility or learning any of the secrets that the laboratories guarded. It would have to be done in such a way as to keep him safe. That was a given. The man was too famous, too loved, too needed by the world to go through with anything that would end with him injured or even jailed. Deported she could work with. She would consult with Joe Kaiphas.

It wasn't until Ammar's voice over the speaker told her that they were passing over Evansville that she broke out of her mental hurricane of planning and thought of an older couple she knew who lived in the city far below. Long ago, when she'd been at college, she had met Curt and Deb when they lectured at a campus astronomy club. They had been so deeply in love, and it was visible in every glance and every gesture between them. At the time, she had compared their love to the cool and controlling relationship her father had with her mother, and she wished her parents had been in love like that.

As she looked down on Evansville, all thoughts of scheming and planning about Stablex fled as she thought of the couple she hadn't seen in years. They had been friends for more than a decade, sharing a passion for astronomy, but as Pilatos became all-consuming, she dropped her interest in the heavens, as she'd done with every other non-Pilatos pastime, and lost contact with them. She had always admired how much in love they were, even after so long together. For an instant, she wondered what it would be like to be in love like that, and then it hit her. Lane had spoken to her. *He had spoken to her.* He had told her she was beautiful, and she was going to throw away any chance of having a relationship with him because her loyalty to Pilatos meant she had to betray him.

It hurt. Everything inside was shattering, but she knew what had to be done. Her father and her life had trained her well. She would put emotions aside and function, as required, as one of the heads of Pilatos.

# CHAPTER TWENTY-ONE

*Hold the light in your heart, walk in sunshine and moonlight, and always help light the way of others. Even when life seems overwhelmingly dark, it only takes a small candle to light the way of lost souls – so let your love shine out and be that candle. Love is light that shines from the soul, and it draws others to it, like moths escaping from the darkness. In essence, we are all creatures of light – from our very atoms, which are more light than mass, to the love we feel when we connect to the world around us. Be light.*

**Lane Dimity, in a documentary where celebrities were asked, 'What is love?'**

### Pilatos Building - New York

Pearce picked Karen up from the airport and took her back to the Pilatos Building. They caught up on the latest news about Alycia's art, and he asked about her time away, listening with interest as she described some of the events in Austria as well as some of the people, like Betsy.

Taking the direct lift from the basement car park to her apartment, Karen showered and dressed in one of her favorite grey designer skirts and shirts so that she could spend the last hours of the afternoon at her desk. It was the final transformation, from the woman she had almost become in the time away with Lane, back to the woman she was born to be: an owner and CEO of Pilatos Industries. The feelings that had overwhelmed her for a short time on Laura's jet were safely locked away in a drawer, in a cupboard, in a vault, in a locked room, in the shadows of her mind, and she could operate logically without emotions interfering.

'Have you seen this?' her father strode into her office less than two minutes after she sat at her desk and held his phone out for her to see.

'Have you seen what he has done?'

'Hello, Father. Lovely to see you, too,' she looked up at his towering figure and offered him a cold smile. 'And, my apologies, because in the two or three minutes I've been in my office, I haven't had the opportunity to view your phone.'

'Don't be smart,' he snarled, obviously worked up over something, 'just look at what your Australian wonder-boy has tweeted.'

The mention of Lane caused the memories of last night to stir, and she mentally shoved rocks against the locked room where they were stored. Taking his phone, she looked at his words that already had over a million likes in less than an hour.

*It is time for all animal lovers to gather peacefully outside Pilatos Farm near Lexington to stop the equine horror being practiced there.*

She swore, sighed, and scrolled up to see his other posts. Nothing in the past five days had touched on anything to do with Pilatos. He'd honored his agreement and waited until their time together was over. He knew she wasn't going to change, so he went on the attack. If ever there was a call to arms, that was it.

Scrolling down some of the few thousand comments, she could see that people responded with promises of turning up at the farm in Lexington. There were even people vowing to travel from overseas.

As she was looking, he posted again, this time with Andy's photo of him resting his head on the forehead of one of the Pilatos Friesians, and the sadness in both his and the stallion's eyes was poignant. *The souls of the Pilatos Friesian stallions are dying, and their bodies are dying, too. This must be stopped.*

The instant it appeared on her screen, the number counter next to the little heart began racing as thousands of likes were recorded every second.

A minute later, another photo appeared, which caused both rage and horror when she saw it - the body of a Friesian stallion being autopsied. The image was shocking, as the beauty of the horse could still be seen in his face and glorious mane and tail, but he was opened down the length of his abdomen. *The Pilatos Farm autopsy room where five or six Friesian stallions end each week after dying of unknown causes. Boycott Pilatos products.*

In the jumble of first reactions to this, she was furious at whoever took the photo. All employees signed a non-disclosure contract. Whether it was a vet, a vet nurse, technician, or forklift driver, they would be found and their employment terminated. She also felt sick thinking about five stallions a week dying. That couldn't be true. They had to prove that this was a fabricated number.

'It's getting worse,' she told her father, handing him back his phone so he could see the new posts.

'I thought you were going to neutralize him,' John accused her.

'I did, for five days, but if this is true - if five stallions or more a week are dying of unknown causes - then nothing in the world will stop him. Is it true?'

'How would I know?'

'Because Stablex has been your baby since the day it began, and I was always kept busy elsewhere, so if horses were dying, you would know.'

'Horses die in paddocks and running wild. It's an acceptable risk.'

'Five or six a week is more than twenty percent of the Stablex stallions dying each year, which would mean twelve hundred dead within four or five years, and there are only twelve hundred horses in the stables.'

'We have replacements,' he shrugged, apparently unconcerned by the death rate.

'So, it's true?' She looked at him incredulously. 'We have this number dying each week, and it doesn't *matter* because we have replacements? That isn't going to sit well with the public now that Lane has informed them of it.'

'It matters,' he scowled, turning away from her desk as though to leave but stopping halfway to the door to face her again. 'It matters because they cost a fortune to replace, and we are trying to find the cause of the deaths, so we don't have to breed so many replacements. We're trying to prevent the deaths. Tell him that. And free or not, they're going to die.'

He continued to the door, saying over his shoulder, 'Meeting in my office in ten minutes. We have to get this under control.'

'Wait!' Karen pushed her chair back and stood, following him to the door where he'd stopped at her command. 'What do you mean that they're going to die whether they're free or not? Do you mean that even if they were turned loose in fields and not locked in stalls all the time, they're still going to have these unexplained deaths?'

'Seems that way,' he lifted one shoulder and then strode back to his own office.

Karen shut the door behind him and gazed into empty space for a few minutes as she sorted through the new information. If her father knew that they died whether stabled or free in fields, then it wasn't a case of their 'souls dying' because they were imprisoned, as Lane was claiming, it was a case of something inherently wrong with the health of the stallions. Genetically wrong? Or was someone within the complex sabotaging Stablex by causing the stallions to die?

With Pilatos betting its future on the success of Stablex, she was sure her father was doing his utmost to find out what was causing the deaths. Welfare might motivate Lane, but profits motivated her father, and with stallions dying, he was very motivated to stop the deaths. She vowed to find out more about what was killing the stallions, not just because it was a public relations disaster but because she cared about the horses. Horses died in the wild, in paddocks, and all manner of ways, but there was something particularly distressing about those Friesian stallions dying at such a high rate with no known cause.

Returning to her desk, Karen tapped her fingernails on the antique wood as she puzzled over the problem of the horses dying. Then, there was the issue of the protesters who would soon be arriving at Pilatos Farm. Damn. How many of them were coming? And she still had the Maine land deal to close, for once and for all. Even while away, she had been finding time to keep up with the latest problems relating to that, and she was beginning to feel confident that enough donations had been made to the right people and organizations to allow the sale, and the subsequent timber harvesting, to go through.

On top of that, there was Lane…an ache began to emerge from the shadows of her mind, and she pushed it away; she didn't have time for a migraine. Strangely, she didn't have one while she was with Lane.

*Lane*, his name repeated in her mind, and the discomfort in her head had a matching pain around her heart. His face appeared in her thoughts, smiling at her, and she pushed the image back into the dark spaces. She wouldn't think of him as a friend, or a lover, or anything else that was personal. He was an opponent on the chessboard of business, and she was playing to win. And to win, he would have to be knocked off the board.

'Sandy,' she called, and within seconds her wonderfully efficient assistant was at her desk.

'Yes, Karen?'

'Can you find the list of crimes an Australian visitor to the U.S. can commit that is punishable by deportation? I don't want an indefinite period in jail, just immediate deportation.'

Sandy looked at her intently, her soft brown eyes troubled. 'Are you sure, Karen?'

'No, but I need that option on the table. Also, can you have one of the researchers focus on collecting all public communications from Lane and his friends and keep me updated hourly? They're going to cause a headache.'

'You look like you already have one. Can I get you something?'

'No, it'll run its course, and I have another hour or two before it peaks. Also, I need to speak to one of the senior vets at Pilatos Farm. Can you get one on the line for me in the next few minutes?'

'Sure thing, boss,' Sandy nodded and reached across the desk to lay a comforting hand on her forearm, 'and it's going to work out. I know it will.'

The touch of Sandy's hand almost brought her undone. For too many years, she had been a citadel apart from others, neither receiving nor giving the sort of empathy that was displayed through a comforting hand. Now, it made her want to cry.

'I wish I shared your confidence.'

Karen was almost ready to leave for her father's office when Sandy handed her a printed list of crimes that would result in deportation and apologetically told her that she was unable to get any of the vets on the phone.

'If I didn't know better,' she said in a tone that implied it was exactly what she knew, 'I'd think they were under orders to not speak to you. But who would do that?'

'We both know who,' Karen grimaced, 'the man who controls sixty percent of the company to my ten percent. The man who thinks his daughter can't be trusted when it comes to emotional reactions to horses.'

'I'd be more worried about your emotional reaction to having your access to employees in your own company restricted,' Sandy observed dryly.

'Maybe you know me better than my father,' said Karen, giving her a warm smile and thinking, as she often did, how lucky she was to have Sandy in her life. 'I'll be in his office if you need me. I'm assuming it's an emergency meeting in response to Lane's calls to rally his followers. It wasn't that long ago that the men in that office were laughing at what one man who liked horses could do to a company like this.'

'Now they're peeing their pants out of fear,' said Sandy, with a wink, as she held the door open for Karen.

'I may not have put it like that,' Karen snorted, 'but, yes, they are. Oh, also, can you let me know how many protesters we have at the Farm? I imagine they'll start turning up fairly soon.'

'I'll keep in contact with my guy in security over there,' nodded Sandy.

In her father's office, she had a sense of déjà vu as she saw three men in suits and one dressed in black. Phillip Reach sat licking his lips in a chair in front of her father's desk. Jeremy Murray was beside him with his usual smug, superior look. Her father was looking ominous on his side of the desk, while Joe Kaiphas, in his black open-necked shirt and pants, was standing against the wall wearing his menacing air like a cloak. She nodded at them and walked to the window to look out at New York, seeing another grey day like the one when they'd first brought up the subject of Lane Dimity. Raindrops made patterns on the glass, and she watched them for a moment before turning to face the four men.

'Joe,' John Lawford began, 'it's been an hour since he tried to mobilize his followers. Any action yet?'

Joe nodded, his stony face not revealing any emotions. 'Five minutes ago, security estimated five hundred people have arrived so far, and the road appears to be a traffic jam for several miles as more arrive.'

'In an hour?' Phillip asked, looking visibly shocked.

'Lots of people live within an hour of the Farm, and he has specifically told his followers to go there,' Joe told him. 'Before this, it was more a game of Chinese whispers, but he has now openly and repeatedly told his followers to get to Pilatos Farm if they can and to boycott Pilatos products.'

'Can't we just kill him?' Phillip snickered nervously at his remark.

Karen shook her head and frowned, not bothering to hide her disdain.

'I've said before,' Joe turned his cold eyes to Phillip, 'you make martyrs out of dead people.'

'We're not murdering anyone,' said Karen, as she looked at each of the four men in turn, finding it hard to keep the contempt from her expression for three of them, 'I have a list of crimes for which he can be deported. It's just a matter of finding the right one for him. Joe?'

She walked over to him and handed him the list, meeting his eyes and suspecting that there was a glimmer of approval there.

'I thought you might convince him to toe the line,' Jeremy slimed at her, his version of a smile that always appeared a little too slimy for Karen's liking, 'if you know what I mean.'

Phillip sniveled a laugh.

'I believe I do,' Karen moved to stand over him, looking down at him with unconcealed dislike, maintaining a pause until he shifted uncomfortably and looked away. 'You meant that I – an owner of this company – would have sex with the man and use that to try and win him to our side. Tell me, Jeremy, just how secure do you think your employment is here?'

'Enough, Karen,' her father raised a hand and shook his head at her. 'Joe, that list – what are the chances of hanging one of those crimes on him?'

Joe shrugged, 'He seems to keep his nose clean. We'd have to cook something up.'

'Where is he staying?' John asked. 'Any chance of planting some drugs there?'

'He's hard to track,' said Joe, 'they deliberately go to ground so we can't find them. Obviously, he was in Missouri this morning with Karen, but where he goes from there, I have no idea. We had trackers on two of the cars he and his friends have used, but they only borrow them, drop them, and pick up another friend's car. They appear to be quite paranoid.'

'With good reason, apparently,' muttered Karen.

'Karen,' her father looked at her, 'do you know where he's going to be in the next few days?'

'Damn! Look at this!' Phillip exclaimed before Karen could decide on what to say.

He turned his laptop around so everyone could see a video of what was happening outside Pilatos Farm. A drone was taking the video and streaming it live. It went up into the sky, looking back down the road that led to the farm, and as far as the eye could see, there was a line of vehicles. The road was usually quiet, with most workers arriving on company buses, but there were miles of vehicles parking along it, with people climbing out of cars and walking towards the gates.

'It doesn't matter how many protesters arrive,' Karen pointed out, 'it's not going to damage the sales of Stablex. We should ignore them.'

'It's not just Stablex,' said John, 'he's calling for his followers to stop buying any Pilatos products.'

'He's just one man,' Phillip curled his lip in distaste at the thought of one insignificant man who couldn't even talk, threatening a goliath like Pilatos.

'With seventy million followers,' said John, his expression dark.

Turning his attention to Karen, he narrowed his eyes. She hadn't answered his previous question. Granted, Phillip had interrupted her, but was she seeking to avoid answering it for some reason?

'If we are to find a way to have him deported, as that seems the best way to deal with removing him at present, we'll need to know where he is or where he'll be. Karen?'

Here it is, she told herself, slowly turning her head to meet the piercing gaze of her father, that moment when I betray him. Here, now, this is the moment. The tipping point. He knew I would. He didn't know how, but he knew I would choose Pilatos over him, and he didn't blame me for it. It's the final small act that removes any chance of any sort of a future with him in it. But he will be alive, she argued with herself, he will be alive in Australia and far from men like Joe who could kill for the good of the company.

'Karen?' her father repeated.

'I don't know where he'll be tomorrow or the next day, but I do know that next Wednesday, he'll be entering Pilatos Farm to do the shift for a security worker known as Sean.'

Ignoring the pounding at her temples and the lump of guilt that sat in her gut like a bucket of cold congealed porridge, she gave them the details of Lane's plans to get into the complex.

'I don't know what he intends, but I do know he'll be there,' she finished.

'Joe could catch him,' suggested Phillip, 'and then the police could find drugs on him. I'm sure we could dig up some to put on him.'

John considered the rough plan, 'It's not going to stop him urging his followers to act against us.'

Joe pointed out, 'But he won't have any way to communicate while in jail awaiting deportation. He's not a U.S. citizen, so he has no rights. Until he's back on Australian soil, he won't be tweeting anything. That has to help.'

'What can we do until then?' Jeremy asked, 'Just sit back and let those protesters screw us over with their sit-in?'

Closing his eyes to think for a moment, juggling thoughts the same way his daughter did, John sorted through possibilities. When he opened them a moment later, he looked at Karen with faint approval and appreciation of actions she'd taken in the past.

'Karen made the right call the first time,' he said. 'We allocate a few hundred thousand to provide free food and drink for the protesters, all clearly marked as being gifts from Pilatos. It's harder to be violent and angry against us when we are feeding them out of the goodness of our hearts.'

'But not toilets,' Karen put in, 'don't provide toilets. We let them fill up with free food and coffee and soda, but they'll have to get in their cars and drive elsewhere to the toilets.'

'Like that will work,' scoffed Phillip, 'the filthy mongrels will just go behind a tree.'

Giving him a flat stare that had him licking his lips at double pace, Karen replied, 'No, they won't, because we will put up signs reminding people that urination or defecation in public is an arrestable offense, and we will ensure the police are on-site in large numbers following through with that. There will be no permits issued for portable toilets, so they will have to line up to use private ones in motorhomes or drive three miles to the public toilets. The last thing we want is conflict with the protesters, so we work on the fact that it is the small inconveniences that often break people.'

Doubt was on the faces of Phillip and Jeremy, her father looked disinterested, but Joe nodded his support of the plan.

'We also need to start a new advertising campaign,' Karen continued, 'highlighting all the good Pilatos does in the world: sponsorship of villages in developing countries, donations to schools, recycling, products that help with a green world. One man and his followers can try to damage our sales, but we can use advertising, celebrity endorsements, and some carefully planned videos intended to go viral to offset that damage. On top of that,' she paused and moved to the window, looking out at the bleak afternoon and blinking back the pain in her head, 'if we discredit Lane Dimity and have him deported, we will get through this. Stablex sales start in a week, and nothing will stop that snowball from becoming an avalanche once the men who can afford it start feeling the positive effects of it.'

'I have my order in,' Phillip leered at the others in the room, 'it was a choice between some investment property or Stablex, but after watching John these past few years, I chose Stablex. What about you, Joe?'

'Not me,' Joe held up both his hands, palms outwards, 'I have a daughter. There's no way in hell I want to outlive her.'

Immediately after his words, there was an awkward silence as everyone jumped to thinking of John using Stablex. Karen realized that her father didn't appear concerned with the notion of burying his daughter and living on long after her death. It didn't surprise her. If she hadn't become the daughter he'd wanted, she'd have been dead and buried to him, anyway.

'Find out about Sean as soon as you can,' John ordered Joe.

'I know who he is,' Joe replied, his voice as flat as his gaze. 'We won't be able to take any action until after Lane has entered Pilatos as him, but suffice to say, Sean won't have a job after next Wednesday, and Lane Dimity will be in custody awaiting deportation.'

The finality of the words made Karen's migraine grab at her brain with clawed hands, and she worked hard to maintain a calm exterior. The countdown was on to the nausea; the brightness of the office was already beginning to hurt her eyes.

'What is he hoping to achieve by getting into the facility?' Jeremy asked. 'He can't bring anything in as he'll have to go through the same security showers that everyone does, so it's not like he's going to be able to plant explosives around the place.'

'Information,' said Karen. 'I doubt he wants to do anything to the facility. One or more of our employees there have been feeding them information about what's going on, and he wants to verify if it's true. I gather he wants to find out about the deaths of the stallions and learn about something that he refers to as the source of Stablex.'

In her peripheral vision, she saw her father's head jerk up from the paperwork on his desk when she mentioned Lane's interest in the source of Stablex. As far as she knew, the source of the drug was the blood of the stallions, something that was already public knowledge, so what was it about that phrase that had shaken her father? Did the drug come from somewhere *other* than the stallions? Was the source of Stablex something else?

'Make sure he's caught as soon as he gets in there,' John growled at Joe, 'don't let him reach the laboratories.'

'I'll do my best,' Joe replied.

John gave him a sharp look as though his best might not be enough. 'I think I'll be at the farm on Wednesday to oversee it all. The world has gone mad when one man like him can cause so much of a problem for people like us.'

There was assent from Phillip and Jeremy while Joe remained unreadable.

'Perhaps you should be there, too,' her father looked at her, 'we might need you to translate if no one knows sign language.'

The last place Karen wanted to be was near Lane when he was caught by Pilatos security, but she nodded.

'And the Maine tract,' John said heavily, 'is that finalized yet?'

'Getting close,' she answered, trying to hold focus as the pain in her head hammered at the inside of her eyes, 'the protests have been small scale, mainly from locals concerned about the importance the timber holds for native wildlife in the area. I had to organize two studies by our people to prove that the animals would relocate to other old-growth areas within the region, and a report showing that our logging would provide employment opportunities.'

'Get it wrapped up, will you? We need that timber. Jeremy – the Chinese factories, how are they panning out?'

The meeting turned to Pilatos overseas investments, something Karen disagreed with when she was an avid supporter of American made, but her father had a vision of Chinese expansion, and the men he was dealing with there wanted guaranteed supplies of Stablex, so he had a strong bargaining chip with them.

There were only another ten minutes to get through as, after the subject of Lane had been dealt with, there hadn't been anything that couldn't have waited for another day. Karen tried to march back to her office, but she knew her feet were beginning to drag. As soon as Sandy saw her, she grabbed her arm and helped her to her chair.

'Another migraine?'

Karen nodded, 'I'll head upstairs shortly. I wanted to spend a few hours here, but this is catching me up. I might lie down for a bit and come back later tonight.'

'Your speech is slurring - you'll be vomiting soon. Get upstairs now, I'll help you. And it's the elevator today, not the stairs.'

As Sandy was helping her into the elevator, the office door swung open, and Isabella made an entrance in a glorious buttercup yellow creation that flounced around her as she walked. She paused for dramatic effect, knowing she looked fabulous in a dress that was so far removed from her usual jodhpurs and polo shirt.

'Darling!' she exclaimed as soon as she saw her daughter being supported by Sandy.

Rushing across the room, she took Karen's other arm and smiled appreciatively at Sandy. 'Thank you, Sandy. She would be lost without you. I'll help you get her to bed.'

'I'm still conscious, Mum,' Karen objected with a crooked smile, 'and I can walk. I just want to go to bed for an hour or two, and then I'll be fine.'

'We'll get you to bed, darling,' her mother cooed, 'won't we, Sandy?'

'If she doesn't thump us for speaking about her as though she's three,' Sandy chuckled.

'Sick people are always three as far as their mothers are concerned.'

Karen rolled her eyes at her mother's fussing, 'Why don't you two stay here and chat about me while I take myself upstairs.'

'If you're right with her,' Sandy smiled at Isabella, 'I have a few things to finish here. She seems feisty enough to get by with one person helping her.'

'Yes, of course,' Isabella steered Karen into the lift, talking to Sandy over her shoulder. 'I was not there for her as I should have been when she was a child, and I am hoping it isn't too late to make up for that now.'

'I hope she allows you to make up for it,' said Sandy, seeing the slight touch of desperation in Isabella's eyes. She *wanted* to be a mother now, but Karen may not accept mothering.

'I'm still conscious,' Karen grumbled, 'and I'm still here.'

'Hush, darling,' Isabella patted her arm, 'we're simply talking about you, not to you.'

Once in her apartment, Karen made a beeline for the bathroom and gave in to the nausea that was sweeping over her. When she emerged, Isabella greeted her with a glass of water and a sympathetic smile.

'I really am sorry I wasn't there for you when you were little,' she spoke softly and sincerely, 'and I do want to make it up to you now.'

'So you've said,' Karen replied, taking the glass of water and sipping, 'and I'm sure you will, but for now, I just want to crawl into bed, turn the lights off, and sleep. This will pass in another hour or two.'

'Of course,' said Isabella, 'I'll sit with you.'

'No need, really.'

Slipping between the cool sheets fully dressed, Karen curled up on her side and clutched a spare pillow to her chest. The pain receded into a haze of exhaustion, and she slept. When she woke, almost exactly an hour later, Isabella was sitting next to the bed, watching her.

'That's actually a little creepy, Mother,' Karen chuckled at Isabella's version of *being a good mother,* 'you're watching me like a serial killer watches his latest prisoner.'

Isabella lightly slapped her daughter's arm, 'Don't be cheeky. I'm watching you like a mother hen watches over her favorite chick.'

'I'm your only chick, I have to be the favorite.'

'Clearly, your migraine has gone if you can be so pedantic. You did look awful downstairs, but the color is back in your cheeks, now.'

'They're mini-migraines. They build slowly, become unbearable, I throw up, sleep, and then get back to life. A bit inconvenient, but the long-lasting ones would be worse.'

'And these are caused by stress?'

'I suppose,' Karen shrugged as she got to her feet and then scowled at her crumpled clothes, 'but I seem to have stress all the time and only get these occasionally, so who knows.'

'Perhaps a doctor knows. You need a better doctor. So, tell me, did you have a good time away with our Mr. Dimity?'

Karen paused as she was pulling out some fresh clothes from her wardrobe, 'I did. Yes, it was…different.'

'Tell me about the horses you saw,' Isabella clasped her hands under her chin like an excited little girl. 'The Lipizzaners – did you get to ride one?'

Karen began recounting some of the highlights of the days away as she showered and put on the new clothes. They moved to the kitchen. Isabella motioned for her to sit and told her to keep talking about the trip while she made coffee for them both. As she spoke, Isabella made encouraging noises and even clapped her hands on several occasions.

'That Lane, he is amazing,' she enthused as Karen finished telling her about how he rode the mustang stallion. 'So, when will you be seeing him again?'

'I don't know,' Karen said evasively.

'But it sounds as though you have become such good friends! You must see him. I know he adores you. He told me so this morning when we were talking. Well, not talking, but texting. Same thing.'

'He tried to convince me that stallions have souls, but he failed in that, and now we are back to being on opposite sides of the fence,' Karen sighed and tried to sound less melancholy over the end of whatever it was they had shared. 'You do realize that the main reason I went with him was to give Pilatos a break from his protesters, as he agreed to that. It wasn't a date.'

'Oh, mwah,' Isabella waved her words away, 'it doesn't matter why you started out, what matters is where you ended up.'

'We've ended up with him telling all his followers to move to the doorstep of the Farm and to boycott our products.'

Isabella laughed, 'Oh, I can imagine how much John is enjoying that. I can hear him now, fuming over an Australian daring to raise a hand to his precious Pilatos.'

'It's serious, Mum, it's likely they'll do tens of millions of dollars damage to the company's profits, if not more.'

For several long seconds, Isabella looked at her daughter, wishing she could peel back the years so she could reach the child who grew to believe that she had to be a certain way to please her father. It should be Karen on the Bisente horses getting ready for international competitions. She should be training with Julian and laughing as she rode her favorite horse around the jumps. She should be getting her hands dirty with cleaning stalls, not getting her hands dirty with corporate filth.

'Your father sees the world in terms of profits and losses and assets, and he has forsaken all else for his beliefs, but you need to remember that Pilatos can fall and wither away, and we go on. We are not Pilatos. We are more than the business we run.'

'Nice sentiment,' Karen leaned over to briefly touch her mother's hand, 'but not all that helpful in real-life scenarios where it's my job to help keep the company running.'

'Well, just remember, you are more than Pilatos. You do not have to sell your soul to run the business. You can do the right thing and still run the business.'

'But what is the right thing?' Karen tensed her lips in what could have been a smile but looked more like a sad reflection of inner turmoil. 'It changes from moment to moment and scene to scene. What seems right in the wilds of Missouri isn't at all right in the boardrooms of New York.'

Isabella nodded sympathetically, 'Life is so very hard at times, and choices don't always seem clear. I think you need to ask yourself what will seem like the right decision when you look back at it from ten or twenty years from now. And, sometimes, you need to make decisions from the heart, not the mind. It is not always about what is good for the company or for the profits; sometimes, it has to be about what is good for you, the people you care about, and the environment. Don't ignore your heart, darling.'

'It's too late for that,' Karen replied bleakly.

'It's never too late,' Isabella countered. 'It's why I'm trying to be a mother now when I failed you in childhood. It's why I want to tell you things, like the fact that I will always be here for you whatever decisions you make. I will support you no matter what you do – my love and support are not dependent on how you make your decisions, they are always there. You can send Pilatos to hell, and you can live with me at Bisente…I don't need the Pilatos money, you do know that, don't you? I give all my Pilatos profits to charity because I don't want John's money.'

'I believe you've mentioned it before,' Karen said wryly, thinking of the numerous times Isabella had made that point clear.

'I don't know how you feel about Lane,' Isabella continued, 'but I know how much he cares for you. If you want to run away to Australia with him, just do it. Leave all this. It can run without you, or without John for that matter.'

'I'm not running away anywhere with anyone,' Karen snorted at the ridiculousness of the idea, then turned pensive. 'Lane isn't going to care about me much after this week, believe me. I've chosen Pilatos over him, and he's going to know that soon enough.'

'He knows you are going to do that,' Isabella said softly, 'and he won't hold that against you. You know he told me that he thinks you are the most beautiful woman he has ever seen.'

Tears began pushing at Karen's eyes as the emotions in her locked room started leaking into her mind. She couldn't reply to her mother as she knew her voice was somehow linked to the tears, and if she responded, they would be released, so she just nodded. *You are so beautiful*, he had told her. He had spoken to her, and she was going to throw him to the wolves of Pilatos so that he'd be removed from her shores, and she'd never see him again.

'Are you alright, darling?' her mother laid cool fingers on her hand.

The empathy in her mother's voice was her undoing, and she shook her head as the tears burned in her eyes, and she wiped her other hand across them so the tears wouldn't fall.

'It is alright, dearest,' Isabella stood and came around to put her arms around Karen's shoulders, 'It doesn't matter. It will all be alright in the end. It will. I promise you.'

'No, it won't, Mum,' Karen sniffed, and then the floodgates holding her tears released, and she sobbed, 'It really hurts. I've lost him, and it hurts so much.'

'Shh,' Isabella crooned. 'You won't ever lose him, no matter what you do. He isn't like your father. There are no conditions or limits on Lane's feelings. And it's good that you're hurting; it is, it really is. You *need* to be able to feel like this to know what is important. This is your heart – let it cry so that it can be heard.'

### Pilatos Farm
### Dr. Edward Klemmer, Chief Veterinary Surgeon in charge of The Source

Driving into Pilatos Farm through the thousands who were lining the approach to the gates had been slow, but after his shift, as he negotiated the Corvette in the dark through the placard-waving protesters, he was driving at a walking pace to avoid hitting anyone. It had been another tough shift, and he just wanted to get home and clean it from his system with a bottle of whiskey.

His hands shook slightly as he drove. It had been too long since his last drink.

*Free the stallions*, a placard screamed at him in red. Another read, *You are evil!* He sighed as he read the words waved at his windscreen. A cardboard sign with *Down with Pilatos* slapped at his window, and two more *Free the Stallions* were waved at him. He had to hit the brakes as a girl riding a huge Friesian danced on the road in his headlights, the horse performing the 'trot on the spot' action of passage that was so beautiful to watch.

His hands began to shake more, and he swore at them, telling them to behave until he got home.

He was nearly through the mile-long line of protesters when another banner was waved in front of his car, this one asking, *What are you doing to those horses?*

'I don't know,' he replied to his empty car, 'I don't know anymore.'

He began to cry.

It was only another five miles to his favorite tree, and he could make it there, he knew he could. A sense of peace settled over him as he thought of the magnificent tree that welcomed him every time he left Pilatos and drove home. An old oak tree with wide branches that stretched out like arms. The self-loathing that ate at him after every shift with The Source began to lift as he approached the tree. His hands stopped shaking. He felt calm.

Once his headlights lit up the ancient tree, he unclipped his seat belt and pressed his foot on the accelerator. He had disabled his drivers-side airbags six months ago in preparation for this moment. The arms of the tree were open to receive him, and he felt like he was going home. His last thought as he hit the trunk at over one hundred and twenty miles an hour was that he should have taken care of The Source first.

# CHAPTER TWENTY-TWO

*Life is short. Don't waste your hours. Ride your horse.*
**Popular t-shirt featuring Lane Dimity.**

### Pilatos Farm - Lane's Last Day

Regretting her momentary weakness with her mother and blaming the migraine for her bout of tears, Karen set about to toughen herself up after that first day back from Missouri. She began her days early, working through the contracts Sandy had put on her desk and attacking the Maine tract problem with ferocity. Another few hundred acres of standing lumber had come up for sale in Washington, and she was pushing ahead to have that ready to fell to ensure the supply to their mills was increasing.

There had been texts on her phone from Lane, but she refused to read them. Reading his social media posts was enough for her to know that there was too much of a gulf between them to ever be anything except adversaries. Those days and nights away had been an enchanted interlude from her world that operated without magic; they were merely memories to be sealed away. Her father seemed pleased with her these days, so she assumed he was still monitoring her phone calls and had seen that she had no contact with the Australian.

Quietly, using Sandy as her intermediary, she had been trying to find out more about the source of Stablex. Sandy reported that Pilatos workers either had no idea at all, or they clammed up and ended the conversation, so she was no closer to solving that mystery if there was one. The death rate was another subject that ended in workers refusing to talk.

The estimated number of protesters at Pilatos Farm had grown to twenty thousand, and people were still arriving from around the country and overseas. At any one time, there could be several hundred Friesians present, being led or ridden around the crowds to show what magnificent animals these proud black horses were, and seeing them made the crowd more determined to free the stallions.

Early on the Wednesday that Lane was due to swap places with the Pilatos employee, Sean, Karen, and her father arrived at Pilatos Farm. It took over an hour to move through the crowd that stretched along the road to the farm. An endless sea of faces peered into the darkened windows of the vehicle, unable to see who was inside.

'We should have used the helicopter,' John hit his hand against his knee, frustrated with the slow passage through the crowds.

Pearce glanced at him in the mirror, 'It's still waiting on parts, John.'

'Then we should have hired another one. It's never taken this long to drive from the airport before.'

'Twenty thousand reasons for that,' Karen said softly.

'We should just be able to shoot the lot of them,' snarled John, looking at the great diversity of people with disgust, 'unemployed rabble living off our hard work.'

'To be fair,' Karen said with her usual coolness, 'most of these people are employed; they have applied for vacations to be here. I've seen how people are pairing up with others so that when their vacations end, someone else's start, and they can take their place here on the line. They're planning for a long stay.'

'Then the sooner we get rid of that Australian, the better. Maybe they won't be so keen to do whatever he wants once they learn he's been making money from dealing drugs.'

'Again, to be fair,' Karen gave him a fake smile, 'he's not dealing drugs. We are going to make it look as though he is.'

John waved her words away, 'What matters is that his followers will see that he's not this perfect leader who should be listened to at all costs. Smear his reputation, and the rest will crumble around him.'

'Let's hope for that outcome, then, shall we?' Karen's smile appeared more like a grimace.

She wasn't happy with the drug set-up, but deportation was better than physical harm, and this circus had to be stopped. And stopped on their terms, not on any terms set by Lane and his followers. The stallions would not be freed. Stablex would be released on schedule in a few days. Pilatos would not be beaten.

Once safe within the secure perimeter of the farm, Karen relaxed a little. The security forces had been quadrupled over the past few days, and, everywhere she looked, guards were patrolling the fences, grounds, and buildings. She didn't think that the demonstrators were likely to be violent, but she understood the nature of the crowd mentality, and one person's aggressive reaction to seeing two of the Lawfords in a vehicle could easily trigger a riot.

Like everyone entering the farm, they went through the process of removing their clothes, showering, and dressing in the outfits that were kept on site for them, then John strode away to have a meeting with some scientists, and Karen decided to go and see the horses. She hadn't been here since the day Andy had visited to photograph the stallions, and she wanted to see if her view of the stallions had changed at all since her travels with Lane. He had hoped she would see them differently; she doubted anything would change.

Opening the doors to the first stable block she came to, she smiled as twenty identical black heads turned to look at her. Friesians were so remarkable, she thought, admiring their beautiful forelocks and manes that tumbled in waves down their faces and necks. The horse nearest her moved its head as though nickering to her, and his nostrils quivered, but there was no sound.

The muted stallions, she thought sadly, listening to the silence of the stalls where two hundred stallions were housed.

'Can I help you?' a pleasant voice asked from the stall on her right.

A slim girl in a Pilatos uniform appeared under the neck of the horse she'd been grooming, and she looked enquiringly at Karen.

'I'm saying hello to the horses,' Karen smiled at her. 'They're lovely animals, aren't they?'

'The best,' the girl replied, continuing her grooming.

'Do you have a favorite?' Karen asked her.

'I loved Thirty Twenty-two and Thirty-one Forty. They were special. But they're all special, really.'

'You call them all by their numbers?'

'Officially, we do. Those two were Max and Echo.'

'Were?' asked Karen, curious, 'Aren't they here anymore?'

'They both died. Echo died a few nights ago. This is his replacement, Forty-two Twenty-nine. I'm calling him Dream.'

The girl finished her grooming and stepped out of the stable. Shutting the door behind her, she gave the horse one last pat on his jaw. Clearly, she loved horses.

'I'm Karen, by the way, and you are?' Karen held out her hand in greeting.

'Jacinta,' she replied, taking Karen's hand tentatively, her expression closing down with suspicion as she realized who Karen was.

'Nice to meet you. I'm sorry about your horses.'

'They were your horses, Miss Lawford. I only looked after them.'

'Do you know why they died, Jacinta?'

'Would you care, Miss Lawford?' Jacinta lifted her chin dangerously, knowing she was probably going to get fired for this, anyway, so she was determined to go down fighting.

'I'm very interested in why the stallions are dying. Have you seen many die?'

'I've held them in my arms as they breathed their last breath,' Jacinta wiped at the tears that sprang into her eyes at the memories that came with her words. 'I've cried for them as they gave up on living. I felt their souls fly free when their bodies gave way. Their deaths are unexplained, Miss Lawford, but that's the official story. I can tell you that Lane Dimity is right. They are dying because their souls have died, and their bodies are just following along.'

Taking a deep breath, Karen nodded, 'Interesting.'

'No, it's more than interesting,' Jacinta insisted, 'it's the truth. You traveled with Lane. I read about it every day as people reported seeing you two together. You have to know that what he says is true. Look at them, Miss Lawford,' Jacinta sniffed and rubbed a hand over her eyes again, 'just look at them. It breaks my heart to see them like this, but I can't leave them because I try to bring them comfort. And now you'll fire me, so I won't even be able to do that.'

Looking into the eyes of the closest stallions, Karen shivered, sensing...sensing something. She walked to the one past Dream and laid a hand on his forehead. He closed his eyes and leaned into her touch. An overwhelming sense of sadness flowed into her, and she felt a wretchedness leaching into her chest. Desolation came with the feelings, and despair, and anguish. The horse opened his eyes and looked at her, and she could see all of that there inside of him and more. A sense of hopelessness that stained her mind with blackness emanated from the horse, and as she looked at the next, and the next, she saw it there, too.

Connecting to the stallions and sensing their misery hurt almost as much as knowing she had betrayed Lane. It was easier to not feel, she thought, it was better to look at them and see healthy horses and not see beneath the surface.

'Are you alright, Miss Lawford?' Jacinta asked, wondering why she was standing so still, looking at the horses as though in a daze.

'Yes, thank you,' she turned towards the younger woman and saw the resigned look on her face. 'You're not getting fired, Jacinta. Keep up the good work looking after these stallions. I want you to know that we are trying to find the cause of the deaths. It costs a lot of money to replace them, and few things motivate action in this company more than a potential loss of profits.'

After grateful thanks from Jacinta, Karen left the stables and walked to the featureless white cube at the heart of the six stable blocks: the Pilatos Farm Laboratories. In the entrance foyer, six security guards stood at various points. Nodding at them, she went to the main reception desk and asked to see the inner laboratories.

'I'm awfully sorry, Miss Lawford,' replied the older woman in an English accent. She had grey hair in a bun, a nose like a pick, and an expression of alertness like a Jack Russell watching a rat hole. She didn't sound at all sorry. 'I can't allow anyone without the appropriate security clearance and accreditation to enter the labs. We're handling some dangerous contagions in there, and the risk is too great to have anyone wander in for a look.'

'I wouldn't have thought one of the owners of this facility would rank as an *anyone*,' Karen's voice crackled with ice, 'and I want to have full access to the laboratories.'

'It can't be done,' the woman's voice was equally chilly, 'many of the regulations are enforced by the government. You cannot access the laboratories.'

Their gazes clashed for several seconds before Karen gave her an insincere thanks for her time and left. She was restless. She didn't want to go back to the stallions and be haunted by the shadows in their eyes. The laboratories were out of bounds. The demonstrators outside made it objectionable to venture out. It had been against her better judgment to be here on this day, but both her father and Joe Kaiphas had suggested that it might be beneficial for the situation if she were present since she understood sign language.

Sighing, she headed back to the building where they entered, intending to find a spare office where she could access a computer and do some work. As she passed the main security room with its bank of screens covering the facility and gates, as well as the road leading to the gates, she heard a couple of the men arguing. She stopped when she heard them mention Lane's name.

'It is him, zoom in. It's him,' said one.

'There's no way Lane is going to be on our doorstep,' the other replied, 'he'll be holed up somewhere safe where Joe's men can't get him.'

'Look at everyone gathering around him. It's him, I tell you.'

Curious, Karen went in to look at the image that had caught their attention and immediately recognized Lane. Judging by the trees in the background, he was not far from the front gates. The changed behavior of the crowd as individuals moved to cluster around him was like a beacon pointing out his location and identity.

'That's him, isn't it, Miss Lawford?' one of the guards asked her.

The man assumed she would recognize him, she thinned her lips in annoyance; perhaps he'd been another one following the gossip about how Karen Lawford of Pilatos and Lane Dimity of horse welfare fame were swanning around the world together.

'Yes, that's him,' she answered.

'He's like a god to them,' said the other one, a touch of awe in his voice, 'look at how they try to touch him.'

The ever-growing circle of people around him had dozens of arms reaching out, and he tried to shake or high-five everyone. Their expressions on the high-definition screen showed what could only be described as fanaticism as they pushed towards him, their faces alight with emotion. Some of the girls and women began to cry when they were close to him. It looked like hysteria to Karen as she watched them surround him, desperate to get close.

He looked in danger of getting crushed by the crowd surging towards him when five riders on Friesians rode slowly through the horde to form a guard around him and give him some space. Karen saw him sign, *Thanks*, to them and his smile knocked on the door of her heart. Damn him for being so attractive, she thought, it would be so much easier to deal with all this if everything about him was ordinary.

A girl, who looked thirteen or fourteen, appeared on the edge of the screen, her face fearful as she looked up at the towering crowd from her wheelchair. She held her arms protectively over her face as one of the horses swung sideways, and its legs almost became entangled in her wheels. Lane stepped forward to stand next to her, holding his hands up at the horses, and they stepped away from him, giving the girl space at the heart of the mob. They were side on to the camera that currently focussed on them, and, when it zoomed in closer, Karen was able to see them signing to each other.

*Thank you so much for that*, the girl's hands said, *I thought they were going to tread on me.*

*You're safe*, he replied, *they didn't see you there in the crowd.*

*They're so beautiful,* she motioned towards the five black horses standing around them, holding back the crowd.

One of the riders bent over to say something to Lane, and though Karen couldn't lip-read, she could guess what she said by what Lane signed next.

*Do you want to pat one of them?*

*I'd like to ride one,* signed the girl, laughing.

*Have you ever been on a horse before?* Lane asked her.

*Dad has taken me horse riding a few times. Last time I even cantered. On purpose.*

Lane looked up at the rider and pointed to the girl, then to the back of the horse, and the rider understood and nodded. She slid from the horse's back and stood, holding the reins behind Lane and his young friend. The big animal appeared a bit nervous, and Lane put his hand on the horse's neck and, immediately, the tension ebbed from the horse's body, and his head lowered as though he was falling asleep. Then, Lane held his hand out to the girl, and she rose from the wheelchair on unsteady legs and leaned on him for the few steps to the horse.

Karen had no way of knowing that, before meeting Lane, the child had not walked since she was five. She was seeing another minor miracle and didn't even know, but other witnesses were aware of the importance of the girl rising from her wheelchair.

Lane grinned at the girl, and asked, *Ready*? before holding her by the waist and hoisting her up onto the back of the horse, while the horse's owner helped position her legs. Once on board, the girl grinned and laughed, patting the black coat and picking up some of the mane that cascaded down the horse's neck.

*I want one,* she signed to Lane, her face blazing with joy, *he's like a dream.*

*Better ask your father, then,* Lane replied, *I don't think you can have this one.*

*And are all the horses in there*, she pointed towards the Pilatos stables, *like this one, only locked up all the time?*

Lane nodded, *Locked up, and never taken out of their stable block until they die.*

*They must be so sad,* her face fell as she gazed at the white stables.

*They are.* He turned and looked directly at the camera, and Karen felt a jolt run through her as though he was looking right at her.

After taking the girl off the horse, he helped her back to her wheelchair and then pushed her slowly through the crowd until they moved off-screen and into a blind spot between cameras.

'He's very kind,' a female voice behind Karen caused her to turn. 'Some people would never bother about helping a child and putting her on a horse. She loved it.'

Several other guards, including the woman who had spoken, were gazing at the screen, their faces soft. Joe Kaiphas was also there, watching the screen closely, his expression inscrutable, as usual.

'Back to work,' he ordered, 'there are plenty of other screens that should be under observation.'

'It was a kind thing to do, Joe,' Karen said, trying to lessen any anger he might feel towards his staff for showing empathy for the enemy of Pilatos.

'Do you want to call off tonight's activities?' he asked her, as though her comment was a sign of weakness.

'No,' Karen said, after the briefest hesitation, 'it has to be done.'

Karen nodded at him and left the room, finding an office further along the corridor where she could do some work and try not to think of what she was doing to Lane. His friends lived in America, he came here often, he helped people here… and once deported, he'd never be allowed back. She pushed the thoughts aside and turned on a computer.

While it was starting up, she stared at the blank white wall in front of her, thinking about the fact that Lane was a kind person. If he had a religion, it was kindness. He not only took the time to speak to the girl in the wheelchair, but he also helped her sit on a horse and filled those moments with delight. The look on the child's face reminded her of herself when she was younger. Oh, how she'd loved horses then, they were her dreams. Dream. Her mind pulled her back to the Friesian stallion that Jacinta had introduced her to. How long before he was dead? How long before they all died?

She shook her head to clear the thoughts and went to work on some documents Sandy had emailed to her.

At lunchtime, Karen ate in one of the cafeterias with other staff, sitting at a table by herself and feeling the eyes of the employees on her. She returned to her temporary office for the afternoon and continued with pushing through the Maine land deal and trying to secure the Washington land. For an hour or so, she toyed with the idea of going to visit her mother at Bisente, but she was worried Isabella might catch a hint of what was going to happen that night, and she would warn Lane. Isabella did not share her loyalty to Pilatos.

During the day, her father had been elsewhere. She suspected he might have been in the laboratories but wasn't sure. It was a huge facility, he could have been meeting with people anywhere in the compound, but he kept his Pilatos Farm activities hidden from her. Stablex was his baby, his dream for Pilatos, his way to ensure the company's future, and he didn't like sharing it with his daughter. She was surprised he wanted her here at all.

She checked on the security room a few times to ask if Lane had made another appearance, but the guards reported that he hadn't been seen since the incident that she'd viewed that morning. Was he preparing to take Sean's place tonight, or had he left to continue the fight from afar? A small voice from a corner of her mind wished that he'd gone so that tonight's plans would be abandoned. Part of her dreaded thinking of him being locked up in a cell, like the horses were locked in their stalls - safe, but not free. It would kill him not to be free. She could message him and tell him to stay away…but she didn't.

The day passed like a jerky countdown to something unpleasant, and Karen had a sense of pieces in a game arranging themselves on the board for that one moment in time, which would alter everything.

As it approached nine that night, Karen sat in the control room in front of the screens, looking at the employees as they approached one of several entry points to the farm. The security guards, stable workers, cleaners, and everyone else followed the same routine when entering Pilatos Farm. There were four guards in the room with her, all watching screens and checking on the security staff patrolling the grounds, but she was the only one who spotted Lane. They had no knowledge of what was happening that night, so to them, he was Sean, if they recognized him at all.

Sitting perfectly still except for the turning of her head, she followed him from one screen to another as he moved through the camera system operating around the farm. There were no cameras in the showers, of course, and she picked him up as soon as he came out the other side and headed towards the cafeteria with some other employees for coffee before their shift started. When he was no longer in the angles covered by the cameras, she used the controls to switch through the cameras until she found him again.

'Are you right with those for a minute, Miss Lawford?' one of the guards asked Karen as he pointed to the square of twenty-five screens in front of her. 'It's nearly change-over, and Jasmine and I need to get the paperwork done. Malachi and Neil will still be here to keep an eye on things.'

Glancing at his name badge, she replied, 'That's fine, Kane.'

'Who's coming in tonight?' Jasmine looked up from the clipboard she'd taken from the wall. 'It should be Daniel, Dillan, Anton, and Kiel, but they're down here as not working tonight. The four of them out? All four? That's unusual.'

Kane shrugged, 'Joe made the changes. He has four of his own coming in here. For training, he said. His people are doing most of the next shift tonight.'

'Who am I to argue?' Jasmine sniffed and followed Kane out of the room.

'Does that happen often?' Karen asked Malachi, who was now monitoring two banks of screens.

'Haven't heard of it before,' he shook his head without taking his eyes off the screens, 'but it makes sense that he'd want his team to be able to run everything, so it's probably a good training exercise.'

Looking back at the cafeteria, where Lane had been sipping his coffee while standing alone at a window, she realized he'd gone, and she began a frantic search through the cameras, trying to find him.

Alarms started to shriek, and Neil swore softly as one of his views showed a large truck plowing through the perimeter fence not far from the main gates. Another camera showed a second truck coming through on the other side of the gates and continuing at full speed towards the high-security fence surrounding the Stablex facility.

Damn, Karen stared at the images as protesters dressed in black began following the trucks through the holes in the fences and headed, at a run, towards the stables. Had Lane been several jumps ahead of her again? Was his part in coming here merely the distraction for the attempt to get to the stallions? Was this going to be the night they tried to free the stallions?

'Code Red! Code Red!' an urgent voice spoke over the radio in the control room. 'We need backup at the main gates and the inner gates, now. And in Stable Blocks One and Two. All available security to those areas, now!'

'Are you right here?' Malachi asked her as he and Neil unlocked the gun safe and strapped weapons to their hips. 'All cameras are recording and storing the images, so no need to do anything with them. I'll lock the door on the way out so you'll be safe. I doubt Joe's men will want to come in here now, they'll be down there handling that.' He pointed at the streams of people that were coming through the fences.

'Go,' she told them, 'I think they'll be trying to release the stallions.'

The door snapped shut behind them as they left, and Karen was alone with all the views of the farm, seeing security staff in most cameras heading at a run to the disturbance.

She went back to looking for Lane, flicking through camera after camera. If he were in the main horde, it would be difficult to see him, but her instinct told her that he would be heading to the laboratories. In a moment of clarity, she realized that his presence wasn't the distraction to allow the release of the stallions; rather, the break-in by the crowd was the distraction to let him reach the citadel at the heart of Pilatos Farm. He was going to the laboratories. He was going for the source of Stablex, as she'd thought all along. And, if most of the security were heading to try and stop the intrusion of protesters, he would have a clear path.

Clicking through the camera angles on the one screen, she stopped when she saw several figures standing in the shadows next to what appeared to be the back wall of the laboratories. Their stillness was unusual when all other people in the views were running.

Zooming in, she was able to see that the furthest figure was Lane, standing with his arms raised. Good, he hadn't made it into the building and completed whatever it was he wanted to do in there, which may have been to only gather information, but she couldn't ignore the possibility that he was going in with the intent to cause crippling damage. The two men who faced him appeared to be Joe and her father, both, to her alarm, were holding handguns. When had guns become a part of the plan to arrest Lane?

A frozen hand reached into her chest and grabbed her heart and lungs, and she couldn't breathe. This wasn't what was planned. Oh, God, no. Oh, God, no. Oh, God, no. A distant wailing voice repeated in her mind. With a horrifying certainty, she knew what was about to happen. They never intended to arrest him and have him deported. This was how they dealt with threats to Pilatos. Please, no, she begged the screen, please, no, no, no.

A flash came from her father's gun, his hand jerked, and Lane stumbled backward. A dark stain immediately bloomed on his pale Pilatos uniform, right over his heart. He stood for a second, clutching at his chest, then fell backward, his legs twitching as though he was dancing a macabre jig.

The enormity of what she was witnessing crashed into her like being hit by a speeding car, and though her body didn't fly through the air from the impact, her internal organs were so damaged that she didn't think she could move or think or live. He was gone. Just like that, he was gone. Her father had taken her hunting enough as a child to recognize a heart shot when she saw it.

He was gone. He was the light and the smiles, the kindness to children, and the speaker of truths. He was the man who spoke to horses and rode wild mustangs, the sunshine on dark days, and the warmth in winter. He was the laughter and the color and the hope of the world, the goodness and compassion, and love. Lane Dimity did not speak aloud with words, but his words were heard by all, and he made the world a better place. And she had led him to his death.

A strange keening noise assaulted her ears, and she realized it was coming from her. Something inside of her had broken, and the noise was coming from somewhere so deep within her soul that she didn't recognize it. It was the sound of grief rubbing against anguish and giving birth to heartbreak.

# CHAPTER TWENTY-THREE

*When You Look For Me*
*The place I was born calls to me,*
*The beat of my heart is her sound.*
*She held me in those early years*
*As I walked on her hallowed ground,*
*Wherever else I want to be*
*To that place, my soul is bound*
*So when I am gone, and you look for me*
*That is the place I'll be found.*
*May I find my resting peace,*
*Back on her hallowed ground.*
**A short poem by Lane Dimity, posted on Facebook about a week before**
**his disappearance. One hundred million shares over the next four weeks.**

### Pilatos Farm

A half-hour before Lane was due to arrive, John Lawford was standing next to Joe in the armaments room where most of the security weaponry was stored. Joe was one of five Pilatos employees who carried the keys to the room as there were enough weapons to equip a small army, so security was tight. They stood in the center of the room and looked around at the lockers, cabinets, and wall racks of automatics, semi-automatics, handguns, tasers, smoke bombs, tear gas, and other items that could be used to defend the compound.

'Impressive,' muttered John, running his hand over a trio of Remington ACRs. 'I wouldn't mind the opportunity to get these on the firing range. Maybe it's time to do some hunting.'

'Adaptive Combat Rifles,' Joe said flatly, 'are not what a hunter would use, John. A single shot to the head with a good bolt action is better hunting than peppering your prey with fifty bullets.'

No one else ever dared to speak to John the way Joe did, never fearing to correct him or point out his errors, and it was one of the reasons he trusted Joe more than he trusted any other person in his life. Not completely. He didn't trust any person entirely, but Joe was as close to that as possible.

'What are we taking out to get this Australian?' John asked, eyeing some of the racks of G19s and Ruger LCPs, picking up one in each hand to compare the weights.

'Check they're unloaded before swinging them around,' Joe told him.

'Of course, they're unloaded,' John continued to bring both guns up to aim at the wall and lower them again, preferring the feel of the Glock to the Ruger. Whenever Joe took him out for some shooting practice on the range, he chose the Glock. It felt good in his hand. Powerful.

'Check them,' Joe commanded. 'Every gun must be checked as unloaded when it is put away. Every gun must be checked as unloaded when it is picked up. Mistakes are made, and it's too often the unloaded gun that kills someone.'

John put the guns back down rather than check them.

Joe picked up a taser and some zip-ties to act as handcuffs. He then reached for a weapon to give John - a shotgun equipped to fire beanbag rounds. It could be dangerous at extremely close range but non-lethal at any distance. He suspected, correctly, that John would not be content to use a non-lethal weapon.

'Here,' he handed it to John, along with some flexible baton rounds.

'What the hell is this?' John held the gun and rounds up, shaking them as though expecting them to rattle and reveal their identity.

'Beanbag gun and rounds,' said Joe, his expression flat.

'I'm not chasing after a criminal with bean bags,' John scoffed at the idea. 'As far as I'm concerned, the man is a terrorist breaking into our facility, and I want to be armed – really armed, not throwing beanbags at him.'

'It's not a good idea, John. As I said, accidents happen – we don't want to kill the man. You could use a taser, like this one.'

'Put the taser away, Joe,' John spoke with the authoritative tone of the head of Pilatos, telling an employee to follow instructions. 'I know we don't want to kill him, but he's smart. He sees a taser pointed at him, and he's going to run. He sees a pair of Glocks pointed at him, and he's going to stand.'

For several seconds, Joe eyed his boss without expression, then acquiesced, putting the taser away. John nodded with satisfaction – Joe understood that a man staring down the barrel of a Glock was more likely to stop when told to than a man who thought he could outrun a taser. No one would outrun the bullet.

Taking two G19s from their racks, Joe released the magazines in both, then pushed the slides back to ensure there were no rounds in them. Next, he unlocked a cabinet and took a box of 9mm cartridges from it, pushing ten into each of the magazines. He clicked the magazines back into the grip and cast a wary glance at John, who was eyeing the guns too eagerly.

'I'm sliding them shut,' said Joe, 'and they'll be loaded. You've used these before on the firing range. You know to keep your finger off the trigger. There isn't a safety to disengage apart from the trigger pull - you pull that trigger hard enough, and it will fire. I don't need bullets flying around because you coughed and squeezed off a round.'

'I know what I'm doing,' John spoke confidently, holding out his hand for the Glock.

With a quick hand movement and a mechanical clicking, Joe loaded the first gun and handed it to John, along with a shoulder holster. Strapping a holster around his torso, he put his Glock in it, then picked up the zip ties and pushed them into a pocket. Locking the ammunition back up, they left the room, secured it, and went on patrol to wait for Lane.

As they walked, Joe talked to his security team with the communication device that was all but invisible. Listening to him, John ascertained that Joe's personal squad was on the lookout for Lane, and the facial recognition technology should locate him as soon as he came through the employees' entrance.

'He's arrived now,' Joe informed John as they made their way between two stable complexes to approach the ominous cube at the center.

They waited in the shadows as Joe's men kept a running report on Lane's visit to the cafeteria, then his departure, and his casual stroll towards the laboratories as though he belonged there.

'He's coming now,' Joe said, 'under no circumstances discharge your weapon, John, no matter what you feel about this man. We stop him, we secure him, and we call the police to arrest him, understood?'

'I know, I know,' said John, annoyed that Joe had such little respect for his ability with a gun and his self-restraint.

'At this stage, it looks as though he'll be approaching the cube from between Stable Blocks Four and Five…'

His voice broke off as the alarms began to screech, and red lights blinked on the corners of buildings. Floodlights came on all over the facility. Joe noted that there was a corridor of shadow behind the cube, and it was his bet that Lane was going to aim for that.

'What the...?' John began, looking around wildly, but Joe waved him into silence as he listened to the information coming through his earpiece.

'There's been a break-in near the front gates,' Joe reported to his boss. 'Two semis drove through the fence, and protesters are entering the facility, presumably to free the stallions.'

John immediately began to turn to go back to where the break-in was taking place, but Joe put a restraining hand on his arm.

'I think that's what we're meant to do,' he said, having to raise his voice slightly to be heard over the alarms. 'It's a disturbance to allow Lane the opportunity to achieve his mission, whatever that is. You have to consider that he may have had the contacts to smuggle in explosives or contagions, as we know he has people within Pilatos working with him.'

'Where is he, though?' John demanded. 'How can we find him?'

'We wait for him,' Joe explained, his gaze resting on the shadows that could hide someone who wanted to sneak, unnoticed, as far as possible towards the laboratories. 'I think he'll be coming through here before long. We wait.'

Torn between staying with Joe to catch Lane and going to see what damage was being done at the front of the compound, John swore and kicked at the ground like a disgruntled bull wanting to charge at something.

'There he is,' Joe pointed to the gap between the stable blocks where his staff had last reported him and took his gun from the holster. John followed suit.

Lane stood in an unlit corner and looked around, not seeing Joe and John standing in another pool of shadow. He strode quickly across the well-lit area to merge into the gloom close to the walls of the cube. He began to approach the two Pilatos men, making his way around the building to reach the main entrance. When he was within twenty strides, Joe took a step forward and raised his gun.

'Lane Dimity,' he spoke firmly, his voice emotionless. 'Stand and raise your hands.'

Immediately, Lane halted and stared at the two men. Their guns were pointed at him, and he raised his hands as instructed, licking his lips that suddenly seemed to have gone dry. This is what looking into the face of death means, he thought, looking at the two dark holes of the gun barrels, like the soulless eyes of Death who had come for him.

Unbidden, his mind took him back to looking at the gun in the hands of his father - the gun that ended the lives he loved that day so long ago. He took a deep breath and found peace within himself for what was about to happen.

Great change sometimes requires great sacrifice, he reminded himself, and I had grown tired of this life, anyway. Every day, it felt like the people were feeding from me like Prometheus's vultures, and it is time to unchain myself from this rock and go free, just as I want to see the stallions run free. I wanted a quiet life at home in the outback with someone like Karen to share it, and now it's time to go home.

He raised his eyes to the heavens above to say goodbye to the stars of the northern hemisphere, then dropped his gaze to stare at the two men. John's face looked angry but also gleeful, like a man in a hunting frenzy as he gloated over his prey. He was a man prepared to kill.

Joe yelled at John to stop, and, in the same instant, Lane saw a flash from John's barrel and a massive thump of pain in his chest over his heart. A split second later, he heard the sound of the shot. He looked down at the mass of blood that was spreading over the material of his shirt and stumbled backward, falling. Falling.

So sorry, Karen, were his last thoughts before he hit the ground.

'What the hell have you done?' Joe roared at John; his usual detachment lost in a fury of unimaginable proportions.

He pointed his gun at John, his voice rigid with rage. 'Put it down, John. Put it down.'

'I didn't mean to do it!' John lowered the gun, pointing the barrel at the ground. 'It just happened. The trigger just fired. I swear, I didn't mean to shoot him.'

'Drop the gun,' Joe trained his gun on John's right arm, ready to shoot if his boss raised the weapon to point it at him.

Not only did John drop the weapon to the ground, but he also dropped to the ground himself, falling to his knees, the blood gone from his face so that he looked a pasty shade of dead in the floodlights.

'I didn't mean it,' he said in a small voice, looking at the still body of Lane Dimity only twenty meters away. 'I swear, Joe, it was an accident.'

'Shut up!' Joe snarled at him, anger on his face. 'Stay there, don't move, and shut up, John. Just shut the hell up.'

Picking up John's gun, he left the head of Pilatos kneeling on the grass, shaking as the enormity of what he'd done punched into him. He had killed someone. He had shot and killed Lane Dimity. The Australian had raised his hands in surrender, and he had shot him in the heart. His stomach churned, and saliva ran from his mouth as though a tap had been turned on, and he heaved his dinner up on the grass.

Joe walked to Lane and leaned over, placing two fingers on his neck. He shook his head and glared back at John. The hole in the shirt over Lane's heart had blood still pumping out of it. Joe watched the blood spreading over his front and dripping down to the grass.

'Is he alive?' John asked, his voice hopeful.

'Of course, he's not,' Joe spat the words, walking back to John.

'What do we do now?' John asked, almost childlike in his shock at what he'd done. 'I can't go to jail, Joe; I can't. I'll pay whatever it takes to fix this up. Just fix it, Joe. Please.'

Joe rubbed his hands over his eyes and shook his head. 'It's murder, John. Plain and simple. The man had his hands raised. What were you thinking?'

'I don't know,' John's voice quavered, and he battled not to vomit again, 'I swear, I didn't mean it. It just went off. I didn't mean it to happen.'

'I told you to keep your finger off the trigger. This is a bloody mess.'

'You can fix it, Joe. I'll owe you. I'll do anything. You can do it. I know you can.'

All the brash confidence of the corporate giant had shriveled into a man terrified of being punished for what he had done, and Joe looked down at him, feeling sick at seeing the man for what he was. He didn't even seem to care for the life he had taken, he only wanted to avoid being punished for what he had done.

'Go, John. Leave the farm, go back to New York, and make plans to leave the country for a few days, at least. Don't mention this to anyone. Don't say a word. Lane will have to disappear, and you have to remain silent about this. If there's no body, it will be hard to pin a murder on you.'

'Thank you, Joe, thank you,' John got to his feet shakily, his face still devoid of color. 'Do you want me to help you?'

'You've done enough,' Joe looked at him in disgust.

At that moment, a figure dressed in grey came running from between the stables and the cube. Karen. Her voice wailed a continuous repeat of, 'No, no, no, no, no, no...'

She stopped a few steps from the two men and stared wild-eyed at her father, tears running down her pale cheeks, her mouth moving, but the sound had stopped.

'Karen...' her father began.

She took one step, drew back an arm, and punched him in the nose with the force of a horsewoman who had grown up hoisting bales of hay and saddles around. His nose shattered under her blow, and blood pumped out onto his face.

'Don't speak to me,' her voice wavered as she found her words. 'I will destroy you.'

'It was an accident. I didn't mean it.'

Her face wrinkled in disgust at his excuses. 'I saw it. You murdered him. You will pay for this, I swear it.'

'It wasn't my fault,' her father spoke in a small voice, cowed by the emotions he saw in his daughter.

She turned away from him and went to approach Lane, but Joe took her firmly in his arms and held her. Struggling futilely against the bear-like strength of the man, she demanded to be released.

'It's too late,' Joe spoke, his voice gentle for the first time. 'It's too late, Karen. He's gone.'

'I have to see him,' she pleaded, looking up into his eyes, her own revealing the raw anguish of her heart that was lying as ruined in her chest as Lane's.

'Don't,' Joe told her, an uncharacteristic level of compassion in his voice. 'You don't want to remember him like this. Believe me, I know. Walk away. Forget you saw any of this. If you care for him at all, honor what you know of him.'

'My father needs to pay for this,' she tried to hold back the sobs that were shoving against her words, trying to break through. 'He has to pay.'

'It will all work out in the end,' he said, repeating a phrase she had heard too often before. This was an end, and it was not working out. 'Leave it be. At this stage, only the three of us know about this, and it can stay that way, and he will still pay for what he's done.'

'You're going to cover this up, aren't you?' she asked accusingly, shocked that Joe would go this far for her father.

'It's for the best. You'll see. Now, go back to the control room or an office somewhere, and let this play out as though you weren't here.'

Her legs felt weak as she looked past him to the body lying in the shadows, and it seemed that everything within was dying. 'I want to see him, Joe,' she pleaded, 'I need to say goodbye.'

'It's not goodbye,' he said, his voice strangely soothing against the background of alarms and flashing lights and distant shouting. 'We'll all meet again, somewhere. I have to clean this up; that's my job for Pilatos. Your job, for now, is to do what you think is right for Pilatos – and for Lane.'

With strength behind his gentle hands, he turned her and pushed her away to get her walking. 'Keep going, Karen. Walk away.'

In her shocked state of mind, she followed the direction of his words, walking unsteadily back to the control room where she found her father sitting, watching the monitors which showed the crowds being pushed back by security. He looked up at her, a hand towel pressed to his nose, his face ashen, and she saw a weak man. All her life, he had seemed to be the strongest man on the planet, but now she saw it was just an exoskeleton of sociopathic tendencies that made him appear to be strong. Underneath, there was nothing of value, no real strength, no character apart from a man who wanted everything for himself, and then more, and more. Always more. Nothing would ever be enough for him. He was the face of greed, and that was what had killed Lane Dimity.

He raised a hand towards her as though about to ask for help, but she turned and walked away from him. There were no words to hurl at him, no accusation, no revelation, nothing damning enough to pierce him the way his action had stabbed her. She simply could not look at him, not now, and maybe not ever again. What did he give of himself to others? What genuine care did he have for others? Where was the kindness? The goodness? All that he was had been channeled into his ambition to have Pilatos earn more and more money, bigger profits, and more power.

Finding the room where she'd worked earlier, she sat in the chair at the desk and stared at the blank computer screen. Her phone rang, and she ignored it. It rang again. When it rang a third time, she picked it up and saw it was her mother calling. Could she speak to anyone at this time and not break in two? Should she tell her mother what happened? Should she keep quiet about it, as Joe had instructed? Decisions seemed beyond her as she kept replaying the scene where her father's gun discharged, and Lane fell. The phone stopped ringing.

What was it all for? What was worth his life? A thousand horses died every day. Maybe ten thousand. What was so important about these horses that he had to lose his life? He should never have challenged Pilatos, as the company was always going to win. Her father had always made sure of that.

Minutes passed. Police sirens wailed. Minutes passed. The alarms ceased. Minutes passed. The faint sounds from outside diminished. Minutes passed. She sat, numb and unmoving, unable to think or respond or react. She just sat, and the minutes passed.

The phone rang again, and her finger hovered over the power button but, instead of turning it off, she answered.

'Hello, mother,' she said flatly.

'What's going on over there?' Isabella asked, 'I saw on the news that there is rioting at the Farm.'

'Not rioting,' Karen spoke without expression. 'The protesters broke in. They've been pushed back.'

'Have you contacted Lane?' she asked.

Tears began to fall from her eyes, and she sat, choking on her words, unable to reply.

'Are you there, Karen?'

'Yes.'

'Lane asked me to ring you.'

Hope suddenly flared. He was alive? He'd rung her mother? How? Had he been wearing a Kevlar vest? Had he survived the shooting? But…all that blood. She'd seen it on the front of his shirt as soon as the bullet hit him.

'When?' she found her voice. 'When did he ring you?'

'He texted a few hours ago. He said he'd been trying to message you, but you wouldn't respond to his texts.'

Hope died. Emptiness remained. She was floating away on nothingness.

'Are you there, Karen?'

'I have to go, Mum,' she forced the words out.

'Wait! He said he had an important message for you, and I was to ring you at this time if I didn't hear from him. It seemed very mysterious.'

A message for her? Did he realize that he wasn't coming back from Pilatos? What did he have to say to her that was so important? Perhaps he was going to blame her for betraying him. She deserved that.

'Yes?' Karen's voice was small.

'I wrote it down as I'm hopeless at reading texts while trying to talk on the phone. Let's see; he said that I was to tell you to check his messages and that he hoped you'd go looking for the source. He said that whatever you did was the right thing for you to do at that time, and whatever you do from this point is also the right thing for you to do, and that you must not regret your decisions or feel guilty about them. There was one more thing.' The sound of a piece of paper being turned over crackled through the phone. 'Here it is. He said, and I quote, *tell her I'm ready to go home and have a rest because I'm tired of all of this*. If that makes sense to you. Why would he go home before finishing his business with Pilatos?'

The significance of his words was not lost on Karen. It seemed that he knew he was likely to die on this night, and he wasn't talking about physically going home to Australia, he was talking about a spiritual return to the land where he was born, to the place where his soul was bound, as he had written in the poem he had posted to Facebook a week ago.

'Does that make sense to you?' Isabella asked, her voice laced with concern as she sensed her daughter's mood was different from any she had known before. 'What's wrong, Karen? What has happened?'

She could not open the floodgates to what had happened that night, as she needed time to think through what her actions would be in the coming hours and days and weeks. For now, Joe's assertive and authoritative command to keep it to herself made corporate sense. Still, she could confide her feelings to her mother without confessing what she had witnessed that night.

'I feel so guilty about the things I've done,' she uttered the words as though speaking in confessional, looking for forgiveness. 'I don't know what decisions to make now. I feel like a sailing ship that has had her masts and sails cut down, and I don't know how to keep on going.'

'You row,' her mother said pragmatically, 'when the sails are gone, you get out the oars. When the oars are gone, you paddle with your hands. When your ship is gone, you swim. When you can no longer swim, you float. What you never do is sink.'

'What if I want to sink?'

'Whereabouts are you at the farm?' Isabella asked briskly, trying not to show alarm at what she heard in Karen's voice and words. 'I'm coming over right now. I don't know what is going on, but I know you need me now. I know that. And whatever it is, we'll make it right.'

'We can't make it right,' Karen shook her head at that notion, and tears continued to roll down her pale cheeks.

'Of course, we can,' Isabella assured her. 'As for your decisions now, either make none at all and wait until I'm there or, if you have to make a choice before I get there, just ask yourself this: when you're ninety years old and looking back on this moment, which decision is the one that makes you proud in your old age? When all else has gone, and Pilatos has faded away, and life is almost over, and you are looking back at this moment, what choice was the right one to make? I'll be there in under two hours. Stay there.'

'Thank you, Mum,' Karen murmured, feeling the faintest hug from the universe at the thought of her mother racing to be with her. Her father might only have an exoskeleton of strength to hide his weak inner-self, but her mother had substance. She could see that now.

And what choice would make her proud in fifty or sixty years? Sitting here, doing nothing and waiting for events to happen to her? Or taking control of her life and making the events go the way she wanted?

Step one, she told herself, was to read Lane's messages in case there was something important there that she needed to know, such as he was wearing a bullet-proof vest or that he wasn't coming in and it was Sean who was on duty as usual. Maybe that was Sean lying out there.

*Are you there?* She read his first message, received the night she arrived home in New York. It was repeated several times.

He then had several telling her how much he enjoyed their time together, and he hoped they could still be friends even though they had gone back to their corners to spar for a bit. A couple reminded her of moments they'd laughed together and of how important it was to laugh like that. It appeared he was desperate to contact her and have her respond to anything, and, in her arrogance, she had ignored him. One that arrived in the early hours of the morning spoke of how he didn't feel lonely when he had been with her, but, without her, loneliness was like a cancer on his soul, surrounded by good friends and followed by so many people, but feeling so alone.

The most recent one was the text she had ignored earlier tonight, sent not long before he would have rung her mother.

*I know I'm going to go too far tonight, and you may never forgive me. I also know that you may never forgive yourself. Can we agree to stop the need to forgive each other, or ourselves, and just be? Whatever we do or say, or whatever happens, it is OK, and there's nothing to forgive because we both just do what we have to do. I need to find out about The Source, and you need to stop me. Those are the cards we are playing with tonight. If we have the chance to meet again when this is behind us, I hope we can start with friendship and keep going. If we aren't to meet again, then I have to say this now – and it doesn't matter if you don't feel the same, it is merely something that I want you to know. I love you. Everything about you. No conditions, no limits, no parameters, no boundaries, no restrictions. Just as you are. I love you.*

The words tunneled through her eyes into her brain and wound themselves around what was left of her ravaged emotions, pulling them back together and providing cohesion for her fractured ability to make decisions. He used the words *The Source* as though it was the name for something, not a general idea about the source of Stablex, but the name of something specific. Something in the cube that he wanted to view tonight. There was no suggestion of him wanting to destroy anything - he wanted to find out about The Source.

Taking several deep breaths, like a diver about to enter the water for a long swim under the surface, she turned her phone to silent, put it in her pocket, and decided, for Lane's sake and her own, that she would find out about The Source. If nothing else, she owed him that.

# CHAPTER TWENTY-FOUR

*Every decision you make is a fork in the road of your life's journey. Look ahead and see where that road takes you before you make the decision.*
**Lane Dimity, speaking to students at a Queensland high school.**

### The Source

No one noticed her walking between stables on her way to the laboratories. All attention focused on the front gates where the protesters were being forced back by police and Pilatos security. The alarms had stopped blaring, but the floodlights were still creating vast pools of brightness surrounded by patches of shadow, and she merely walked as though she belonged there, and she did. She was the owner of all of this, and she had the right to go wherever she wished.

The horses were devoid of calls and whinnying, their voices barren, though banging came from some stalls as though the horses were beginning to find another way to express themselves, and it wasn't a pleasant sound. Stopping for a moment, she listened to the banging and realized it echoed across the entire establishment. Knees and hooves and even heads banged against stable walls and doors, and it became a disturbing background noise as she sought The Source.

Avoiding the area where Lane was shot, she entered the cube through the front door. A different disapproving woman was on duty at the reception desk, and she tried to deny access to Karen.

'I am Karen Lawford,' she spoke in a quelling voice, hoping her red eyes did not make her look weaker than the intimidating figure she was trying to create. 'I am one of four owners of Pilatos. I will go where I wish. If you deny me access, you can consider your employment terminated immediately.'

The woman's eyes bulged, and she stuttered before saying, 'It's not our regulations, Miss Lawford. We have to enforce government regulations about bio-security.'

'Screw the government,' Karen spat the words, knowing that her father would have gone wherever he wanted here in the cube without giving a damn about government regulations. Reading the woman's name tag, she said, 'Give me full access to the facility now, Angela, or I'll get it anyway, only you won't have a job.'

'Perhaps if Mr. Lawford...' Angela began.

'Mr. Lawford is not fit for anything at present,' Karen interrupted her, 'I am in charge of Pilatos as of now, not my father. You will give me a security tag that gives me entrance to all of the facility. Now.'

Reluctantly, feeling that she was in a *damned if I do, damned if I don't* position, Angela unlocked a drawer in the reception desk and withdrew a plastic tag on a lanyard. There was a photo of her father on it.

'This one is your father's, and it grants access to all areas,' she said in a small voice, somewhat daunted by the tall, angry woman in front of her.

'Does it require fingerprints or facial recognition to enter anywhere?'

'The alarm automatically triggered those safety measures,' said Angela, trying to appear less nervous than she felt. She realized she wanted to keep this job.

'Can you disable them?'

Angela's eyes narrowed as she considered the question. 'I'm not meant to be able to,' her voice was hesitant, 'but I know the codes. I shouldn't know them, but I've seen them used.'

'Good,' Karen nodded at her. 'Use them. And don't contact anyone about me being here, as that would imply that you don't believe I can be trusted in my own facility. I don't want employees around who don't trust me.'

'Of course, ma'am,' Angela nodded, comprehending that if she wanted to continue working for Pilatos, she needed to demonstrate loyalty to Karen Lawford. That idea appealed to her. She had never particularly liked John Lawford when she met him, but this strong, capable woman was a leader she was prepared to follow.

'And ma'am,' she said as Karen began walking towards the lifts, 'I can be trusted. I'm glad you're taking over. We need changes.'

Karen stopped and looked at her keenly. 'Any particular reason for that?'

'We've had three suicides in the last month. Whatever they're working on up there is destroying lives.'

Three suicides? Karen shook her head. How on earth did Pilatos keep that quiet? Why wasn't she informed of that?

'Thank you, Angela. I trust I will be making changes to prevent further tragedies. We don't need people dying for Stablex, do we?'

At the lifts, she scanned the information next to the floor levels, her mind so focused that she was able to move her feelings about Lane's death to the side as she fixated on the problem before her. She imagined whatever she was looking for would be in the center of the facility since it was something that needed to be protected. The Source. She narrowed her eyes, considering the names of the different sections, not seeing anything that hinted at something so top secret that her father felt compelled to murder someone who was looking for it.

It could take days to explore all the sections on all the levels of this vast building. Turning away from the lifts, she strode back to Angela.

'Do you know what The Source is and where it's located?'

Angela shook her head, 'I'm sorry, Ma'am. I don't know what it is, but I do believe you are looking for Level 5 in the blue area, which is in the center of the building. You can exit the lift there and follow the blue line on the floor. I know the three who died all worked in that area, and the people there have very little to do with the rest of us.'

'Thank you,' Karen tried to smile at her, but her mouth didn't want to respond with anything that hinted at joy, it was still reeling from the shock and grief of Lane's shooting, and smiles could not be found.

'You'll find PPE in the lift, Miss Lawford. I suggest putting it on before going there. I don't know what is there, but perhaps it would be wise to protect yourself from whatever it is.'

In the elevator, Karen found several bags hanging from a hook with the label *PPE* – Personal Protective Equipment. Taking one, she donned a green disposable biohazard suit, pulled on disposable boot covers that went over her footwear, as well as a plastic cap and face mask with a high-grade filter for breathing. Her reflection in the mirrored walls of the lift gave the impression she was about to enter an Ebola outbreak.

The blue line on the floor of Level Five led her down several corridors and through doors that required her to tap her father's card against discs that controlled the locking systems. True to her word, Angela had proven trustworthy, and no lock required the fingerprints or facial scans located next to the tap-and-go locks.

At this time of night, there were almost no people working in the offices and laboratories. A young man in PPE passed, wheeling a tray of vials and medical equipment. He nodded at her without any hint of concern about her presence. It seemed the biohazard suit allowed her to fit right in.

Various small robotic cleaners hummed quietly around the hallways and rooms. They vacuumed, polished floors, emptied bins, and scurried back to discard the contents in rubbish chutes set low in the walls so the little machines could access them. It made sense that Pilatos did not want cleaning staff around something as top-secret as whatever they hid here.

The blue line ended at a blue door. Several signs on the door warned about nuclear material, hazardous chemicals, and admission restricted to classified staff. Bracing herself for whatever lay beyond, she tapped her father's security card on the disc and waited as several locks clicked back. As the door slid open, she felt a rush of warm air that pushed past her in a constant *whoosh*. It occurred to her that they weren't worried about a contagion or hazardous chemical escaping from this section; they had a positive air pressure maintained so that no contagion could enter.

 Stepping in, the door closed behind her, and she stood for a moment to peer around. There was a dimly lit wide passage with a dozen wide doors along its length and an elevator at the far end that was far larger than the one that brought her to this level. Twelve rooms at the heart of the Pilatos Farm laboratories. Is this where The Source existed?

One of the doors opened, and a man walked out, his eyes expectant for a moment as he looked at her, then all expression disappeared behind a mask of wariness. Like her, he wore the full PPE, including the filtered breathing apparatus, but she was beginning to suspect it was less about protecting the people wearing them and more about protecting whatever was contained here in the blue section.

Had he been expecting Lane? Her gut told her that he had. Unless he had organized a clandestine meeting with a fellow worker because his eyes had clearly shown anticipation, even hope, before he slammed the window down on his emotions.

'I'm Karen Lawford,' she said, her voice sounding muffled yet too loud in this dim, quiet hallway.

His eyebrows twitched in surprise as he recognized her name. She noticed that his eyes looked as red as her own. Was he having a reaction to chemicals here, or had he been crying? Was he Lane's contact here in the center of the Stablex building? Were there security monitors in this section, and had he seen Lane shot? Her mind threw questions out like a rapid-fire tennis ball launcher, and she wanted answers.

'And you are?' she prompted him.

'Dr. Hannaford,' he said, his voice cautious. 'I do the night shift here.'

'And what does that involve?'

'Monitoring, checking, filling in forms,' he responded, not questioning her authority for a moment.

'Who else is here?' She looked around at the doors, hearing no indications of other people, just the quiet hums and beeps of medical equipment.

'Only me, tonight,' he answered, wiping a bead of sweat from his forehead, 'Dr. Klemmer often does this shift with his assistant, but they're both...they're no longer with us.'

'Did they resign?'

'No,' he blinked nervously.

'Have they both died?'

'Yes.'

'So, Dr. Hannaford, what is located here that would cause three staff members to kill themselves?'

'I don't know what you mean,' he responded, looking past her, unable to meet her eyes.

'I am beyond playing games,' her voice was savage, and she stepped in closer to the man who was looking everywhere except at her. Poking a finger at his chest, she said, 'I'm here to learn about The Source. You are here to tell me about it. Get talking.'

'I can't,' his voice shook slightly as he stared down at his shoes. 'We can't discuss him with anyone.'

'*Him*?' she asked, surprised. 'The Source is a *him*?'

He nodded, his skin pale.

'Explain,' she demanded.

Noah remained silent as he thought through his options. Lane was supposed to have stepped out of the lifts to see The Source for himself. That is what he and Abhirka had organized. Why wasn't he here? Karen had traveled with him recently. Were they friends? Was she here on his behalf, or was she here in her Pilatos role to find out if he had betrayed the firm?

As he thought of what lay in the room at the end of the corridor, he realized he didn't care if she knew that he had called Lane about this. He had moved his immediate family members into hiding in preparation for this night, so Pilatos could not touch them. He knew he would lose his job, but he'd been prepared to leave after this night, anyway. And he had made enough recordings and notes, stored in various places to be released to the media if he died or disappeared, that he hoped it would prevent Pilatos from following through on the implied threats of what would happen to anyone who betrayed this inner sanctum.

'If anything happens to me,' he glared at her, 'I have over ten copies of video and photos documenting what is going on here, and they will be automatically released.'

Karen widened her eyes at him, 'Do I look like I'm here to kill you? And if Pilatos has been making those sorts of threats against employees, I want to know more about it, so please have one of those copies sent directly to me. Now, The Source. Tell me what you know.'

He wasn't sure he could trust her since she was Pilatos, but he may as well tell her. Since she'd spent so much time with Lane, perhaps she would share his attitude towards horses and do something about it. If she didn't, then he had to walk away. He couldn't spend another night working here or performing autopsies on dead stallions, or he'd be at risk of adding a fourth to the list of suicides.

He raised his eyes to hers. 'There is only one source of Sevv's Gene. Around here, they call him The Source.'

Karen took a moment to absorb his words, then rejected them. 'There are twelve hundred stallions in the stalls surrounding this building, all carrying Sevv's Gene. There isn't a single source.'

'Yes, there is,' his expression hardened. 'He's in that room.' He pointed towards the end of the hallway.

'Show me,' she commanded.

They began to walk towards the door he'd indicated.

'Tell me, Dr. Hannaford, were you expecting Lane Dimity?'

He hesitated, then felt the time for deception, lies, and wariness had passed, so he nodded. 'I wanted him to see this for himself.'

'You risked your job for this?'

'Others died for this,' he shrugged. 'At least, they died so that they wouldn't have to see this anymore. Maybe when you see him, you'll understand. If you have any compassion, any care for horses, maybe you'll understand.'

His hand hesitated on the door handle as he steeled himself to enter the room. Taking a breath to calm his nerves, he opened the door and invited Karen to step in.

She did.

She stopped and stared.

In the center of the room was a large bed, and on that lay a black horse, or what remained of a black horse, as it looked like a large skeleton draped with an incomplete black hide, so that bare flesh and bones poked through in places, creating a gruesome patchwork of mutilated death. The horse's legs and neck, and head were secured to the bed by straps so that he was unable to move.

Tubes protruded from his neck and muzzle and chest and gut, connecting him to all manner of machines. There was a mechanical ventilator thumping and wheezing as it forced air into the sealed muzzle of the horse and sucked it out again. Tubes carried tired, dark blood away from the horse's neck and ran it through a dialysis machine, adding nutrients and saline solution and returning bright red oxygenated and nutritionally enhanced blood to the animal. Another tube was feeding what looked like a concentrated mush of food directly into the horse's stomach through a hole in his chest. The raw flesh around the tube was shrinking away from it, revealing layers like an anatomy diagram. A hose through the loins of the horse siphoned a slop of manure from the horse's gut, while another dripped urine from his barely-functioning kidneys.

As Karen stared at this pitiful abomination of a horse, he opened his eye in the sunken socket and swiveled it to look at her. There was so much fear, pain, and misery in that eye, so much desolation, unhappiness, horror, and distress, that she felt it like swords being thrust into her. The anguish of this horse was beyond imagining.

A feeling of nausea swept over her, and she held a hand over her mouth, unable to comprehend what she was seeing.

Noah's hand came to her elbow to steady her.

'What is this?' she turned a stricken face to him, seeing her horror reflected in his eyes.

'This is The Source of Stablex, Sevvodarray the Third, being kept alive because once he dies, Stablex will be no more.'

Karen shook her head. That didn't make sense. All those stallions in the stalls. They carried Sevv's Gene. Glancing at the body on the oversized bed, she took in the many sores where his black hide pulled back from raw flesh. How could any living creature suffer that much damage and still be alive?

'But the stallions...' she began, then stopped as the sight of this horse and the look in his eye overwhelmed her. Queasiness rose, and she knew she was going to throw up.

Seeing the look and knowing it well, since he experienced it every time he worked here, Noah took her by the arm and led her out of the room. There was a bathroom across the corridor. He opened the door to the toilet and left her to remove the breathing filter and respond to the revulsion that churned her stomach.

After several minutes, she flushed the toilet, washed her face and hands, and came back out, looking pale and shaken, the mask abandoned. Wordlessly, he handed her a glass of water and led her to an office a few doors away where they could sit. He assumed that Karen would want to sit, think, and talk after seeing The Source.

'How can he be the only source of the gene?' she asked him when they were sitting opposite each other across a small table.

Noah removed his breathing filter and his cap and placed them on the table. The regulations stated that they were to be worn at all times because there was to be no risk of bacteria or viruses reaching Sevv from anyone's breath and no DNA contamination of human hair. He didn't care about the regulations now.

'The gene doesn't breed on,' he explained, leaning forward to rest his elbows on the table and drop his face into his hands. 'They used his semen to inseminate hundreds of mares, but there were only two outcomes: healthy foals born without the gene and fetuses with the gene that were aborted by the mares. His one copy of the gene is a unique mutation that should never have been, and perhaps he had the one in a million or one in a hundred million genetic code that allowed an individual to survive with the gene. Whenever the gene appeared in one of his offspring that carried a different genome, because half the genes came from the dam, it died and was aborted within the first two months of gestation.'

'But the Stablex stallions are his sons,' she objected, wondering why they existed at all if they weren't providing the extract needed to make Stablex.

Noah shook his head, 'Not his sons. They are him. They are all Sevvodarray the Third. Clones. After many years of trying, it became apparent that the only way for the gene to exist in a living horse is if the horse has the exact same genome as Sevv. A lot of this facility is set up to use Sevv's cells to clone new versions of him, which are then implanted into mares on Levels Two and Three. Not all the clones become viable foals, but your father has ensured that all healthy foals remain in these stalls and under guard until they are old enough to become the replacements for the stallions that are dying. Some mares are out in the fields, but they don't carry the little Sevvs - they are used for breeding more mares that will carry the clones.'

Like a moving puzzle, Karen's understanding of Pilatos Farm, Stablex, the stallions, as well as her father, was changing, moving around, and creating a different pattern from the one she had held in her mind until a few hours ago.

'But the clones provide another source of the gene.'

'Only as long as they live. As I said, it can't be bred on, and it only exists in him and his first-generation clones. We're not sure why, but second-generation clones are not viable – they have to be cloned from the original cells of The Source. Storing his cells or the cloned embryos cryonically is not successful either, so a supply of future clones can't be created. This horse is the only true source of Stablex.'

He paused for the enormity of his information to sink in, trusting that she had the necessary scientific knowledge to understand the implications.

'When an animal ages,' he explained, 'a part of the chromosome that we call a telomere acts like a clock for the cell. When the animal is young, telomeres tend to be long, and, as it ages, the telomeres shorten. Some cloned animals seem to defy this with long telomeres in the clones even though the donor animal was older and had short telomeres, and some are unusual in that some tissue cells have long ones, and others have short ones. With Sevv, unfortunately, every single one of his clones is born with telomeres on the chromosomes as short as his own. They are born as foals, they look young, but the clock in their cells is saying that they have already lived more than seventy years. No one here has been able to change that, and they are dying young because their cells are old, and the chemical we extract from their blood simply can't work on cells that old – it doesn't make an individual immortal, it merely adds thirty percent or so to their life, and these stallions have cells that are already past that use-by date.'

Thoughts and ideas began branching out in her mind like a spreading web, growing and multiplying. Once this horse died, Stablex could only be produced until the last of his first-generation clones died. This gene should have never existed and would not continue to exist. Something unique about Sevv allowed him to live with the gene when none of his offspring could live with it. The genome in Sevv and his first-generation clones allowed it to exist, but they could not be used to keep creating copies of the horse. The stallions were dying unexpectedly because their cells were already near the end of their lives when they were born.

What would she do? Decisions had to be made. If all of Pilatos depended on the success of Stablex because her father had obsessed about this drug, then when that horse died, it would only be a matter of time before all his clones also died. Had they produced enough of the drug to keep the company going for many years? Were they close to creating a synthetic version of it? Could they find a way to have the gene breed on?

Did any of it change the decision she had to make now?

'Do you know if my father has seen that poor creature?' she asked Noah, hoping the answer would be no, but the way she viewed her father was undergoing a transformation, and she knew her hope would be in vain.

'At least once a month,' he replied. 'He keeps pushing us to find ways to make him live longer. He would have died five years ago without all the life support.'

'Five years?' She was in equal parts astounded and disgusted. 'He's been like that for five years? Strapped on that bed like that?'

Noah nodded, looking faintly sick as he thought of it. 'He is rolled over and sometimes held upright in a cradle arrangement attached to the bed, but he is so fragile now, movement is very restricted.'

He wished he had never been asked to work in this part of the facility. He had begun to detest his job when so much of it was about dealing with dying horses and autopsies, but this work…watching over a horse that was forced to live when he so desperately wanted to die - needed to die - was distressing beyond belief.

Only a handful of people could access this inner sanctum of the laboratories. Hardly anyone who worked in the building was aware that Sevv lived because John Lawford knew that few people could look on this horse and accept what was being done to him. The scientists and laboratory assistants who worked on Sevv's genetics did not know that he existed like this – they merely received cell samples. The few who worked with Sevv had managed to put aside any empathy for this one animal in exchange for the massive financial gain offered by John and for a lifetime supply of Stablex. Those who developed a conscience understood that it wasn't just their job at stake if they spoke up – John had made it clear that Pilatos could harm their families, so they maintained their silence.

As one had told Noah, 'It's just one horse. Right now, as we speak, there are tens of thousands of horses out there, all over the world, suffering dreadfully, and this is just one horse. Sure, it's not pretty, but his few years of discomfort will give decades to the lives of so many people. If one horse has to suffer so that a million men can live, then that is a price that will be paid.'

It was a logic that Noah could never accept. He was not a man who would allow another to suffer so that he could live longer.

If Abhirka hadn't convinced him to contact Lane about The Source, he imagined that he could have joined those staff whose consciences drove them into depression and then to the point where they saw death as the way out of their mental pain. Seeing this animal was soul-destroying. He had studied veterinary science to work with horses, but this, this wasn't working with them; this was extinguishing the essence of what it meant to be a horse.

Karen felt her rage rising. The image of her father pulling the trigger to kill Lane overlapped with the knowledge that he visited this laboratory and looked down on that poor suffering creature and only cared about keeping him alive so the damned drug could be made. He had risked all of her family's company to develop a drug to give himself longer life – it had always been about him, not the company, or her, or her mother; it was for him. He needed projected profits to justify the expense at this site so that he could have thirty more years. He condemned that horse to inconceivable misery so that Stablex could be made for himself and wealthy men like him, but she was sure it was mostly about his desire to extend his own life.

She had no doubt that he had poured all the research and development money from Pilatos into this project at the expense of all other research. In growing awareness of the extent of his obsession, she realized that the embezzlement of funds that had been discovered in the Pilatos Agricultural Chemical division would turn out to be a movement of funds to this section, which was why he took over the investigation. It would not surprise her if her father were siphoning funds from all divisions of Pilatos to prop this up and ensure Stablex was produced. Of course, when Stablex failed, Pilatos would fail. It was like an enormous inverted pyramid with its point balanced on the life of one horse. And if that suffering creature was the foundation on which the future of Pilatos was built, what did that say about the company?

Standing, Karen asked to go back to see Sevv. This time she was prepared for the horror that was the existence of that once majestic horse, now strapped to a bed, being forced to breathe, and having machines do the work that his body could no longer do so that his cells remained alive. Cells that had been dividing and copying themselves for over seventy years and now that incredibly unique genome was failing due to age. Copying the genome into clones was also failing because the new cells had aged chromosomes, and although the clones were chronologically young, they were genetically ancient. The freak of nature that had allowed the existence of a gene that created a hormone to prolong the life of male mammals should have ended years ago when Sevv's life was due to end, but it lingered on at the heart of Pilatos Farm.

Approaching the Friesian stallion, she felt weighed down with the knowledge that the future of the company she loved, Pilatos Industries, was based on prolonging the suffering of this animal.

She reached out a hand and laid it gently on his forehead, and he opened his eyes again, beseeching her with all his soul to be let go. In that touch, she felt his thoughts. She felt the memories of him running free, of feeling the grass under his hooves and the sun on his back. The joy of life was a distant memory for this horse, and he begged her to be released from this hell constructed for him by her father. The horses who had gone before him called to him, and he wanted to gallop free again. He wanted to die.

The horses she had met in the days traveling with Lane cantered joyously into her memory. Horses that worked with people but were not enslaved, horses that earned their keep but had liberty, horses whose souls were not imprisoned within four walls. As her hand lingered on the great forehead of this once mighty horse, she accepted that Lane had been right: horses did have souls. It was not something that could be proven by science, but neither could it be disproven. In her connection with this horse, she felt the energy trapped in his dying body which hungered to be set loose from that prison.

All of Stablex, she thought, and the future of Pilatos was based on this tragic figure at the heart of it all: this emaciated, barely alive horse. The horse gave a shudder under her hand as though he was trying to call to her, but, like all the other versions of him in the stables around them, he was surgically muted, and there was no sound apart from the noise of machinery.

She closed her eyes, and she could feel it: his pleading to be dead, his wish that she end his life so he could be free of this torture on which Stablex was built.

This night was becoming too much for her, and she wanted it to be over. Her mother was right: the decision to be made had to be one she could look back on in decades to come and know it was the right one, regardless of the consequences. On the one side was her father, her company, the employment of thousands who worked for Pilatos, the contracts for Stablex that had to be honored, profits, and business. On the other side, there was this horse, his clones, and the beliefs that Lane had tried to reawaken in her.

There was only one choice. She took hold of the tube that pumped the refreshed blood back into the horse and wrenched it from his neck. It fell at her feet, and a pool of blood began spreading, pumping onto the white laboratory floor and making its way to the drain.

It shouldn't be painful, she thought, he would just grow faint and then unconscious, and, as the last of his life force pumped into the drains of the laboratory, he would be set free.

Noah laid a supporting hand on her shoulder, overwhelmed with emotions and unable to speak. This was something he had longed to see, but, like the others, he feared the retribution from John Lawford if they had attempted the act that came easily to Karen. It had been known that anyone who facilitated the death of this horse would not only lose their job, there was the threat of harm to both them and their families, and the small number of people who knew about Sevv justified keeping him alive by believing it also kept their loved ones safe. Or, as he realized, they were just cowards: it was easier to accept an atrocious situation rather than find the courage to change it.

At last, the misery of this horse would be over, and he felt a weight lifted from his shoulders as he watched the horse slip away into the welcoming arms of sleep.

Karen switched off the ventilator once the horse looked to be unconscious, and as the air stopped going into his lungs, he opened his eyes one last time and looked at her. The eye that met hers was soft and thankful, all fear had gone, and he looked as though he was looking beyond her to never-ending fields that beckoned him home.

They both sensed the moment that he was gone. A feeling of gratitude passed lightly through them, like the faintest of breezes rustling leaves as it passed.

Karen wanted to sit and cry, but there was more to be done. Her mind was racing in several directions, trying to cover all the problems that she had to deal with, not the least of which was her father and how he would react to the death of this horse. She began plotting the possible moves ahead of her from that night on, and she began to see her way through. It could be done.

'This was an accident,' she told Noah, her eyes narrowed as she tried to find a way to stall for time before the inevitable showdown with her father. She wanted it to be on her terms, not his. She wanted him to pay for what he had done to Lane, to this horse, and to all the horses in this facility whose lives were abused to produce Stablex. And to her.

'No one will believe that,' said Noah.

'They don't have to,' she shook her head slightly, 'they only have to see it's possible. You are down on staff here, you are working alone, you are depressed over the deaths of your colleagues. You fell asleep and woke to this.'

'Woke to machines that are turned off?' he looked doubtfully at the ventilator.

Knowing that Sevv was dead and gone, and all that remained was his body, Karen switched it back on and turned away from the slightly macabre rising and falling of his chest.

'Somehow, he moved his neck enough to dislodge the needle, and he bled out. I wasn't here, and, believe me, my father is going to be too preoccupied to worry about any of this for a few days. I'll remove any video records, and I'll give you my personal guarantee that you will still have employment here if you want it – all those other Sevvs are going to need your care until they die.'

'No more autopsies?' he asked, knowing that the stallions would keep on dying.

'No more autopsies. They will live – and die – in peace.'

She wasn't sure how she would achieve this, but the watershed moment of seeing this stallion, and giving him the peace he craved, was changing everything. She could feel her priorities crumbling and reforming, her resolve shifting and moving in different directions. When she considered what Pilatos had stood for when its future was dependent on one drug, which was, in turn, dependent on the life of one horse, she realized it had represented the worst of humanity – it was about greed and her father's obsessive desire to live longer. It was madness.

'But your father...'

'My father can go to hell,' she replied, her eyes cold as she thought of him. 'In fact, he is going to hell, and I'm driving the bus that's taking him there.'

She removed the green biohazard suit and handed it to him. 'Wait an hour before reporting his death. There are enough distractions going on that no one will know.'

'Distractions?'

'The break-in...' she started, then realized that he probably had no communications with anyone outside this section since it started, so she explained about the protesters breaking through the fences in a failed attempt to free the stallions.

'I think it was a ruse to give Lane the chance to come here and see Sevv for himself,' she fought back the rising sorrow at the mention of his name. There wasn't time for that; she would grieve later. 'He couldn't make it, so I came instead.'

'Where is he?' Noah asked.

'I don't know,' she replied honestly, knowing that, by now, Joe would have moved his body, 'but I do know what he would want to be done, and it will happen.'

# CHAPTER TWENTY-FIVE

*Don't fight your horse on his terms. If he learns that he's bigger than you, he will win. Out-think your horse. Hopefully, he'll never learn that he's smarter than you.*
**Lane Dimity, Working with Horses, p. 98**

### Pilatos Farm - Change is Coming

In the foyer of the cube, Karen handed her father's security pass back to Angela.

'Thank you for your help,' she spoke quickly, anxious to be gone from this building. 'Are you able to access the video that is recorded throughout the building?'

Angela nodded, 'I can from here, as well as from the security office on Level Three. The two men on duty there tonight are out front handling the protesters if you want them.'

'I don't want them,' Karen shook her head, 'I want you to erase the last hour of footage if it's possible.'

'That's against company regulations…' Angela began, only to be stopped by a raised hand from Karen.

'Yes, I understand all that, but company regulations are changing as of now. If you feel unable to erase it, perhaps you could just put it aside for a few days. That would work – for both of us. I thought you might prefer not to be seen handing me that security pass until we put all this behind us.'

That hit its mark, and Angela nodded, 'I think I can take care of that. It's above my security level, mind you, but I can get around that. It will be here if you need it, but it will not be available in the usual place or to anyone except you.'

'I appreciate that,' Karen inclined her head in gratitude. 'One more

393

thing, does the control room here get video feed from elsewhere in the compound?'

'No, only our internal cameras,' Angela informed her. 'All external footage goes to the control room in the building near the front gates. They don't get any of our internal feed, though; it doesn't leave this building.'

'Excellent,' Karen responded, turning to leave.

'Oh, Miss Lawford,' Angela called, making her stop again.

'Please, call me Karen.'

'Karen,' Angela smiled at her, 'I gather you haven't been here at all tonight?'

'Exactly.'

Leaving the building, Karen headed back the way she'd arrived, crossing the lawn so that she could walk between the stable blocks. Halfway to the stables, she stopped, then detoured so that she could look down beside the cube at the area where her father shot Lane. As expected, the area was clean. Joe had done the work he was paid to do, and that part of the evidence about John Lawford's crime this night was already gone. She had to move fast.

Breaking into a run, she moved between the stables and back to the control room, where she had started the night. There was only one man on duty when she walked in, Malachi, the others were still helping to contain the protesters, and there was no sign of her father.

'Any problems, Miss Lawford?' Malachi asked, looking away from the screens for a moment.

'Have you seen my father?'

'He left a few minutes ago,' he told her, turning back to scrutinize the video feed that usually took four or more to watch it. 'His car went out one of the back gates, not through the front, obviously.'

'That makes sense,' she tapped her fingers against her leg, her brow pinched in thought. 'Malachi, I thought your shift was ending, and Joe's men were going to be running this.'

'Lucky me, overtime,' he responded with a shrug. 'Everyone is still busy out there, and I was nearly ready to leave when Joe asked me to take over here, so as of five minutes ago, I'm back on duty.'

'Before I left, I was watching the video feed from cameras that cover the lawns between the stables and the cubes. I'm particularly interested in the lawn on the western side of the cube – how do I get a copy of that footage?'

'You won't find it,' Joe's sharp voice carved through the air.

Swinging around, Karen found her father's henchman standing in the doorway, leaning against the door frame as though nothing untoward had happened that night.

'Pardon, Joe?' she asked, hiding her revulsion at the sight of him.

She had thought he was a man who provoked a sense of trust, but that belief had been replaced with fear and misgiving. Clearly, he would do anything to protect John Lawford.

'You won't find the video you're looking for,' he said, 'it's been taken care of.'

'Has it?' she asked, stalling as her mind raced. 'Thank you,' she decided to play along and pretend to be on his side. She didn't want him *taking care* of her. 'That saves me a job. Has my father returned to New York?'

He regarded her with hooded eyes, and she tried to hold her calmness under his stare. It would not do for him to guess at any of her plans before she had the opportunity to think them through carefully and put them into play.

Joe nodded, 'He has. Do you have a message for him?'

'No,' she forced a smile, 'I'll catch up with him tomorrow.'

'He is busy tomorrow,' Joe told her, his expressionless face somehow chilling, 'he's going overseas for a couple of days. Unexpectedly. He'll be back here for a media conference we are organizing for Monday, all going well.'

Karen took a few seconds to reshuffle some of her thoughts and plans. That could work. She would make it work.

'Darling!' Isabella's voice cut short any further conversation between Joe and Karen.

The diminutive powerhouse burst into the room, filling it with her energy and warmth. Judging from her make-up and hair, she had ignored the rule about showering before entering the complex and had flounced through the shower and change rooms without pausing.

Karen found herself fighting the urge to fling herself into her mother's arms and weep uncontrollably, something she had never done. It simply wouldn't do with the attentive Joe, watching her closely to see how she was reacting to the night's events. She had to show him that she was unperturbed by anything she had seen that night, that she was her father's daughter and loyal to Pilatos.

'I'm glad you came,' Karen attempted to make a smile.

'Of course, I came!' Isabella exclaimed. 'These riots and break-ins are all over the news. It is dreadful,' she tut-tutted, her eyes far more perceptive than the airiness of her voice indicated. 'What is the world coming to? People charging through fences onto private property. They have no respect.'

'It's under control now,' Joe assured her.

'Thank goodness for that!' Isabella gave him one of her winning smiles before taking Karen's hand. 'You will come back to Bisente with me for the night, won't you? I simply will not have you staying out here any longer with all these angry people wanting to break in.'

'I'll get my bag,' Karen agreed to the plan to return to Bisente.

She went to the office where she had left her handbag earlier. Joe followed, and as she picked up her bag, he blocked the doorway, his presence menacing.

'Do you have any questions about anything?' he asked. 'Any thoughts about what we need to do?'

'I'm sure you and my father have everything under control,' she replied coolly, hoping he couldn't hear her heart racing. 'I need to concentrate on closing the Maine land deal, and I don't have the time to worry about this. Stablex is, and always was, my father's concern.'

'Are you sure?'

'Yes,' she met his dark eyes with her own and refused to flinch. 'Please stand aside.'

'It might be…' he hesitated, looking at her closely, '…wise to keep quiet about anything you've seen tonight. I'm sure Isabella doesn't need to be involved in something that might prove detrimental to her health.'

'Are you threatening me and my mother, Joe?' she raised her chin and met his gaze with a defiant stare.

'Merely offering advice,' he stepped aside so she could pass. 'Without evidence, any accusation becomes one person's word against another.'

'How fortuitous you have that evidence, then,' she remarked as she rejoined her mother.

All she wanted to do was escape from him. She couldn't think straight with him near her, reminding her of what her father had done that night and of how far Joe would go to protect him. Would he harm her? She had no doubt he would if he thought she was a threat to John. Distance was what she needed to get perspective and plan the strategies that would bring her father down.

There was nothing else she could do at Pilatos Farm once she realized that Joe had already removed the recordings of her father shooting Lane. She had thought to use those as leverage to force her father to hand over control of Pilatos to her, and once she had that, then she would hand the tapes to the police and fix this mess that was Stablex. Or would she become an accomplice if she had the evidence and didn't give it to the authorities immediately? It didn't matter now, anyway, without the tapes, she and Joe were the only witnesses to what had happened that night, and he certainly wasn't going to talk.

As her mother steered her Mercedes sports car along the circuit road of the farm and out the double security gates at the far side where fewer protesters gathered, Karen leaned back in the seat and thought hard. Two things had to be achieved. If there was any chance of saving Pilatos, she had to remove her father from control. He also had to stand trial for murder. Both required the sort of intricate planning at which she excelled, but her mind was crashing into a wall, and she couldn't see any way forward.

'Talk to me,' Isabella commanded once they reached the road outside the compound and left the picketers behind them. 'There is more going on tonight than that protest.'

'What do you know of The Source?' Karen asked her.

'Do you mean sauce that goes on food, or like trying to find the source of the Nile?'

Karen's first reaction was one of relief. Her mother had no idea about what was going on inside the cube. She had hoped, no, she had been sure that would be the case, and could not imagine Isabella ignoring the plight of Sevv, but she had to be sure.

She asked a few more questions to determine that Isabella had no inkling of an ancient stallion that should have died years ago and all his clones, then proceeded to tell her about what was happening with the Stablex stallions. She told her about killing Sevv and her dream of setting the stallions free so they could feel the grass under their feet and run in fields until they died.

'And they won't live long,' she sighed as they passed through Lexington on their way to Bisente. 'They are dying, mother, because they were cloned from such an old horse. The wonder drug that we can take from them to help men live longer doesn't help *them* live longer because their genetic code is already breaking down as though it is seventy years old.'

'With the DNA from Sevv already that old,' Isabella nodded, 'yes, it is conceivable that, at a cellular level, they are dying of old age. Those poor animals.'

'Part of me feels that father has done all this so that he would have a source of Stablex for himself. He wasn't thinking of the company, only himself.'

'Oh, I'm sure of it,' Isabella said with conviction. 'I don't like speaking ill of your father to you, but the man is a narcissist of the highest order. He would think nothing of twisting all of Pilatos and sending it down burning if it would provide him with the extra thirty years Stablex offers. Like most narcissists, he has the happy knack of looking as though he is doing everything for the right reasons, but always, they are only motivated by what is good for them. An extra thirty years of life would override everything else in John's mind.'

'I don't know how to stop him,' Karen shook her head, looking out at the passing lights of the city. 'I know I have to, and I know I will, but my ten percent of the company isn't enough to challenge him, and I haven't had time to plan this. It only came to me in the last few hours that this is what I have to do. I thought I had some leverage, but Joe is protecting him.'

Isabella glanced over at her daughter. 'You do realize that your father's sixty percent is dependent on John Senior letting him control his thirty percent? If you want control of Pilatos, darling, by lunchtime tomorrow, you can have control of seventy percent of the company. I would be delighted to give you power over my thirty percent, and John Senior will not put up any argument once the plight of those horses is known to him. He adores horses, and he has very little time for John, which was probably the start of John's problems. It's just been easier to have him run everything. But if you want control of Pilatos, consider it yours. I never really wanted my thirty percent, anyway, but it was fun to take it away from John in that meeting with Lane and his friends. I think that moment took at least ten years off his Stablex-augmented life.'

Was it as easy as that? Karen stared at her mother. 'Even if I take control, I'm worried he has taken the company too far into dependency on the outcome of Stablex. I don't know if I'll be able to save it.'

'Then you don't save it,' Isabella shrugged and patted her daughter's hand, her eyes back on the road. 'If Pilatos is still there next year, well and good, if it isn't, then you will be, and that is more important than a company that can do what was done to that stallion so that wealthy men can live longer. Personally, I believe the world needs far fewer wealthy men, not having them live longer to get even wealthier. Without Pilatos, the world will go on. I know your father tried to make you believe that Pilatos was the world, but it isn't. It isn't even an important part of it. So, if it fails, don't be hard on yourself because it is John and his obsession with that awful drug who has taken it to that point. You can only do what you can do.'

For the first time in her life, Karen could understand her mother's cavalier attitude towards Pilatos. It wasn't holy ground or a divine institution, it was a business run by her father to benefit himself, and she was merely another tool in the organization to be used by him. It was strangely liberating to consider that she could have a life without Pilatos after all these years of believing it was her life.

She tried to coalesce the changes she had undergone in the past few hours into words. Tonight, she had gone from looking at the world from inside Pilatos, trying to find ways to make that world serve the company, to standing in the world looking in at Pilatos, trying to find a way to make the company serve the world.

Yes, she nodded to herself, that was part of the shift in her mind. That is what Lane wanted her to see when they traveled, picking at the one thread that should have had meaning to her: horses. If she could see that one part of Pilatos was so horribly wrong and gangrenous, the part that surgically muted those stallions and locked them up for their entire lives, then she should have been able to see that the infection was spread through the entire body of Pilatos. It wouldn't be a case of merely removing the necrotic tissue that was Stablex, it would have to be a treatment for the entire company, and it may not survive. But she would.

At Bisente, she had a hot chocolate with Isabella as they discussed plans for the coming days. The only thing glaringly missing from their conversation was any mention of Lane. For Karen's part, she could not bear to think of him, and since she felt that she was unable to do anything about what happened, she pushed all thoughts of him aside until she could find a way to act and make her father accountable. It was only when she lay in bed, alone with her thoughts, that she picked up her phone and reread his last messages. And again. And again. Sobbing quietly in the night, she kept reading. The last thing she did before going to sleep was to text back to him, *Are you there?* No reply came.

The next morning, Isabella turned her energies to ensuring her daughter would have control of Pilatos. She contacted John senior, gave him the bare details of The Source and his clones, and that was all it took for him to demand that Karen take over his share of Pilatos. He was approaching ninety, but his mind was as sharp as it had ever been, and he would help Karen. Like Isabella, it had suited him to let John run Pilatos as it was just one part of his assets, but it was a simple matter to have his lawyers apply the clause that reverted control immediately to him and then hand it over to his granddaughter. A call to Isabella's lawyer had him drafting the paperwork to give Karen power over her share, as well.

By early afternoon, while John was hiding in a foreign country trying to gather his wits to return to America, Karen had quietly seized control of Pilatos, but she was not yet prepared to act as head of the company as she wanted to make a public spectacle that would destroy her father and, hopefully, help send Pilatos in a new direction where it could survive the demise of Stablex. She needed public support, so she had to give them a show that would cement the new Pilatos in their minds as a company worth supporting. Lane had shown her never to underestimate the power of public support.

She spent the next two days in the Bisente office, making phone calls and ensuring the world's media was going to be out in full force at the media conference her father and Joe had organized for Monday. It was expected that John would address the issue of the protesters along with the release of Stablex, but Karen was planning something different.

In those days, Karen made several visits to the Stablex stallions, speaking to management, security, vets, and other staff. They removed the cannulas and there was to be no more blood collected from them. Fences were being built, and orders were given to bury any dead stallions without further autopsies. The atoms from their cells would go back to the earth, and Sevv's gene, which should never have existed in the first place, would be given back to the planet.

On each trip in and out of Pilatos Farm, she noted that the numbers of protesters continued to rise, with estimates reaching thirty thousand people quietly holding up placards to all visitors. There were no acts of violence or any more attempts to break through the fence; they simply gathered and waved signs. Word was leaking out that changes were taking place at the farm, and they waited, wanting to witness whatever was coming.

With a heavy heart, she noticed the appearance of signs asking, 'Where is Lane?' His silence was echoing across the world, and posts on social media began asking the same question. Andrea had tried contacting her several times, but she would not take her calls. It was impossible to talk about him or to consider what had happened. All she could do was act in such a way as to make his sacrifice have some worth. He had said that great change required great sacrifice, and she wanted to make changes that rippled out from Pilatos and helped change the world for the better. That was what he deserved.

Each night, alone in bed, she wept and read through the messages they had sent each other. Thousands of texts, funny and serious, angry and careful, filled with emotion and light, laughter, and kindness. And each night, before going to sleep, she texted, *Are you there?* in the hope that he would answer, and the world would seem whole again. He never responded.

When her father arrived back in the country on Monday morning, he rang to thank her for running everything in his absence. He also asked her to be present at the media conference that afternoon at

Pilatos Farm. His voice was subdued. He said he hadn't been feeling well and that he might need her to help with his speech. It took great effort to overpower the desire to hyperventilate at the sound of his voice, and she answered him in clipped tones, which he didn't think were unusual. He would email her the speech he had written to celebrate the release of Stablex on to the market, and she could make any changes she required.

There would be changes; she gritted her teeth as she read through the script he had sent her. The speakers from the welfare organizations that had been paid so well by her father were not going to get the chance to speak. In fact, her father wouldn't be allowed to deliver his speech. It was her show, dedicated to Lane and made for the benefit of the stallions.

She had to keep the changes hidden from him until he was on that stage in front of the television cameras and the thirty thousand protesters, with her own security team surrounding them. Her father and Joe had to have no inkling of what was going on so that she could control the proceedings. John Lawford thought he was organizing some publicity for Stablex while she was organizing a coup to take place in front of the world.

# CHAPTER TWENTY-SIX

*Horses have served us for thousands of years. They carried our soldiers, our explorers, our settlers. They plowed our fields and pulled our coaches. They gave us greatness. We owe them. Don't ever forget what we owe the horses. Respect.*
**Lane Dimity, Thoughts on Horses, p. 22**

### Pilatos Farm - Freedom

A portable stage stood next to the front gates of Pilatos Farm and temporary fencing erected around it to hold the protesters back from the media area. Several hundred security workers stood quietly along the inside of the fence on Pilatos land, reminding protesters to stay out. Within the fenced media area, scores of cameras were set up, pointed at the stage, while roaming cameras took in the waiting crowds on one side and the clean, white stables with the featureless cube rearing up in the center of them on the other.

Before her father arrived, Karen walked through Stable Block One, patting horses, talking to staff and visitors, occasionally even hugging someone, and thanking them for being present. She left the Stablex compound and went to the boundary fence of the farm where Pilatos met the protesters. Trying to control her emotions, she moved to the marquee behind the stage and tried to keep her grief, nerves, and fears at a distance as she focused on her breathing. In and out. In and out.

The silence from thirty thousand people was unnerving. There was the shuffle of feet, the sound of signs bumping each other occasionally, even a cough, but no voices. Silence.

When the limousine carrying her father and Joe Kaiphas pulled up at the gates, the crowd silently raised their heads, revealing a scar drawn on every throat. Men, women, and children, horse people, animal lovers, those with a sense of justice who had never owned an animal, old people, young, employed, those with degrees, those who were homeless. They stood silently, heads raised, showing the hand-drawn scar on every throat to signify their support of the stallions that had been silenced by Pilatos. Perhaps, thought Karen, it also referenced Lane. But she couldn't think of him now, not now. There were changes to be made.

John Lawford stood in front of his daughter, and she regarded him without showing any emotion. It seemed that murder did not sit as comfortably on his shoulders as he may have expected. There were dark rings under his eyes, and, even with his beloved Stablex coursing through his system, he appeared to have aged ten years in a few days. She felt no sympathy for him. She felt nothing for him.

'Ready?' he nodded to her before climbing the steps onto the stage.

'Of course,' she replied.

Joe looked at her strangely as she stepped in front of him, cutting him off to follow her father and leaving him to follow her. Once on the stage, he looked around suspiciously, sensing that things were not as they appeared. Karen had changed, he could see that, and his eyes rested speculatively on her as she took her place next to her father. She was wearing a military-red skirt and jacket with a bright yellow silk shirt and a colorful scarf with black horses around her neck. It was a bold statement from a woman who had worn neutral greys for more than a decade. The red looked like a warning, and he wondered if John had taken note.

Scanning the protesters, Joe ran his eyes over hundreds of faces in the first few rows, and he noticed Isabella and John Senior standing next to each other, a couple of rows back. His eyebrow twitched. Things were afoot. There was a far larger media presence than John had organized, and as he looked around at the farm behind them, he saw new fences. It seemed Karen had been busy. He glanced at her, his expression blank, hiding his thoughts. She stared back at him with a combative lift to her head.

Looking around again, he noticed certain men and women almost blending into the crowd of protesters, among the media and Pilatos workers. He knew the look of police, soldiers, mercenaries, and security well enough to recognize what they were. Their own eyes scanned everything, returning to Karen and moving around her before scanning the crowds again. He hid a smile. She had organized her own army. The girl had balls.

'Welcome,' John took the microphone and motioned to the media and the crowd. 'Thank you to the protesters for being so well behaved. We've organized free refreshments for you again today...' His voice faltered when he saw several people silently raise signs that asked *Where is Lane?* and *What have you done to Lane?*

His skin looked several shades paler as he read the placards, and he swung to look at Joe, who waved a hand to tell him to keep talking. Karen saw the touch of panic in her father's eyes, and she felt pleased. He was on edge, not knowing if he would be arrested for murder, not knowing if this crowd would turn on him, and he wasn't handling it well. Suffer, she told him silently, like you made Sevv suffer as you stood over the bed he was strapped to and watched him live in agony to create the drug you wanted.

'As you all know, Stablex will be on the market later this week, and I wanted to clear the air with the protesters today, and anyone else having concerns about the horses here, by having some of the vets and leading welfare experts speak to us about the care of our stallions. We want everyone to feel assured that no horse is harmed in the making of Stablex.'

More signs about Lane and *Free the Stallions* were raised by the silent crowd, and John looked faintly sick.

'My daughter, Karen, is here to explain about the care of our horses in the stalls behind us.'

He almost ran from the microphone and sat heavily in his chair between Joe and Karen, mopping at his sweating face with a tissue. As Karen stood, she motioned for a tall, athletic man to take her seat. The bulge under his jacket was apparent to Joe, as was the lethally cold expression on his face. He was there to protect Karen. Two similar men moved to stand beside Joe's chair and behind him, and he held his empty hands out for them to see, inclining his head to them to show that he understood he was neutralized. He could do nothing to stop the coup that was underway.

'Stablex is a drug that only men can use,' Karen began, causing her father to sit upright as she departed from the speech he had given her.

Joe laid a restraining hand on John's shoulder to keep him seated and whispered, 'Sit still. We are surrounded by Karen's security forces, John, I count at least thirty, and judging from the looks on their faces, they will kill to protect her.'

'An expensive drug that only the wealthiest men will be able to afford,' Karen looked around at the cameras and at the crowd who listened, riveted by her words.

She noticed Andrea, Matt, and Tom moving to the front of the crowd, pushing a wheelchair with the girl Lane put on the Friesian last week. One of the journalists in the media section, Vicki Marshall, a woman Karen knew to be opposed to the emotional and financial tricks used by charities and welfare groups like ADOR, turned and reached out to Tom. He smiled warmly at her as he held his hand towards the fence that separated them.

'Stablex will give them an estimated thirty extra years of good health, and they will watch their sisters and wives and daughters die of old age while they have the time to amass more wealth. Today, the richest one percent of people in the world hold over fifty percent of the world's wealth. The fifty wealthiest individuals on the planet, most of them men, have more wealth than over four billion of the poorest people combined. Stablex will ensure that those wealthy men get wealthier, and the rest of the world suffers.'

She paused at the end of the sentence as she saw journalists scrambling for phones to tell their television stations that this was to go live rather than waiting for the regular news broadcast. Looking down at her bright-colored clothes, she drew in strength from the crowd who loved Lane and wanted to change the world.

'A good friend of mine told me that he lived his life by a set of rules, the first being to always choose kindness, and one of the others was to do no harm. He said to not harm yourself, or the people around you, or the animals, or the world around you. Stablex harms horses, it will harm lives, and it will make the world a worse place, and, as the new head of Pilatos Industries, I pledge that we will cease production of the drug.'

'No!' her father roared at her, held in his seat by Joe on one side and Karen's bodyguard on the other.

'Ten percent!' he yelled at her in disbelief. 'You only have ten percent!'

Karen looked at him with cold disdain and turned again to face the cameras and crowd, her voice firm. 'It will come as a surprise to my father, but my mother and my grandfather have given me control of their sixty percent of Pilatos, so I now control seventy percent of the company, and Stablex will cease. The stallions who have been locked in stalls all their lives will be freed, though they may not live long as they are all cloned from the original horse with this unique gene, Sevvodarray the Third, who died last Wednesday, aged well over seventy years. His cells were to clone the Stablex stallions because the Sevv Gene responsible for producing the hormone that slows or reverses aging does not breed on and cannot exist in any horse whose genome differs in any way from Sevvodarray himself. Unfortunately, because of the age of his cells, the cells in his clones behave like they are already over seventy years of age, and the stallions are dying.'

A collective gasp came from the crowd.

'We cannot stop them from dying, but we can give them dignity in life until that time. The Friesian stallions of Pilatos Farm are to go free.'

Stopping, she turned to raise an arm towards Stable Block One, where Dr. Noah Hannaford led the first stallion into the sunlight of the late afternoon. The huge black horse walked with high steps, the silken feathers on his legs rippling as he walked. He tossed his head in excitement, and his long mane and forelock flicked through the air with every movement of his head. He was a warhorse, carrying the blood of countless generations of warhorses, and he walked with pride in every step.

'In the past few days, we have built over one hundred yards for the first of the stallions to be released from their stalls, and in the coming weeks, we will ensure that every stallion will have access to grazing and sunshine and fields for at least six hours every day. They will still be stabled at night to protect them, but the stallions will now know freedom.'

Behind Noah, Abhirka led another stallion out of the stable block. This one trotted in piaffe beside her, raising his legs high as he expressed his delight in being outside in the sunshine. Housemates Jacinta and Nia followed with two more stallions, one walking calmly, gazing around at the world that was so much larger than he ever imagined, and the other appeared frightened of such space after living all his life inside four walls.

'The people leading the stallions out for their first taste of the world outside their stalls include the vets, vet nurses, stablehands, security, and other workers of Pilatos Farm.'

A few people began to clap, but Karen held up her hands to stop them. 'Please don't applaud. These horses will have enough to cope with today without the sound of applause scaring them. So, if you care about them, continue to show your appreciation in silence, thank you.'

The first horses reached their grassed fields, and the handlers led them around the perimeter so that each horse could see and touch the solid fences and learn that they would have to stop at them. One horse to a field. The Noriker stallions were used to being released together every year and used their voices to communicate intent and consent, but Karen was not prepared to risk these stallions by turning them out together.

'We're also lucky to have Lukas Waldberg, one of the riders at the Spanish Riding School, with us,' Karen indicated Lukas as he led out a stallion, and he waved to the cameras and the crowd, 'and his friend, Simon.'

Lukas looked at her and smiled, then put his hand to his heart and pointed at her. True to his promise, when she had asked him to come and pick up her shattered pieces, he and Simon had arrived at Bisente within a day.

As horse after horse was led from the stables, Karen continued to introduce the people leading them. Julian O'Sullivan and Julie from Bisente. Molly Vitale in her trademark bright purple jodhpurs and sunflower yellow polo shirt with a black armband for her son, Betsy from Missouri, and others she had met on her trip with Lane. The Pilatos driver, Pearce, and his daughter Alycia were also there to lead horses.

Once Noah had led his stallion around the small rectangular field, shown him the water trough, and let him push against the fence to check that it was not something to try and run through, he carefully removed the halter and stood back. The stallion took a step to move with him. Noah patted him on the neck and gave him a small push to show him that he could walk away. Stepping back from the horse again, he moved towards the closed gate. The horse watched him, then turned his head to gaze around his grassy field. He lowered his neck to snort at the grass and take a tentative bite of it, then, with green grass hanging from the side of his mouth, he began to walk to the far end of his field, then trot, then canter.

His legs moved in a climbing action, and he enjoyed covering ground for the first time in his life, moving from one place to another. He slowed as he neared the fence and turned rather clumsily before cantering back to the gate, throwing in a leap and a buck as he went.

One by one, in the other small fields, the stallions were released, and their reactions ranged from explosive joy about being able to canter and play to tentative steps as they walked carefully across the strange green substance underfoot. Everyone watched the horses, entranced. Except for her father. The men on either side of him restrained his arms, forcing him to remain in his seat. His face had changed from pale to a rage of red, but Karen pushed on, insensible to his fury.

'I don't know if our company can survive this change in direction,' she told the media, 'but Pilatos will now serve the world rather than expecting the world to serve Pilatos. Half of the Stablex that has been produced will be available for purchase by auction. The money raised from that will go to fund the other half of Stablex, which is being donated to health centers around the world to help those men and boys who have diseases that can be temporarily alleviated by Stablex. It will also be available to ethical pharmaceutical companies that wish to work on developing a synthetic version of the hormone, an objective that Pilatos has been unable to achieve, as well as a version that will work with the female genome.'

John Lawford raged at her, held tightly in place by Joe and her security officer, and she turned to look down at him with contempt for all he'd done to these horses, to Sevv, their company, and Lane. And to her. She wasn't sure if he would face trial for what he had done to Lane, as it would be her word against Joe's and her father's, without any evidence apart from the fact that Lane was missing. There was no proof Lane was on the farm that night, even though his friends could say he intended to be there. She knew Joe well enough to know that the tapes, the guns, the bullets, and the body would never be found unless he wished it to be so.

Watching her father struggle, his face mottled with anger, she sighed. At least he had received some punishment, and if he never faced the justice system for what he had done, life was punishing him. The world had seen him humiliated by his daughter, and he would never recover from that.

As the stallions continued to be led out and released, journalists started calling to Karen with questions about Pilatos, Stablex, the stallions, and other topics, including Lane. She could not face them and cast a beseeching look at her mother, who entered the media pen with John Senior and took over the microphones so that Karen could escape.

Slipping away from the crowds, she went to the car she'd borrowed from her mother and drove away from the farm back to Bisente. It was quiet there, as most of the workers were over on the other side of the city, releasing the first one hundred stallions, and she wandered through the stalls where horses snorted and nickered to each other, making the sounds that horses were meant to make.

Reaching a stall marked Bisente Shandy, she saw the head of the little chestnut she admired poking over the door to greet her, his eyes shining brightly.

'Hello, boy,' she patted him, and he nodded his head. 'Even among all these giants, you would be my pick. I've always admired heart.'

The horse snorted food over her shirt and jacket. She laughed, then stopped. She hadn't laughed since the night she lost him. Lane would want her to laugh. She looked at the horse. Lane would want her to ride.

Kicking off her shoes, she picked them up and ran barefoot up to the house. Changing into riding jeans and a bright orange safety shirt, the least grey color she could find, she slipped on her riding boots and ran back to Shandy.

'How do you feel about being ridden bareback?' she asked him.

He refused to answer but flicked his ears back and forth.

'I'll take that to be a yes.'

In the tack room, she found a snaffle bridle hanging on a hook under his name, grabbed a helmet in her size, and returned to Shandy. She led him out on to the jumping arena, looked around to see that she was alone, and then vaulted lightly on to his back. He skittered sideways, and she moved with him, asking him to go forward, hearing almost every riding instructor's voice in her head telling her, *Whatever the question, whatever the problem, forward is always the answer.*

Soon, they were trotting and cantering around the arena, doing figure of eights with simple and flying changes, and she felt her soul begin to soar with the freedom of this horse. On a soft rein, she set him at one of the practice jumps, and he took it straight and true, without hesitation.

The girl who had loved horses raised her voice from within and sang a song of joy. She was free again. Karen felt at home on the back of this horse, happier than she had ever been in an office overlooking the streets of New York. She turned Shandy towards the railed fence that surrounded the jumping arena and asked him to canter. He sprang forward, willingly, following her directions to lengthen or shorten his stride so that he was placed perfectly for take-off, and he sailed over the fence. The fields of Bisente stretched out before her, just as they had when she was a child riding her horses bareback, wild and free, and she urged Shandy up into a ground covering, big striding canter, heading down to the cross-country course where they could jump logs and banks, picnic tables and upturned boats.

For the time that she was on his back, all the problems of her world were blown away by the wind in her face and the power of this horse. She vowed to continue to change her life to allow for the time to go on riding. She would run Pilatos, but she would not forsake the other loves of her life to be a slave to the company.

Later that night, after dinner with her mother and grandfather, as well as a couple of the security staff assigned to protect her while her father was out for revenge, she lay in bed reading one of Lane's books.

Before going to sleep, she texted his phone again. *Are you there?*

There was no answer. She stared at her message and all the repeats of the same question above it. If she closed her eyes, she could imagine him holding his phone and wanting to answer, but having an important reason not to answer. She imagined him thinking of her, wanting to be with her, wanting to answer her messages… then she fell into an exhausted sleep, tears dampening her pillow.

Over the next few weeks, she spent more than sixteen hours every day trying to save Pilatos and restructure it so that it could continue to exist without the income from Stablex. The forensic accountants found evidence of her father siphoning tens of millions of dollars from other areas of Pilatos into the development of Stablex. With him mortgaging the future of the company on the production of a drug that would cease when the clones died, it was going to be difficult to save it. She banked on winning the support of the public by their moves to become an ethical and moral company, making changes to improve the world.

John Senior came out of retirement and back to his office, and he convinced her father that if he hoped to inherit any of the Lawford fortune, he would do well to avoid Pilatos and Karen for at least a year. Also, he would agree to never, under any circumstance, act in any way that could be detrimental to his daughter. He was given a decade's worth of Stablex, not that anyone knew if it would be viable beyond its two-year use-by date, and he withdrew to one of John Senior's houses in Tuscany. There would be a reckoning, Karen accepted that, but for now, he was hobbled by his desire to inherit the family fortune, and by his hunger to keep Stablex in his system.

The purchase of the Maine land tract finally went through after the months of negotiating, and she immediately drew up contracts to ensure the land remained a managed wildlife habitat that was a refuge for the black bear, moose, whitetail deer, beaver, and other animals and birds, and it was never to be developed or used for commercial gain. She followed through with the same deal on the Washington land and ran a media campaign patting themselves on the back for their acts of generosity to the environment. They received a good deal of support from the public and the media for preserving the forest habitats, and Karen hoped that would translate into customers supporting Pilatos by choosing their products.

With the source of timber being lost to environmental kindness, Karen then set up a think-tank to come up with ways to re-purpose the lumber mills so that the employees there had continued work. Another media campaign was started, stating how Pilatos cared for the environment and its employees.

Jeremy Murray and Phillip Reach were removed from their positions and were replaced with people who would work to make an ethical Pilatos successful, something Jeremy and Phillip could never have done because ethics and morals were anathema to them.

One issue she could not deal with was thinking about the loss of Lane, and how to make her father accountable for that. The *Where is*

*Lane?* movement grew in the days after Sevv died and the stallions were released, and she felt physically ill every time she saw something to remind her of the Australian. There had been phone calls, texts, and emails from Andrea that she would not take or return. Everything about Lane had become an enormous pile of emotions that she pushed back and back, until it reared high over her, threatening to crash down on her life at any moment.

Unexpectedly, it was Joe Kaiphas who saved her from that. He had accompanied her father to Tuscany and then returned to the Pilatos Building in New York.

'My loyalties lie with Pilatos,' he told her in his emotionless voice when she allowed him into her office, 'and while your father was in charge, they also lay with him. Now that you are in charge, my loyalties lie with you.'

'Get me the tapes and the gun, then, Joe,' she challenged him, her eyes flashing with specks of ice as she stood near the window, the New York skyline serving as her background.

'Impossible,' he responded, 'they are gone.'

'Leaving me to handle Lane's friends, and see his fans ask about him hour after hour. Great.'

She turned and rested her forehead against the cool glass, gazing down at the street and footpaths below. From above, it was a meaningless flow of life, something to look down upon with the emptiness of a lesser god watching leaves blow across a dead lawn. Closing her eyes, she told herself that it wasn't meaningless, every life below had their own story, their own loves, and their own heartaches. Every life in the flow had meaning. And the emptiness she had once felt was now filled to overflowing with emotions. She was just another human, filled with love and grief, fear, hope, sorrow, and joy, and all the other emotions that she had removed herself from for too many years. It hurt now that they were back, but hurting was still better than having that emptiness within.

'I will take care of those problems,' Joe assured her. 'Leave it to me.'

Giving him a skeptical look, she asked, 'And how do you intend to do that, Joe? Can you raise the dead? Do you think his friends will listen to any advice at all from Pilatos?'

'Trust me,' he inclined his head slightly, 'I will take care of it. As long as his friends are prepared to start posting on social media as Lane, the *where is* campaign will go away.'

Karen waved a weary hand at him. 'Do whatever you can do,' she sighed, unconvinced he could do anything, and even less convinced that she should keep him in her employ. 'But apply limits, Joe. No murder. No framing people for crimes they didn't commit. Be ethical. And when you're ready to prove your newfound loyalty to me, let me know, so we can go to the police and report what we both witnessed that night.'

He left without saying anything further, and to her surprise, the social media posts from Lane's accounts started up again that afternoon. She didn't know how he had convinced Lane's friends to post as him, but he had done it, and the *where is* comments and signs disappeared almost immediately.

Day after day, she worked to pull Pilatos back from the brink of disaster. Surprisingly, even with all the long hours, her migraines were leaving her alone. Perhaps the stress of working with her father, and always feeling like she was never good enough for him, was the trigger for the headaches. Now she was free of him, they had gone, too.

'Give yourself a break,' her grandfather told her in the fifth week after her coup. 'You've plugged a lot of holes in this leaky boat over the past few weeks, and it can stagger on without you for a while. You may have forgotten, but I ran it for quite a few decades before your father took over.'

'I know you can run it better than anyone, even me,' she answered, perching on the edge of his desk in her blue jeans and royal blue shirt, 'but are you OK with this new direction I'm taking things?'

'I'm more than OK, honey,' he smiled fondly at her and patted her hand. 'The older I get, the more I realize that I can't take the money with me. Go back to Bisente and ride that chestnut horse your mother keeps in the stables for you.'

That night, sitting on the floor of Shandy's stall at Bisente, Karen tapped another, *Are you there?* into her phone as she listened to the comforting crunching of her horse chewing grain.

Her phone pinged. *Always.*

She stared at it. Did Andrea write that? Matt? Tom?

It pinged again. *Except for these past few weeks when Joe Kaiphas made it absolutely clear that I had to leave you alone to fix up the mess that was Pilatos. I'm sorry.*

## CHAPTER TWENTY-SEVEN

*I dream of living at home in the outback, enjoying the peace of a vast and ancient land, and having a friend to share it with. And horses. I dream of horses.*

**Lane Dimity, when asked of what he dreamt. On-line interview.**

### Joe Kaiphas

When Joe heard that Karen had organized Andrea to photograph the Stablex stallions, he knew that Lane would be with her, and he made sure that he was also there that day. He intended to find time alone with Lane to speak to him, and when he wandered off, looking at horses down other corridors, Joe followed.

He watched Lane pass each horse, placing his hand on their heads or necks as though communicating with them. Then, when he was sure they were far enough from the others and that there were no other employees in this twenty-horse section, he stopped Lane.

'I've been wanting to speak to you,' Joe said, his voice low.

Lane turned and looked at him inquisitively, *Do you sign?*

'Yes, my daughter's deaf,' he told him.

*What did you want to talk about?*

'I want to talk about what's happening here. I've read some of your books. My daughter likes horses. I know it's not right what's happening here.'

*What is happening here? I'm told they are happy, but I'm not seeing that. What can you tell me?*

Joe looked around, making sure they were alone. He had disabled the cameras and microphones in this entire stable block an hour earlier, so he wasn't concerned about them. 'I can tell you that Karen's father keeps her away from here as much as possible, as he doesn't want her to know what's going on. It's not just the horses in these stables; there's several hundred broodmares in the cube at the center of this, plus young horses that are kept in the cube stables until they're old enough to come here. My daughter would cry if she knew how these horses lived. Karen Lawford used to be the sort of girl who would cry for that, but she doesn't know.'

*What do you want me to do?* Lane looked at him speculatively, wondering if he was being set up by a loyal Pilatos employee.

Joe took a deep breath and looked at the kind heads of the stallions around him. 'I want you to do whatever it takes to get these stallions freed and to end what is going on inside the cube.'

*That's what I intend to do, though I didn't know about the horses in the cube.*

'Neither does Karen. This is John's project; he doesn't want her here.'

*Do you care about Karen?* Lane narrowed his eyes and regarded Joe curiously.

'I watched her grow up. We named our daughter after her because I wanted her to be a strong-willed woman who would stand up for herself in this world. But Karen has changed. I think you could bring her back. She's not the cold person that you see; she used to laugh. A lot. I remember her riding her horses bareback around Bisente like a wild child joined to those horses.'

*I'll do what I can.* Lane was hesitant about trusting this man.

'I'll work with you,' Joe lowered his voice even further and passed Lane a small white card with some handwritten numbers on it. 'The phone numbers there are for phones that John doesn't know about. He's become paranoid in recent years, and anyone close to him has their phone records perused so he can see who they are contacting.'

*How do I know I can trust you?* Lane arched his eyebrows questioningly. *You are the head of security in Pilatos; after all, it would be your job to try and have me trust you.*

'I understand,' Joe nodded and thought fast. It was essential to have Lane trust him. They didn't have much time. 'Will you call me soon? Perhaps we can meet somewhere, and I'll bring my daughter. I think if you meet her, you'll understand me more. My daughter thinks I'm a hero, Lane, but when I walk in these stables and see these horses, I know I'm not.'

He paused and pointed at the horse next to Lane. 'Look at their throats. They have been surgically muted so that John doesn't have to listen to their voices when he visits. All these horses, silenced. John made that happen. He has to be stopped. When you learn more about Stablex, you'll understand.'

Lane called a few weeks after they'd talked in the stables, and they organized to meet in Central Park. Joe took Karina to meet him. In his heart, he believed that once Lane met Karina, he would understand that under the rock-hard surface that he had learned to show the world, there lived a man who cared about life, and Karen, and those horses.

When Karina was five years old, Joe's wife, Chelsea, was driving him to work with their daughter in the back seat. There was a single second that replayed eternally in Joe's mind: he was looking at Chelsea, thinking how beautiful she was. She glanced to the left to see a speeding car coming through a stop sign, then turned to look at Joe. At that moment, as she met his eyes, there was so much love, and yet so much sorrow, as she knew it was goodbye. The car slammed into her door, knocking Joe unconscious. When he came to, Chelsea was still looking at him, only she was dead, and blood ran from her ears, nose, and mouth. Karina was crying in the back seat, covered in blood. He managed to crawl back to her and hold her until the paramedics arrived.

She had been in a wheelchair since the accident, and the head injury had left her deaf and unable to talk. Her mind was bright and active, she loved horses, and she loved everything about Lane Dimity, wearing t-shirts with his quotes and covering her bedroom wall with images of the outback horseman. It was not something that Joe could explain, but he felt that it was important for Karina to meet Lane, perhaps because he was her idol, and Joe felt that he was one idol who wouldn't let her down. Karina deserved to believe in her dreams of goodness.

When Lane met them in Central Park, he knelt by the wheelchair and chatted with Karina in sign language. Her face lit up like it was Christmas as they talked with each other. Lane went to give her his hand but looked to Joe first for permission to touch his daughter. Joe nodded. Holding her small hand in his, he smiled at her, and she grinned back. He touched her knees with his other hand and looked at her closely.

*Do you want to ride horses?* he asked after releasing her hand, his eyes creasing in kindness.

*I want to walk, first,* she signed to him.

Touching each leg lightly, he looked at her eyes, his own burning with something that Joe could not describe. Joe knew that there was no physical cause preventing Karina from walking. The doctors told him it was a mental barrier – it was as though she had given up on believing she could walk.

*Then walk. You can walk.*

He stood and held a hand out to her to help her from the chair. Looking up into his eyes, Karina believed his words. On shaky legs, she rose and balanced, leaning weight into his hand. He moved a few steps, and she walked with him. Karina giggled and glanced at her father, looking happier than he had ever seen her. She was walking.

Tears filled Joe's eyes. The Australian was more than he had ever expected him to be, and to see his daughter walk alongside him made him realize that this man had to be protected. He might work for John Lawford, but Lane Dimity was someone who had to be kept safe at all costs. And he would make sure he would do that job, no matter how it damaged his career at Pilatos.

After meeting Karina, Lane believed that he could trust Joe, and they stayed in contact, often discussing events at Pilatos or elsewhere in the world. Lane used the text-to-voice feature so they could have phone conversations rather than the texting that he and Karen indulged in.

Although Joe did not actively help Lane with the sabotage of the launch of Stablex at The Pilatos Centre in Lexington, he failed to report several Pilatos employees that he suspected of working with Lane and his friends. Also, he enabled his security forces to be less effective than they usually were on that night.

Together, they came up with the idea of taking Karen on tour to see the stallions. Joe had told him that if only she could remember how she used to work with horses, then perhaps she would open her eyes to what was going wrong at Pilatos Farm. It was Joe who suggested that Karen was likely to agree to the trip if Lane promised to ask his protesters to go quiet for the time that he was away. Joe had a knack for knowing what motivated people and what they were likely to respond to, and he had been correct about Karen.

While they were away, Joe had spent many hours trying to develop a plan that could neutralize John and have him hand control of Pilatos to Karen. Joe believed that John would destroy the company because of his obsession with Stablex, and he needed to find the leverage to remove John from his position. Once he was gone, Karen could do what was right by those horses who did not deserve the life that Pilatos had given them.

At first, his plan focused on John. If they could make John believe he had committed murder, then Joe could convince him that his best option would be to leave the country and have Karen run Pilatos. He knew that John would be terrified of the prospect of jail, so it might work if Joe could convince him to flee. He came up with the idea that Karen had to overhear a conversation where Lane and his friends discussed Sean at Pilatos and how Lane was to take his place on a particular night. Her loyalty to Pilatos would force her to reveal her knowledge of the identity swap, and that allowed Joe to invent the scene that had John believe he had shot Lane.

On that Wednesday, Joe had swapped all loaded cartridges for blanks in the armaments room at Pilatos Farm and rigged up a remote-control device in the gun he would hand to John - the Glock that he always favored. Lane wore a movie-prop vest with synthetic blood in a bladder over the heart. The intention was to have John pointing the gun at Lane, and then Joe would activate the remote, which would pull the trigger and fire the blank, at the same time that the small charge in Lane's vest ripped open the bag of blood.

It was only when Joe saw Karen watching the security videos in the control room that his idea evolved to the next level. While she watched Lane lift Karina onto the back of the big Friesian, Joe realized that if she believed her father had killed Lane, it was likely that she would carry out Lane's work and find out what lay at the heart of the cube and at the foundation of Stablex. He was sure that once she saw the atrocity that was Sevv, she would move heaven and earth to remove her father as head of the company, and she would try to make things right.

It was a gamble, more so for Lane than anyone else. In those moments when two guns were pointed at him, Joe saw the doubt in his eyes. He'd realized that he had placed his life in the hands of a Pilatos employee, and if there were real bullets in those guns, he was in the last seconds of his life. In the instant that the small charge on his vest went off, he thought that he'd been shot, his eyes widening in alarm as he staggered and fell without any acting required.

As he lay there, it was a relief to feel his heart beating normally, if rapidly, in his chest.

'I didn't let you down, son,' Joe whispered to him as he pretended to feel for a pulse.

Lane winked at him, thankful for that.

When Karen appeared, desperate to see Lane, Joe used the lines he'd been practicing to trigger the response he wanted.

'Don't,' he told her. 'You don't want to remember him like this. Believe me, I know. Walk away. Forget you saw any of this. If you care for him at all, honor what you know of him.'

Once alone with Lane, he'd carried him as if he were dead, in case Karen or John were watching and placed him on the back seat of his car.

As Joe had predicted, Karen did honor what she knew of Lane by going into the cube to find The Source. While she was there, he removed the tapes of the shooting, convinced John that he needed to leave the country for a few days in case the police learned of the 'murder,' and drove Lane outside the farm compound where Andrea, Matt, and Tom picked him up.

He knew Lane felt guilty about letting Karen think he was dead, but Joe convinced him to stay silent so that she could take control of the company and act in accordance with her true character.

'Now that she's seen what lies at the heart of all of this,' Joe flicked a hand to indicate everything on the other side of the fence, 'nothing will stop her. If you want those stallions set free, you have to leave her alone to do her work.'

*But she thinks I'm dead,* Lane argued.

'Yes, she does, and that will be the fuel that will keep her fires burning. Her father spent most of her life trying to make her stop feeling, and you've brought a lifetime of feelings back to her. She'll do the right thing by those horses, and by the company. They both need saving. She does, too. Just leave her alone and let her do it.'

*Keep her safe,* Lane's eyes beseeched him.

'I will. You go home to the outback and enjoy some time to yourself. You were growing tired of this public life, anyway,' Joe smiled at him. 'I'll bring her to you when it's time.'

# EPILOGUE

*When the world becomes too much for me, I will be going home.*
**T-shirt featuring Lane Dimity.**

### Ellamanga Station, Outback Queensland

Lane sat on the bare back of his black stock horse; his arms stretched wide to the sun as he caught the light that had left the star eight minutes earlier. Wearing a deep blue shirt and jeans, with an Akubra on his head, he looked like a typical outback horseman. He waited at the top of the jump-up behind the Ellamanga house for the plane to arrive, and he gazed out over the land he loved. The rolling plains of the outback stretched away on all sides, rich with grass after several good seasons. It was like looking across heaven to see the land so green.

The buzz of the twin propellers caught his attention, and he watched the eight-seater plane approach from the east, coming out of the sun. It banked over him, and the pilot waggled his wings as they made a large circle around the hills to find the right approach to the section of road that served as the landing strip. Waving to the plane, he urged his horse off the jump-up, and it willingly launched itself over the edge to slide, leap, and step its way down the steep incline.

It took less than a minute to reach the house, where he released the horse and jumped into one of the vehicles. By the time he drove the few hundred meters to the section of road that doubled as a runway, the plane was taxiing to a stop. He stepped out of the car and tried to look calm, but he felt like jumping from one foot to the other in excitement. It took some effort to stand still and raise an arm in welcome as hands inside the plane waved to him.

Joe disembarked first, holding out his hands to help his daughter. Then came Karen, dressed in a bright yellow sundress with the scarf he'd given her draped around her neck. Lane felt ridiculously happy to see her standing on his land. Any fears about her being angry at him for what had played out at Pilatos Farm and afterward were abandoned as soon as her eyes met his.

*Welcome,* he signed, grinning.

*Good to be here,* she signed back.

She began to make her way towards him as Andrea, Matt, and Tom climbed out of the plane. Joe motioned for them to stay back so that Lane and Karen had a moment to themselves before everyone joined them.

Joe found himself smiling as Lane's arms wrapped around Karen, and she melted into his embrace. They were home.

THE END

Lane, Karen, Tom, Andrea, Matthew, and Joe return in Book 2 of The Dimity Horse Mysteries: **RESCUED – Saving the Lost Horses**

# ABOUT THE AUTHOR

Leanne Owens is an English teacher with a Master's in Education who has written freelance articles for horse magazines for decades. She also wrote and reported for Horse Talk TV before she started writing novels. Leanne has spent her life around horses – riding, training, breeding, competing, and judging, and has won scores of state and national titles with her horses. Because of her years on her husband's family properties past Longreach in outback Queensland, most of her books contain outback scenes. Leanne lives with her husband on their 100-acre farm in south-east Queensland along with their horses and dogs, and she hopes to write many more books in years to come.

Made in the USA
Middletown, DE
29 June 2023

34178519R00257